Man and landscape in Australia

TOWARDS AN ECOLOGICAL VISION

AUSTRALIAN UNESCO COMMITTEE
FOR MAN AND THE BIOSPHERE

Publication No. 2

GF
801
.M35
1974

Man and landscape in Australia

TOWARDS AN ECOLOGICAL VISION

Papers from a symposium held at the
Australian Academy of Science, Canberra
30 May–2 June 1974

Edited by George Seddon and Mari Davis

Australian Government Publishing Service
Canberra 1976

First published 1976
Reprinted 1977

Printed by Courier-Mail Printing Service, Brisbane

An ecological vision of Australia has been slow to develop,
partly because her white settlers have come from an energetic,
transforming race with a culture that has evolved in a very different
environment. Australia might have been settled by Spaniards, or
perhaps by an agricultural people five hundred years ago, using the
genetic material to hand – grasses, seeds, fruits, marsupials – for
centuries of selective breeding, parallel with that of Eurasia and the
Americas, to evolve an indigenous agriculture. Prize kangaroos
might have been kinder to the Australian landscape than the sheep
and the rabbit, and would have fostered a different understanding
of it. But this is fantasy. What happened was the superimposition of
European practices, with varying degrees of adaptation, and a
generally limited perception of natural ecosystems. The theme of
the seminar is thus the interaction between imported cultural
notions – economic, social, aesthetic – and response to the
indigenous environment. It begins historically, and then turns to
implications and the future, to ask what kind of Australian
landscape we can have and want.

Acknowledgments

George Seddon is responsible for the general editing of these papers, and Mari Davis for the technical editing. We thank the contributors for their co-operation, and all those at the symposium on *Man and Landscape in Australia*, 30 May–2 June 1974 in Canberra, whose comments and questions helped contributors to revise their papers. The Unesco Secretariat in Canberra has been unfailingly helpful, and we thank especially Robin Savage and Ruth Trotter. Members of the Symposium Planning Committee are responsible for the form of the symposium:

Professor G. Seddon (Chairman) – Centre for Environmental Studies, University of Melbourne

Dr R. Darroch – Department of Psychology, Australian National University

Dr P. Ellyard – Department of Environment and Conservation

Mr B. Mackenzie – Bruce Mackenzie and Associates (Landscape Consultants)

Dr J. Philip – CSIRO Division of Environmental Mechanics

Mr C. Pugh – Hurstbridge, Victoria

Mr K. Storey – National Capital Development Commission

Mr D. Yencken – Merchant Builders Pty Ltd

The sources of illustrations are acknowledged with the caption when relevant.

Contents

Contents

Introduction

Introduction

The publication of this book is a part of Australia's contribution to the Unesco *Programme on Man and the Biosphere* (MAB), 'an intergovernmental and interdisciplinary programme of research emphasising an ecological approach to study of the inter-relationships between man and the environment, and to problems relating to rational use and conservation of the resources of the biosphere'.[1]

The Australian Unesco Committee for MAB was established in 1971 to guide Australia's participation in the international program. As a part of Project 13 (described below) a symposium was held at the Academy of Science in Canberra from 30 May to 2 June 1974, with the title *Man and Landscape in Australia*. It was a lively seminar, but the participants were necessarily few, and we recognised an obligation to make the ideas generated there accessible to a larger audience. We also felt that the subject of the symposium – perceptual attitudes to the Australian scene – is moving so fast that it was desirable to aim at relatively speedy publication. What follows, then, is not offered as uniformly solid scholarly work – but neither is it a simple transcript of the proceedings. The papers have been revised by their authors for publication, and edited with varying degrees of brutality. One new paper was solicited – that by Professor Ledgar – to fill a gap. Some material offered at the symposium has been abridged or omitted.

MAB Project 13, 'the perception of environmental quality' was outlined as follows:

THE PROBLEM

The social, natural and man-made environments are closely related in the dimension of environmental quality. Approaching the question of environmental quality, man should be aware that he is himself a member of the biosphere, sharing the same roots with all other living beings and thus being in partnership with them. On the other hand, he has, because of this knowledge and power, the full responsibility for the biosphere. Empirical studies emphasise the importance of man's perception of the environment. The mutual interrelationship between humans and their environments can be isolated for separate discussion at different scales, e.g. in terms of personal space, large architectural space (aesthetics), roads and pathways, neighbourhoods, the city, larger conceptual regions (natural beauty and open space), and countries.

Perceptions vary with different cultural groups, each seeking to utilise the environment which they perceive in different ways.

Regardless of human preferences, certain environments set limits upon human numbers and forms of land use. The establishment of ecological and cultural criteria which can guide the shaping or modification of the environment is essential. Man can tolerate a wide but not unlimited range of environmental conditions. In order to establish the ratios and relationships between quality and quantity, sets of indicators need to be developed to plan for future changes.

The escalation of man's impact on the landscape due to the effects of technological advance and the diversity of circumstances imposed by physical constraints imply a flow of resources and a constant reinvestment thereof.

Effective methods of measuring the parameters, e.g. the effects of sensorial stimuli in urban and non-urban populations, is a formidable task requiring research which is interdisciplinary in nature.

POSSIBLE FIELDS OF ACTION

(1) Analysis of perception of environment in different regions and cultures, to seek the major cultural determinants affecting environmental perception in various societies. This analysis should include different kinds of cultures and might be approached for example, through studies of:

  (a) perceptions of environmental hazards;
  (b) perceptions of visual or acoustic surroundings;
  (c) perceptions of landscape, in both its aesthetic and historic aspects, and in terms of its past or proposed remodelling by man.

(2) Cross-cultural studies of environmental preferences.

(3) Studies to establish socio-cultural and physical indices of environmental quality, with tests of their predictive effectiveness.[2]

A working group of the Australian Unesco Committee for Man and the Biosphere met on 22 June 1973, in Canberra, with Professor Ralph Slatyer in the Chair, to consider Australia's contribution to Project 13, and the symposium was the outcome. As Macquarie University was about to hold a specialist seminar on the search for indices and indicators of environmental quality (since held at Macquarie, November 1973), the Committee were inclined to parts 1 and 2 of the fields outlined above, especially part 1(c), and I was asked to chair a working group to organise a seminar along these lines.

In setting up a symposium on environmental perception in Australia, the Committee had problems. The field is vast, ill-defined, and yet much work in it is highly specialised. If we take the view that the topic 'is better approached from the point of view of understanding the man-environment interface'[3] then it is hard to see what is excluded. Theology is not, because it is abundantly clear that religious views have a profound effect on environmental behaviour and environmental perception. The social environment cannot be divorced from the physical environment, and neither can be described other than through one man's or another's perception of them. This topic has no natural boundaries.

The topic lacks definition because there are four basic questions, no one of which can be answered independently. The questions concern:

What there is
What we have done to it
What it has done to us
What we can and should do in the future

Each question is hard. If we ask what there is, what the Australian environment is like, we are asking a question about perception, one that is not answered by the blithe assumption that *we* know what it is *really* like, and so the accuracy of the perceptions of others can be assessed by this yardstick. Is it, for instance, a harsh environment? Many of those who write about it will say so, yet live in a coastal city like Sydney, which has a remarkably equable climate by world standards. Even Melbourne is mild in comparison with the rigours of the United Kingdom, from which most of our forebears came.

'What have we done to it?' is a question about our environmental behaviour, itself a measure of perception, the one that behavioural psychologists choose to study, but it is a complex measure, because our behaviour is the resultant of many forces and motives, including economic ones. Economic motives themselves are complex. Farmers may shoot eagles and ring-bark every tree on the property from what they take to be economic motives, protecting their flocks and improving their pastures, although there is evidence to show that eagles may be an ally in controlling rabbits and rodents, and that the amenity of shade trees on a pastoral property may be money in the bank in real estate terms.

'What has it done to us?' is perhaps the most interesting of all the questions. How far has the Australian character and way of life been shaped by the Australian environment? The range of interpretation ranges to the extremes, from geographical determinism ('Sydney life sparkles like its harbour; Melbourne runs conformably between narrow banks like the Yarra', to invent a quotation) – to the other extreme of supposing that the environment is a trivial backdrop, as have so many of our professional historians, describing political and economic history as if it all happened in Birmingham or Leeds. Our behaviour is clearly an adaptive response to the environment in some ways – by the addition of a verandah to the Georgian box, for instance, although both word and practice were Indian imports. Yet in a later phase of our architecture, we returned to the unshaded box, made it bigger, walled it with glass, and installed air conditioning, thus preferring to adapt the environment to us. There are also quite conscious elements of defiance in our national response, for example in the still fairly common practice of eating plum pudding on Christmas Day, even in the middle of a heat-wave, showing the environment who's boss.

And that takes us to the last question. 'How far should we adapt, or respond?' No matter how earnestly they are implored to do so, Australians are not likely to learn the ways of the Aboriginal inhabitants. We will continue to live as technological man, and this holds both for the Collins Street lawyer and the Nimbin drop-out; the difference between a new Mercedes and an eight-year-old utility is trivial. We will keep on adapting the environment to our needs, and so in some ways we should. Pastures that are 'improved' with superphosphate and subterranean clover, for instance, are indeed improved, a long-term increment in the life-sustaining capacities of the continent. At the other extreme, consider the following: a second-generation Australian of my acquaintance, who has lived in a dozen country towns in two States, is a great gardener, and knows the names and cultural requirement of literally thousands of exotic garden plants. She was asked to identify an unfamiliar garden specimen. 'Is it a native?' she said. 'If it's a native, I won't know it.' That was said with neither pride nor shame, but was a simple statement of fact, and common for her generation.

It is fair to say, therefore, that we are still, by and large, aliens in an alien land. Does it matter? It might matter in at least three ways. The first is practical. Without a better understanding of the environment we are not likely to understand its constraints, the limits to what we can and cannot do with it, especially in those cases where the effects of our behaviour reveal themselves only in slow and long-term changes. The second is in environmental design. The third is in the shadow land of identity, national consciousness, a subject that is hard to talk about intelligibly, as fundamental questions often are.

This book answers few questions, but it may help readers to formulate some of them more precisely. The papers are grouped into five sections, in a way that is necessarily artificial, for the reasons given above. *Section One* sets the context of inquiry, with an introductory survey of the evolution of perceptual attitudes, a paper on perception from a psychologist, and one on the responses of the first European settlers to the new land. *Section Two* turns to the physical setting, with a paper on the biological structure of the landscape, and three synoptic histories of our major transformations of it by way of farming, gardening and engineering. *Section Three* considers the evolution of attitudes to the landscape as reflected in the arts, especially poetry, painting and the novel. This grouping is, at first sight, logical and self-contained, but it is incomplete – we would like to have had a paper on perceptions as reflected in advertising, the history of film in Australia, and of television, but ran out of time and space. Moreover, some of the papers show the artificiality of the grouping. Frank Moorhouse's paper, for instance, is in this section because he writes short stories, but it would have been equally appropriate in either of the following two sections. His account is of social perceptions, especially of the young and footloose. His characters 'live in the old urban core', yet are often refugees from the claustrophobic social environment of country towns, yearning in Kings Cross for self-sufficiency, the return to Nature and a rural life-style.

Section Four* gives a history of the built environment; the buildings, towns and cities we have made. *Section Five* looks to the future and at some rapidly changing perceptions. Because the contributors to this section have such different backgrounds, it also offers in itself a wide range of responses. The student of perception might indeed regard this whole book, both its parts and its organisation, as raw material for further studies in perception and as a contemporary record of attitudes. The last contributor, Professor David Lowenthal, a guest from the other hemisphere, does just that.

GEORGE SEDDON
December 1974

References

1. International co-ordinating council of the Programme on Man and the Biosphere (MAB). First session. *Final Report*. November 1971. Paris, Unesco, 1972, p. 5.
2. *op cit.*, p. 25.
3. WALMSLEY, D. J. and DAY, R. A. *Perception and man-environment interaction: a bibliography and guide to the literature*. Geographical Society of New South Wales, New England Branch, Armidale. Occasional papers in geography, no. 2, 1972.

1. The context

*George Seddon**

The evolution of perceptual attitudes

The common aim of these papers is to show the evolution of the perceptual attitudes of Australians to their land. Some are descriptive: that is, they attempt to show how Australians have in fact perceived their environment through time (and for this reason, much of the book is historical). Some are also prescriptive, suggesting ways in which our environmental perceptions might be heightened and more finely attuned to the needs of the land that is now home. The *Programme on Man and the Biosphere* which occasioned this book is biologically oriented, and the subtitle, *Towards an ecological vision of Australia*, derives from that orientation. All contributors to the book would agree with the general proposition that Australians should become more sensitive to the special needs of their unique landscapes, but agreement probably ends there. We have different prescriptions, and different diagnoses of the past, some of them primarily cultural, some economic (for example, Bruce Davidson shows very clearly the major economic constraints that have determined the broad patterns of Australian agriculture, and suggests in doing so that they could hardly have been different from what they were).

It is not surprising that there are differences of opinion. It cannot be assumed that we know a great deal either about what Australians 'see' or about the forces that have shaped their perceptual worlds. Further, there is no such thing as 'the Australian environment': Balmain is not much like Eucla. Thirteen million different people see a great variety of different places, in different ways, at different times, and any one person sees the same place in many different ways in the course of a day. For example, in 1971 Melbourne had 108 000 people of Greek origin, most of them living in and around South Melbourne, and thus a city within a city. There have been a few studies of this Greek community from specific points of view (e.g. housing), but none of their perceptual responses to their environment. Contemporary perceptual studies of any kind are few.[1] We have been a little better served by historical studies, especially by Bernard Smith's subtle and provocative *European vision and the South Pacific*[2], Geoffrey Blainey's *The tyranny of distance*[3] and studies such as R. L. Heathcote's *Drought in Australia: a problem of perception.*[4] Sir Keith Hancock's history of land-use, *Discovering Monaro*[5], may mark a new beginning among professional historians, who have generally ignored the land.

Part of the difficulty with such studies is that it is not always clear what should count as evidence. The only perceptions we know directly are our own. We guess at the perception of others from what they say they perceived, what they record, what they omit, how they behave. Poetry, painting, old films, advertisements and newspapers, are all records, but they all need interpretation – early pictorial artists drew the indigenous flora and fauna, topography, Aboriginals, in certain ways, partly because of current traditions of draughtsmanship, and because of the function of their

---

* George Seddon, Director of the Centre for Environmental Studies at the University of Melbourne since 1974, was formerly Professor of History and Philosophy of Science at the University of New South Wales. He is a member of the Australian Advisory Committee on the Environment.

work (e.g. to serve as scientific illustration rather than decorative wall hangings),
partly because of individual idiosyncrasy, or limitations of skill with the pen, partly
because of cultural preconditioning (which led, for example, to the portrayal of
Aboriginals first as Noble Savages, and a few years later, in reaction, as comic
scarecrows) – and partly as a genuine visual response to the object before them. This
last component, the only one which some would call the genuinely perceptual
component, is not in fact separable from the cultural and biological predisposition to
see in certain ways, as John Ross shows in the next chapter.

If it is hard to interpret individual perceptions, it is harder to make useful
statements about those of a community. From the outset, individual responses varied
widely, as the following early descriptions of the site of Sydney show well enough:

The first is from Major Robert Ross:

> I do not scruple to pronounce that in the whole world there is not a worse country
> than what we have yet seen of this. All that is contiguous to us is so very barren
> and forbidding that it may with truth be said here that Nature is reversed; and
> and if not so, she is nearly worn out . . .

The second is from Lieutenant Ralph Clark:

> This is the poorest country in the world – over run with large trees, not one acre
> of clear ground to be seen . . .

The third is from Captain Watkin Tench:

> The general face of the country is certainly pleasing, being diversified with gentle
> ascents, and little winding vallies, covered for the most part with large spreading
> trees, which afford a succession of leaves in all seasons. In those places where trees
> are scarce, a variety of flowering shrubs abound, most of them entirely new to a
> European, and surpassing in beauty, fragrance and number, all I ever saw in an
> uncultivated state: among these, a tall shrub, bearing an elegant white flower, which
> smells like English May, is particularly delightful, and perfumes the air to a great
> distance.

The fourth is from Mrs Elizabeth Macarthur:

> The greater part of the country is like an English park, and the trees give it the
> appearance of a wilderness or shrubbery, commonly attached to the habitations of
> people of fortune, filled with a variety of native plants, placed in a wild, irregular
> manner.

The fifth is from Surgeon Bowes:

> To describe the beautiful and novel appearance of the different coves and islands
> as we sailed up is a task I shall not undertake, as I am conscious I cannot do
> justice to the subject. Suffice it to say that the finest terras's, lawns, and grottos,
> with distinct plantations of the tallest and most stately trees I ever saw in any
> nobleman's grounds in England, cannot excell in beauty those which nature now
> presented to our view.[6]

Yet despite the apparent range of responses expressed here, they are easily sorted,
and a much wider sample would fall under much the same headings. The two
unfavourable responses are utilitarian ('not one acre of clear ground'); two of the

three favourable respond to the scene as 'picturesque', and this division has persisted
to the present day, with one group taking the picturesque view ('superb and unique
tract of *E. camaldulensis* riverine woodland') while the utilitarian has a bleaker
response ('a muddy paddock with a few scruffy old gum-trees'). It is a misfortune that
these two responses are so sharply distinct in Australia – many of the finest landscapes
of Europe are man-made, productive and yet harmonious with the natural environment. The Australian landscape, by contrast, was not as a rule immediately hospitable
to human needs, so that utility and natural beauty have become sharply defined
alternative categories. The heart of our environmental design problem, in my view, is
to fuse those categories.

Other elements in the responses quoted above that recur again and again are the
reason given for liking the landscape by Mrs Macarthur and Surgeon Bowes, that it
is 'park-like'; the rather open woodlands have an imported value attached to them,
in that they suggest a noble estate (these responses are discussed more fully by
Heathcote). The comment that 'Nature is reversed' and 'worn out' by Major Ross are
also much repeated. This is the Antipodes, where all things are topsy-turvy. It is also
tired, the last of lands (see Alec Hope's 'Australia'). This latter view is another potent
myth, although it is a biological and geological absurdity, not so much 'wrong' as
meaningless. In the sense that Australia probably broke off from the Antarctic
land-mass in the Eocene, only fifty million years ago[7], it is one of the youngest
continents. It has large exposures of ancient Precambrian rocks, but so do Europe
and North America. The soils are old, and some of the landforms are old. The flora
has been evolving continuously to the present; it is certainly not 'ancient' in any sense,
and since it is predominantly angiosperm, with fewer gymnosperms than any other
continent, it is at least in that sense a 'young' flora. Its mammals are marsupials
rather than placental, and thus represent an ancient lineage, but they are not, of
course, Cretaceous mammals, or even Pleistocene ones (the Pleistocene fauna was
quite different): they are the outcome of quite recent evolutionary events – as, of
course, are the gymnosperms of the other continents.

When they called it old or tired, they meant that it was strange, harsh, rugged –
unlike the green and gentle, temperate homeland. If Australia had been settled by
Spaniards, for example, the responses and behaviour might have been very different.
Spanish agricultural experience, respect for water, styles of architecture and of
shaping towns might have led to a society more in harmony with the Australian
environment, although it would probably have lacked the Anglo-Saxon virtues – for
example, the talent for political stability – which also characterise our society. But
whatever might have been, it was the Anglo-Saxons (and Irish) who came, thus
generating the central paradox, that of a people whose cultural traditions and
aspirations derive from a fundamentally different physical environment.

Of course the strangeness can be exaggerated; some visitors to Sydney in the 1820s
remarked on the familiarity of the vegetation in its natural setting, because they
knew the flowers already from English gardens. Visiting botanists generally had a good
knowledge of the flora before they set foot in Australia, and flowers from all over the
continent were illustrated in works such as Robert Sweet's *Flora Australasica: or a
Selection of Handsome and Curious Plants, natives of New Holland, and the South Sea
Islands – most proper for the Conservatory or Greenhouse* (1827–28)[8], drawn from
flowering specimens in English gardens before Perth, Adelaide or Melbourne were
settled. Thus the strangeness obviously depended on the experience of the observer.

11

The strength of the Anglo-Saxon cultural tradition can also be exaggerated. In some ways, behaviour was modified rather quickly to suit local conditions – for example, the evolution of dry-farming techniques – yet the Anglo-Saxon conditioning was, and is, strong. The shortness of our pre-industrial history is also significant. By the end of the nineteenth century, Australians were beginning to accommodate themselves emotionally to their new setting (as Brian Elliott shows); and physically, as illustrated by country towns like Beechworth, Clare, York, Bathurst. But evolving local tradition did not have long enough to establish itself firmly before it was overwhelmed by the homogenising technology of this century, in which so many forces are at work to over-ride regional differentiation. Americans had stronger resources; for example, the landscape tradition established by Olmsted persisted into the twentieth century, and has been a base from which schools of landscape design have been able to tackle the new problems of a new century. Guilfoyle's work in Australia in the nineteenth century was as good as Olmsted's, but the skills died with him, and we have almost had to start all over again in the last decades.

Some of the dissonance between expressed perception of the environment in Australia and environmental behaviour is due to the speed of urban and industrial growth, so that the way we see ourselves and our setting is often at odds with the way we behave. The Man from Snowy River still rides through the advertisements of the tobacco companies, although he is rarely met in Pitt Street. The bronzed Anzac, the lifesaver, the Great Australian athlete, the skilled bushman, lurks within us all, although by generally accepted health standards, Australians are among the least healthy groups living in 'developed' societies.[9] We are aware of these inconsistencies, and many of our perceptions of the environment have undergone rapid evolution in the last few years: for example, the 1972 election, which brought Labor to power, marked the effective political recognition that most Australians lived in cities, and this recognition, if belated, will never again be neglected politically. Our perception of our cities themselves has also undergone rapid changes, as Bernard Smith shows – within a period of ten years, Paddington, for example, passed from an official slum, 'totally substandard' suitable only for demolition, to the most expensive real-estate in Sydney. Our perceptions of our social environment are also changing very quickly, as Frank Moorhouse shows.

Our capacity to adapt and evolve new responses is real, but we are still in trouble, I think. There are basic incompatibilities in our responses which we are reluctant to face. For instance, most Australians are perfectly sincere in saying they 'love the bush', including its fauna. Of British stock, they also love cats and dogs. To live in the bush without destroying its native animals, for example at the Bend of Islands outside Melbourne, residential co-operatives find it essential to ban cats and dogs. This has met with passionate resentment: it is hard to accept the stark incompatibility. Ecologists have been saying that the Australian environment is fragile for so long that 'fragile' is now a part of the popular vocabulary, but it does not seem to control basic thinking about our future in any significant way (for instance, population policy is still not a major political issue). No other western, highly urbanised and industrial country is as ecologically vulnerable as Australia. Advanced technology makes massive demands on natural systems. Flushing of pollutants, for example, depends on natural rainfall, yet the sum of the run-off from all Australian streams at their outlets is less than that of any one of the world's major rivers, for example the Mississippi. Our large cities are all in exceptionally favoured corners of the continent,

12

but even in those corners flood, fire, and drought are recurrent realities, although we seem to be taken by surprise with every renewal. Both city and country life in Australia are dependent on massive power consumption, much of it currently drawn from non-renewable sources, as is the fertiliser on which Australian agriculture depends so heavily.

The cities are in many ways insulated by technology from environmental realities, and thus generate a world in which myths can grow and flourish, the most pernicious of which is the myth that Australia is a big country, whereas in terms of permanent life-supporting systems it is a relatively small one, with about the same amount of arable land as France, much of it of inferior quality, with a high variability in rainfall. (Although Australia could undoubtedly increase both her total cereal production and her yield per hectare if it were profitable to do so, present yields are very low by world standards, yet the average Australian is incredulous on being told that in 1972, for example, the United Kingdom grew one and a half times as much cereal as Australia, on one third the area.)[10] It is a large country only as a communication system – the tyranny of distance still rules, to use Blainey's phrase. Australia is a small country with long journeys. Much of our wealth, the wealth that has directly and indirectly supported our massive urban growth, has come from mineral resources, from gold in Victoria, silver-lead at Broken Hill, gold again at Kalgoorlie, through to the present boom. Geoffrey Blainey called his book on mineral exploitation in Australia, *The rush that never ended*[11], but there could be a postscript, and I can imagine a complacent and well-fed New Zealand economic historian two hundred years hence writing an epitaph for Australia, as for Nauru: 'She was cursed with great riches in non-renewable mineral wealth'.

Although the riches are great, they are not inexhaustible, a fact to which our ghost-towns bear witness. This is no argument against using them, but it would be unwise to base estimates of the permanent carrying capacity of the continent on current rate of resource consumption. Mineral wealth seems to engender a recklessly expansive view of the future, while the evidence that Australia is *not* a big country is disregarded, even though it dominates our lives. We are, in fact, already short of land, and absurd though this may seem at first sight, we read about it in every newspaper (but with a different set of perceptions, not our 'Big Country' perceptions, but our 'Urban Problems' perceptions). When the newspapers report a shortage of land, we know that not enough building blocks are coming on to the market around the capital cities. We may then urge the Government to make more land available. The outward expansion of the cities can be speeded up in various ways, but no Government can make more land – except, perhaps, the Dutch. All, or almost all, the habitable land in Australia is already under competing pressures (for housing, for farming, for mining, for roads, for recreation), a fact starkly illustrated by the cost of land of any kind for any purpose within eighty kilometres of the major cities. An even clearer example of the shortage of land for specific purposes is the difficulty of finding an acceptable new site for almost any substantial enterprise in Australia – an airport for Sydney, a container terminal, a new power station in Melbourne. Every new freeway site, major housing subdivision, sewerage works, dam site, quarry application, is bitterly contested, usually with good reason, namely that the site already has valid uses, and the new uses would conflict with the old. The curious feature of this situation is that an acute community awareness of all these specific problems has not yet become a national perception that Australia is already short of land for some of its needs, which are primarily urban. Because of its geology and latitude, Australia is short of water and good soils. These observations are commonplace. (Because of her latitude, Australia was exempt from the extensive glaciations of the Pleistocene that so profoundly modified the lands of the northern hemisphere, in ways that contribute greatly to their capacity to sustain large populations.) It is less well known that, compared with the other continents, Australia is poorly supplied with natural harbours, estuaries and wetlands. The limited supply of estuaries and wetlands presents us with acute problems in land use, because they have a special biological function (as nurseries) that is incompatible with the demands that technological man makes of them. This conflict is to be found in all industrial countries, but it is exceptionally acute in Australia.

These are all essentially problems of urban and industrial landuse. Meanwhile, down on the farm things may be worse. Sir Keith Hancock has said of his own childhood:

> In *Country and calling* I commented as follows on the privileges and deprivations of my boyhood in Gippsland: 'As a healthy young barbarian I found vivid joy with the Australian outdoors; but might not my joy have been deeper if somebody had taught me to read the story which time had written upon Australian earth?' (p. 53). My teachers could not help me to use my eyes, because nobody had helped them to use their eyes. I wonder whether things are different today in Gippsland?[12]

A country boy may now be lucky enough to find people who know something of the land he lives in, but it is still likely to be an impoverished environment. One of the most telling comments for me in Donald Horne's *The education of young Donald*[13] is his account of his upbringing in Muswellbrook, in the heart of the country, but cut off from nature. Horne learnt about nature in the city, on his trips to Sydney, where he could walk the beaches and explore the Royal National Park and Port Hacking, much richer than the paddocks of the upper Hunter.

In a book published in 1966, a few years before its time and therefore without the impact it should have had (*The great extermination*, edited by A. J. Marshall[14]), there is a chapter with the title, 'The decline of the plants' by John Turner. Writing of the basaltic grasslands of western Victoria, he remarks that 'the native flora was virtually exterminated over hundreds of square miles'. He quotes an estimate of 2200 native plant species for Victoria, with 550 aliens – 'about five new weed species established themselves every year between 1870–1930. This is an index of the progressive deterioration of the natural plant communities, for these are rarely invaded when in the natural state'. In fact, of the native plants, some 277 species are either extinct or survive only in isolated pockets. But the loss of individual species is less serious than the loss of whole communities: 'throughout the better watered pastoral belt' of Australia 'the original vegetation was a mosaic of many different plant communities, dominated by different species of *Eucalyptus* (White Box, White Iron-bark, Yellow Box, etc.). Each had its characteristic topography, soil, climate, flora and fauna. With pasture improvement all these diverse communities are losing their individuality and are converging to one more or less uniform pasture, carrying a few exotic species of grass and clover – the surviving trees themselves are rarely allowed to regenerate; they are a diminishing asset.'

Some Australians who 'love the bush' have in mind such cleared pastures with a few stands of remnant eucalypts. Many have no idea of what an undisturbed

14

environment is like. I have heard a tattered few acres that has been logged, cleared and burned three times in a hundred years, and is now tertiary regrowth eucalyptus woodland choked with blackberry and watsonia, described and ardently defended as 'natural bushland'. I have been shown degenerate rain-forest (a so-called National Park) from which all of the valuable timber was removed over a century ago, beginning with the cedar-cutters, so that little remains today other than lawyer vines and the Giant Stinging Nettle Tree (*Laportea*), a weed species. This sorry relic was presented as pristine rain-forest.

Many Australians know no better, because they have had little opportunity to learn. To be sure, they would have had no opportunity at all if we had never settled this continent, thus preserving the pristine environment in its entirety. Given settlement, of course the land had to be cleared, the trees felled, the native grasses ousted. Yet in Europe, the fields have been tilled for centuries without obliterating the indigenous flora. In England, and China or Japan, and equally in much of North America, the native flowers and grasses and shrubs and trees survive in meadow and hedgerows, and along the roadsides, as well as in woodlands and natural reserves. The difference lies in the isolation of the Australian flora, which rarely survives competition with introduced species in disturbed areas – that is, in most of agricultural and pastoral Australia – whereas the native flora of the temperate lands of the northern hemisphere can often co-exist with the species of agriculture, themselves plants of the northern hemisphere, with relatives among the natural communities of the regions in which they are cultivated. In Australia, the original communities are wiped out directly by clearing and indirectly by competition along the roads and elsewhere; where the original communities were rich and diverse, the flora that replaces them is very poor in species, consisting of a few agricultural species, together with their attendant introduced weed species, and it is in this sense that the environment is impoverished. Of course, much depends on the region. The young Keith Hancock had riches on his doorstep in east Gippsland, and his deprivation was the lack of a natural history tradition in his upbringing. But Donald Horne had neither the riches nor the natural history at Muswellbrook; and my own experience was closer to Horne's than Hancock's.

I spent a part of my youth in the Wimmera. I do not believe that I had a deprived childhood – it was a happy one for the most part – but it was deprived in three significant and inter-related ways. First it was socially deprived. Like most country towns in Australia, ours was quite rigidly socially stratified. As I and a very few others went away to boarding school, I was not on holidays at the same time as the children who went to the local State school, and I hardly even knew them. This spelt alienation of one kind. I also had Sir Keith Hancock's problem of environmental education. Although I must have had a latent interest in natural history when I was young, there was no-one to foster it, no-one to tell me about the birds or the plants or the geology, or even the history of settlement of my own countryside. (We were familiar with names like Muller and Dahlenberg in the district, but knew nothing of the cultural history of the German settlers in the Wimmera, nor of their traditions of land use, other than that they were respected as 'good farmers'.)

Finally, much of the Wimmera was and is an impoverished countryside. I do not recollect ever seeing a marsupial (except the possum) in its natural setting while I was young, and the natural vegetation had nearly all gone, replaced by exotics that certainly serve man's economic purposes better, but are very few in number of species, so that a complex ecosystem has been replaced by a monotonous and simple one. There was no Walden Pond at Horsham or Nhill, and could have been no Thoreau or Gilbert White, or even Huck Finn. Most English and American country children enjoy much greater natural history resources than most Australian country children, except perhaps in part of the American mid-West, although there at least the corn is indigenous. If I seem to labour this point, it is because it is contrary to the popular view. Many English children have seen, sometimes even studied, rabbits and foxes, weasels, stoats, squirrels, water-rats, badgers perhaps, occasionally even otters. At least fifteen native mammals are to be found today within the confines of metropolitan London, and some of them, including the fox, mole, vole, shrew and hedgehog – together with the non-native grey squirrel – are common.[15] Many children know at least the popular names of the wayside flowers, and many of the birds, including those of the wetlands and the migratory species. This is partly the tradition of a culture biased to country pursuits, partly opportunity.

I grew up among paddocks of wheat, planted sugar-gums from South Australia, weeds, a few surviving eucalypts, and the limited range of exotics common to country-town parks and gardens. The only animals with which I was familiar were dogs, cats, rabbits, horses, sheep and cows. There were birds, but I knew little of them, other than the magpie, and around the houses, sparrows, starlings, and mynah. None of this is to deny that the resources *potentially* available to me were richer than those of my English counterparts. I *could* have explored near-pristine bushland in the Grampians, and we did sometimes 'go for a drive' or even a picnic in country such as this, but it was not my day-to-day environment. I was obscurely drawn at this time of my life to a swamp down behind the town (Nhill, in this case) and to the Little Desert, long before it became a *cause célèbre*, but I did not know why, and never learned much about it. Almost the only other places where indigenous grasses and herbs were to be found in the area were the graveyards, but I did not know that either. I did not begin to learn until years later, and then at first out of books. I had to learn to begin to see Australia. Alec Hope's account of us as 'Second-hand Europeans, pullulating on alien shores'[16] has been quoted too much, but it sums up much of our history to date. I think my experience is typical, and it is not therefore surprising that we have among the lowest standards of environmental design in the world. Australians are still learning to see where it is they live. The imaginative apprehension of a continent is as much a pioneering enterprise as breaking the clod.

References

1. WALMSLEY, D. J. and DAY, R. A. *Perception and man-environment interaction: a bibliography and guide to the literature.* Geographical Society of New South Wales, New England Branch, Armidale. Occasional papers in geography, no 2, 1972.
2. SMITH, B. *European vision and the South Pacific 1768–1850: a study in the history of art and ideas.* Oxford, Clarendon Press, 1960.
3. BLAINEY, G. *The tyranny of distance: how distance shaped Australia's history.* Melbourne, Sun Books, 1966.
4. HEATHCOTE, R. L. Drought in Australia: a problem of perception. *Geog. Rev.* 59:175–94, 1969.
5. HANCOCK, SIR W. K. *Discovering Monaro: a study of man's impact on his environment.* Cambridge, Cambridge University Press, 1972.
6. See GILBERT, LIONEL. Botanical investigation of eastern seaboard Australia 1788–1810. B.A. Honours thesis, University of New England, 1962.

7. See, for example, VEEVERS, J. J. 'Phanerozoic history of Western Australia related to continental drift', *J. geol. Soc. Aust.* 18(2): 89–96, 1971.
8. SWEET, ROBERT. *Flora Australasica.* London, James Ridgeway, 1827–8.
9. HETZEL, BASIL. *Health and Australian society.* Harmondsworth, England, Penguin 1974.
10. *Australian yearbook, 1972.* Canberra, AGPS, 1973, and FAO. *Production yearbook, 1972.* v. 26. Rome, FAO, 1973.
11. BLAINEY, G. *The rush that never ended: a history of Australian mining.* Melbourne, MUP, 1963.
12. HANCOCK, SIR W. K. Book review of G. Seddon. 'Sense of place, a response to an environment', *Canberra Historical Journal.* February 1974, p. 72.
13. HORNE, D. *The education of young Donald.* Sydney, Angus and Robertson, 1967.
14. MARSHALL, A. J. (ed.) *The great extermination: a guide to Anglo-Australian cupidity, wickedness and waste.* London, Heinemann, 1966.
15. GILL, DON and BONNETT, PENELOPE. *Nature in the urban landscape: a study of city ecosystems.* Baltimore, Md, York Press, 1973.
16. HOPE, A. D. *Selected poems.* Sydney, Angus and Robertson, 1973.

*John Ross**

Perceptual worlds

The eye is so much like a camera that it has been said, probably correctly, that no instrument made by man resembles a working part of his body more closely. It is the image forming property of the eye which has led to the misconception that visual perception deals in images which we interpret in order to comprehend our environment and to deal with it. Philosophers might read 'sense data' for 'images'.[1]

Perhaps the boldest attempt to characterise perception in general was Helmholtz's statement made in 1865 at the start of a chapter entitled 'Concerning the perceptions in general'. Helmholtz's formula was as follows:

> The sensations aroused by light in the nervous mechanisms of vision enable us to form conceptions as to the existence, form, and position of external objects. These ideas are called visual perceptions.

There is no reference to images in the formula. There is instead an assertion that it is reactions within what we would now call the visual system which enable us to form conceptions or ideas about the external world, with the implication that the visual system deals not in images but in conjectures about the environment. The difficulty with Helmholtz's formula for perception has been to explain how the inferences about the world are made within the processes of perception themselves. Helmholtz appealed to the notion of unconscious inference, which had the effect of introducing mind into perception and making perception too intellectual an activity for most people's taste. Perception seems too direct to have to wait for an act of mind before we see what we do.

The realisation that networks constructed from logical components – that is to say, electronic or biological components which perform elementary jobs of logical analysis – can automatically make inferences has eliminated, or at least sharply reduced, the force of the objection to Helmholtz's formula.

THE FROG'S EYE

In 1959 four MIT scientists, Lettvin, Maturana, McCulloch and Pitts published a remarkable paper under the title 'What the frog's eye tells the frog's brain'. They intercepted messages being sent from the eye to the brain. Objects were shown to a live, awake frog inside a hemisphere. Electrodes detected the signals sent from eye to brain.

The study began earlier, in ponds. Lettvin put himself in the frog's environment to try to discover the objects and events of significance to a frog. They turn out to be bugs, for eating, moving shadows, since they are usually cast by predators, and edges, since they occur where the water of the pond meets the shore, or where the frog's path is obstructed. These observations were important clues in understanding the significance of the experimental findings.

The attitude of the investigators is best expressed by a paragraph of their own:

---

* John Ross is Professor of Psychology at the University of Western Australia.

18

The assumption has been that the eye mainly senses light, whose local distribution is transmitted to the brain in a kind of copy by a mosaic of impulses. Suppose we held otherwise, that the nervous apparatus in the eye is itself devoted to detecting certain *patterns* of light and their changes, corresponding to particular relations in the visual world. If this should be the case, the laws found by using small spots of light on the retina may be true and yet, in a sense, be misleading.

In other words, the question in their minds is: What if the eye is not there to record images, and pass them on to the brain, but to detect patterns of significance within the environment?

Very briefly what was found was that the frog's eye did not send image copies to the brain, but signalled four, and only four classes of event: stationary edges, moving shadows, dimming or brightening, and a fourth, again described by the authors:

A delightful exhibit uses a large colour photograph of the natural habitat of the frog from a frog's eye view, flowers and grass. We can move this photograph – waving it around at a seven inch distance: there is no response. If we perch with a magnet a fly-sized object 1° long on the part of the picture seen by the receptive field and move only the object, we get an excellent response. If the object is fixed to the picture in about the same place and the whole moved about, then there is none.

This fourth signal is sent only when a small object moves erratically in front of a complex texture. It means that a fly is there, and to be eaten.

The images of the frog never get past his eyes. All the brain is told is about patterns of crucial biological and environmental significance to the frog.

OTHER EYES

Are our eyes like frogs' eyes? The answer is that they are not, but that the search for significant pattern and the signalling of pattern rather than the mosaic necessary to carry the image from eye to brain, is common to all visual systems so far investigated. The visual systems of rabbits, cats and monkeys, while different from one another and from the frog's, all seem to be specialised for the detection of significant pattern. Evidence for this proposition – which I shall not attempt to summarise – has been accumulating for more than a decade. Much of the important work has been done in Canberra by physiologists at the John Curtin School of Medical Research.

There is, however, one important difference. Much of the analysis of patterns of concern to a frog is done early, in the retina of its eyes. Animals who live in more complicated environments, and who move more rapidly within them, seem to analyse by stages and undoubtedly leave provision for modification of the analytic process by experience. The way they see is not fixed, as it seems to be for the frog. It changes with experience.

INFERENCE IN VISION

Very probably, almost certainly, our experience affects the way we see the next figure. Figure 1 was invented by Kanizsa. It consists only of three identical figures, each in a different position and a different orientation. We see a triangle where there is none. It has contours, where none exist. It is whiter than the area surrounding it, thought objectively there is no brightness or colour difference. And it stands out in depth, though the picture is flat.[2]

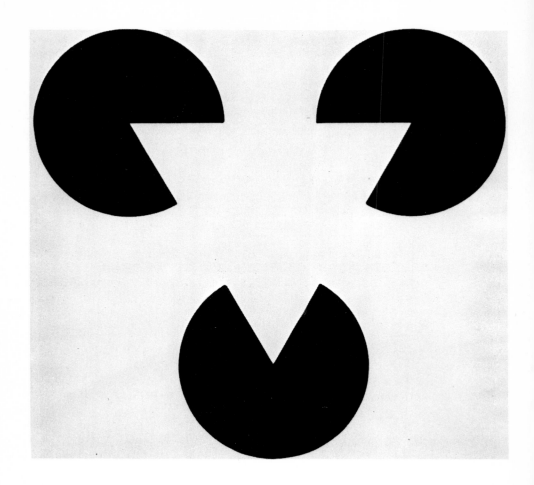

Figure 1. A figure invented by Kanizsa to show contour without gradients. Several other compelling examples are reported in Kanizsa (1974). Note especially the difference in surface quality of the inferred triangle.

Although it is present only by inference, the induced figure is visible, and vividly so. We sense that the incomplete circles are completed behind the triangle, but we do not see them as complete. We are caused to make two types of inference, one resulting in a vivid misperception, the other resulting in comprehension, which is not made visible.

Why do we see the figure as we do? Why is it so difficult to see the figure objectively? A complete answer would take too long, and involve too much speculation, but the brief answer is that our visual system structures the world by inference. When it has enough clues to indicate a structure, it leaps to the inference. Like the frog's eye, our visual system is hunting for significant pattern. Here it finds enough to tell us that there is a triangle, and exaggerates the point by giving it contour, differential colour, and a different position in depth. In doing so it draws not only on the preconceptions with which it was endowed, but on what it has learned about interposition.

SYMMETRY AS A PREDILECTION

Whereas the frog's eye has a predilection for bugs in the grass, or the pattern they cast on the eye, we respond to more abstract relationships of more general significance.

Figure 2 shows a random strip of dots within a rectangular display area. The strip is repeated, so that two identical strips of random texture stand side-by-side. Not much need be said about the collection itself except that it is conspicuously devoid of pattern, meaning or interest.

The point is that the repetition is not obvious. It requires close scrutiny to verify that each detail on the left is repeated on the right of the midline. Knowledge that there is repetition, whether given in advance, or discovered by perceptual investigation, does not lead to any direct revelation within perception of the fact of repetition.

Figure 3 shows the same random strip again, this time with its mirror image. The symmetry is immediately evident, without scrutiny, as a perceptual fact.[3] Moreover the symmetry is not *passive*. It causes an immediate organisation of the whole display into animated patterns, especially near the midline, or axis of symmetry. The collection is no longer devoid of pattern, but full of it, and no longer dull.

Vision is immediately responsive to symmetry in a way that it is not to repetition. It is more responsive to vertical than to horizontal symmetry. It is most responsive to two-fold symmetry (Figure 4), which yields brilliant Persian carpet effects. Note how powerfully the random configuration is now organised into patterns. The most spectacular effects of symmetry occur when it is displayed dynamically, as a pattern in constant change, but always symmetrical. Symmetry is not detected in an image.

Symmetry has been detected by the time we look, and by then has already structured what we see. We see symmetrical patterns in a way which is conditioned by the structure of our visual system as an instrument specialised for the interpretation of the world in terms of biological significance. Apart from man-made objects, the only frequent instances of symmetry in the world are living creatures. Our sensitivity to symmetry, and the sense of animation it creates, is probably a specialised sensitivity to life forms, and to approach and retreat by them or ourselves.

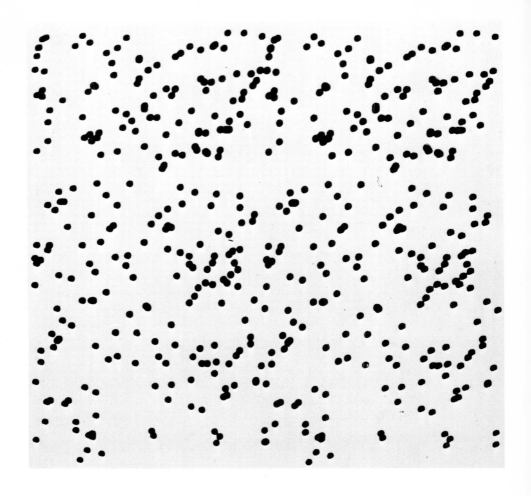

Figure 2. Identical random strips repeated side by side. A strip of random texture formed by plotting points at random with a rectangular region. The photograph is taken directly from an oscilloscope controlled by a computer. Random thermal activity decides where each point will fall. Repetition is not obvious without careful comparison of the two strips.

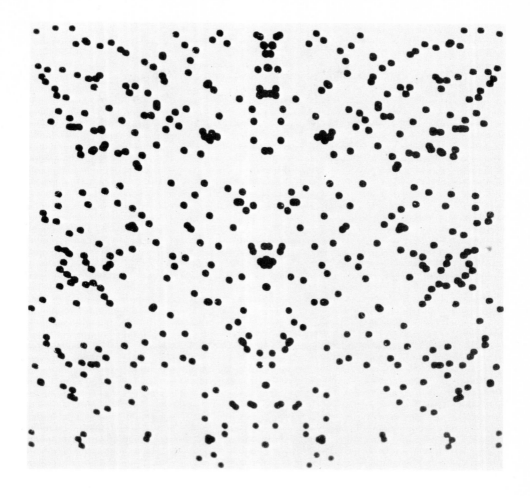

Figure 3. The same identical strips repeated side by side, but with one reflected, as in a mirror. Symmetry is immediately evident, especially near the midline. Neither strip now looks random.

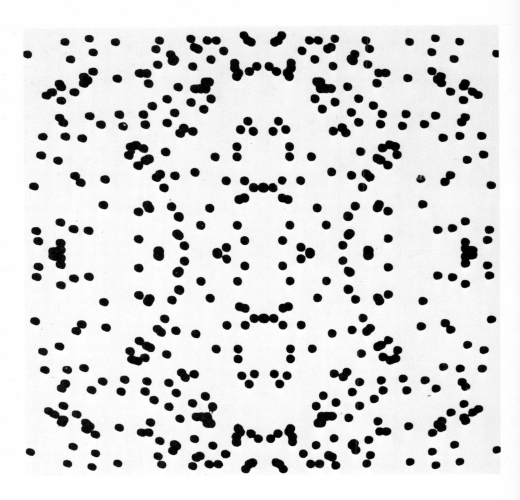

Figure 4. An example of two-fold symmetry, about the horizontal as well as the vertical midline. Vertical symmetry predominates, as can be seen by turning the page sideways.

THE STRUCTURE OF SPACE

We see the world as solid despite the fact that it reaches the first stage of the analytic systems of vision as a pair of images projected on flat surfaces, the retinae of our eyes. The most direct cause of solidity is the disparity between the images formed by the left and right eyes.

In 1838 Wheatstone invented the stereoscope to demonstrate the remarkable fact that we see solid when each eye is shown a separate picture of a scene as it would appear from its position.[4]

Until 1960 it was believed that the impression of solidity, *stereopsis*, depended upon a comparison of features from eye to eye. The information for depth is disparity in the relative position within the fields of view of the two eyes. How could disparity in position be established except by a comparison of new features recognised to be the same features but in different relative positions as seen by each eye?

In 1960 Bela Julesz showed that impressions of depth occurred when each eye was completely deprived of recognisable features. The next illustration (Figure 5) shows a pair of random dot stereograms, invented by Julesz.[5] Each by itself presents a uniform random texture. When each is seen by a different eye, one by the left eye and one by the right, you see a square standing out in depth from the background. It is solid and it has sharp edges.

Where does it come from? The two stereograms are identical except for a square patch which is slightly displaced in one of them. In order to detect the displacement the visual system has to compare the eyes' views element by element. The task of finding the displaced segment would be enormous, even with the aid of a computer. Our eyes not only do it automatically, but they also go on to draw the necessary inferences.

Julesz calls his stereograms 'cyclopean stimuli', since the scene they portray is visible only to a single, central eye. The left and right eyes alone are blind to them. He draws a comparison with contrapuntal melody, in which two tunes work together to produce a third. More convincingly than any of the previous demonstrations, these illustrations show that what is seen may be quite different from the images formed by the optical systems of the eye.

Quite complex patterns can be portrayed. The interested reader is referred to Julesz's book, *Foundations of cyclopean perception*, for many beautiful examples.

The fact that without the aid of meaning or memory, we can so rapidly detect the structure which is hidden in the relationships between the pictures seen separately by the eyes, underlines our extraordinary appetite for information indicating structure, and our remarkable skill in benefiting from it.

The vast amount of information presented to our eyes in these stereograms is stored for them on the photographic transparency. But such is the determination of the interpretative systems built into our vision, that we see just as clearly when the same information is presented to the eyes, one point at a time, requiring them to store the information themselves. That is to say, depth, like symmetry can be seen as the result of a process rather than by viewing static scenes presented as pictures.

ON THE ENVIRONMENT

What I hope I have shown is that when we perceive we do not perceive images of the world but we perceive a perceptual world constructed for us by our visual system. We must understand the visual system through which we construct our

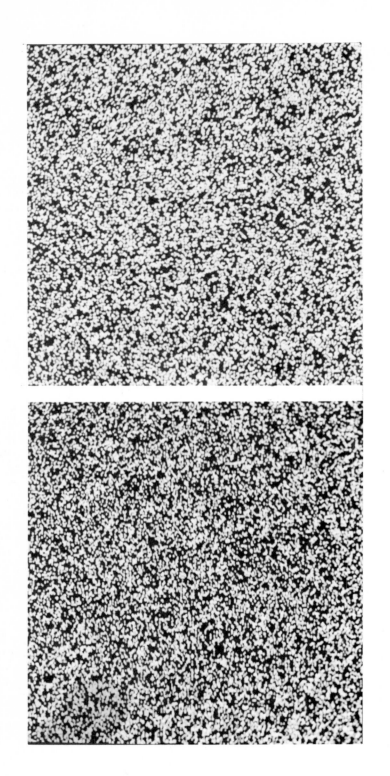

Figure 5. A random stereogram. Each of the two pictures displays a uniform random texture, with no hint of form or depth. To achieve binocular vision, cross your eyes, so that the left eye sees the right picture, and *vice versa*. This is not easy without practice, but can be done, with patience, by holding a pencil half way between your eyes and the page, and fixating on the pencil's point. When it is in the right position, both eyes are aimed at their proper targets, since they are converged on the pencil. Don't give up! The result is well worth the struggle. If intrigued, frustrated, or both, consult Julesz (1971, 1974), who provides glasses with his publications to eliminate the need to cross the eyes.

perceptual world as a complex biological system which has evolved genetically and learned by experience to deal with the environment in which we have to live.

I have stressed our inherited sensitivity to symmetry and to the binocular disparities that specify depth, rather than the sensitivities we acquire by experience. I have chosen to do so in order to show, by the most powerful demonstrations available, that we literally perceive the world as we construct it to be. The objects constructed for us by cyclopean perception are as plainly visible as a gum tree, a kangaroo or a plaster gnome.

But we also learn to see. The inherited machinery of vision undergoes constant modification and change as we learn to cope with the environment in which we live. It is therefore possible to speak of individual and cultural vision, and to mean much more than that different people in different cultures interpret what they see in different ways. Different people and different cultures live in different perceptual worlds, because the world is made manifest by conceptions which become built into the very process of perception.

Notes

1. 'Image' is used in two different senses here. The image on the retina is an image in the optical sense, formed by focussing light onto its surface. When visual perception is said to deal in images what is meant is something different, primitive visual sensations not yet subjected to interpretation. The one is, however, often thought to be the source of the other, and the undoubted fact that the eye does form images is used to justify speaking about images in the second sense. Some other contributors to this symposium run together the notion of an image in this second sense with something different again, namely a general conception of the way things are or might be construed to be in imagination. I think they believe we have a 'vision', a capability for ordering scenes in our minds, by means of which we filter, select and piece together into coherent wholes the fragments of experience collected by our senses. If what I am saying is true, this is rubbish.
2. Kanizsa has numerous other examples to consolidate the main points made by this demonstration, and to support a reformulated version of Helmholtz's theory with, as he says, 'the appropriate modernizations made possible by developments in modern information theory and in computer programming'. The interested reader is referred also to two books by Gregory, listed in the references.
3. The point here is that seeing repetition and seeing symmetry require comparisons of the same kind. Both depend on the relative position of texture elements. That one is detected spontaneously and the other not, means that vision is alert for symmetry, probably because of reciprocating transactions about the midline of the eye. It will be noticed that symmetry is less easy to see if the page is held sideways, or at an angle, and also if the gaze is fixed away from the centre of the picture. Symmetry can be detected even under heavy camouflage, which underlines our receptivity to symmetry.
4. Wheatstone's invention provided parlour room amusement for the nineteenth century as well as a powerful tool for the study of perception. Artists have made little use of stereoscopy although it has long been known that stereoscopic fusion leads to a 'decided improvement in beauty', to quote a New Zealand letter writer of the 1860s. Salvador Dali has one painting which is designed for viewing through lenses to help stereopsis. As if by magic a halo appears, to arouse religious awe in the breast of the spectator.
5. This figure was constructed by John Hogben, of the University of Western Australia, who wrote the computer program. The photographs are taken directly from point plotting oscilloscopes, which provide a dynamic version of this display, and others. They are rather more spectacular than their static equivalents.

References

VON HELMHOLZ, H. 1866. *Treatise on psychological optics*, v. 3. Translated from the third German edition; edited by J. P. C. Southall. New York, Dover Publications, 1925.

LETTVIN, J. Y., MATURANA, H. R., McCULLOCH, W. S., and PITTS, W. S. 'What the frog's eye tells the frog's brain', *Proceedings of the JRE.* 47(11): 1940–1951, 1959.

KANIZSA, G. 'Contours without gradients or cognitive contours?', *Italian Journal of Psychology.* 1(1): 93–113, 1974.

JULESZ, B. *Foundations of cyclopean perception.* Chicago, University of Chicago Press, 1971.

JULESZ, B. 'Co-operative phenomena in binocular depth perception', *American Scientist.* 62(1): 32–43, 1974.

WHEATSTONE, C. 'On some remarkable, and hitherto unobserved phenomena of binocular vision', *Phil Trans. Royal Soc.* London, pp. 128, 371–394, 1838.

GREGORY, R. L. *Eye and brain.* London, World University Library, 1966.

GREGORY, R. L. *The intelligent eye.* New York, McGraw-Hill, 1971.

R. L. Heathcote*

Early European perception of the Australian landscape: the first hundred years

'The southern unknown region, or Terra Australia incognita, is a vast tract of land as we judge by the coasts . . . The inhabitants are white, of a large stature, strong, industrious and courageous . . . Some modern relations tell us that in all that vast country they have neither King nor Prince, all the people being combined together in several factions in the form of a Commonwealth. They choose governors only to make the lazy work, punish offenders, and render justice to every man. They are idolators, and have oratories to pray to their idols in: they observe certain feasts and wash their bodies on certain days every year.'   *H. Moll, 1722.*[1]

Herman Moll's speculations that were made some 48 years before Cook's landfall in eastern Australia, opened up new sources of information but possibly two hundred years and certainly 116 years after the *first* European landfalls[2], illustrate the two fundamental problems implicit in the discovery and exploration of unknown lands. First there is the problem of lack of knowledge leading to often erroneous speculation, while second there is the problem of the interpretation or understanding of such information as is available, information often of a contradictory and apparently inconsistent nature. The century following Cook's landfall was to provide abundant evidence of these two problems; and, in particular, European perception of the Australian landscape was to provide plenty of evidence of erroneous speculations and to much conflicting information – sufficient indeed, as one contemporary put it, 'to confound and bamboozle the public mind'.[3]

But first some definitions. In this paper I shall be concerned with perception and attitudes, and Yi-Fu Tuan's recent explanation is relevant:

Perception is both the response of the senses to external stimuli and purposeful activity in which certain phenomena are clearly registered while others recede in the shade or are blocked out. Much of what we perceive has value for us, for biological survival, and for providing certain satisfactions that are rooted in culture.

Attitude is primarily a cultural stance, a position one takes *vis-à-vis* the world.[4]

Perception is essentially then the process of finding out – in our context, about the Australian landscape: the attitudes to the landscape are the result of that process. The scope of the term 'landscape' will be limited here to the visual components, the patterns of the weather, landforms and soils, plants and animals. The Aboriginal inhabitants will not be considered since they would require a separate study in their own right, and a competent literature already exists and has been recently added to.[5]

The process of environmental perception is currently under examination by both psychologists and geographers and the complexities and ramifications have been

---

* R. L. Heathcote is Reader in Geography at Flinders University of South Australia.

demonstrated.[6] For simplicity, however, in this paper the perception process will be considered as having three major components which mutually interacted to provide the final attitudes. First was the object about which information was sought, that is the continent itself, its characteristics insofar as they might have affected the perception process. Second were the observers, the variety of persons, groups or institutions who had an interest in or concern for the continental landscapes. Finally there were the media, the methods by which information of the continent was made available to the observers. We need to examine the nature of each in turn before we can understand the attitudes which they helped to create.

TERRA AUSTRALIA

From hindsight it appears obvious that the character of the continent influenced the perception of the landscape. The global location of the continent was not only responsible for the relative lateness of European contact but affected, and still affects, the flow of knowledge from Australia. By comparison with information from North America, 'intelligence' from the Antipodes took at least six times as long to arrive and most was virtually a year out of date by the time it was available in Europe. Indeed, the first hundred years of European settlement had almost elapsed before the first telegraphic communication link was opened in 1872. Perhaps significantly one of the major movements of British capital into Australia took place in the decade which followed the installation of this rapid communication system.[7] Remoteness reduced the volume and dated the information flow from Australia, and in the colony produced an isolated community out of step with events and philosophies in Europe.[8] Remoteness further discouraged potential emigrants by comparison with the nearer Americas, and even deterred the Scottish explorer Mungo Park, who declined Sir Joseph Banks' offer to provide the opportunity to duplicate his African successes in outback New South Wales.[9]

The very size and compact shape of the continent hindered the European explorers. The mariners were faced by a compact landmass unbroken by gulfs from which easy examination of the interior could be made. The mangrove mudflats of the Gulf of Carpentaria and the shoals and saltbush plains of Spencer's Gulf were not encouraging, and before the development and application of railway technology, the land routes to the interior were too costly for commerce.[10] As a result, the initial settlements were peripheral and isolated (by land) rather than central and consolidated.

The arid core of the continent, some forty-nine percent of the total area according to current thinking[11], meant that explorers from the peripheral settlements generally found a deteriorating environment the further they went, and the discouragement this produced delayed basic exploration of the interior until well into the twentieth century.[12] In other words even the basic continental patterns of terrain, vegetation or drainage had not been clearly established by 1870.

Not only was the continent apparently less attractive the further inland one went, but the condition of the environment changed significantly from season to season and from year to year. Most of the continent experienced a dry season when surface water disappeared and forage for livestock withered and often blew away, and there was abundant evidence of both floods and droughts at irregular intervals over the years. As a result, explorers experienced a variety of conditions, and their reports often differed even when describing the same locality.[13]

To these problems of a changeable environment must be added the novelty of the flora and fauna for European eyes. In 1825 the London *Quarterly Review* summed up the prevailing opinions:

> There is something so strangely different in the physical constitution of Australia, from that of every other part of the world; – we meet with so many whimsical deviations . . . from the ordinary rules and operations of nature in the animal and vegetable parts of the creation, that he must be a dull traveller indeed who does not glean something new and amusing from these regions, which are yet so imperfectly known to us.
>
> Here too we find the ferns, nettles, and even grasses, growing to the size of trees; – rivers running from the sea and lost in interior swamps; – trees that are evergreen in spite of frost and snow; – extensive plains on which, as one writer tells us, 'one tree, one soil, one water, and one description of bird, fish, or animal prevails, alike for ten miles, and for one hundred'; – and, as it is said, though we do not believe it, a climate diminishing in temperature as cultivation extends itself.[11]

In the face of such contradictions and uncertainties the evaluation of the usefulness of such phenomena to the new settlers was to take time and often to be a painful experience.

THE OBSERVERS

A variety of persons, groups and institutions had an interest in acquiring information about the new continent. At least ten groups might be identified as potentially holding different perceptions of the landscape because of either their particular experiences, calling or motives. Probably the smallest group was the explorers, yet they were the initial observers, and upon their reports were based many of the perceptions of others. In addition, however, we must identify the officials, both in Europe and Australia, the politicians and promoters, the scientists and philosophers, the technicians and refugees, and the convicts or free settlers. Each group had differing motives in its examination of the Australian landscape, and often contrasting perceptions resulted.

For the British officials, the landscapes were of relevance as strategic patterns of land and water, or sources of supply of scarce naval stores, or potential locations for convicts or free emigrants. The politicians and promoters saw opportunities for speculative gains and commercial exploitation, and occasionally joined with the philosophers in forecasting new societies in the new lands. The scientists regarded the patterns of vegetation and soils (in their own right) as phenomena to be classified and explained, while the technicians had interests more in common with the free settlers, looking more specifically at those patterns as they might provide a basis for capital investment and 'development'. The refugees brought traditional, or at least preconceived, ideas of how their society could be reconstructed in the new land and the land's resources fitted into that reconstruction. In contrast, for many of the convicts, the land was a hell on earth, although for some, artists and philosophers, the landscape had a fascination which never dimmed.

To illustrate the complexity of the perception process which such a variety of observers implied, it is worth looking briefly at two, possibly extreme, ends of the spectrum, the perception problems facing the explorers and those facing the free emigrants.

The perception of the landscape of the explorers was influenced in part by their motives, whether their search was for specific routeways or qualities of land, whether

spelt out in official orders or merely in their mind's eye. But this was only part of
what psychologists have recognised to be a complex relationship between psychological and environmental phenomena (Figure 6). In particular, the physical problems of survival in the arid interior often dominated their experiences, and an empty
stomach or malnutrition could give a jaundiced view of the landscapes.[15] Further,
the explorers had only a very limited time to formulate their impressions, and were
at the mercy of seasonal and even chance weather conditions. We need to remember,
for example, that the decision to direct the First Fleet to Botany Bay was based
upon only eight days' observations by Captain Cook's party, and it took Governor
Phillip less than 48 hours after his arrival on 19 January 1788, to decide he had been
sent to the wrong place, and less than a further 48 hours to relocate his settlement
at Sydney Cove. [16] Impressions had to be gained and decisions made quickly: once
made, however, they tended to be permanent.

At the other end of the spectrum of observers were the free emigrants – those
individuals and groups who made a conscious decision to emigrate to a new land,
which they perceived to offer them advantages over their own. Although they were
to experience at first hand the character of the landscape once arrived, their initial
perception had to be based upon information from other observers. Further, research
on migration movements suggest that while published descriptions had a role in
the general decision to migrate, specific movements may have been the result of
private communications and information-chains which did not form part of the
published 'information field.'[17]

In fact, despite the potential variety of views which the array of observers might
have been expected to provide, two basic problems confronted them all. First, how
to transmit their experiences to their fellow men, and second, how to interpret the
experiences of other observers. These were problems which the English
philosopher Francis Bacon (1561–1626) had spelt out in 1620. According to
Charles Singer:

> As an insurance against bias in the collection and error in the consideration of facts,
> Bacon warned men against his four famous *Idols*, four false notions, or erroneous
> ways of looking at Nature. There were the *Idols of the Tribe*, fallacies inherent in
> humankind in general, and notably man's proneness to suppose in Nature greater
> order than is actually there. There were the *Idols of the Cave*, errors inherent in our
> individual constitution, our private and particular prejudices, as we may term them.
> There were the *Idols of the Market-place*, errors arising from received systems of
> thought. There were the *Idols of the Theatre*, errors arising from the influence of mere
> words over our minds.[18]

Each of the four idols, or perhaps a better metaphor for our purposes is four
lenses (Figure 7), distorted the process of acquiring knowledge of the landscape.
Each, as we shall see, had relevance in explaining European perceptions.

Opposite

Figure 6. One interpretation of the relationship between psychological and environmental
phenomena in the perception process.

Figure 7. Some distortions of the perception process.
A. Bacon's four idols which lead men astray from the path to truth.
B. The four idols conceptualised as four distorting lenses through which the observer
   regards the object.

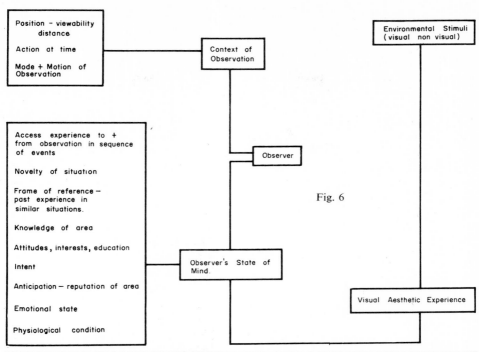

Fig. 6

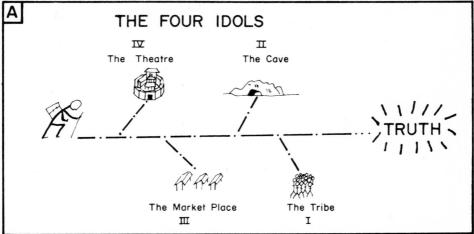

A

THE FOUR IDOLS

IV
The Theatre

II
The Cave

TRUTH

The Market Place
III

The Tribe
I

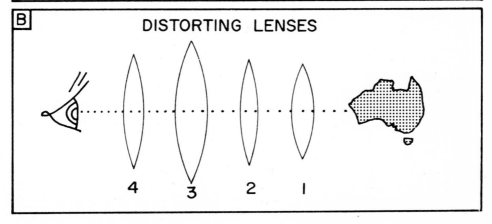

B

DISTORTING LENSES

4   3   2   I

Fig. 7

33

THE MEDIA

Between the 'object' and the 'observer' however lay the media, the means by which information of the one was brought to the attention of the other. The late eighteenth and nineteenth century context of the exploration and settlement of Australia meant that the process of that exploration and settlement was well documented by both literary and graphic sources at official levels, and even unofficial activities were marked by the keeping of personal journals and sketch books, extensive private correspondence to and from the continent, and reports to superiors, much of which seems to have survived. This mass of evidence is still relatively unresearched, but isolated examples and some prior work do allow some recognition; first, of the various channels by which information concerning Australia reached European observers; secondly, of the problems implicit in the interpretation of the information field provided by such channels; and thirdly, the role of those individuals who appear to have exercised an abnormal influence upon the transfer of information from one side of the world to the other – the gatekeepers.

The channels by which information reached the European observers are tentatively outlined in Figure 8. From the observations of the explorers the channels of information spread and multiply, some broader, some possibly cul-de-sacs, until the composite 'information field' is outlined from which the observer abstracts what he considers relevant information. Each subsequent stage reflects an increasing quantity of information (much of it of course repetitious and plagiarised), and an increasing component of individual choice, and an increasing possibility of error.

The existence of the channels, however, did not automatically imply communication. We have no real idea how many or what proportion of the Europeans read about Australia in the first hundred years. Indeed, we have only a scant idea of how many Europeans could read at all – for England, Raymond Williams estimated that only about twenty per cent of the public could read by the early nineteenth century.[19] The numbers of editions of some of the guidebooks suggest a wide variation in actual circulation – Carol Lansbury noted seven editions (one thousand each) of *Sidney's Australian Handbook* sold in five months in 1848, many more than Wakefield's rival *Hand-book for New Zealand*.[20] Averaging a shilling a copy, such were not sources of cheap information for the masses, but aimed more likely at the small capitalists. The early nineteenth century was the heyday of the literary periodicals such as the *Quarterly Review* and *Edinburgh Review*, which, as we have seen above, reviewed most of the serious publications on the new lands, and in the 1820s–1830s their circulations were between 9000 and 11 000 for each issue. A different order of magnitude however applied to Charles Dickens' works, several of which had Australian associations. Thus *David Copperfield*, wherein Mr Micawber found his fortune in Australia, sold 25 000 copies within a year of publication in 1849, and 83 000 copies of a penny edition in three weeks in 1871[21].

Just what kind of information was presented via the media would need a massive constant-analysis of the available literature. For the English-language sources, the prospect is too daunting, but some work on the much smaller German-language sources has enabled the sequence of topics covered to be identified and analysed[22]. An arbitrary categorisation of the subjects covered showed identifiable sequences (Figure 9) and a crude analysis suggested a wave-like sequence of first 'general' studies, then more specific or 'special' categories (Figure 10). In terms of information available in books, theses and journals (but excluding the newspaper

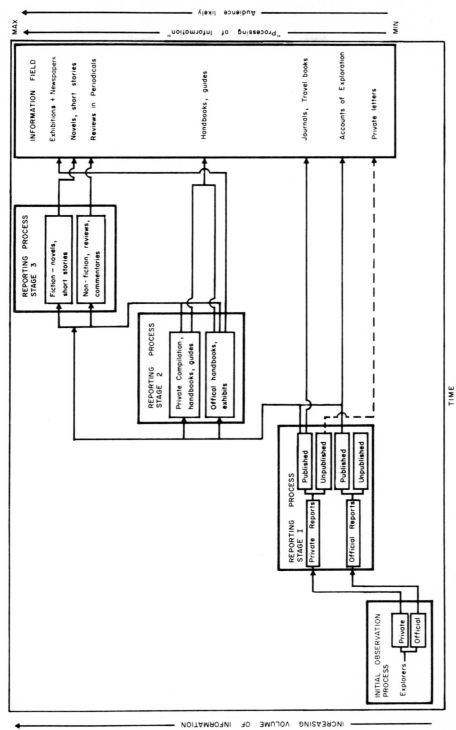

Figure 8. The possible evolution of the 'information field' available for European perception of the Australian landscape.

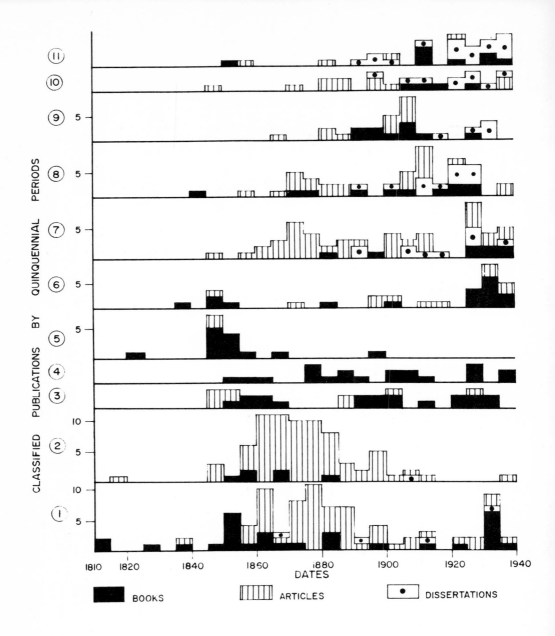

Figure 9. Sequence of German publications on Australia, 1810–1940.

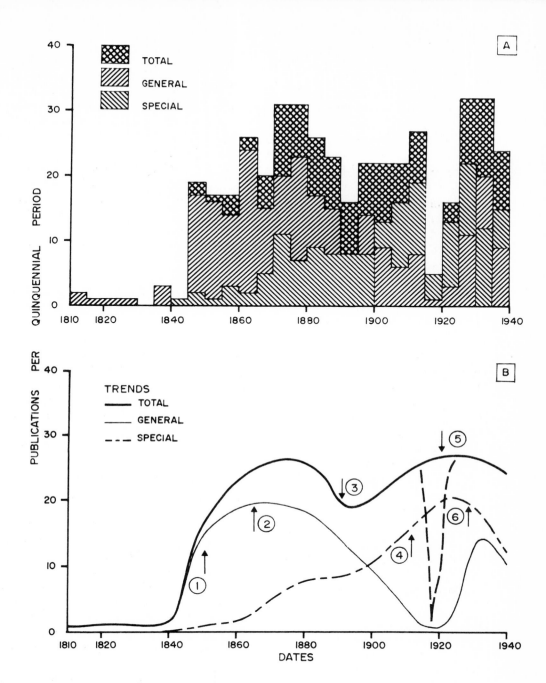

Figure 10. Summary of the sequence of German publications on Australia 1810–1940.
A. Actual sequence summarised. 'General'—total for categories 1 to 6 of Figure 9.
'Special'—total for categories 7 to 11 of Figure 9.
B. Trendline model of apparent sequence. Arrows indicate apparent stimuli/depressants which affected the trends: 1—1848 declaration of Federal Republic with interests in emigration, and the Australia gold rushes beginning. 2—Exploration of the interior under way and influence of Petermann's publications. 3—End of major land explorations and death of Petermann. 4—Specialist studies (in particular biological and anthropological topics). 5—First World War. 6—Specialist studies (in particular thematic geographies, economic and socio-political topics).

accounts) the sequence was from first, general studies of the whole continent, through the immigrant guides, exploration and travel accounts, to specific studies of the settlers, their institutions and organisations, the Aboriginal cultures and specific items of contemporary scientific interest.

The literary sources, however, were of limited value in many cases because of the problems of semantics (Bacon's Idol of the Theatre) and analogous reasoning (Idol of the Tribe). A major problem resulted from the use of traditional descriptive terminology, for words used in descriptions did not always mean what the reader might be expected to think they meant. Thus 'plants, birds and fishes were often called by the English names of the species they most resembled'.[23] Terms such as 'river', 'lake' and 'stream' gave a false sense of permanence to what were often occasionally dry watercourses, while other names, such as 'creek' had their meanings modified to fit the new circumstances. Prior to the mid-nineteenth century, literary descriptions of the landscape were couched in a terminology often much less than precisely depicting for the reader what the original observer had seen[24].

Authors uncertain of the facts tended to fall back upon the use of analogy to fill in the details of an obscure but hopefully rational pattern of Nature. The latitudinal zoning of climatic patterns, vegetation and even geological zones was claimed in proposals for settlement by the Dutch in Nuyts Land at the head of the Great Australian Bight, and was used by Stirling in his assessment of the prospects for the Swan River[25]. That all land had potentially equal population carrying-capacity was implicit in Captain Vetch's division of the continent into eight convenient units—each to have by analogy with its European equivalent (Spain and Portugal) a future population of 19 millions![26]

In the graphic descriptions there were similar problems of interpretation. Bernard Smith's analysis of the constraints within which the contemporary draughtsmen and artists worked shows that not only was the process of landscape illustration one including a deliberate search for, and identification of, a limited 'relevant' range of the total environmental stimuli, but also involved the tailoring of the end-product to the particular audience in mind, with the whole set within the framework of the contemporary conventions of graphic illustration.[27] The British Admiralty draughtsmen were interested only in the profile of the landscape visible from offshore to the captain using it, to locate his safe anchorage or establish his position: the first official land explorers were mainly concerned for the profile of landforms and 'skylines' as reference landmarks and triangulation points for future surveys to establish the basic dimensions of the land. Once their official commitments had been met, however, many were prepared to transform their official sketches for the public view, usually by adding items thought to be of interest and attempting to create at the same time an aesthetically pleasing impression.[28]

The channels of information were the creations of both officialdom and the private sector of society. They reflected not only official policies and the propaganda to support them, but the roles played by various private institutions and the influence of particular influential individuals—the gatekeepers as we shall call them. Apart from the information available in the Government Gazettes, the main sources of official information were the reports of the various consuls appointed to the new colonies by the European nations, once trade and migration began to flow, and the rival reports of the Agents General of the colonies in London, established shortly after responsible government was granted. Of particular importance in that it potentially was available to a much larger audience, was the information contained in the international exhibitions, for which official displays were prepared by the various colonies.[29]

Independent organisations and philanthropic societies attempted to provide their own, supposedly less biased, accounts of the new lands. The Society for the Diffusion of Useful Knowledge issued maps of parts of Australia from 1829 to the 1850s, as portions of a Family Atlas (which was reissued *in toto* by Stanford in London in 1857) and in 1845 the Society for Promoting Christian Knowledge produced its own map of Australia.[30]

Equally, if not more, important in their influence upon the information available were individuals who by their position, experience or interest attempted to channel information on the continent along certain directions. Cameron's recent study of the role of Stirling in the initial British perception of the Swan River area not only illustrates the process of perception but suggests the main actors in that process:

> Stirling not only discovered an area which he believed would support a substantial agricultural and commercial settlement, but was able to convince Darling and Arthur, officials at the Colonial Office, and John Barrow of the Admiralty, the recognised British authority on the southern hemisphere, of its suitability. More importantly, he attracted the support of several groups of speculators, particularly Thomas Peel and his associates, for his colonisation proposals.[31]

With such men convinced, and actively fostering the optimistic image of the future colony, a 'Swan River mania' resulted—only to be destroyed by the letters from the first colonists.

In Germany a significant gatekeeper for knowledge of Australia was August Petermann who was founding-editor of what became known as *Petermann's Mitteilungen* from 1855 to his death in 1878. This journal created a highly respectable professional image as a medium for the reporting of the contemporary European discoveries of 'new lands' and at the same time had a large audience in the German educated public. Petermann was particularly interested in anything to do with Australia and sought out all available information for relay to his audience. The explorer Giles acknowledged Petermann's role, when he named the Petermann Range in central Australia in 1872:

> . . . after Dr Augustus Petermann of Gotha, the celebrated geographer, who has laboured so strenuously in the furtherance of all plans of Australian discovery and who has produced the most excellent and reliable maps of this continent, which have ever appeared.[32]

The impact in terms of information flow was obvious after his death (Figure 9).

In Britain the role of Banks in the early perception of New South Wales was central to official thinking and actions. Both as President of the Royal Society and official 'expert' on the new colony, he was consulted on its potential, was invited to nominate its officials, and himself encouraged all who would provide more knowledge of the new lands. And all this even though his private opinions did not always coincide with those expressed in public.[33] For the general public, however, at least the one in ten who supposedly read his works, Charles Dickens' image of Australia was more important, even though founded upon the shaky, if popular, evidence of Samuel Sidney's handbooks. The image particularly of the Social

39

Arcady, where each settler happily tilled his own small farm untroubled by droughts or landlords, had a strong appeal, to which in rapid succession was added the glitter of the goldfields.[34]

ATTITUDES TO THE AUSTRALIAN LANDSCAPE 1770–1870

What were the attitudes which emerged over the century from this complex interplay of the perception process? Three overall, but often conflicting, themes may be recognised and since some examination of these has appeared elsewhere, the intention here is merely to summarise and where necessary complement those prior studies.[35]

The scientific attitude: landscape as phenomena

Captain Cook's voyage, which revitalised interest in the continent, was both a part of and stimulus for European scientific interest in the lands of the southern Pacific Ocean. As Hazard has demonstrated, the late eighteenth century was a period of rapidly expanding interest in the natural sciences among European philosophers.[36] On the one hand Christian philosophers were seeking evidence of Divine Order in nature, while others sought merely for evidence of some rational patterns amid the multiplicity of newly-discovered life forms. Glacken has suggested that much of this interest concerned ideas which were to become increasingly pertinent to thinking in the nineteenth and twentieth centuries:

> . . . the idea of a primordial balance in nature which civilised man interferes with at his own risk; the contrasting idea of purposeful change to create a better environment, the effects of [land] clearing on climate, of clearing and drainage on health, the cultural aspects of forest protection and torrent control.[37]

Whatever the reason, however, there is no doubt of interest in the continent and the Pacific Islands, which were seen as one of the last great natural laboratories for the scientists to explore.

As a result, most of the official explorations by sea and later by land were mounted as *scientific* expeditions which were required to keep observations of weather, collect samples of the flora and fauna, and comment on the soils, as well as to map the patterns of land and water. Many of their collections found their way to the conservatories of the nobility in Europe as well as the newly founded Kew Gardens in London and the Jardin des Plantes in Paris, while their narratives were widely published both in Government Gazettes and independently by their leaders.

Of particular interest to the philosophers was the evidence which led to modifications of the prior Linnaean system of plant classification, and the evidence from four British naval expeditions 1836–1850, on which most of the radical theories of plant and animal evolution were to be based.[38]

The aesthetic attitude: landscape as scenery

The late eighteenth century in Europe, however, was not merely the age of the new scientists, but also the age of the new aesthetes. Interest in the landscape as scenery – as something to be looked at for its aesthetic qualities, not merely as a place to live, arose from the stimulus of the increasingly popular landscape painting. By the latter half of the century, earlier interest in the 'civilised' landscapes of classical Italy, with their bare brown countrysides dotted by the ruins of antiquity, was being challenged by the cult of the picturesque – the irregular and varied, but none-the-less carefully composed, 'pictures' of Claude Lorrain. As scenery,

40

landscapes were examined as to their potential to make a picture, convention requiring the view to be framed and tinted the requisite golden shades by being observed through a Claude 'glass'.[39]

Not only was the composition and the role of the scenery being re-examined; the cult of the romantic landscapes added a specific content – wilderness, whether of mountain or forest, always mysterious and often exotic in their location and human activities depicted. By implication primitive and uncivilised, such scenes appealed to the new aesthetes and were used as the setting for Rousseau's philosophical comments upon the nature of man himself.[40]

This re-evaluation of landscape produced two significant activities which were to affect the attitudes to the Australian landscape. The late eighteenth century was the heyday of the Grand Tour – the educational travel through European countries in search of historical and aesthetic stimulation. From the awe-inspiring ruins of Rome to the sublime majesty of the Alps, the tourists – some 45 000 'English gentry' in 1785 – travelled in search of the scenery which the landscape painters had first brought to public notice. While many journeyed abroad in search of scenery, a smaller group created their own scenery at home in the English landscape gardens which were being transformed in the eighteenth century. The formal geometric baroque gardens became the landscape parks of Humphrey Repton and Capability Brown – parks where the entire view (covering several hundred hectares) was carefully engineered to present the irregular pattern of clumps of trees and shaven lawns.[41]

The Europeans therefore, who came to Australia as officials or settlers, brought with them an interest in the aesthetics of landscape and preconceptions of the optimal scenery. Some indeed were artists who brought with them the picturesque conventions of Europe or who, like George French Angas, came 'activated by an ardent admiration of the grandeur and loveliness of Nature in her wildest aspect'.[42] Individual settlers appreciated the aesthetics of the wilderness they were about to transform:

> There was a wonderful charm in exploring country [Victoria in 1840s] thus uninhabited except by natives and wild birds and animals. These occupied, without altering the face of nature . . . The creeks were then all fringed with reeds and rushes [which] formed a beautiful edging to dark solemn pools overhung by water-loving gum trees.[43]

Occasionally they showed an awareness of how that scenery would be transformed through the painter's brush into the contemporary European conventions of beauty. A South Australian J.P., looking across the Adelaide Plain in 1850, thought that:

> Our good friend Henry Warren would have made something of it, particularly a very brilliant and unclouded sun, would have favoured our talented relative's camel-loving and Turner-like propensities.[44]

Henry Warren, President of the New Society of Painters in Water Colours, London, from 1839–1873, never got the chance, but there were many who did, as Bernard Smith's studies have shown.[45]

Even the scientists were not insensitive to the scenery they were to catalogue. A dour explorer such as Sir Thomas Mitchell could be occasionally impressed by the view. The Fitzroy Downs of northern New South Wales were:

> . . . the finest country I had ever seen in a primeval state. A champain region, spotted with wood, stretching as far as human vision, or even the telescope, could reach . . . A noble mountain mass arose in the midst of that fine country.[46]

41

And Captain Sturt, retreating defeated from his furthest sortie into the desert and
passing en route through a patch of low well-grassed woodland around a salt pan:

> ... could not help reflecting with how much more buoyant and pleasurable feelings we
> should have explored such a country, when compared with the monotonous and
> sterile region we had wandered over. The transition however from the rich to the
> barren, from the picturesque to the contrary, was instantaneous. From the grassy
> woodland . . . we debouched upon a barren plain.[47]

While barren plains became more evident the further the explorers pushed inland,
there were some parts of the scenery able to measure up to imported preconceptions.

One aspect in particular had general appeal. In the thinner stands of the
sclerophyll forest on the east coast, but more often on the savannah woodlands of
the slopes beyond the mountains and the plains of South and Western Australia,
the open woodlands with native grass undercover reminded many of the English
landscape parks. From Elizabeth Macarthur in 1795 describing the Hawkesbury
River valley, Colonel Light describing the Adelaide Plains in 1836, the English
economist Jevons describing the western slopes of southern New South Wales in
1859, and many individual settlers whose writings have been preserved, the
similarity was greeted with general enthusiasm. In part the scenery was itself
aesthetically pleasing from the composition of the masses of woods broken by the
open grasslands – the 'champaign region' of Mitchell – but also because it gave the
impression of a 'managed' and 'improved' landscape, 'more like land in the
possession of persons of property rather than left to the course of nature alone' as
Colonel Light put it.[48] It seems to have brought comfort to some, that the wilderness did not always appear to be as wild as at first glance and herein lies a clue to
the third – materialistic – attitude to the landscape.

Materialistic attitudes: landscape as a resource

For many officials and settlers the landscape had but one character – its
potential for economic exploitation. From such a standpoint the scientific interest
was relevant only to the extent that it was applied to the practical problems of
resource identification and use. The explorers from the 1830s onwards were
specifically instructed to look for potential agricultural and grazing lands. The local
botanical gardens, originally founded to cultivate the native plants for transmission
to Europe, became in turn one medium by which exotic plants were introduced to
Australia by the various horticultural and acclimatisation societies. Kew Gardens in
London were rejuvenated in the 1840s with a new role, to disseminate practical
information on commercial plants coming from and going to Australia and other
British colonies.[49] Geological studies gained considerable stimulus from the gold
discoveries of the latter half of the nineteenth century.

If science was to be applied, the scenery for many was to be decried. It lacked
any picturesque qualities according to Barron Field[50] and, from long established
settlers to fleeting visitors, repelled aesthetes by its monotony. Even Charles Darwin,
who should have known the dangers of generalising from limited experiences,
depreciated the views seen on his eighteen-day visit in the summer of 1836:

> The scenery is singular from its uniformity. Everywhere open forest land; the trees
> have all the same character of growth and their foliage is of one tint.[51]

Even the attractive 'parkscapes' were commended for their ease of land clearance
for cultivation as much as for their aesthetics.[52]

42

Captain Cook's forecast that what was wanted to transform the landscape was 'the hand of Industry' was to be effectively verified by the following century of European contact with that landscape. His sentiments were echoed by the surveyor Mitchell who saw the deficiencies of the continent as but a challenge to European skills and ingenuity:

> If there be no navigable rivers, there are no unwholesome savannahs; if there are rocky ranges, they afford, at least, the means of forming reservoirs of water; and, although it is uncertain when rain may fall, it is certain that an abundance of rain does fall; and the hand of man alone is wanting to preserve that supply and regulate its use.[53]

The transformation of the landscape which resulted was not merely the clearance of woodland for agriculture and the importation of exotic grasses for the new flocks and herds, it was the creation also of an improved scenery. The transformation was material – in productivity of crops and livestock, and aesthetic – the creation of new scenery in the patterns of farmland and urban architecture, the new colours, shapes and textures of exotic, natural and man-made forms. From paintings such as *John Glover's House and Garden* 1835 to S. T. Gill's series of seasonal vignettes of South Australia 1847 (perhaps modelled upon the fifteenth century French *Book of Hours* of the Duc de Berri), the impression is of a man-made landscape carved out of the original nature.[54]

THE SITUATION CIRCA 1870

By 1870 there was evidence of all three themes still present in attitudes to the Australian landscape. The scientists – as explorers – were still at work, Ernest Giles was considering his expedition to the interior and others such as the Forrest brothers and Colonel Warburton were to follow. Each of the colonies had its scientific circle, its learned societies; in Sydney and Melbourne the universities were at work and in Adelaide another was being contemplated. While Anthony Trollope was about the visit the Antipodes and add his condemnation of the monotony of the bush, there were others who still warmed to its 'weird charm' or were encouraged to experience the stimulating and therapeutic atmosphere of the Australian Alps.[55]

The dominating theme by 1870, however, was the materialistic view. The next two decades were to see the apparent triumph of materialism in attitudes to the landscape. The gold rushes were continuing to find the precious metal and source of capital for further resource development in ever remoter locations;[56] the eras of the golden fleece and the golden grain were at hand. Everywhere, it seemed, the hand of industry was at work transforming nature to the benefit of man. By 1870 only some 1.2 million hectares (3 million acres) had been cleared for agriculture; in the next thirty years a further 3.5 million hectares (8.5 million acres) were to be similarly transformed.

Alongside the old themes there was evidence of some innovations. Even in the midst of the triumph of materialism there was concern that the unlimited transformation of nature would bring its own problems. Fears for the scarcity of resources, particularly timber, had been voiced earlier, but the first effective attempts to create reserves and encourage replanting began in South Australia, New South Wales and Queensland in the 1870s, and the first reserves of a scientific-cum-scenic type – the Jenolan Caves of New South Wales – had been set up in 1866.[57] The same railways which were bringing out the wool bales and the wheat bags to the ports, and which were to bring out the mallee roots from the

newly cleared farmlands to the suburban hearths of Melbourne and Adelaide, were
to carry Henry Lawson and his mates outback to evoke the 'Australian Legend',
and from the Melbourne suburb of Heidelberg the 'plein-air' painters such as
Arthur Streeton, Tom Roberts and Frank McCubbin were to venture out into the
still-adjacent bush to create a national school of art. The European perceptions
were to be seriously challenged in the next century of Australian history.

Notes and References

1. Quoted in BAKER, J. N. L. *The history of geography*. London, Blackwood, 1963. pp. 186–7.
2. SHARP, A. *The discovery of Australia*. Oxford, Clarendon Press, 1963.
3. SMITH, S. *Where to go, and whither . . .* London, 1849, p. 45.
4. YI-FU TUAN. *Topophilia: a study of environmental perception, attitudes, and values*. Englewood Cliffs, N.J., Prentice-Hall, 1974, p. 4.
5. See MULVANEY, D. J. 'The Australian Aborigines 1606–1929: opinion and fieldwork', *Historical Studies of Australia and New Zealand*. 8:131–151 and 297–314, 1958; SMITH, B. *European vision and the South Pacific 1768–1850: a study in the history of art and ideas*. Oxford, Clarendon Press, 1960; and DUTTON, G. *White on black: the Australian Aborigine portrayed in art*. South Melbourne, Macmillan, 1974.
6. For the geographers see LOWENTHAL, D. (ed.) *Environmental perception and behaviour*. Chicago, University of Chicago, 1967; SAARINEN, T. F. *Perception of environment*. Washington, Association of American Geographers, 1969; and TUAN, 1974, *op cit*. For the psychologists see CRAIK, K. H. 'Environmental psychology', *New dimensions in psychology*. 4:1–121, 1970 and PROSHANSKY, H. M. *et al.* (eds.) *Environmental psychology: man and his physical setting*. New York, Holt, Rinehart and Winston, 1970.
7. British capital investment in Australia was averaging £2.3 millions per year in the decade pre-1872. The decade post-1872 saw this rise to £5.6 millions per year and in the decade post-1882 to £18.2 millions per year, before the crash of 1893. BUTLIN, N. G. *Australian domestic product, investment and foreign borrowing 1861–1938/39*. Cambridge, Cambridge University Press, 1962, p. 424.
8. MOZLEY, A. 'Evolution and the climate of opinion in Australia, 1840–76', *Victorian Studies*. 10:411–430, 1967.
9. CAMERON, H. C. *Sir Joseph Banks: the autocrat of the philosophers*. London, Batchworth Press, 1952, pp. 89–90.
10. BLAINEY, G. *The tyranny of distance*. Melbourne, Sun Books, 1966.
11. MEIGS, P. World distribution of arid and semi-arid homoclimates, in UNESCO. *Reviews of research in arid zone hydrology*. Paris, Unesco, 1953, pp. 203–310.
12. PRICE, A. GRENFELL. 'Moving frontiers and changing landscapes in the Pacific and its continents', *Australian Journal of Science*. 19:188–98, 1957.
13. BAUER, F. H. *Historical geographic survey of part of Northern Australia, Part I*. Canberra, CSIRO, 1959.
14. *Quarterly Review*, 32:311–2, 1825.
15. A forthcoming publication of the Diary of Daniel Brock, a member of Sturt's 1844 Expedition, edited by K. Peake Jones for the Royal Geographical Society of Australasia (S.A. Branch) Inc. will illustrate the mental stresses to which Captain Sturt was exposed during the isolation of his party at Poole's Glen in the winter of 1845.
16. CLARK, C. M. H. *A history of Australia*, Vol. 1. Melbourne, Melbourne University Press, 1962, pp. 49 and 86.
17. JACKSON, J. A. (ed.) *Migration*. Cambridge, Cambridge University Press, 1969.
18. SINGER, C. *A short history of scientific ideas to 1900*. Oxford, Clarendon Press, 1959, p. 266.

19. WILLIAMS, R. *The long revolution.* Harmondsworth, Penguin, 1961.

20. LANSBURY, C. *Arcady in Australia: the evocation of Australia in nineteenth-century English literature.* Melbourne, Melbourne University Press, 1970, p. 62.

21. ALTICK, R. D. *The English common reader: a social history of the mass reading public 1800–1900.* Chicago, University of Chicago Press, 1957. Phoenix ed, 1963, pp. 384 and 392.

22. HEATHCOTE, G. E. A. and HEATHCOTE, R. L. 'German geographical literature on Australia 1810–1940: a preliminary bibliography and comment', *Australian Geographer.* 12:154–75, 1972.

23. TURNER, G. W. *The English language in Australia and New Zealand.* London, Longmans, 1966, p. 3.

24. HEATHCOTE, R. L. *Back of Bourke: a study of land appraisal and settlement in semi-arid Australia.* Melbourne, Melbourne University Press, 1965, pp. 18–20.

25. See PERRY, T. M. 'Climate and settlement in Australia 1700–1930: some theoretical considerations', in ANDREWS, J. (ed.) *Frontiers and men.* Melbourne, Cheshire, 1966, pp. 138–154; and CAMERON, J. M. R. 'Prelude to colonisation: James Stirling's examination of Swan River, March 1827', *Australian Geographer.* 12: 309–327, 1973.

26. VETCH, CAPTAIN. 'Considerations of the political geography and geographical nomenclature of Australia', *Journal Royal Geographical Society.* 8: 157–69, 1838.

27. *op. cit.* SMITH, B., 1960, and SMITH, B. *Australian painting 1788–1960.* Melbourne, Oxford University Press, 1962.

28. See the contrasts in the official and popular versions of William Westall's illustrations in T. M. Perry and D. H. Simpson (eds.) *Drawings by William Westall* (London, Royal Commonwealth Society, 1962), and the contrasts between the sketches of the surveyor Thomas Mitchell in the Mitchell Library, Sydney, and as published in T. L. Mitchell, *Journal of an Expedition into the Interior of Tropical Australia . . .* London, Longmans, 1848.

29. None of these sources has to my knowledge been adequately researched. In particular the exhibits prepared for the Great Exhibition London 1851, Paris, 1855, London 1862 and 1873, Philadelphia 1876, Chicago 1893 and Paris 1908, would be worth examining as the changing projection of an official image of the colonies. Carol Lansbury has hinted at the impact of gold discoveries in popular interest in the 1862 London exhibition in contrast to the 1857 display (*op. cit.* Lansbury, p. 115).

30. TOOLEY, R. V. (ed.) *Map Collectors' Circle*, nos. 60, 64, 66, 72 and 79, London, 1970–72.

31. *op. cit.* CAMERON, J. M. R., 1973, p. 310.

32. GILES, E. *Geographical travels in central Australia from 1872–1874.* Melbourne, McCarron Bird, 1875, p. 172.

33. *op. cit.* LANSBURY, 1970, p. 15.

34. *op. cit.* LANSBURY, 1970, Chapters 5 and 7.

35. Two parallel but independent investigations have appeared as R. L. Heathcote, 'The visions of Australia 1770–1970', in RAPOPORT, A. (ed.) *Australia as human setting.* Sydney, Angus and Robertson, 1972, pp. 77–98, and POWELL, J. M. 'Images of Australia, 1788–1914', *Monash Publications in Geography.* 3: 1–21, 1972.

36. HAZARD, P. *European thought in the eighteenth century from Montesquieu to Lessing.* London, Hollis and Carter, 1954, translated by J. Lewis from original edition 1946.

37. GLACKEN, G. J. *Traces on the Rhodian shore: nature and culture in western thought from ancient times to the end of the eighteenth century.* Berkeley, University of California Press, 1967, p. 657.

38. Australia was visited by H.M.S. *Beagle*, with Charles Darwin on board in 1836; by H.M.S. *Erebus* and *Terror* with the botanist J. D. Hooker in 1840, by H.M.S. *Fly* with the geologist J. Beate Jukes and the zoologist J. MacGillivray over the period

1842 to 1846; and by H.M.S. *Rattlesnake* with the zoologist T. H. Huxley over the period 1847 to 1850.

39. CLARK, K. *Landscape in art*. Harmondsworth, Penguin, 1956.

40. CLARK, K. and HEATHCOTE, R. L. 'The artist as geographer: landscape painting as a source for geographical research', *Proc. Royal Geographical Society Australasia* (*S.A. Branch*). 73: 12–15, 1972.

41. HUSSEY, C. *English gardens and landscapes 1770–1759*. London, Country Life, 1967, and PRINCE, H. C. *Parks in England*. Newport (I.O.W.), Pinhorns, 1967.

42. ANGAS, G. F. *Savage life and scenes in Australia and New Zealand*. London, Smith, Eldon, 1847, preface.

43. BRIDE, T. F. (ed.) *Letters from Victorian pioneers*. Melbourne, Government Printer, 1898, p. 216.

44. YELLAND, E. M. (ed.) *Colonists, copper and corn in the colony of South Australia 1850–51, by old colonist*. Melbourne, Hawthorn Press, 1970, p. 20.

45. *op. cit.* SMITH, B. 1960 and 1962.

46. MITCHELL, T. L. *Journal of an expedition into the interior of tropical Australia*. London, Longmans, 1848, pp. 152–3.

47. STURT, C. *Narrative of an expedition into Central Australia*. London, T. and W. Boone, 1849, p. 408.

48. For descriptions see STIVENS, D. 'Landscape in Australian literature', *Westerly*. 3: 47, 1964; MOON, K. 'Perception and appraisal of the South Australian landscape 1836–1850', *Proc. Royal Geographical Society Australasia* (*S.A. Branch*). 70: 47, 1969; and JEVONS, W. S. *Letters and journals of W. Stanley Jevons*. London, 1886, edited by Harriet A. Jevons, p. 122.

49. See JOSE, A. W. and CARTER, H. J. (eds.). *The illustrated Australian encyclopaedia*. Sydney, 1925–6, 2 volumes, 'Botanic gardens' and 'Societies, learned'; and GARDENER, W. 'A love of flowers', *The Listener*. London, 25 November 1965, pp. 847–9.

50. *op. cit.* SMITH, B. 1960, pp. 181–2.

51. BARLOW, N. *Charles Darwin and the voyage of the* Beagle. London, London Pilot Press, 1945, p. 132.

52. *op. cit.* SMITH, B., 1960, p. 186, and *op. cit.* STURT, C., 1849, p. 264.

53. BEAGLEHOLE, J. C. (ed.) *The journals of Captain James Cook on his voyages of discovery*. Cambridge, Cambridge University Press, 1955, p. 397 and *op. cit.* MITCHELL, T. L., 1848, pp. 421–2.

54. *op. cit.* HEATHCOTE, R. L., 1972, plate 11, and DUTTON, G. (ed.) *Paintings of S. T. Gill*. Adelaide, Rigby, 1962.

55. BIRD, S. D. *On Australasian climates and their influence on the prevention and arrest of pulmonary consumption*. London, 1863.

56. BLAINEY, G. *The rush that never ended*. Melbourne, Melbourne University Press, 1963.

57. MOSLEY, J. G. 'Towards a history of conservation in Australia', in RAPOPORT, A., *op. cit.*, 1972, pp. 136–154.

2. The physical landscape

*Sir Otto Frankel**

The biological structure
of the landscape

In this contribution I am discussing biological aspects which I believe are basic to our perception of the Australian landscape. I am excluding any specific consideration of the impact of land use on the landscape since this is the subject of the contributions which follow.

INDIGENOUS AND EXOTIC ELEMENTS

Under my all-too-general title I shall speak about what appear to me as the overriding and unifying features in the perception of the Australian landscape: the distinctiveness and the ubiquity of the native elements of the landscape, and the relationships, and indeed the contrast between the native and the exotic elements. In Australia this contrast is peculiarly prominent, more so than in most other places; so much so, as I have ascertained in casual opinion polls, that most people are conscious of the personality split in the Australian landscape, and that they not only perceive and register it, but that it is a subject of interest and of some concern.

Now, what is so peculiar about the Australian situation, and why should one care? Perception is essentially a personal thing, so I feel justified in starting from personal observations. My life has been spent in about equal portions in three places, Australia, New Zealand, and Europe. They differ greatly in their biological structure in the sense in which I am using the term. In large parts of Europe there is little left of the indigenous structure of any landscape, thanks to the age and intensity of land use, and the extent of exchange within and between continents. Few Englishmen or Germans would know whether a plant was native or introduced, nor would they care. In New Zealand – and especially in the South Island – native and introduced plants are, in the main, segregated ecologically and geographically. In the agricultural and pastoral countryside native trees are uncommon and confined to specific ecological niches such as river beds or gullies. The trees sheltering South Island homesteads – indispensable in so windy a country – are usually pines or cypresses from California or eucalypts from Australia. In or near almost any New Zealand township the native species – except the relatively few which have become garden plants – are few and far between. Most New Zealanders live in a 'transformation landscape'[1], a man-made landscape with a flora which is almost entirely alien to the country. Indigenous plant communities are mainly in rugged, mountainous, inaccessible or otherwise unusable parts of the country. New Zealanders rarely notice this marked dichotomy in their landscape. I became aware of it only on my first return from Australia when, looking out of a laboratory window near the small city of Palmerston North, I could not see a single native plant. This would be a rare occurrence in similar sites in Australia.

* Sir Otto Frankel is Senior Research Fellow at CSIRO's Division of Plant Industry in Canberra. Sir Otto was formerly Chief of the Division between 1951 and 1962 and was a member of the CSIRO Executive during 1962–1966.

INDIGENOUS AND EXOTIC – ECOLOGICAL ADAPTATION

In contrast, there are few Australian landscapes even in intensively used areas, which are altogether devoid of natives, whether remnants or derivatives of the original flora, or deliberately established in gardens, parks, plantations or roadsides. In those areas where ninety per cent or more of Australians live and the landscape is greatly modified from its original structure, native plants, and especially native trees, are still prevalent. No doubt this is so largely for ecological reasons. As one would expect, indigenous plants throughout their evolution have become adapted to and tolerant of the climatic and edaphic (or soil) limitations of the Australian environments – moisture stress, often combined with temperature stress, and the widespread deficiencies of major and minor mineral nutrients. They are able to take advantage of good seasons, survive exposure to exceptional stresses, and at any time require little or no looking after.

But, of course, Australian plants are not unique in this regard. In the south of the continent this is obvious from the large number and wide distribution of successful introductions and invaders from the Mediterranean region and from the corresponding climate zone in the western United States where conditions are similar to those of our 'mediterranean' zone. Introduced mediterranean species have changed the face of the pastoral landscape of southern Australia, and subtropical and tropical introductions from Latin America and Africa are on the way to playing a similar role in the northern half of the continent. Some of these plants came as intruders, and with many others which have failed to reach the ranks of crops, they became naturalised in congenial environments. Mostly annuals or short-lived perennials, without fertilisers they tend to be as inconspicuous in Australia as they are in their countries of origin. There are not many naturalised shrubs; and exotic trees are mainly confined to plantations, gardens or roadsides. There are significant exceptions in particular ecological niches such as the riverbed sites in the temperate zones where willows and poplars have become 'natural', though strikingly alien, trees (Figure 11).

INDIGENOUS TREES IN A TRANSFORMATION LANDSCAPE

Here there is a marked visual clash, compared with the subdued visual impact of exotic pastures. The ground cover provided by phalaris – subterranean clover pastures in the south, by paspalum or Townsville lucerne in the north, is distinctive in colour, yet diffuse, unstructured, and basically ephemeral. But trees are enduring, structural, individual, like hills, only more so because they are alive and subject to the vagaries of life, reproduction and death; and though their normal life span may exceed ours, their continued existence is increasingly subject to our own social and individual attitude and decision making (Figure 12). We are *involved*, aesthetically and socially. And here we have come up against the real issue we are discussing: our perception, appreciation and value judgement of the place of the indigenous and exotic species in the Australian landscape. This is not simply a rhetorical question, to be answered something like this: 'Introductions have found their place in agriculture and forestry, in parks and gardens, and to a very limited extent in more or less natural environments. In the broad expanse of countryside where two-thirds of our sheep and cattle on introduced pasture species, native trees where two-thirds of our sheep and cattle graze on introduced pasture species, native trees still dominate the landscape, and elsewhere the indigenous flora in unchallenged'. But this is not the whole story. Over large parts of the pastoral belt the

C. Totterdell, CSIRO, Division of Plant Industry

Figure 11. Willows along Yarralumla Creek, A.C.T.

C. Totterdell, CSIRO, Division of Plant Industry

Figure 12. Grazing land near Canberra with natural woodland trees—some native grasses but predominant ground cover of introduced pasture grasses and clovers.

51

C. Totterdell, CSIRO, Division of Plant Industry

Figure 13. Ground cleared for grazing—a few relics of *Eucalyptus blakelyi* offer sparse shade. Paucity of trees and continuous grazing inhibit regeneration of savannah woodland in such a site. Distant slope has not been intensively cleared.

O. H. Frankel, CSIRO, Division of Plant Industry

Figure 14. Ghost gum. (*Eucalyptus papuana*)

52

remaining native trees are in uneasy balance with the environment, and with time. Many of the trees are old. In some areas the residual tree populations are heavily parasitised. Grazing and cultivation prevent replacement by natural regeneration (Figure 13).

But tree replacement does not come without trouble and expense. It requires fencing off and some cultivation to encourage reseeding of the established and locally adapted population.[2] So far, very little indeed is being done.

For the moment let us leave the problem of the trees in the rural landscape, significant as it is; but we shall return to it after we have considered the more general issue of the perception of the indigenous plants themselves, irrespective of their relationship to exotic plants or their role in partially transformed landscapes. The focus is primarily on the indigenous *flora*, not only because I know a little more about plants than about animals, but also because, important as animals are in the context of man's involvement with nature, they do not by themselves determine the form of the landscape to the extent that plants so obviously do.[3] The observations I am going to make are an attempt to integrate scientific interpretations with aesthetic and emotional perceptions. You may find them suggestive, but they can be no more: they are personal reactions of questionable validity, and, as you will see, they mainly serve to introduce an issue with which I shall deal with much greater confidence in the final section of this paper.

THE INDIGENOUS FLORA – DIVERSITY AND CONTINUITY

What do I find remarkable about Australian wildlife? First and foremost, the degree of its diversity: diversity of species, of life forms, of communities, of individuals; of minute niches occupied by a few uncommon species; of vast plains with interlacing communities rich in the diversity of plant species and equally in bird and marsupial and insect species. I shall shun statistics, and I deplore records. I don't care whether the flora of Brazil is richer – as it probably is – or whether China or India have more insect species: the number in Australia is enormous, and many have yet to be recorded. But let us not overlook another source of diversity, intrinsic in the stress conditions which are a prominent environmental factor over the greater part of the continent, and this is the diversity induced by climatic oscillations. This source of diversity has a dramatic effect on the landscape. The desert is parched, and even the dust-laden atmosphere is part of the landscape; or the desert is a luscious green, the desert blooms. Only the great trees remain the same.

Two features are particularly significant. One I would call the 'continuity of diversity', the sequence of environments from coast to desert to coast, from south to north, from east to west, with the great variety of latitudinal and longitudinal transects which the size of the land mass and the diversity of environments afford. And, let it be emphasised again, transformation landscapes, in Seddon's sense[4], as yet are not so completely transformed as to destroy this continuity, which is of course the case in the North American continent. This, need I say it again, is mainly due to the great trees which remain.

This continuity expresses itself in life forms which are so characteristic that even a botanical ignoramus like myself has no difficulty in recognising from a distance the Australian section of any botanical gardens; and that one is not often in doubt whether a plant is indigenous or exotic. If there is one group of plants which

signally contributes to this continuity, it is the great genus *Eucalyptus* which spans
Australia from the tropics to the cool temperate zone, from rain-forest to desert to
treeline, in fact wherever trees will grow. Thus it unifies Australia; and some
nationalists may be pleased at the thought that it does not extend beyond New
Guinea and the Phillipines. The oaks of Europe and the Near East may once have
played a similar role of linking diverse environments within a large continuous
land mass.

The eucalypts, to my mind, are the epitome of the Australian landscape,
expressing, in the one genus, its essence and distinctiveness (Figures 14, 15). We are
aware of them even on the fringe, or in the distant background, as on the treeless
plains in the tablelands; and the impact of the riverine plains, occasioned by their
treeless vastness, is grand rather than monotonous because, at the back of one's
mind, there are the great trees by the river some few miles away.

What is it that gives these trees such strength of character that they impose
themselves so forcefully on our perception of the landscape? Above all, their
enormous diversity: genetic diversity of species, ecotypes, individuals; diversity in
the response to the macro- and micro-environment; diversity of the individual
resulting from all these factors, but more particularly from the informal,
opportunistic growth form: casually shedding leaves or growing new ones; lopping-
off branches when they are too long; sprouting new growth when half devoured by
insects, incinerated by bush fires, or decapitated by man. All these lesions leave their
marks; but while they would mangle almost any other tree, they make eucalypts
expressively beautiful and give them their mark of individuality – like the face of a
beautiful old lady who has gained distinction in a full life. It may even be that the
exposure of the individual trees which the thinning of the original stands has
brought about, has given those which remain more scope for individual development, and has made them more conspicuous and notable for the observer. The
remarkable trees by Australian roadsides[5], often remnants of communities which
have all but disappeared, are a joy to the traveller and no doubt a continuing joy
to the people who see them daily – just like the colourful, lively, tortuous trunk of
of the yellow box outside my study window which is so beautiful that I find it
hard to take my eyes off it to write these words. I believe it is the casual
informality of form, so much in keeping with what one has come to regard as the
national character, which has given the eucalypts their unrivalled place in the
Australian landscape, and in our perception and consciousness of Australia.

I have already stressed that in spite of their enormous diversity, the distinctiveness and ubiquity of the eucalypts give them a unifying role in the Australian
landscape. So have other genera, foremost among them another ubiquitous genus,
Acacia (Figure 16). However, this unifying quality is not confined to one or the
other genus, but is reflected in the indigenous flora as a whole, perhaps more so
than in any other continent. Yet, although grey-green, sparse-crowned plants
characterise the landscapes of temperate, and of the major part of sub-tropical and
tropical Australia, one must not overlook the fact the northern tropical parts have
an intricate vegetation pattern of their own. Here broad-leaved, dark-green trees and
shrubs, sometimes deciduous, including palms and other unusual life forms, form
dense canopied islands in a sea of grey-green sclerophylls. They greatly add to the
interest and attractiveness of the landscape, without detracting from the essentially
Australian character of the landscape as a whole.

O. H. Frankel, CSIRO, Division of Plant Industry

Figure 15. Mallee eucalypt, Riverina.

C. Totterdell, CSIRO, Division of Plant Industry

Figure 16. Myall (*Acacia pendula*) is one of many species of Acacia which range throughout the semi-arid and arid zones of Australia. These trees are near Deniliquin, N.S.W.

There is much more that could – and has been – said about the part of the
Australian wildlife in the life of Australia of today and tomorrow, and I shall do
so myself before I conclude. But at this stage I should like to venture some guesses
on what the perception of Australian wildlife means to Australians as individuals,
rather than to an idealised 'Australia'.

One may perhaps generalise by thinking of three kinds of landscapes in which
native plants and animals are seen. First, there are the native plants and animals
in or near cities, around farm homesteads, or in the agricultural and pastoral
countryside. These have already been discussed at length. Second, there are the
sites visited for recreation and relaxation, for various sports such as fishing, ski-ing
or bush walking, or for the pursuit of special interests such as bird watching, seeing
the fabulous wildflowers in national parks and elsewhere, or the equally – if not
more – fabulous life on the coral reef. This takes people to the sea, to rivers, lakes,
mountains, the Great Barrier Reef, and of course to many other easily accessible
environments where, in spite of considerable disturbance, enough of the wildlife
remains to form a major part of the environment and of the attraction for the
visitor.

Third, there are the areas where the landscape and especially the indigenous
wildlife, is the principal interest and attraction, and these are the national parks and
nature reserves (Figure 17) and the remote and relatively undisturbed areas, chiefly
the centre of the continent, the south-west of Tasmania and the rain-forests and
monsoon forests in the tropics. I shall return to these shortly.

THE EXOTICS

Now I should give a similar treatment to the exotic flora; but this I must
cut to the aesthetic bare bones if I am not to invade in force the territory of the
next two chapters. I have already ascribed, perhaps somewhat contentiously, a
minor aesthetic role to the exotic pastures and crops, describing them as the background colouring of a landscape still dominated by the indigenous trees. How
right this is, becomes evident in a corresponding landscape of exotic pasture
without the trees – such as the Esperance district in the south of Western
Australia – which to my mind is one of the dreariest landscapes on this continent.
Here there had not been any trees due to the extreme deficiency of the soil, and
roadside remnants of the original scrub – very beautiful in the spring – are all that
is left to break the monotony.

So let us again turn to the trees, but now the exotic ones. First, there are many
species, both deciduous and evergreen, in parks, in gardens, surrounding sports-
grounds, lining drives (Figure 18). They add variety, interest, and something of a
cosmopolitan air to urban and suburban landscape; they demonstrate that other
parts of the world also have their trees of distinction and beauty. And this goes of
course for many other plants in the 'paradise gardens'[6]. Let me admit it, sometimes
I recall with some nostalgia the rich green and the deep shade of the oaks and
limes in our Christchurch (New Zealand) garden, especially on a hot day.

Second, there are the exotic forest plantations, and here I make only one
comment as a geneticist. Forestry plantations are mainly pines. The most widely
used, *Pinus radiata*, is derived from a few small relic populations on the central
California coast (Figure 19). Forest geneticists have shown that they contain a good
deal of variation; but this is too slight to be noticeable in a population. Our

Figure 17. Coastal forest, Nadgee Nature Reserve, N.S.W., showing density and diversity of vegetation, which includes *Eucalyptus gummifera*, *Angophora floribunda*, *Casuarina* sp., bracken fern and many flowering shrubs.

C. Totterdell, CSIRO, Division of Plant Industry

J. Simpson, CSIRO, Division of Plant Industry

Figure 18. Ornamental exotics bordering Lake Burley Griffin, A.C.T. Claret ash and poplars.

C. Totterdell, CSIRO, Division of Plant Industry

Figure 19. Pine forest near the Cotter Dam, A.C.T. These forests replace native eucalypts in many parts of temperate Australia.

plantings appear homogeneous, of unrelieved monotony. How different from the natural conifers of the Californian sierra, with their altitudinal procession of species, their varied undergrowth, their admixture of deciduous species; or from the pine, spruce and larch forests of Switzerland, with the great christmas trees standing over meadows or snowfields or alongside gashes torn by avalanches or mountain torrents. We cannot blame the foresters; but their creation, to my perception, is a landscape of lifeless monotony, more so even than the agricultural landscape of Northern France and Belgium after the trees had been destroyed in the first war. No doubt there are good economic reasons. But are they the whole answer in our increasingly environment conscious era? With forest development rearing to replace native forests in geometric progression, would it be conceivable to mitigate this impoverishment of vast tracts of our landscape by more imaginative planning, albeit at some loss in economic efficiency?

COMMUNITY ATTITUDES

Having pretended to say all this in the first person singular I now boldly assert that I am far from alone in my, now obvious, partisanship. Certainly, the present-day wide-spread interest in, and concern for the Australian wildlife is of relatively recent origin, though preceding the current wave of the new nationalism. It is easy to appreciate how formidable and, indeed, hostile the enormous, impenetrable, seemingly featureless landscape with its unbelievably strange plants and animals must have appeared to settlers from the 'old country', generating fear of many kinds – of getting lost, of bush fires, and, strangely enough, until the generation only just past, of fears of the bush linked with fears of Aborigines.

These days are gone, and when only yesterday bush clearing, in whatever situation, was regarded as a national service generously rewarded by the tax commissioner (which it still is), we have begun to question the long-term wisdom of this policy. Today the passionate enthusiasm of conservationists is so great that it is risking a violent backlash. Clearly, the interest in our wildlife is strong and growing, and so is the demand for greater protection and for accessibility to areas where wildlife survives.

In response to this demand, and in anticipation of its gaining greater force with growing population, education, and leisure, it is essential that the recommendation by the National Estate Committee, 1974, against 'further alienation of natural or near natural areas close to cities' be adopted and implemented without delay. It is such areas which give greatest enjoyment of the native wildlife to the largest numbers, and make many familiar with the unique character and the beauty of the plants and animals which their country has evolved. This is not the place to discuss selection of sites, management, or other operational features: suffice it to say that, for the sake of both the users and the protection of the landscape, such areas should be as extensive as possible.

THE TIME SCALE OF CONCERN

In Book XI of *War and Peace*, Tolstoy discusses the ancient sophism of Achilles being unable ever to overtake the tortoise which is proceeding at one-tenth of his speed, because every time he would attempt to catch up, the tortoise was one-tenth of the distance further along the track; a sophism arising from the atomisation of time. Tolstoy argues that history is not simply the result of the episodic impact of this or that emperor or general, but is a continuous process. I suppose we tend to look at contemporary events to a degree in the atomistic manner, with a time scale of concern not far beyond our own life span. The worst consequences of this primitive conceit – which we share with all the other animals – is avoided by the fact that some of us are born every day so that the period of concern is automatically integrated in time.

Yet in a period of drastic change the leisurely laissez-faire of the past is out of date; the consequences of our actions are so tremendous that they implicate the future immeasurably more than had been imaginable even half a century ago. The rapid evolution of numbers, demands, know-how and technical resources could make us change the face of the earth, let alone of any part of it, well within a single life span. We are recognising that we have become not only our brother's, but our grandson's keeper. It is natural for a geneticist's thoughts to bridge the generations and centuries, since his experiments seek to illuminate the evolutionary past and his models to explore future generations.

Our thoughts and actions relating to future consequences of our own activities have inevitably a time dimension which I have called the time scale of concern.[7] This may be the next 50, 200 or 10 000 years. In terms of the Australian landscape, a realistic time scale of concern for the trees of the agricultural and pastoral zone would be much shorter – say, 50 to 100 years – than that for major nature reserves which should, I believe, be notionally without end.

We may pause to consider the difference. By comparison with the time scale of evolution, the works of man come and go on a time scale of a different order of magnitude. Evolution at the will of man, whether of plants and animals or of a landscape, is pretty rapid. Our oldest crops began their evolution under domestication a mere 10 000 years ago, and the Australian landscape changed to what we now see, in a century and a half. Ecosystems transformed by man are subject to the rhythm of his biological system and the dynamics of social change. This is as true of buildings as it is of the elements of the Australian landscape. To preserve a transformation landscape used by man, or any elements of it, requires *action as incisive, as deliberately planned and executed*, as has been, and continues to be, necessary to establish and manage such a landscape. In our example, to maintain the tree population in our rural landscape would require opportunities for reseeding.[8] This would require an intensive campaign over, perhaps, 20–30 years, and presumably financial and other inducements. But whatever the success of this endeavour, no-one could venture to foresee the future face of the Australian agricultural landscape, say, beyond the middle of the next century.

Diametrically the opposite is true of those areas which are *not* transformed and, for the most part, not irrecoverably disturbed. Here I refer to *national parks and reserves* and the as yet little disturbed areas in the centre of the Cape York Peninsula, and elsewhere. Here the need is for *non-action*, at least in principle. Natural communities can only persist and continue to evolve if left to their own devices, i.e. with the minimum of management measures which may be needed to maintain the ecosystem in ecological balance (e.g. population control of a dominant species). The only drastic, positive act required is to *establish and secure adequate, well designed areas*, selected to represent to the largest possible extent the diversity of Australian wildlife. For let us be clear that perhaps in the course of the next century there will be few native species left under natural conditions outside of reserved areas.[9] The survey of plant communities in Australia and Papua New Guinea, which was recently conducted as an Australian contribution to the International Biological Program[10], will be of great assistance in identifying the representative ecosystems and communities in need of protection.

We must recognise that the time scale of concern relating to nature reserves depends on the purposes of a reserve. The nature reserves near cities, with maximum user access, or the small reserves in many parts of the country designed to protect scenic or attractive sites or communities will be time limited by the very nature of use and size. Nevertheless they serve an important social and educational function and deserve strong local and government support. Certainly, they play a role in diversifying and enriching the landscape. They have an ancient tradition, alas not upheld by the white settlers. Dame Mary Gilmore[11] wrote of the 'native sanctuaries' for fish, birds and animals in the Riverina, which were carefully managed to maintain populations at reproductively viable levels by the first Australians, but which were neglected and rapidly destroyed by the first white settlers.

Reserves designed to perpetuate the wildlife of a region must not only be physically and legally, but biologically secure. Since they are to serve for an unlimited time span they must provide the scope for *continuing evolution* by genetic adaptation to changing environments. Hence they must contain adequate population size and diversity to provide the raw material for natural selection.[12] [13] Generally speaking, genetic considerations reinforce the ecological requirements for size and diversity of reserved areas.

Thus the interest of the present generation in safeguarding the biological heritage coincides with our responsibility towards the future. We are beginning to regard ourselves as the trustees of this heritage, well knowing that any generation after us has it in its power to break the trust. But, in appreciation of what we recognise as the unique glory in the Australian landscape, let *ours* not be *that* generation.

Notes and references

1. SEDDON, GEORGE. *Swan River landscapes*. Nedlands, University of Western Australia Press, 1970.
2. JOHNSON, L. and BRIGGS, BARBARA G. 'Unplanted trees – the value of regrowth', *Agr. Gazette NSW*. 82:34/35, 1971.
3. Yet animals play a vital role in the landscape, as Dr L. J. Webb comments: 'Fauna conveys a dynamic quality in a landscape, whereas vegetation is immobile, like a frozen cine frame. Flocks of white cockatoos, pink and white galahs, the green and gold sheen of clouds of budgerigars, solemn processions of water birds . . . Without animals, a landscape restricted to vegetation is somehow diffuse and two-dimensional, like a town at dusk: animals provide movement and luminescence – just like when the lights come on!'
4. *op. cit.* SEDDON, 1970.
5. WALLING, EDNA M. *The Australian roadside*. Melbourne, Oxford University Press, 1952.
6. *op. cit.* SEDDON, 1970.
7. FRANKEL, O. H. 'Genetic conservation: our evolutionary responsibility', *Genetics*. 78: 53–65, 1974.
8. *op. cit.* JOHNSON and BRIGGS, 1971.
9. DAY, M. F. 'The role of national parks and reserves in conservation', in COSTIN, A. B. and FRITH, H. J. (eds.) *Conservation*. Ringwood, Vic., Penguin, 1971, pp. 190–213.

10. SPECHT, R. L., ROE, ETHEL M. and BOUGHTON, VALERIE H. (eds.) 'Conservation of major plant communities in Australia and Papua New Guinea'. *Aust. J. Bot. Suppt. no 7*, 1974.
11. GILMORE, MARY. *Old days, old ways.* Sydney, Angus and Robertson, 1934.
12. FRANKEL, O. H. 'Variation – the essence of life', *Proc. Linn. Soc. NSW.* 95:158–169, 1970.
13. UNESCO. Programme on Man and the Biosphere (MAB). *Conservation of natural areas and of genetic material they contain:* project no 8. Paris, Unesco, 1973.

*Bruce Davidson**

History of the Australian rural landscape

Agriculture as it exists in Australia at present is the result of an attempt to found a system of farming which was developed in the temperate regions of Europe in a country with a climate ranging from the Mediterranean to tropical and dry desert types. The different physical environment, the long distance from its principal markets and the very different ratio of land to labour in Australia, led to the development of systems of farming and rural landscapes which bore little relationship to those found in Europe.

THE ORIGINAL LANDSCAPE

When the European arrived in Australia in 1788 he found an environment which was only slightly affected by man. The Aboriginal was a hunter and fisherman, and apart from using fire as an aid to grazing, he had little effect on the landscape.

The vegetation chiefly consisted of open eucalypt forest in the wetter coastal regions which decreased in height and density as the climate became drier further inland. There were some areas of closed rain-forest, but these were limited to isolated regions of high rainfall on the east and south-eastern coasts (Figure 20). The overall effect of decreasing rainfall with increasing distance from the coast in the south of the continent was for the open forest on the coast to grade into savannah woodland further inland and for this in turn to give way to eucalypt scrub, commonly known as mallee (*Eucalyptus* spp.) then to herbaceous salt bush and blue bush (*Atriplex vesicaria* and *Kochia sedifolia*) which in turn gave place to almost treeless heaths (*Epacridaceae* complex) and spinifex (*Triodia*) grassland, and finally to a dry desert. All of the southern forests and woodlands carried an understorey of grasses in which tall perennials such as kangaroo grass (*Themeda australis*) were dominant. In the north of the continent, the succession was similar, except that the savannah woodlands gave way to scrubs of non-eucalypt species such as brigalow (*Acacia harpophylla*) and mulga (*Acacia aneura*) rather than to the base-branching mallee form of many *Eucalyptus* species. There were exceptions to this general pattern. In some areas where even the coastal regions were dry, as on the Great Australian Bight and on the central coast of Western Australia, the heath lands extended to the sea. In other areas such as the Mitchell grass plains of north-western New South Wales (dominated by *Astreleba* spp.) and in parts of the Western District of Victoria the pattern was modified by the soil. The cracking clays made eucalypt tree growth impossible and savannah woodland was replaced by grass land.[1]

---

* Bruce Davidson is Senior Lecturer, Department of Agricultural Economics, University of Sydney.

63

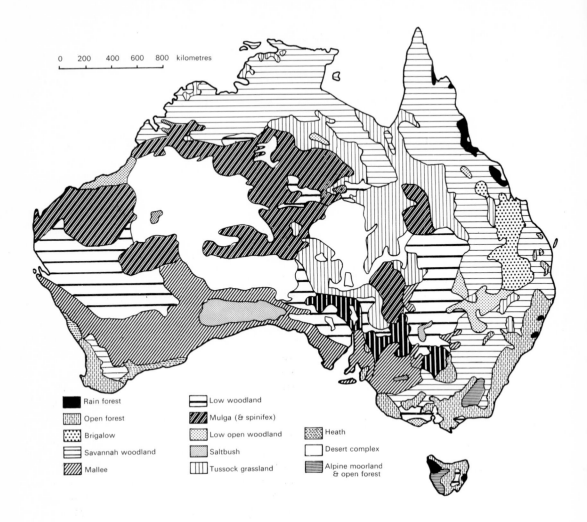

0 200 400 600 800 kilometres

Rain forest

Open forest

Brigalow

Savannah woodland

Mallee

Low woodland

Mulga (& spinifex)

Low open woodland

Saltbush

Tussock grassland

Heath

Desert complex

Alpine moorland
& open forest

Figure 20. Australia—pattern of vegetation formations.

FIRST SETTLEMENT

The initial aim of the original European settlers was to produce enough food to make the colony self-supporting. They rapidly discovered that Australian soils in the vicinity of Sydney were infertile and that crops could only be produced on the limited areas of rich alluvial soils on the Parramatta, Nepean, Hawkesbury and Hunter Rivers. On these rivers the land was cleared and maize and other food crops were produced. At the same time it was realised that the cedar trees in the coastal forest were a valuable timber that could be exported to Britain. From 1822 trees were removed, first from the south coats and later from further north until by the 1870s this species had largely vanished.[2] It is sometimes forgotten that for a long time timber and whale oil were the only major exports from Australia. Until 1830 whale oil and seal oil were a more valuable export than wool.[3] Thus the first years of European settlement affected the landscape only in areas where fertile soil existed and where a valuable species of timber existed.

MARKETS, LAND AND LABOUR

Until the beginning of the nineteenth century, agriculture in Australia had developed to satisfy the needs of the local population for food and fibre. However, Australia differed from the older European countries because the area of well-watered land on which crops could be grown and animals grazed was extremely large in relation to its population. This difference became even more marked once the Blue Mountains were crossed in 1813. It has been estimated that Australia could support a population of 50 million before it is as short of well-watered land as the United States is at the present time and 130 million before the ratio of well-watered land to population equals that of Western Europe.[4]

Because the Australian population was small, large agricultural industries could only be developed if a large overseas market existed for the commodities produced and if these could be transported to European markets without deteriorating. The small population also meant that wages were higher in Australia than in Europe. Thus for any agricultural industry to be successful it had to be developed and operated using a small labour force. The only advantage Australia possessed was a large area of well-watered land.

The history of Australian agricultural development and of the rural landscape which resulted from it, is largely a history of the development of techniques which made it possible to supply the European market with commodities which could be produced with a small labour force using large areas of land, and the effect that these techniques had on the landscape.

THE DEVELOPMENT OF THE WOOL INDUSTRY

No one was more aware of the economic factors controlling agricultural development in Australia than John Macarthur. As early as 1792, he realised that 'a petty population established at so vast a distance from other civilised parts of the globe, could have no prospects of ultimately succeeding, unless by raising as an export some raw material which would be produced with little labour, be in considerable demand, and be capable of bearing the expense of a long sea voyage; that only by production of some such commodity, whatever might be the natural fertility of the country, could it hope to escape the alterations of abundance and scarcity even of bread'.[5]

65

Clearing of the tableland forests for sheep grazing was too expensive to be undertaken because of the high cost of labour, and without clearing their carrying capacity was low. The importance of this point can be appreciated when it is realised that between 1820 and 1825 wool exports from Tasmania exceeded those from New South Wales because the savannah grasslands of Tasmania in their uncleared state had a higher carrying capacity than coastal New South Wales[6]. In 1813 the Blue Mountains were crossed and sheep graziers had access to the savannah land west of the mountains[7]. The squatters rapidly occupied this region and by 1840 sheep stations had been established in all of the savannah woodlands from the Darling Downs in Queensland to South Australia.

As the savannah woodlands were grazed without clearing the initial changes in the rural landscape were not particularly marked. Stocking with sheep meant heavier grazing than by the native marsupials and this in turn led to the disappearance of the dominant tall perennial grasses such as kangaroo grass (*Themeda australis*) and its replacement as the dominant species by shorter grasses such as wallaby grass (*Danthonia* spp.).

Similarly, man-made structures must have made little impact on the landscape. The sheep stations were extremely large; even in well-watered Victoria they averaged 16 000 hectares (40 000 acres) in area.[8] As the sheep were shepherded, no fences were constructed. At night they were herded into moveable yards to protect them from the dingoes. Permanent structures were limited to a homestead, normally with a detached kitchen, huts for the men and a shearing shed. Initially these were either constructed completely of bark or were built with slab walls with a bark roof.[9] The early shearing sheds were built without walls and all buildings had earth floors.

THE EARLY COUNTRY TOWN

During the first half of the nineteenth century, as the sheep men were occupying the interior, the Australian country towns began to emerge. At first these were mainly limited to the coast, as the squatters were sparsely settled and their needs could be met by a drinking shanty or at the most, a general store. Most of the towns were extremely small. (It is curious that the words 'hamlet' and 'village' have no place in the Australian vocabulary. No country had more need of them. 'Township' is sometimes used to denote a small town, but even it has fallen into disuse.)

The general uniformity of country towns in Australia might be said to be the successful or the disastrous result of centralised town planning. As early as 1829, Governor Darling decreed that all towns in New South Wales were to be laid out in a rectangular pattern. Main streets were to be 100 feet (30.5 metres) wide, subsidiary streets 80 feet (24.4 metres) wide, and both were to be bounded by footpaths 10 feet (3 metres) wide. Buildings were to be erected at least 14 feet (4.3 metres) from the street, although this space could be occupied by a verandah. Building allotments in the main streets were to be 66 feet (20.1 metres) wide and 330 feet (100 metres) deep. All allotments were to be fenced.[10] So the Australian country town was born and so it remains in plan although allotments, particularly in the main streets, were later subdivided so that a 20 feet (6.1 metres) or even a 12 foot (3.7 metres) frontage was common and the regulation requiring shops to be 14 feet (4.3 metres) from the pavement has disappeared.

A town plan for Lake Cargellico, drawn up in 1878, still fits Darling's plan except that the allotments are 33 feet (10.1 metres) wide and 200 feet (61 metres) deep[11]. The following description of Wollongong, New South Wales, in 1855 gives a picture of the smaller country town which persists to this day:

> Like most country towns Wollongong consisted of one main street pretty well filled with buildings and a number of parallel and cross streets which each boasted but a few houses. Each principal religious denomination had a good church. The most striking building was the national school, a new structure of brick.[12]

Originally, country town buildings like farm buildings were of slab construction with bark roofs. Brick structures were extremely rare. The typical weatherboard buildings did not emerge until the late 1850s when steam saw-mills made sawn timber cheaper and cheap wire nails made the construction of such dwellings a practical proposition.

THE EFFECT OF THE GOLD RUSH

Unlike the squatters, whose influence on the rural landscape was slight but widespread, the immediate effect of the gold rushes of the 1850s was to lead to large changes in the landscape, but only in very limited areas. Gold bearing ground was confined to minute areas of the continent. In these areas, camps, or if the gold field was extensive and long lasting, towns, were established. The earth was either stripped of its surface soil to reveal the gold bearing gravel, or disfigured with mullock heaps if underground mining was undertaken. Unless the gold town became a centre for agricultural activities, as in the case of Bendigo and Ballarat in Victoria, it was abandoned when all the payable gold was mined. The ghost town and the mining scars in the form of eroded gravel hillsides and grassed mullock heaps are all that remain of this age.

The other immediate effect of the gold rush was to rob the squatter of his shepherds, who rushed to the gold fields. This forced the squatter to fence his run and it was fortuitous that cheap methods of manufacturing wire and nails were developed at this time.[13] Seven- or nine-wire fences were the rule on the squatter's domain, but the paddocks were still large, and fences in the savannah woodlands must have been scarcely noticeable. Nevertheless it set a pattern for wire enclosed paddocks which were to dominate the Australian landscape in the future.

FREE SELECTION AND CLOSER SETTLEMENT

The major effect of the gold rush on the landscape of Australia was not that caused by mining, or fencing by the squatters, but that resulting from the large increase in the population which occurred at this time. Between 1840 and 1860, the Australian population increased from 200 000 to over 1 000 000. Once the alluvial gold was exhausted, attempts were made to settle a large proportion of the ex-miners on the land. It was from this settlement that the largest changes in the Australian landscape were to arise.

Much of the land suitable for settlement had already been taken up by the squatters. The only way to settle large numbers of farmers was to pass laws which enabled selectors to take up limited areas of the squatters' leasehold land.[14] The squatters combated this, either by selecting the maximum area permitted in the names of themselves and their families, or by bribing their employees to select land and then purchasing it from them – a process known as 'dummying'. As land without water was useless for grazing, squatters could sometimes select land around permanent sources of water, making the remaining land unsuitable for settlement, a process known as 'peacocking'.[15] It was by these means that most of the large properties which still exist in the better rainfall areas of Victoria and New South Wales were established.

Later, more effective laws made settlement possible both on the squatters' leases in the savannah woodlands and on crown land in the open forests along the coast.[16] The squatters had been able to make a satisfactory living in the savannah woodland without clearing by grazing sheep at a rate of one sheep to two hectares (5 acres).[17] However, once farms of 130 hectares (320 acres) were established it was impossible to make a living for a family at these light stocking rates. To overcome this problem, the selector destroyed the trees by ringbarking and as more light penetrated to the ground and competition for moisture from trees was removed, stocking rates increased. The same procedure was followed in the open forest on the tablelands in New South Wales. In both regions the leaves and smaller limbs fell from the ringbarked trees but the trunks and larger limbs remained.

The selector, as he hoped to own his land, was keener to build permanent improvements than the squatter. In fact numerous regulations required him to carry out a certain amount of clearing and fencing before he obtained a title to the land.[18]

The initial result of closer settlement was a series of holdings of 130 hectares (320 acres) in area, covered with grey ringbarked trees and fenced in a variety of ways. As family labour was not otherwise employed for long periods of the year, and capital was scarce, many of the fences in the open forest were made of large logs separated by chocks with panels at an angle to each other. These chock and log fences zig-zagged around the coastal settlers' holdings. As timber became scarcer, they were replaced by rail fences. At first these were simply rails supported between two posts and separated from each other by chocks. But as saplings of the right size for rails became scarcer they were replaced by split rails fitted to morticed posts. Further inland in the savannah woodlands, where timber was smaller and scarcer, the selector like the squatter before him was forced to rely on wire fences. In all areas slip rails were the common form of gate.

The selectors' first homes, like those of the first squatters, were made of slab and bark. Later, as the settlers became more prosperous – and in many cases this change was delayed until the early 1900s – the original slab and bark houses were replaced by weatherboard structures with corrugated iron roofs. Two basic designs were favoured. The larger, which was mainly limited to the wealthier sheep stations, consisted of a bungalow surrounded by a verandah with a separate kitchen and men's huts. The selector's house was normally hip-roofed with a verandah in the front and a skillion at the back which could be extended as the family grew[19]. Both types of houses had farm buildings, either of slabs or weatherboard, at the rear and yards of timber rails for handling livestock.

As neither house nor farm buildings were painted, they, the fences and the ringbarked eucalypt trees, weathered to a silver grey which stood among the wallaby grass, grey in summer and autumn and green in winter and spring. Landscapes of this type can still be found, for example on the old Bridle Track Road from Bathurst to Hill End, New South Wales, and in the more isolated parts of the Hunter Valley and in East Gippsland. Reactions to this landscape varied; to most English visitors used to neat green fields enclosed by hedges, the grey ringbarked trees were hideous. Henry Lawson[20] considered them appallingly dreary, but to Dorothea Mackellar[21] they were a thing of beauty.

THE DEVELOPMENT OF THE MODERN FARMING SYSTEM

Although much of the old savannah woodland had been subdivided into small holdings the new settler was still a poor man. His clearing had raised the carrying capacity from 2 hectares (5 acres) per sheep to one sheep to 0.4 hectares (1 acre) on the best land and 0.8 hectares (2 acres) per sheep on the poorer land, but the income from 130 hectare (320 acre) holdings was still insufficient to give a satisfactory living. The solution to this problem depended on two factors. First, the establishment of large sheep runs in the previously unsettled dry interior with a growing season of less than five months. Secondly, on the development of new technologies which were to make the areas with a growing season of more than five months more productive, and to give Australia distinct farming regions each with its own dominant commodity. The zones can be defined as follows:[22]

The Southern Pastoral Zone
The Northern Pastoral Zone
The Irrigation Zone
The Wheat and Sheep Zone
The Beef and Sheep Zone
The Dairying Zone

The location of these zones is shown in Figure 21.

Each was to develop its own landscape or landscapes and each was the product of the new technologies which increased the productivity of both land and labour.

THE SOUTHERN PASTORAL ZONE

The limits to settlement prior to the gold rush had been imposed by the availability of drinking water for livestock. With the subdivision of much of the old pastoral lands, the pressure to utilise land with a growing season of less than five months increased. Even before the gold rush, areas away from the rivers had been developed by building large earthen dams in which run-off from the surrounding land could be stored for livestock. In the 1860s and 1870s much of the drier land in western New South Wales was rapidly occupied[23] and this was to be repeated at a slightly later date in South Australia and Western Australia. Further inland it was discovered that artesian water could be tapped[24], and although it was highly saline it was suitable for livestock. Using these supplies of water, it was possible to graze sheep on the native vegetation south of the tropics in all but the driest regions such as the Simpson Desert, the Gibson Desert and on the Nullarbor Plain. The other limiting factor was the dingo, which made sheep grazing impossible in the brigalow, mulga and mallee scrubs.

The new sheep runs were large, ranging from 2000 hectares (5000 acres) in the better areas such as the western Riverina to almost 800 000 hectares (2 million acres) on Lake Eyre. By 1890, the western division of New South Wales carried 16 million sheep. Although the saltbush was an excellent fodder, it would not stand heavy grazing, and began to disappear. Its disappearance was hastened by the hordes of rabbits which spread across Victoria in the 1860s, New South Wales and South Australia in the 1880s, and finally crossed the Nullarbor Plain and entered Western Australia in 1894.[25]

In most parts of the Pastoral Zone, the earlier seven- or nine-wire fences were replaced with wire netting to help control the hordes of rabbits and these fences became a permanent feature of the landscape. Some States even netted part of their

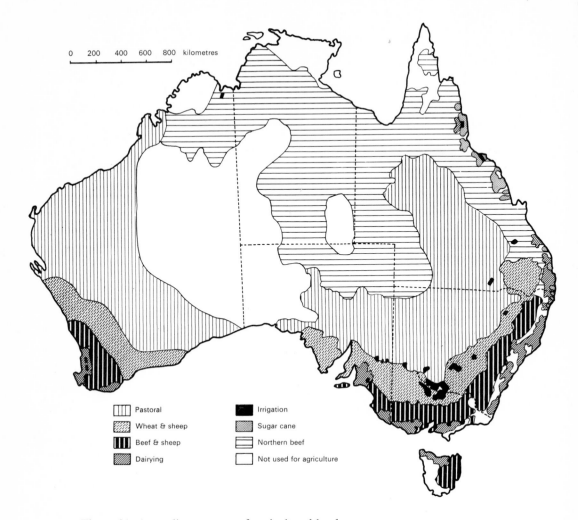

0 200 400 600 800 kilometres

	Pastoral		Irrigation
	Wheat & sheep		Sugar cane
	Beef & sheep		Northern beef
	Dairying		Not used for agriculture

Figure 21. Australia—pattern of agricultural land use.

boundaries in a futile attempt to exclude the plague. Two such fences were built in Western Australia from the Southern to the Indian Ocean. One of these over 1600 kilometres long is still maintained to control the entry of emus onto the grazing land.

Rabbits and heavy stocking changed the dominant salt bush vegetation to one dominated by grassland, and the carrying capacity dropped. Between 1890 and 1900 sheep numbers in western New South Wales declined from 16 million to 7 million sheep. Even in the 1950s, when sheep grazing was extremely profitable, there were only 8 million sheep in the western division of New South Wales.[26] Modern stocking rates range from one sheep to 1.2 hectares (3 acres) in the wetter parts of the Pastoral Zone such as the western Riverina, to one sheep to 80 hectares (200 acres) in the gibber desert near Lake Eyre. Although the change from saltbush to grassland has often been described as one of the worst examples of man's effect on vegetation, it is doubtful if any method of grazing would have given this region a higher carrying capacity than at present. It should also be remembered that in terms of the ratio between returns and resources used, it is one of Australia's most efficient forms of land use (Table 1).

In spite of the change in vegetation, this Zone, with the exception of the northern Pastoral Zone, is the area in which an early explorer, if he returned, would notice least change. The fences of its large paddocks can scarcely be noticed. Where trees exist, they are untouched and its large verandahed homesteads are too far apart to have much effect on the landscape. Even the fauna is less affected than in other regions. Although many of the smaller species have disappeared, the larger species increased in numbers when water was introduced for sheep. The larger marsupials

Table 1. The national efficiency of Australia's farming zones

	Unsubsidised net return to total farm capital + State capital — unimproved capital value
	%
Southern Pastoral Zone	6.7
Northern Pastoral Zone	
(1) Kimberleys	5.2
(2) Northern Territory	8.9
(3) Queensland	7.9
Wheat and Sheep Zone	8.0
Beef and Sheep Zone	4.5
Dairying Zone	0.7
Irrigation Zone	
(1) Rice and Sheep	2.6
(2) Sheep	2.3
(3) Dairying	1.0
(4) Cotton (Namoi)	3.7
(5) Large citrus orchards	4.7
(6) Small citrus orchards	—0.3

Source: DAVIDSON. B. R. 'The comparative profitability and efficiency of agriculture in different regions of Australia'. *Review of Marketing and Agricultural Economics.* 35:198, 1967; and AUSTRALIA. BUREAU OF MARKETING AND AGRICULTURAL ECONOMICS. *Supplement to the Australian Beef Cattle Industry Survey Report,* 1962–63 to 1964–65. Canberra, 1970.

now compete with sheep for grazing, as do the previously domesticated livestock such as camels, donkeys, goats and horses. The latter now breed in the wild state and like their marsupial counterparts can reach plague proportions in some regions.

THE NORTHERN PASTORAL ZONE

Although the tropical regions in Australia were too wet for sheep, it was rapidly discovered that light stocking with cattle was possible. The open eucalypt forest of coastal northern Australia, the Mitchell grass plains of western Queensland, the brigalow of southern Queensland and even the mulga scrub of central Australia were all taken up as huge cattle stations between 1860 and 1890.[27]

At first all runs were unfenced, but the better country in Queensland was fenced in huge paddocks at a later stage, and some ringbarking was undertaken. Creeks, dams and artesian bores were relied on as a water supply. As these stations were held on leases and the profits to be obtained from improvements were doubtful, particularly in the Kimberleys and the Northern Territory, few permanent improvements were made. In these remote regions no clearing, not even ringbarking, was attempted. Cattle were simply allowed to graze, mustered once a year, the older male stock taken out for sale, and the calves branded before they and the females were released to graze and breed for another year. In these conditions the only change in the environment was erection of a homestead, and several outstations with huts and cattle drafting yards.

Unlike the tall grasses of the temperate region, the tropical species persisted under grazing. The mulga scrub of Central Australia was one of the main sources of cattle feed and in drought periods was often lopped to provide additional fodder for cattle. In the 1880s the brigalow was invaded with prickly pear, but this was destroyed by the *Cactoblastis cactorum* caterpillar in the late 1920s. Thus the Northern Pastoral Zone remained the region of Australia least affected by hand of man, an area in much of which man's activity was limited to hunting wild cattle. In spite of its primitive form, agriculture is efficient, and the unsubsidised returns to capital are higher than in more closely settled areas (Table 1).

Only recently has man begun seriously to change the remote northern landscape. It has been discovered that the legume Townsville stylo (*Stylosanthes humilis*) can be established in the tropics and has a much higher carrying capacity than the native grasses. Although the additional profits are not high enough to justify its establishment in the remote Northern Territory and the Kimberleys[28], the converse is true in the better rainfall areas in Queensland, particularly where the soils are fertile as in the brigalow scrub lands. In the last decade, large areas of brigalow, and even some of the open eucalypt forest on the coast of Queensland, have been cleared and sown to tropical pastures.[29][30] Clearing is complete, and the effect is one of large paddocks, green in the wet summer, and brown in the dry winter, with only the occasional bottle tree (*Brachychiton rupestre*) as a reminder of the former scrub or forest.

THE IRRIGATED INTERIOR

The first attempt to improve the income of the small farmers on the subdivided stations in southern Australia was by irrigating the native pasture. When closer settlement first occurred, wool was still the only product which could be exported, and it was thought that the carrying capacity and incomes could be increased if water were available to mitigate the effect of the long summer droughts. Irrigation had been economically successful in California, southern France and northern Italy, and it was thought that the same might be true in Australia. What the the protagonists of irrigation overlooked was that in the former countries, permanent snow water was available throughout the summer and only light diversion weirs were needed to divert it from the rivers. In Australia there were no large permanent snow fields, and large reservoirs had to be erected to store winter rainfall if it were to be available for irrigation in summer. With its small population, the market available for high priced fruit and vegetables, which might have made irrigation economically feasible, was extremely limited. Today, less than ten per cent of Australia's 1.2 million hectares (3 million acres) of irrigated land are used for these products. Irrigation is a labour intensive form of agriculture and the large labour force required rendered it even less profitable. The results of all these factors is that irrigation gives a lower unsubsidised return to all of the capital invested in it (including State capital) than any other form of agriculture (Table 1).

Early irrigation schemes were established along the Goulburn and Murray Rivers in the 1890s and extended to the Murrumbidgee in 1913. At first, farms of from 0.4 to 40 hectares (1 to 100 acres) were attempted, but these proved totally unprofitable. By the 1930s, by which time dairying and rice growing had become possible, 240 hectare (600 acre) rice and sheep farms, with the area of rice limited to 32 hectares (80 acres) because of lack of markets, and 16 hectare (40 acre) fruit farms were the accepted form of irrigated land use in New South Wales. In Victoria, the 40 hectare (100 acre) dairy farm became the most common type of irrigated holding. Both sheep and dairy farms were sown to exotic pasture species.

The large reservoirs in the mountains, the diversion weirs on the rivers with their large canals which branch into even smaller canals to take water to the farms, have become part of the Australian landscape.[31] So have the rectangular paddocks with their irrigation bays and the rice paddies with their contour banks. Many Australians are proud of this, mainly man-made, landscape but few realise it is the most uneconomic form of farming in Australia. It is also forgotten that if irrigation succeeded in turning arid land into a garden, it also in some areas turned arid land into a desert. In an attempt to irrigate cheaply, drainage schemes were not introduced, and in large areas the high salt content of the soil made farming impossible. The large areas of useless Dillon bush (*Nitraria schoberi*) between Echuca and Kerang are the only evidence that this is the site of what was fondly hoped would be a rich farming area.

WHEAT

Before a successful wheat industry could be established in Australia, several problems had to be overcome. In Europe wheat was harvested with a scythe and the high cost of labour made this form of production impossible in Australia. However, with the development of Bull and Ridley's stripper harvester in 1843, the first mechanical harvester in the world, this problem was overcome.[32]

Cultivated lands in Europe were completely cleared of trees and large roots. The high cost of Australian labour made this impossible. The trees could be pulled down with horses or bullocks, but the large roots remained. It was only when Smith developed the stump jump plough in 1876 that large scale ploughing without wrecking cultivation implements became possible.[33]

The coastal regions were too wet for wheat, which was destroyed by rust or smut. The red brown earths of the savannah woodlands west of the mountains were too dry to grow wheat unless it was planted in the autumn and set its seed during the lengthening days of spring. This was the converse of Europe, where wheat was sown in the spring and matured in the autumn, when the days were shortening. Because of this effect of light, English varieties were unsuitable for Australian conditions. To some extent this problem was overcome in the 1880s and 1890s by breeding early varieties. However, varieties which would ripen during a lengthening day were not developed until Farrer crossed English with Indian wheats in 1902.[34] The red brown earths, like most Australian soils, were deficient in phosphate, and low yields were obtained until Custance discovered this deficiency in 1879 and remedied it with superphosphate.[35] Even with these developments, wheat growing would have been impossible without the development of railways. The cost of carting wheat the 160 kilometres from the nearest red brown earths at Bathurst to Sydney in New South Wales or from north of the Great Divide in Victoria to Melbourne, was greater than the value of the wheat.[36] It was only with the development of railways in the 1870s and 1880s that the final ingredient of a successful wheat industry was added.

The landscape which developed in the wheat belt depended to some extent on the initial environment. Although there were common features, a correct overall description can only be made if each environment is described separately.

THE RED BROWN EARTHS OF THE
SAVANNAH WOODLANDS

The initial effect of the wheat industry on the landscape was the removal of the ringbarked timber from large areas of the red brown earths in New South Wales, Victoria and South Australia. It was quickly discovered that high yields could only be obtained if the ploughed land was left fallow from spring until sowing in autumn, so that organic matter would break down and give a readily available supply of nitrogen for the next crop.

With the introduction of wheat, paddocks became smaller as wheat land was fenced off from grazing land. The paddocks were still large by European standards, 20 to 40 hectares (50–100 acres) were common. Australian wheat yields were and still are less than half those obtained in Europe. Wheat grown in Australia and shipped half-way round the world could only compete in European markets because the area of wheat grown by an Australian farmer was four times as large as that of his European counterpart.

The typical rotation was ploughed fallow, wheat, oats. Nearly all farms still used the steeper land for sheep grazing and it retained its former ringbarked trees. The net effect of the introduction of wheat was to change the ringbarked savannah woodland into a mixture of small, completely cleared rectangular fields, and larger grazing paddocks covered with grey ringbarked trees and wallaby grass. After 1890, all fences were built of wire netting to control rabbits. In early spring, the arable land was a mixture of red fallowed fields and green paddocks of wheat and oats. By late spring the crops were in head and the sea of waving oats and wheat changed from green to brown. Harvest in early summer left the brown wheat stubble fields, which persisted through the autumn until they were ploughed and sown again to oats. The ploughed fallow was sown to wheat in autumn and the uniform green of wheat, oats and native pastures was broken only by the brown stubble of last year's oats, until it in turn was ploughed as fallow in the spring.

Around the wheat grower's house were his shearing shed and sheep yards. Once wheat was introduced, a stable for working horses often consisting of posts with thatched or sod roof began to appear on the scene. As oats were harvested as hay, and later cut into chaff for horse feed, large hay stacks became a feature of the landscape. Machinery was left in the open, and beneath a tree near to each homestead lay a mass of rusting, worn-out equipment. These machinery graveyards persisted until the demand for scrap iron before the Second World War caused them to disappear. The ploughed fallows were easily eroded by heavy rains, and erosion gullies became a common feature of the landscape in the early 1900s.

In 1907, Howard discovered that the legume subterranean clover would carry more stock per hectare than the native grasses.[37] Its ability to do so chiefly depended on its high protein content and its ability to set seed in early summer and dry off, leaving a protein-rich hay which could be grazed throughout the summer until the autumn rains caused the seeds to germinate and re-establish the plant. The introduction of subterranean clover into the wheat belt in the 1930s and 1940s led to the disappearance of the native grasses. As it was grazed heavily, it gave the paddocks the appearance of green mown lawn in winter, of lush pastures in spring and of dry bare ground in early autumn.

As tractors replaced horses in the 1940s oats disappeared from the rotations, and as the subterranean clover fixed nitrogen, the fallow became less important. The scene changed to one of wheat fields and subterranean clover paddocks, green in winter and spring and bare and brown in summer. As the grazing land was also sown to subterranean clover, the brown waving wallaby grass disappeared and so the grazing land too, apart from its grey ringbarked trees, assumed a green, heavily grazed look in winter and a bare brown look in late summer and early autumn. Contour banks which diverted the water across the slope and onto permanently grassed water ways which would not erode were superimposed on this scene in the late 1940s and 1950s to create the rolling wheat country of the red brown earths as it is today.

THE MALLEE SCRUB

The very good mallee lands of York Peninsular in South Australia were cleared for wheat growing in the 1890s. After the First World War, the mallee scrub in northern Victoria, western New South Wales, South Australia and Western Australia was also rolled flat, burnt, and sown to wheat.[38] In these areas, yields were lower and paddocks larger than in the savannah woodland. The sandy soils when fallowed were easily eroded by the wind and in some areas formed vast sand dunes which constantly moved. It was not until the 1940s that these were fixed by establishing rye on them. By the 1950s it was discovered that medics would grow in the alkaline mallee soils, and the mallee land too assumed the legume-cereal rotation of the older wheat belt. The main difference in its appearance was the small sand hills as opposed to the rolling hills or plains of the older wheat belt and the absence of any trees except the remaining branched mallee scrub along the roadside.

Settlement of the mallee land was by no means a continuous process. The drier parts of the mallee which were settled in the 1920s were abandoned in the 1930s and re-settled after the Second World War. Wheat varieties with a shorter growing season made the second settlement a more practical proposition. It was not until the late 1960s that the wheat belt in New South Wales reached the limit of expansion in the 1920s. In Western Australia, the area cultivated expanded rapidly in the 1960s and the land was being settled at the rate of 405 000 hectares (one million acres) a year until low wheat and wool prices in the 1960s halted this expansion.

THE BRIGALOW SCRUB AND BLACK SOIL PLAINS OF NORTHERN
NEW SOUTH WALES AND SOUTHERN QUEENSLAND

Although the climate of the southern brigalow lands in northern New South Wales and in Queensland was suitable for wheat, cropping was impossible until the prickly pear was controlled by *Cactoblastis*.[39] The black cracking clays in these regions, unlike most Australian soils, were rich in both nitrogen and phosphorus and crops could be grown every year. The only difficulty was to control the weed growth.

It was not until tractors replaced horses, and large cultivating machinery was developed, which enabled large areas to be cultivated rapidly, that the weeds were controlled effectively. Thus much of the brigalow land and the neighbouring Mitchell grass plains were not sown to wheat until the 1950s. In this region, the stubbles were burnt after harvesting in the spring, and the land was ploughed immediately and worked to control weed growth until the crop was sown in May or June. The landscape is dominated by cultivated black soils in summer and autumn and green wheat in winter and early spring. As wheat was only established on the plains in the 1950s and 1960s when large machinery became available, the paddocks are large and crops of 200 to 400 hectares (500 to 1000 acres) are not uncommon.

Sheep grazing is an auxiliary enterprise on all Australian wheat farms. As the number of sheep grazed and area of wheat grown varies with the profitability of each enterprise, so the landscape can vary from one with a high proportion of pasture, to one with a high proportion of wheat. Thus in the early 1950s, when the price of wool was high, pastures dominated the landscape. In the mid-1960s, when wool prices were low, practically all the land which could be cropped was sown to wheat, and pasture was limited to the steeper slopes.

With the introduction of the tractor and more sophisticated cultivating machinery after the Second World War, machinery began to be housed, and the large open corrugated iron machinery shed was added to the farmer's collection of buildings. Sometimes it was accompanied by galvanized iron silos as an on-farm store of grain for livestock.

Until the 1930s, all wheat was handled in bags, and large stacks of these could be seen at all railway stations in the wheat belt. In the late 1930s bulk handling was introduced, and the tall cylindrical silos became part of the landscape of every wheat town. During the Second World War it was realised that large rectangular corrugated iron storages were cheaper than concrete silos and as the area of wheat increased, these were added to the silos at the railway siding of all wheat towns.

THE BEEF AND SHEEP ZONE

On the tablelands of New South Wales, on the borders of the ranges in Victoria, in south eastern South Australia and on the edge of the plateau in south western

Australia, the topography made the land unsuitable for wheat growing using large scale Australian methods. After the gold rushes, many of the large holdings were subdivided into family farms of 130 to 260 hectares (320 to 640 acres). The timber was ringbarked to increase the carrying capacity, but over time much of the rung timber has been burnt. As in other areas, wire-netting fences were introduced to control rabbits. All of this land south of the latitude of Sydney was capable of supporting improved pastures of subterranean clover if it were topdressed with superphosphate. The native pastures of wallaby grass were converted to improved subterranean clover in Victoria, Western Australia and South Australia in the 1930s and early 1940s.

The final effect in the winter is a park-like appearance of wire-netting enclosing closely grazed green pastures. In summer the subterranean clover dries off and as it is consumed throughout the summer it gives the land a barren look. This is deceptive as the subterranean pastures will carry twice or even three times the number of sheep that the native grasses they replaced would support. In the northern part of the Zone, such as the Hunter Valley, the climate proved unsuitable for subterranean clover and the tall native grass pastures, brown in summer, green in winter, can still be seen.

Close grazing by rabbits led to serious erosion in all of the area before rabbits were controlled first by myxomatosis in the 1950s and later by 1080 poison. The erosion gullies are still a feature of the landscape, although they are slowly being covered by grass in many areas.

Farm buildings are limited to a machinery shed and a wool shed with its attached sheep and cattle yards. In the early period these were built of slabs, and later replaced by weatherboard structures. Since the Second World War, with increasing timber prices there has been a tendency for all farm buildings to be constructed of corrugated iron.

THE COASTAL DAIRYING LANDS

The establishment of a dairying industry in Australia depended on the development of the three following techniques in the 1880s:

(a) The cream separator which enabled cream to be extracted efficiently from large quantities of milk on the farm.
(b) The Babcock tester which gave an accurate measurement of the quantity of butterfat in cream.
(c) Refrigeration, which made it possible to transport butter to European markets without rotting during the voyage.[40]

The open eucalypt forests of south eastern and south western Australia were too wet for either wheat growing or sheep grazing. In the pastoral era, if they were used at all it was as large cattle runs. The advantage of this region was that it had a growing season of nine months and could support perennial pastures such as perennial rye grass, white clover and cocksfoot, which produced large quantities of fodder. These have been the main grasses and clover of Britain for centuries. Such pastures were ideal for dairying as their productivity was high at all seasons except the winter. As the dairy cow's lactation period was nine months, the cows could be dried off during the three-month winter and hand feeding and housing of cattle was unnecessary.

Australian butter could be sold at a lower price in Britain than domestically produced butter, because dairy cattle could be maintained by grazing alone in winter and because the Australian farmer and his family could milk 30 cows compared with the average of 10 milked by his British counterpart.

The disadvantage of the region was the very dense stands of large rain-forest and wet sclerophyll forest, which had to be destroyed before pastures could be established. The soils varied from infertile sands and podsols to rich forest soils (kraznozems), and naturally the forest was densest where the soils were most fertile. The timber was initially destroyed by ringbarking and the smaller limbs, leaves and scrub burnt. The pasture seeds were normally sown in the ashes, as much of the land, such as the Strezlecki Ranges in Gippsland, was too steep to plough. In some areas, clearing resulted in a dense growth of bracken, which had to be continually cut until it was destroyed. As timber was plentiful, post and rail fences were built, or in some areas such as on the north coast of New South Wales even fences of split palings.

The initial landscape was one of enormous ringbarked trees with lush pasture beneath, grazed with dairy cows at a rate of one to 1.2 hectares (3 acres) in the better areas. Development of this kind continued up until the 1920s, when attempts were made to clear the giant Karri forests in Western Australia. Low butterfat prices in the 1930s and the high cost of clearing forced much of this attempted settlement to be abandoned. In northern coastal New South Wales and Queensland it was difficult to establish legumes, and dairying became a poor man's industry.

In the early period, the dairy farmer's house, like that of his sheep farming counterpart, was of slab and bark. These were later replaced with the typical weatherboard structures, although in the cooler coastal region the wide verandah was not such a prominent feature as in the drier inland. Behind each house was the milking shed, at first of slab with an earth floor, but later, weatherboard structures were built. With the passage of years many of the large ringbarked trees which were such a striking feature of the dairy country have been burnt, leaving it uniformly covered with permanent pasture with the occasional shade tree. As the timber was destroyed, the post and railing fences were replaced with wire fences and later with wire-netting as a means of controlling rabbits. In some areas such as north western Tasmania and at Berwick in Victoria, hedges rather than fences were established, but the high cost of cutting hedges made the English method of enclosing fields impossible in Australia.

THE GROWTH AND DISAPPEARANCE OF THE COUNTRY TOWN

By 1870, the Australian country town was a collection of weatherboard shops along a main street, with verandahs supported by posts shading the pavement. Houses in the adjacent streets were also of weatherboard and followed the pattern of the farm houses. They were either bungalows surrounded by verandahs, or hip-roofed structures with a skillion of various lengths at the back. All towns still adhered to the rectangular plan laid down in 1938. South Australia was the only exception: in this State the same style of building was constructed of stone rather than of weatherboard.

The prosperity which came with successful wheat farming, grazing and dairying after 1890, slowly changed the country town. Large hotels were built, often with two storeys and wide verandahs and balconies, and the narrow-fronted shops were replaced by wider structures. Bungalows became the dominant form of housing, rather than the hip-roofed houses of earlier years.

Development, however, was by no means uniform. Towns in favoured positions, particularly at railway junctions or at major river crossings, grew rapidly and had a high proportion of new buildings. Others in less favoured situations retained their original population and architecture.

Until the 1920s, towns were normally located about 30 kilometres apart, with a hotel between each two towns. However, the motor car was to have a serious effect on the country towns. With shorter travelling time, fewer towns were needed. The first victim of the motor car was the hotel halfway between towns; most of them had vanished by 1930. Faster cars and better roads after the Second World War led to the decline, and in some cases the virtual disappearance, of the small country towns, and the increase in the size of the larger towns. The census figures indicate that in many country towns with less than 2000 people, population declined between 1966 and 1971, while in most of those with more than 2000 people, population increased.

The car was to bring other changes. The verandahs over the foot paths, which had been one of the most attractive features of the country towns, hindered parking, so they were replaced by the cantilever type of verandah, or simply abolished. In many towns the large leafy trees which lined the streets and gave shade in summer suffered the same fate.

After the Second World War, the only international form of architecture was introduced into the Australian country towns. The traditional garage, which was sometimes a converted weatherboard blacksmith's shop, or a corrugated iron structure built in the 1920s, was replaced by the modern service station with its standardised flat-roofed buildings, petrol pumps, advertisements and brand of fuel.

The trend was to make all buildings more like those in the large cities. The low bungalow with a verandah was replaced by the verandah-less suburban bungalow. Weatherboard was replaced by brick and in imitation of city hotels, country hotels were faced with tiles. (It is curious to find the last country hotels being faced with tiles in the present decade just when they are being removed from most city hotels.) Perhaps the two worst features of the Australian countryside are the semi-derelict small country town and the transplanted miniature city, complete with suburban dwellings, which the larger country town has become.

The towns at any one period of time tended to have exactly the same style of architecture. The only regional difference was that in northern Australia houses were built 1.8 metres above the ground to allow air to circulate beneath, and to make regular inspection for invasion by termites a simple matter. As insulation was useless in the tropical climate, the walls sometimes consisted of a single layer of tongue and groove boards with the supporting studs on the outside. The southern houses always had the studs inside the weatherboards, and the interior was lined, at first with hessian and paper, and later with fibro-plaster. However, with air conditioning and better chemical control of termites even this regional difference is disappearing, and the new houses in Queensland are similar to those being built in the southern States. In southern Australia only the surrounding environment or the presence or absence of some functional structure, such as a wheat silo or a butter factory, distinguish a town in one farming zone from another.

CONCLUSION

The Australian countryside is a dynamic entity. It has altered as new farming and building techniques have been introduced, and will continue to do so, perhaps more markedly than in the past. The demand for vegetable protein as a source of animal feed could easily lead to the large scale introduction of new crops such as soya beans, linseed and lupins. Increasing beef prices could cause the clearing of the open eucalypt forests in northern Australia and the replacement of these with tropical pastures.

Economies of scale favour larger farms, but an offsetting factor is the desire of many people for a small holding on which to spend their leisure time. The countryside of the future might consist of a mixture of large agricultural holdings and small hobby farms. It is difficult to understand the New South Wales State Planning Authority's objection to such farms. In many countries in Europe the average size of holding is less than 4 hectares, and it would be difficult to argue that the countryside there is less attractive than the Australian countryside.

Notes and References

1. SPECHT, R. L. 'Vegetation', in LEEPER, G. W. (ed.) *The Australian environment*. 4th edn, Melbourne, MUP, 1970, pp. 44–67.
2. JERVIS, J. 'Cedar and cedar cutters', *J. Roy. Aust. Hist. Soc.* 25:131–155, 1939.
3. SHAW, A. G. L. 'History and development of Australian agriculture', in WILLIAMS, D. B. (ed.) *Agriculture in the Australian economy*. Sydney, Sydney University Press, 1967, pp. 3, 14.
4. DAVIDSON, B. R. *Australia wet or dry?: the physical and economic limits to the expansion of irrigation*. Melbourne, MUP, 1969, pp. 31–35, 48–73.
5. ELLIS, M. H. *John Macarthur*. Sydney, Angus and Robertson, 1955.
6. WADHAM, S. M., KENT WILSON, R. and WOOD, J. *Land utilisation in Australia*. 3rd edn, Melbourne, MUP, 1957.
7. *op. cit.* SHAW, 1967.
8. BILLIS, R. V. and KENYON, A. S. *Pastoral pioneers of Port Phillip*. Melbourne, Macmillan, 1932.
9. ROBERTS, S. H. *The history of Australian land settlement, 1788–1920*. Melbourne, Macmillan, 1968 (first published 1924).
10. DOWD, B. T. 'Town planning in New South Wales', *J. Roy. Aust. Hist. Soc.* 32:318, 1946.
11. DOWD, B. T. 'Lake Cargellico: beginnings of district and village', *J. Roy. Aust. Hist. Soc.* 29:129–207, 1943.
12. JERVIS, J. 'Illawarra: a century of history, 1788–1888', *J. Roy. Aust. Hist. Soc.* 28:65–108, 1942.
13. JERVIS, J. 'The western Riverina: a history of its development', *J. Roy. Aust. Hist. Soc.* 38:1–30, 1952.
14. *op. cit.* ROBERTS, 1968.
15. *op. cit.* ROBERTS, 1968.
16. *op. cit.* ROBERTS, 1968.
17. *op. cit.* BILLIS and KENYON, 1920.
18. *op. cit.* ROBERTS, 1968.
19. BOYD, R. *Australia's home: its origins, builders and occupiers*. Melbourne, MUP, 1952 (paperback edition 1961), p. 8.
20. LAWSON, HENRY. 'In a dry season', in *Prose works of Henry Lawson*. Sydney, Angus and Robertson, 1948, pp. 49–51.

21. MACKELLAR, DOROTHEA. 'My Country', in *My Country and other poems*. Sydney, Honey, 1945.
22. DAVIDSON, B. R. 'The economic structure of Australian farms', in WILLIAMS, D. B. (ed.) *Agriculture in the Australian economy*. Sydney, Sydney University Press, 1967, pp. 29–56.
23. *op. cit*. SHAW, 1967.
24. *op. cit*. WADHAM *et al*., 1957.
25. FRITH, H. J. 'The herbivorous wild animals', in MOORE, M. (ed.) *Australian grasslands*. Canberra, ANU Press, 1970, pp. 79–81.
26. *op. cit*. WADHAM *et al*., 1957.
27. *op. cit*. SHAW, 1967.
28. McLINTOCK, G. 'The economics of pasture improvement for beef production in the Northern Territory. *Quarterly Review of Agricultural Economics*', 23:89–96, 1970.
29. AUSTRALIA. BUREAU OF AGRICULTURAL ECONOMICS. *The economics of brigalow land development in the Fitzroy Basin, Queensland*. Canberra, 1963.
30. MOYLE, R. G. and HAUG, N. F. 'Some economic aspects of increasing beef cattle production in the spear grass zone using improved pastures', *Quarterly Review of Agricultural Economics*. 28:45–57, 1965.
31. *op. cit*. DAVIDSON, 1969.
32. CALLAGHAN, A. R. and MILLINGTON, A. J. *The wheat industry in Australia*. Sydney, Angus and Robertson, 1956.
33. *op. cit*. CALLAGHAN and MILLINGTON, 1956.
34. *op. cit*. CALLAGHAN and MILLINGTON, 1956.
35. DUNSDORFS, E. *The Australian wheat growing industry*. Melbourne, MUP, 1956, p. 144.
36. BLAINEY, G. *The tyranny of distance*. Melbourne, Sun Books, 1966, pp. 122–5.
37. DONALD, C. M. 'Temperature pasture species', in MOORE, R. M. (ed.) *Australian grasslands*. Canberra, ANU Press, 1970, p. 309.
38. *op. cit*. CALLAGHAN and MILLINGTON, 1956.
39. *op. cit*. CALLAGHAN and MILLINGTON, 1956.
40. *op. cit*. WADHAM *et al*., 1957.

*Peter Spooner**

History of gardening

The full history of gardening in Australia, or for that matter in the world as a whole, has yet to be written. Gardens more than any other of man's spatial creations are fugitive, for they change with the seasons and the passage of time, leaving nothing for the historian save legend, an occasional description or painting. We are indebted to the bas-reliefs decorating tombs for our knowledge of ancient Egyptian gardening, to carpets and miniatures for Persian influences and to romantic manuscripts for much of the development prior to the Renaissance period. Of the gardens which succeed Dante and Boccaccio in Italy, France and Britain, few indeed remain to be studied, and those that do owe their continued existence to a kind of temporal stand-down wherein the normal processes of growth and decay are minimised by crafty nocturnal replacements. What we see of historic gardens, apart from their geometry and architectural embellishments is therefore many times removed from the original. Not only plants are subject to change. Lawns, paths, planting beds, steps and stairs are all vulnerable as any enthusiastic improver must know. Gardens in excess of two hundred years old have a great deal in common with Lewis Carroll's Cheshire cat! Having thus established a tone of scepticism sufficient to cover all minor inaccuracies, it is now appropriate to examine, albeit briefly, the gardening background from which our earliest settlers came.

England had been slow to accept the grand formality of Renaissance gardens as epitomised by Vaux le Vicomte and Versailles, and one senses in her retention of the smaller Elizabethan and Tudor gardening tradition, a stubborn distrust of ostentation. One would like to think that the English desisted on account of greater sensitivity and respect for nature, but there is little evidence to support such a view. Indeed, whilst her mazes, knot gardens and parterres were on a smaller scale than their French counterparts, they illustrated an equal disregard for natural forms and an equal preoccupation with straight lines and precise geometric solids, frequently executed in clipped yew or box.

Notwithstanding the Englishman's instinctive distrust, a considerable number of Renaissance-style gardens were constructed in the latter part of the seventeenth and early eighteenth centuries. Blenheim, Chatsworth, Melbourne Hall, Hampton Court and Stowe all owed their initial layout to French influence, and whilst most have since been changed beyond recognition, enough remained to imprint a vestigial awareness upon the consciousness of our early developers. The Renaissance landscape grew out of a need to accommodate large numbers of people with all the pomp and splendour of an outdoor theatre production. Port Jackson was a far cry from Hampton Court; nevertheless, formal ceremonial occasions were essential aids to the maintenance of law and order, and elements suggestive of Renaissance formality may be found in the early gardens of our Government Houses, both in Sydney and at Rose Hill, and in many a subsequent city and suburban park.

---

* Peter Spooner is Professor of Landscape Architecture at the University of New South Wales.

Not only was England slow to follow the French lead in gardening, she was also quick to discard it in favour of a more naturalistic approach. As early as 1720, there were indications of a forthcoming revolution, and by 1750 the English landscape school, represented by no lesser a person than Capability Brown, reigned supreme. Brown eschewed the rigidity and straight lines of the earlier style, developing instead the arcadian landscapes of undulating pasture punctuated by tree belts and copses cleverly disposed to accentuate the site's picturesque qualities. Roads and paths swept through these landscapes with gracious curves, whilst a ha-ha cunningly separated the house and inmates from the picturesque, but sometimes hostile, cattle so necessary to complete the scene. Vegetable and flower gardens were banished to the remotest corner of the estate.

By the time Governor Phillip arrived in Port Jackson, Brown's leadership of the new landscape movement had passed to Humphrey Repton whose famous Red Books bore out the movement's picturesque overtones. Repton was a more versatile designer than Brown, and was prepared to acknowledge his client's frequent wish for flowers and other diversifications. Thus the movement was already losing some of its original clarity when the first fleet set out. Reflections of the eighteenth century landscape tradition movement may be seen in the estates of northern Tasmania and Camden Park near Sydney, but one looks in vain for arcadian parklands during the first few decades of settlement.

There are two reasons at least: (a) the Brown formula called for hills and valleys, woodlands and pastures, and these things spelt broad acres beyond the capacity of the settlers to clear and maintain; and (b) the colony's urgent need was food. Fruit and vegetable gardens played no part in a Brown parkland.

One may also speculate upon the social class and living conditions from which the great majority of our early settlers came. In all probability, their knowledge of gardening and garden design extended no further than a small vegetable patch.

Beatrice Bligh divides the history of gardening in Australia into five sections, the first of which she entitles *Gardens for food and survival* and she makes abundantly clear that gardens for decoration came considerably later. Joseph Banks, who had seen and reported upon the native flora of eastern Australia following his voyage with Captain James Cook, 'personally supervised the loading of plants and seeds onto the sailing ships of Governor Phillip's First Fleet, and advised on their care and maintenance for the long and hazardous journey'.[1] This concern arose from his observation apropos Australia, that 'upon the whole the fertile soils here bear no kind of proportion to that which seems by nature doomed to everlasting barrenness'.[2] Banks' concern was well founded for the settlers found the soils around Sydney Cove unproductive in the extreme. Their sandy nature meant that precious water was quickly lost, and many of the tender plants brought from England must have died in the first few weeks. Indeed it is remarkable that any survived the double ordeal of an eight-month sea voyage and ultimate introduction to our harsh summer climate. However, survive they did, but not in quality enough or with sufficient vigour to support the young colony. In the face of this alarming situation, Governor Phillip pressed inland by water, reaching Parramatta which he subsequently named Rose Hill after Sir George Rose, Treasurer to the Navy.

At Rose Hill the soil was clearly more fertile than at Sydney Cove, and fruit and vegetable gardens were immediately established. Henry Dodd, an experienced farm hand who had supervised the clearing and cultivation at Farm Cove in 1788, was

sent to Parramatta by the Governor in March 1789 to supervise the Government
Farm. In less than a year, 31 hectares in the Government Domain were planted with
corn.[3] Watkin Tench, Captain of Marines, visited Rose Hill in 1791, and reported
as follows:

> Vines of every sort seem to flourish; melons, cucumbers, and pumpkins run with
> unbounded luxuriance; and I am convinced that the grapes of New South Wales will,
> in a few years, equal those of any other country. That their juices will probably
> hereafter furnish an indispensable article of luxury at European tables has already
> been predicted in the vehemence of speculation. Other fruits are yet in their infancy;
> but oranges, lemons, and figs, will I dare believe, in a few years become plentiful.
> Apples and the fruits of other climes also promise to gratify expectation.[4]

James Ruse reported to Captain Tench on his work at Experiment Farm as follows:

> I have now $1\frac{1}{2}$ acres in bearded wheat, $\frac{1}{2}$ acre in maize, and a small kitchen garden . . .
> my land I prepared thus: Having burned the fallen timber off the ground, I dug in the
> ashes, and then hoed it up, never doing more than perhaps nine rods a day, by which
> means it was not like the Government Farm, just scratched over, but done properly;
> then I clod-mouled it, and dug in the grass and weeds . . . My straw, I mean to bury
> in pits, and turn to manure, I have no person to help me, at present, but my wife,
> whom I married in this country; she is industrious.[5]

With that laconic statement, Ruse paid tribute to the pioneer womenfolk who
braved backbreaking toil coupled with indescribable loneliness in their efforts to
establish homes in the new land. Slab huts with earthen floors and bark roofs provided
their only shelter, yet the urge to humanise the immediate surroundings was
irresistible. Roses, lupins, wallflowers, larkspurs, and hollyhocks provided a precious
link with the mother country. In small clearings, under the burning sun and set about
by the silent, brooding bush, the pioneer women undertook the pathetic, but
necessary, task of keeping house, and maintaining their self-respect.

It is difficult for us some two hundred years later to appreciate the sense of infinite
remoteness which must have influenced their every thought and action. The garden
was familiar, as were the specific plants brought out by ship, and the constant attention
it demanded was an insurance against despair. It is reported that, when the first potted
primrose was brought out on one of the ships, people stampeded onto the wharf to
gaze with nostalgia at this small emblem of English gardens. Weeping willows,
oak, elm, Lombardy poplars and the locust tree of North America were amongst
early deciduous trees introduced to the country.

By 1800 a significant number of hitherto unknown indigenous plants had been
collected and planted at Rose Hill for eventual shipment to London, but it was not
until George Cayley arrived with Governor King that the bulk of this material was
sent. Botanical interest was intense, for the settlement of Australia had coincided with
the age of great plant explorers. A lively exchange of exotic and indigenous material
was accompanied by an equally lively correspondence between both trained botanists
and enthusiastic amateur collectors. King's term of office was marked by the growth
of private agriculture and a period of relatively plenty, attested by the fact that the
proportion of population drawing government rations dropped from seventy-two per
cent in 1800 to thirty-two per cent in 1806.[6] King was followed by Bligh, whose interest
in plants found outlets in his Model Farm near Windsor, and then by Johnson,
Foveaux and Paterson, before Macquarie the builder assumed control on New Year's

Day in 1810. During Macquarie's time, the grounds of Government House, Parramatta, were fenced and took upon themselves the superficial characteristics of a parkland, with widely dispersed clumps of trees and gentle slopes descending to the river.

Meantime the gardens associated with cottages in Parramatta, Sydney and Windsor supported mature fruit trees as well as a wide variety of vines and flowering shrubs. From the contemporary illustrations available to us, we gather the impression of strict formality and orderliness, each garden being surrounded by a fence of vertical pales with pointed tops, presumably to keep at bay the wandering goats and other domestic animals. Within this enclosure plants were arranged in orderly rows, and the various sections of the garden separated by straight paths edged with stones.

With the gradual establishment of order in the colony, an increasing number of visitors came to inspect the new settlements. The days of primitive pioneering were at an end and by 1830 gentlemen of property were being encouraged to emigrate to Australia. Gardening took on a new dimension, and the theories of landscape design espoused by Brown and Repton found ardent support through the advocacy of Mr Thomas Shepherd, a nurseryman-cum-landscape designer, who arrived in Australia about 1826.

Shepherd had studied under Mr White, a contemporary of Lancelot Brown, and had the distinction of telling Mr Repton how to construct a garden. He sought to set up a nursery for the commercial production of plants which had hitherto been made available to the public from Government gardens.

Governor Darling had encouraged Shepherd, but it appears that the venture was unprofitable. In 1834 Thomas Shepherd delivered four lectures on the horticulture of Australia, and in June 1835 the first of seven lectures on landscape gardening. He was a very sick man, and died in August, before completing his series, however, the text of his lectures was subsequently presented to the Hon. Alexander McLeay, Secretary for the Colony, and published in 1836.

In his initial lecture, Shepherd refers to the poor state of the landscaping art in Australia:[7]

> With a very few exceptions, Landscape Gardening has been totally neglected. The wants of the early Colonists were objects of too much consideration to permit them to devote much of their time to embellishment . . . We have a few orchards it is true, and some romantically situated country residences, most embellished within the last few years, where attention appears to have been paid to the principles of this delightful art by gentlemen of taste and capital. But there is certainly much that remains to be effected . . . In place of cutting down our splendid forests, right forward without distinction, we have only to thin out and tastefully arrange and dispose them to produce the most pleasing effects.

In referring to his erstwhile master, the redoubtable Mr White, Shepherd says:

> If Mr White had a fault, it was his unlimited ambition in the extent of his designs. A number of estates cost an immense expense in their execution, indeed so much, that many gentlemen were ruined by it, and were under the necessity of disposing of their estates to pay their debts. In my opinion, this ruin was more occasioned by gentlemen being over desirous of doing a great deal in one year towards the execution of Mr White's designs than to the extent of the improvements which he designed.

and here comes the punch line:

It is incredible the immensity of extent and work in Landscape Gardening which may be completed in the very first style of elegance without running the risk of ruin to any landed proprietor of moderate income.

In his third lecture, Mr Shepherd gave a fascinating feasibility study for the establishment of an independent gentlemen of 30 000 pounds capital, and his wife and six children – independent indeed! The budget is worth quoting as it often happens that lists of this kind give a clearer insight than voluminous prose.

	£	s	d
To passage money from England to N.S.W.	500	0	0
To purchase of 7,000 acres of freehold land, at 10 shillings per acre	3,500	0	0
To purchase of 2,000 ewes and rams	2,500	0	0
To the erection of a mansion and outbuildings	5,000	0	0
To purchase of furniture to furnish the mansion	1,000	0	0
To fencing for enclosing 1,000 acres of land	300	0	0
To disbarking trees and burning off and clearing 100 acres for agriculture, kitchen garden, orchard, vineyard, flower garden, shrubberies, etc.	300	0	0
To making an approach from the high road, and pleasure grounds, kitchen garden, orchard, vineyard, etc. as necessary at the first commencement	1,000	0	0
To a coach, four coach horses and harness	600	0	0
To two saddle horses, saddles and bridles	70	0	0
To carts, ploughs, harness and other implements	100	0	0
To pigs and poultry	30	0	0
To two teams of four working oxen for each team	24	0	0
To twenty store oxen, from 3 to 5 years, for slaughter	40	0	0
To twelve milch cows at £3.0.0 each	36	0	0
To fifty ewes and one ram	50	0	0
To fifty wethers, for slaughter	25	0	0
Total capital outlay	**14,575**	**0**	**0**

And the annual running expenses!

	£	s	d
To salary for competent tutor to teach six children	100	0	0
To salary for an experienced horticulturalist, to be employed as superintendent over all the out-door establishment	100	0	0
To a free gardener, as foreman under superintendent	20	0	0
To a free farming man, as foreman under superintendent	20	0	0
To twenty assigned labourers, for clothing and rations	300	0	0
To salary for a free butler	50	0	0
To salary for a free coachman	40	0	0
To a postillion and groom – assigned servants	20	0	0
To two footmen, assigned servants, for clothes	30	0	0
To a free housekeeper	40	0	0
To a free lady's maid	30	0	0
To a free cook	30	0	0
To four free maid servants, at £10 each	40	0	0
To repair of equipment, coach and harness	60	0	0
To wine, spirits, ale, sugar, tea, coffee, spices, and clothing for the family	300	0	0
Total yearly expenditure	**1,180**	**0**	**0**

Clearly, by 1835, the days of subsistence living had passed, and it is reassuring to learn that an independent gentleman could set up house for such a reasonable expense. Once in his stride, Mr Shepherd was not to be distracted and he proceeds in his fourth lecture, to show how persons possessed of £20 000, £10 000 and £5000 could establish themselves. Even the last named did reasonably well, because his yearly expenditure of £415.0.0 covered a tutor, working overseer, ten servants, a maid and manservant and 'necessary articles for the family'.

Shepherd concluded his lecture series with a detailed description of the gardens of *Elizabeth Bay* and *Lyndhurst*, both of which he admired enormously, although his catalogue of *Elizabeth Bay* plantings leaves one with the impression of a botanic garden. Its lawns and polished shrubberies were to be furnished with choice trees and plants from England, China, Mauritius, the East Indies, North and South America, and from Moreton Bay, Norfolk Island, the Cape of Good Hope and other places.

Australia had fallen a victim to the nineteenth century passion for collecting, and her gardens henceforth were to contain as diversified a range of specimens as the climate, aided by man, would permit. Illustrations from 1830 on to 1870 show carriage drives circling before the façades of imposing mansions, many furnished with a bunya pine, and all displaying a wide variety of imported trees and shrubs.

Beatrice Bligh sees the 1860s as the peak of creative landscape design in Australia, claiming that gardens of that period were designed with sympathetic relation to their surroundings, were spacious and simply planted, but it was not long before the country's increasing wealth led to the construction of more elaborate, less tasteful establishments. Indeed, the author draws attention to the Italianate Victorian houses of the seventies and eighties and the incredibly ornate mansions of Victoria's Western District, where the gardens sported statues of Venus, Napoleon or Captain Cook, and as many as 1000 guests would be assembled for croquet and other genteel games.

By comparison with what has preceded it, the history of Australian gardening in the twentieth century seems rather colourless. The final extravagances of the late Victorian era gave way to a period of uncertainty culminating in the Great War, and the days of Victorian pomp and material splendour were over. Labour costs rose to a point where garden maintenance became a serious problem, and this, coupled with the depression years, and the rapidly growing number of small home owners and suburbanites produced a do-it-yourself attitude. Unfortunately, it was all too frequently coupled with a notion that neatness and beauty were synonymous, and that the garden's purpose was to impress rather than serve as a pleasant environment.

There were exceptions, Edna Walling and Jocelyn Brown being foremost amongst them, but the general standard of landscape design throughout Australia did not show improvement until the Second World War was over, and even then the change was relatively slow. One is always tempted to speculate upon the reasons for change, and in this instance it is my belief that a number of factors conspired to encourage the change:

1. The rapid urbanisation of Australian society, and rising land costs, had the effect of reducing residential block sizes.
2. Greatly increased mobility, coupled with higher earnings and more leisure time enabled people to pursue sport and recreation wherever it was to be found. The large private garden consequently lost some of its earlier value.
3. A world-wide change in outlook relative to the pursuit of pleasure. It was no

longer considered necessary to earn rest and relaxation through hard work. Gardens therefore should be things to enjoy lightheartedly rather than the strange love-hate syndrome of the confirmed garden martyr.

The combined effect of these influences showed itself in a general reduction in garden size and labour-intensive treatments. Carports, barbecues and swimming pools have taken the place of decorative statuary and geometric flower beds, whilst paving materials of one kind or another are gradually reducing the extent of the manicured lawn. More recently, and I believe for the same fundamental reasons, there has been a strong move towards the use of hardy indigenous plants and perennial ground covers in preference to the somewhat less appropriate exotics. It is argued, and with considerable justification, that the environmental character or quality attainable through sensitive use of native plants is superior to that achieved with exotics – superior in the sense of its being a true reflection of our ecology.

A history of gardening would be incomplete without reference to and acknowledgment of the part played by nurserymen, for in embarking upon commercial production of plants, they have inevitably favoured popular lines and thereby reinforced the current fashions. More than this, they have from time to time taken the lead in initiating new trends, an undertaking which, whilst being highly commendable from a philosophic point of view, is highly dangerous economically. Progressive nurseries throughout Australia are now increasing the range of native material available to the public, and it is hoped that this trend will continue, not, I might add, to the total exclusion of exotics, but to a better balance than we have had heretofore.

Nor can this history be considered complete without reference to Australia's Botanic Gardens, especially that of Sydney, established in 1816, and of Melbourne in 1846, and an outstanding example of picturesque design. These gardens, together with those of other States, have contributed to the development of agriculture, silviculture and horticulture in innumerable ways, not least of which is the identification, and exchange of plants with and from other parts of the world, and the friendly assistance offered to any gardener with a problem.

It would seem that in some respects the history of Australian gardening has come full-circle. We have returned to the concept of a garden as a place rather than display, our gardens are small, and we maintain them with our own hands. However, here the similarity ends, for we are reintroducing native species which the settlers cleared in their attempts to establish ascendancy over the menacing bush. Does this new acceptance of our indigenous environment imply that we have at last come of age?

References

1. BLIGH, BEATRICE. *Cherish the earth: the story of gardening in Australia.* Sydney, Ure Smith, 1973.
2. *op. cit.* Bligh, 1973.
3. PROUDFOOT, HELEN. *Old Government House: the building and its landscape.* Sydney, Angus and Robertson, 1971.
4. *op. cit.* Bligh, 1973.
5. *op. cit.* Bligh, 1973.
6. *op. cit.* Proudfoot, 1971.
7. SHEPHERD, THOMAS. *Lectures on landscape gardening in Australia.* Sydney, John McGarvie, 1836.

Further reading

CLIFFORD, DEREK. *A history of garden design.* London, Faber & Faber, 1962.

MAIDEN, J. H. 'History of the Sydney Botanic Gardens', *Royal Historical Society Journal.* 15:1–42, 1928; 17:145–162, 1931.

PESCOTT, R. T. M. *W. R. Guilfoyle, 1840–1912: the master of landscaping.* Melbourne, Oxford University Press, 1974.

SEDDON, GEORGE. *Swan River landscapes.* Nedlands, University of W.A. Press, 1970.

WALLING, EDNA. *The Australian roadside.* Melbourne, Oxford University Press, 1952.

*Ken Green**

History of engineering works
on the Australian landscape

INTRODUCTION

What is landscape in the context of this paper? My dictionary says: 'a stretch of country seen from a single point' with the implication that the stretch of country can be in its natural state or 'unnatural', i.e. changed by man or some force other than nature. This point is made here because many landscapes which are the result of past ignorance or carelessness can be modified and improved by engineering works, and indeed this is happening in Australia today, as I hope to demonstrate. There is no doubt that engineers have exercised a considerable impact on Australian landscapes since the earliest European settlements. It could also be argued – and no doubt will be – that this impact has, on the whole, been adverse. This belief can also be challenged.

MILESTONES

The first engineering impact on the Australian landscape probably came from the rudimentary roads radiating outwards from Sydney Cove, the early water supply works, and the crude port facilities developed for the ships from Britain.

Subsequent significant milestones in engineering developments include in more or less chronological order:
– the railways
– the motor car
– the commercial airlines
– heavy earthmoving machinery
– prestressed concrete
– major water conservation and hydro-electric projects
– the computer

Some of these innovations are dealt with below in more detail, but some general points can be made by way of historical introduction. Development of the early roads, for example, was hampered by topography, primitive vehicles and limited means of construction.

The railways changed this by providing a relatively fast method of transporting large and heavy goods to the inland and allowing rural cities and towns to grow and develop their own distinctive townscapes which, in many cases, had begun to emerge during the goldrush days.

Next came the early motor car, and with it, a steady and growing demand for more and better roads. Areas inaccessible by railways were now opened up to the axe and the fire in the name of agricultural progress, as roads were pushed out into the scrub, often with great difficulty and considerable disruption of the environment. South Gippsland and the south coast of New South Wales provide two typical examples.

The commercial airlines probably came next, for they helped to open up new

---

* Major-General Green is Secretary, Department of the Premier, Victoria.

History of engineering
works on the
Australian landscape

areas far away from the capital cities and at the same time provided new vistas for the intrepid traveller, though their full impact was not to develop until after 1945.

The advent of heavy earthmoving machinery in Australia just before World War II was probably the largest single force for landscape change up to that time. Gone was the reliance on horses and primitive tractors. In their place came the bulldozer, the giant mechanical shovel, the scraper, new explosives and the ability to harness many thousands of horsepower in the quick and flexible movement of whole hillsides of earth and rock.

All kinds of new engineering works were now possible in a fraction of the time previously necessary. New highways, land reclamation schemes, tree clearing projects, quarries and mines could be put in hand overnight and landscapes could be changed in the same time. Bigger and bigger machines could be developed, and are still being developed. This ushered in an era of technological capacity, imbalanced by other considerations, which we are still living with, though it is much more civilised than before.

Prestressed concrete was the next major development in this field because of its effect on the nature and size of buildings, bridges and similar large structures. It was now possible to design and build, meccano-fashion, to great heights, using repetitive shapes, at relatively low cost, and in association with steel and glass – hence many of the economical, clean but so monotonous matchboxes which grace our Housing Commission estates and many of our commercial streets. Prestressed concrete can be used as a tool for new and graceful designs, as some of our more imaginative bridges testify, but this is all too rare. Prestressed concrete shapes and forms are also likely to be with us for a very long time, because it is a remarkably strong and durable material and will resist demolition much more than the brick and rubble of the last century, which yields so easily to the bulldozer.

Major water conservation and hydro-electric projects of the past thirty years deserve a special mention because they have provided an opportunity for many people to visit and enjoy vistas and experiences that would otherwise have been denied them. Whatever their other features, the Snowy Mountain Scheme, the Ord River Project, and even the Lake Pedder Scheme, have all opened up new country to virtually everybody instead of merely to the affluent or energetic.

Finally, in this recital of milestones comes the computer. This new and fascinating tool enters all fields of engineering endeavour and has opened all kinds of new options. No longer does one have to make a judgment on a highway location on examination of only two or three alternatives. The computer can throw up ten or twenty for you to examine. Properly programmed, it can take account of environmental, social and other factors, as well as cubic metres and money cost. We have not yet learned to use the computer to the fullest advantage. But as we do, it will offer the best chance to marry technology to all the other considerations in planning and building engineering works, provided that it is in sensitive and competent hands. It is truly the ultimate aid in protecting the environment and the landscape.

THE COST OF TECHNOLOGY

If one assumes that technology, like rape, is inevitable, then the landscape will be changed. It need not always be for the worse – but reduced effects on landscape will almost always lead to increased costs, and the engineers have generally been trained to produce the lowest cost solution to technological problems, in the belief that this is in the public interest. If preservation of landscape is also in the public interest, most engineers will be happy to oblige, but on the understanding that the public appreciates that this will often cost us all more in money, at least in the short term.

A UNIQUE LANDSCAPE

It should be remembered that the Australian landscape is probably unique in the world. We have the oldest and flattest continent; much of it is arid and featureless, and there is no permanent snow, even in Tasmania. The spectacular views of Europe, America or Africa are not for us. Our scenery is not so obvious; it must be sought out and appreciated at leisure.

At the same time, the vast area and small population of this land have resulted in less exploitation of the natural landscape than in many other countries, although we have worked hard on this in recent years! The monotonous topography has made our engineering, particularly civil engineering, less costly than in other countries with more relief. Straight alignments for the early roads and railways were not only cheap, they were obvious – but often bad for the landscape.

Another important general factor is the fragility of much of our countryside. Even the best of this ancient land has only a very thin layer of top soil. It is easily removed or made unstable, and impossible to replace. So apparently inexpensive road alignments which ignore even our mild contours may lead to costly or perhaps insoluble problems.

ROADS

Roads probably represent the engineer's first major impact on the virgin Australian landscape. The coach tracks of the early settlers became the main roads of the surveyors, who hemmed them in with monotonous north-south and east-west grids of parish roads a kilometre or so apart to facilitate the early subdivisions. The flat topography was largely to blame for this seemingly practical but unimaginative pattern, which took little or no heed of natural drainage lines. It has been the bane of many later engineers and planners.

The main roads gradually became the highways with the spread of the motor car. Much of the early alignment of these roads had been dictated by natural crossing places over Australia's erratic rivers, and these were not always the best places for the bridges demanded by the modern automobile. Furthermore, the general routes were restricted by the extensive alienation of public lands into private ownership, and relocation has often been difficult and costly.

Landscapes were given little, if any, consideration in early road design. Fortunately, in many areas, as private clearing and development proceeded, trees were left standing on the road reserves (Figure 22), many of which were wide (mostly for use as stock routes) – including St Kilda Road in Melbourne. As a result, the roads were – and often still are – very pleasant places on which to travel, especially in the summer, when all else was dry and bare. These precious strips of trees are still obvious and attractive, particularly from a light aircraft at low altitude, and provide a welcome relief to the cleared and often neglected land outside.

The growing needs of the motor car led to massive new road building programs, and these were matched by the coming of great earthmoving equipment developed during the Second World War. The design of these roads tended to be dominated

Figure 22. Trees lining the original Hume Highway reserve contrast with the bare paddocks outside.

Figure 23. Carefully spaced plantations of native trees reduce the monotony of the divided highway—Hume Highway near Melbourne

by direct economics, with little conscious thought to the preservation or enhancement of landscape except by the planting of rigidly spaced tree belts and the provision of occasional parking areas at particular vantage points (Figure 23).

Similarly, in designing the early divided highways, insufficient attention was paid to visual separation of lanes, and the need for curves and other alignment changes to reduce monotony and to enhance an awareness of the countryside traversed by the highways (Figure 24). Wayside facilities and traffic signs were often out of harmony with their surroundings, roadside batters frequently slumped or were left bare and road verges were unadorned (Figure 25).

There have, however, been significant improvements in recent years. Road engineers' attitudes have changed with the realisation that the public expects roads to be attractive – and there are safety factors as well as aesthetic factors in this expectation (Figure 26). The modern super-highway itself can offer an attractive complement the natural contours; with strategically placed plantations of trees and bushes indigenous to the area and with roadside batters shaped to suit the local landforms and planted to trees or grass as appropriate (Figures 27, 28, 29). Where all these things are done, pleasant landscapes appropriate to the speed value of the road can also be built into the design and the result will be a happier, safer motorist who will receive some mental stimulus from the journey to compensate for the stress of driving in present-day high-speed traffic.

Today's highway engineers endeavour to achieve all these things, as an inspection of some recent construction will show. Design standards are comparable with the world's best (Figure 30).

Simultaneously, there have been improvements in roadside installations, although further improvements are warranted. Local materials are used wherever possible. Toilets, tables, seats and fireplaces are made unobtrusive and off-highway parking areas are located where they will not interfere with views from passing traffic. Road signs must obtrude to some extent to be effective.

Most of what I have said relates to the view *from* the road. Road designers must also regard the view of the road from other vantage points *outside* it. A road occupying a reservation 100 metres wide cannot be hidden, but its effect on the external landscape can be minimised by careful siting and by adherence to the design principles already enumerated. The colour of the road surface can also be important in the context of the adjacent land surface and land form, and there is often opportunity to choose appropriate pavement materials. A well-designed roadway can even enhance the landscape from a distant viewpoint, particularly in the Australian countryside.

One difficult area deserving special mention is the urban freeway. Highway designers are often under great criticism because of their fondness for locating these in the valleys of watercourses. Perhaps this is because the flood plains in the cities were previously used largely for noxious trades and municipal tips, and land was relatively cheap and unencumbered by housing. The Tullamarine, South-Eastern and Eastern Freeways in Melbourne are typical examples (Figure 31).

Our views on the appropriate use of the flood plains have changed at about the same time as the freeways have come along. Before we are too critical, we should ask ourselves what the alternatives are. Public transport is not the complete answer, and I believe some urban freeways have to be accepted, but we can do much to improve their appearance and lessen their impact on the urban landscape. This will be costly, but it must be attempted.

Figure 24. Smooth curves and modern safety fencing on a mountain road—Omeo Highway, Victoria

Figure 25. A beautiful old masonry bridge is preserved in today's road, though it may have been less costly to demolish it—Goulburn Valley Highway at Avenel, Victoria

Figure 26. Spraying road batters to promote grass cover—mixture of grass seed, bitumen and various chemicals

Figure 27. Batter protection in a National Park—Wilson's Promontory Road near Tidal River, Victoria

Figure 28. Grassed batter after full growth—Princes Highway East, Victoria

Figure 29. Flower and creeper treatment of road verges in a highly scenic area—Olivers Hill, Frankston, Victoria

Figure 30. Decorative treatment of an urban freeway—St. Kilda Junction

Road engineers, like many specialists, once tended to work in isolation in the conceptual and planning stages of major projects. Those days are largely past. Today's highway experts consult with planners, sociologists, foresters, conservationists and certainly with landscape architects.

RAILWAYS

The next engineering marvel to assault the Australian landscape was probably the railway. I suggest that the iron horse has on the whole made a positive contribution to the scenery. After all, there are not many railway lines, and they are not as pervasive as the roads. Because of their gentler grades, they follow the natural contours more closely. They do not occupy much land and the traffic is intermittent.

There was always something romantic about the steam locomotive, drawing its burden across the scene, leaving the sound of its whistle and a few wisps of water vapour in the air. The stone bridges and stations of the early days were built of local material, and had an obvious integrity which blended easily with the view. The early railway engineer had a good eye for country and I suggest that the railways have become part of the fabric of the countryside in Australia. They have certainly become so in England, where they have attracted the attention of artists from the days of Turner. The advent of the diesel locomotive and the aluminium carriage has done little to change this picture. The train still remains an article of sentiment, a thing we would like to keep, even if few of us ride in it!

The worst landscape feature of the railway system today is the typical railway-station complex – a forest of billboards, unpainted fences, dilapidated buildings and weed-infested platforms. Although these are hardly engineering features, railways are

*History of engineering
works on the
Australian landscape*

Figure 31. Tree planting in a built-up area—Tullamarine Freeway

largely managed by engineers, and they deserve some blame for this state of affairs.
The occasional exception shows how attractive these complexes can be, both to the
rail traveller and the non rail traveller. Perhaps the railways' contribution to a better
landscape could be the loss of revenue from the advertisements that disfigure so many
stations.

IRRIGATION, WATER SUPPLY AND DRAINAGE

Water engineers have had a significant effect on Australian landscape from the
earliest days. There is a wide divergence of opinion as to the nature of this effect,
particularly because many of the works are quite old and there is little if any knowledge of the original landscapes.

The earliest dams were built of masonry or earth, as in Britain, and, because they
were not very high, did not affect the countryside to any extent. The valleys they
flooded had often already been cleared for agriculture and the environmental impact
was probably slight. Outlet works and appurtenant buildings were usually built from
local materials and the general effect was, and remains, pleasing.

At a later stage, concrete was used extensively for dam construction, and much of
the earlier harmony with the land was lost. There were some exceptions, such as the
arched Glenmaggie Dam in Gippsland, Victoria (Figure 32) and the massive wall of
the Hume Dam near Albury, but the appearance of these structures has been
spoiled by later additions of spillway gates and operating gear.

In recent years, the trend has been towards earth and rockfill dams, built from
local materials and generally harmonising with the land. Spillways are separated
from the main structure and incorporate local materials where possible (Figure 33).

Figure 32. An attractive concrete arch dam spoiled by new superstructure—Glenmaggie Dam, Gippsland, Victoria

Figure 33. Water, trees and a modern earth and rockfill dam—Lake Bellfield, Grampians, Victoria

100

*History of engineering
works on the
Australian landscape*

Increased care is given to appurtenant works and buildings, and considerable attention is paid to the landscaping of the immediate environs of the dams so that the public may have best possible conditions for viewing these public assets.

The stored water behind the dams also provides a wide range of visual impacts, and increasing opportunities are available for public access to reservoirs, both old and new. There is no doubt about the attraction of large expanses of water for the average person, whether it be for sailing, power boating, water skiing, swimming or just plain contemplation. Dams and reservoirs provide a host of landscapes, moving and static, and the general public is making ever-increasing use of them. They provide a welcome relief in the often arid Australian countryside.

The Victorian Government has recently provided an example of new enlightenment in the water-supply field by deciding to change a previously approved site for a dam on the Mitchell River in Gippsland. This followed an environmental impact study which showed that the original site would adversely affect the landscape and the environment by flooding a unique gorge. The study group recommended an upstream site, yielding the same amount of water, which would protect the gorge and would even enhance the landscape, albeit at an additional cost of $1.5 million. This site has been adopted. Such a decision would have been unthinkable ten years ago.

The irrigated areas of south-eastern Australia which have been made possible by the great reservoirs in the mountains provide their own kind of visual impact. The sudden change from the broad and dusty acres of dry-farming areas to the richness of the pastures, orchards and vineyards of the irrigation districts is very striking, whether seen from the ground or the air. Even the climate seems different! The houses are closer together, the towns are larger, the roads are better. And all this was conceived by the water engineers in partnership with other specialists.[1]

There are blemishes, of course. Australia's irrigated areas are usually very flat and, after a while, monotonous. The houses are too much alike, the crops are often the same in one area, the road verges are tropically lush and unkempt. But the overall effect is one of variety in the larger landscape.

Drainage of wetlands is a different story. This has frequently converted areas of great natural interest and attraction, even if they were untidy, into neat and orderly farmlands, indistinguishable from those elsewhere except by the rectangular grids of weed-infested drainage channels, taking the farm wastes away to pollute some river or estuary nearby.

Today, the developer is the villain here, rather than the engineer, and natural swamps which provided some welcome relief to the cityscape as well as to birds and other creatures, are now being filled in for yet more suburbs, or more farms. Only a multi-disciplinary approach can change public attitudes sufficiently to save the remaining wetlands of any significance.

The river improvement engineer is probably one of the most criticised specialists in his sincere efforts to improve the flood-carrying capacity of a stream by cutting off bends, removing snags and other growth and dredging sandbanks and gravel bars. This engineer is a relative newcomer in Australia. As the value of flood-plain lands has increased, there have been pressures from many farmers to reduce the frequency and severity of local flooding by river improvement works. This has been achieved very often only by changing the natural appearance of the riverscape – for better or worse according to your point of view – and by transferring the flooding to some hapless farmer or township further downstream.

There is a growing realisation that the effects of these works should be much more carefully evaluated before they are put in hand. There is often significant difference between river 'protection' and river 'improvement'. Perhaps rivers, Australian style, were meant to look untidy after all!

POWER AND TELECOMMUNICATIONS

The Australian power engineer has probably come in for the greatest criticism of all engineers for the effect of his work on the landscape. A relative newcomer on the scene, he has festooned the countryside and the city with dams, power stations, transmission lines, overhead wires and substations. These works are inevitable, as part of the price of technology. What was not realised in the early days was the desirability of siting and designing them so as to minimise the effect on the observer – or where this could not be done, to display them free of clutter, with a simple integrity of their own.

Sylvia Crowe[2] has pointed out that many of the new shapes created in electric power structures have no direct counterpart in nature. They are too large to be merged into the landscape and must therefore be seen in their own right. This may be acceptable, as some have simple shapes. For example, cooling towers, huge though they are, have some affinity with ancient brick kilns and appear to rise naturally from the earth, if properly sited (Figure 34).

Similarly, transmission lines marching across the country have a particular grace of their own and can be tolerated if they are located away from the skylines and are kept free of the backdrop of appurtenant works which so often detract from their uniqueness (Figure 35). The locations of two high-voltage transmission lines in

Figure 34. A very large thermal power station, dominated by the simple grace of giant cooling towers—Yallourn, Victoria

History of engineering
works on the
Australian landscape

Figure 35. Modern transmission lines do not conflict with the open countryside

Victoria were the subject of inquiries in recent years[3] and landscape effects were important amongst the factors considered. In one case, the location was changed to avoid skyline effects inherent in the original proposal. It can be said that the State Electricity Commission, Victoria – SEC(V)[4] – is very conscious of its responsibilities in this matter, and it has used landscape consultants in its planning of major transmission lines for some years. (It is worth noting that, in the 1970 inquiry, the relative capital costs for overhead and underground transmission lines of 500 kV capacity were $90 000 and $4 000 000 per mile.)

The history of thermal power stations with respect to landscape has been more clouded, because of the nature of the problem. The Latrobe Valley complex of the SEC(V) is situated on the brown coalfields some 176 kilometres east of Melbourne, and its sheer bulk creates a unique landscape of its own, expressive of the energy being generated from the fossil fuel beneath it. Smoke emissions have been reduced to a minimum for environmental reasons, and the SEC(V) has concentrated on cleaning up the surrounds, so that the impact of size and technical efficiency is not reduced by visual distractions. Recent relocation of the main highway past the area has reduced the length of time the complex is on view to the motorist, but has probably enhanced the impression at the viewpoints which remain.

Power stations in or near capital cities raise other visual problems, mainly from the giant size of the components, which make them stand out even in industrial areas. Controversy over the proposed Newport Power Station in Melbourne has concerned itself among other things with the height of the main chimney stack, which at 182 metres will be visible from virtually the whole of the main metropolitan area, and will be completely out of scale with its surroundings (Figure 36). Is this a major reason for moving the power station? Some would agree that it is.

Substations and overhead wires in cities have been mentioned because of their effect on the urban landscape. Unless we live in Canberra or Tasmania, we have been accustomed all our lives to the untidy forests of poles, transformers and wires that bedeck every street and the red brick substations passing themselves off as windowless villas (Figure 37). Cost has always been put forward as the reason for not under-grounding power cables. However, subdividers are now offered an option by the SEC(V) at the cost of about $400 per block, and many new areas of Melbourne show the beneficial results of this policy (Figure 38). Perhaps this points the way for Government action in the future to make undergrounding compulsory.

I have included the communication engineer here, because he is another breed of electrical specialist. He attracts the attention of the landscape lover because he likes to place large structures on the tops of mountains and prominent landmarks. Once again, some compromise is necessary if we are to enjoy the benefits of telephones, radio and television throughout the land at reasonable cost. I think one grows used to the relatively modest size of the normal repeater installation used to transport TV signals to rural areas and even other States.

One interesting example of a successful battle in this area was the terminal facility at Wilsons Promontory for relaying TV to northern Tasmania. The original towers were reduced in height by some 27 metres by the PMG engineers after impassioned pleas from Dr Len Smith, Victoria's Director of National Parks. The rest of the facility is neatly tucked away behind a hill. As a result, the whole installation is visible from only a small part of the Park – and it seems to serve Tasmania well enough at less cost than the original scheme! The lesson once again is consultation and consideration by all interested parties before it is too late.

Figure 36. The proposed Newport Power Station—an environmental hazard?

*History of engineering
works on the
Australian landscape*

EXTRACTIVE INDUSTRIES

Extractive industries are also of particular concern to the landscape lover. Those with the strongest impact, because they are seen by the most people, are probably quarries yielding material for roads and concrete. There is the permanent effect – the scar on the hillside or the ugly hole in the ground – and there is also the transient effect of dust, of unattractive crushers and ungainly vehicles which assault the ear as well as the eye.

John Turner[5] has written powerfully and at length on this topic from the conservationist's viewpoint. I agree that there is much in the past (and in the present) that the quarry engineer and the road and construction engineer must answer for. Nevertheless, it is a fact of life that we need roads and concrete in ever-increasing amounts and, preferably, at the lowest cost.

It is also true that the community at large was concerned, until quite recently, only with the production of these articles at the lowest money cost. Now there is an acceptance of the need to plan for the lowest total cost, including social costs. It is accepted by a majority of people that development of resources must continue, but it must be planned so as to cause the minimum practicable interference with the environment, including landscapes.

The Arthur's Seat quarrying decision in 1973 by the Town Planning Appeals Tribunal in Victoria was a milestone in this field, stipulating the most rigorous conditions ever imposed in Australia for a quarrying operation.[6] The operator will have to rehabilitate former quarries in the area as well as the new workings, and the whole design of the operation is aimed at maintaining and improving the present environment and ecology of the area. Engineers were closely associated with this case

Figure 37. The ugliness of electric wiring in a modern subdivision

Figure 38. Underground wiring enhances a housing estate

and the preparation of the conditions of the quarrying lease. In many parts of Victoria, road engineers have developed a new conscience in the location and working of quarries for road materials and much care is given to rehabilitation of areas after excavation has ended.

A new field of extractive industry has developed in recent years with the vast mineral mining operations in the north-west of northern Australia (Figure 39). These are virtually all in uninhabited regions far from any cities, and landscape and environmental values have so far received scant consideration from the mining engineers. It can be argued that landscape here is unimportant, that the natural raw, harsh scenery may even be improved by mighty heaps of overburden, the stark framework of a crusher, or the belching fumes of a massive pelletising plant on an open coastline.

I think it is too early for us to be sure about this, one way or the other. What is repugnant at Gladstone may be acceptable at Port Hedland or Dampier, at least for the time being As the populations of these outposts grow, so will their social conscience and improvements will follow – but no-one seems to care at present.

PORTS AND HARBOURS

The port engineer has escaped much of the criticism levelled at his colleagues, because ports have always been with us and there is still something romantic about the big ocean liner berthed at a massive wharf, with cranes and tugs and all the other impedimenta which go with ships.

Artists have made much of all this, and it is accepted into the folklore of landscape. Even today's huge container ships have a compelling force in their simplicity and

History of engineering
works on the
Australian landscape

Figure 39. Extractive industries disfigure the open coastline—North-west Western Australia

bulk, which harmonises with the straightforward efficient outline of the container terminal.

The port engineer is, however, a potential villain as he develops larger and larger harbour facilities (Figure 40). He cannot expand landward and so is forced to think of filling in the shallows of an estuary or an open shore. Thus one of the most precious ecological regions is in danger, and so too is the unique landscape of the tidal mud flats – something which can never be replaced. A solution to this problem will demand all our ingenuity.

AIRFIELDS

The airport engineer has moved with the times and can claim to have made a positive contribution to the present-day landscape with the newest airports. The bulk and clean lines of the Tullamarine Airport Terminal, for example, look well against the background of Mt Macedon when first seen on the way out from Melbourne. There is very little clutter of outbuildings or of extraneous aircraft in contrast to older terminals. The only discordant note, as one approaches the airport, is the largely unused shopping centre and that is a problem of patronage rather than purpose.

The jetliners contribute to the overall sense of unity with their smooth shapes and birdlike grace, and a sense of power which complements the sturdiness of the terminal itself. The enforced absence of urban development nearby means that nothing detracts from the sense of unity of the whole terminal facility. Compare this with the old Essendon Terminal nearby, with its multitude of untidy buildings, hemmed in by houses, tramlines and roads, and one can see how far we have come in the past fifteen years.

107

Figure 40. Loading wharves and stockpiles of iron ore contrast with the Indian Ocean—Port Hedland, Western Australia

Figure 41. The ultimate ugliness of municipal engineering—St Kilda Junction

History of engineering
works on the
Australian landscape

MUNICIPAL ENGINEERING

This is a field in which many dreadful things have been done to the landscape –
most of them quite unnecessary (Figure 41). That they are still being done is usually
a testimony to the shortsightedness of some councillors as well as their engineering
advisers. Typical examples are the bitumenised parking areas along beach fronts;
urban subdivision in sensitive coastal sand-dunes; marinas; comfort stations on
cliff tops; and box-like community halls on the edges of public parks.

Education of engineers in this field is improving as it is elsewhere, but not fast
enough, probably because of failure to appreciate the major effect of relatively minor
works, often conceived in isolation from other aspects and because many councils
cannot afford to hire the specialist advisers now commonly used by larger authorities.
Until a broader view is taken on these matters at the local government level, planning
controls through regional or State planning authorities are the only answer. The
mechanism largely exists already, but it often works too slowly to prevent a *fait
accompli* by the local council.

THE PRESENT

The engineer's present position with regard to landscape matters is generally one
of willing involvement. There are grey areas, to be sure, but these are being reduced
year by year. McHarg's planning techniques[7] are being employed by engineers in road
location and in land use planning in sensitive catchments such as the Macedon
Ranges in Victoria. Environmental impact studies are accepted and used as an essential
tool in evaluating new developmental projects such as reservoirs and urban freeways.
These new projects are being implemented largely by engineers working in teams
with other professionals – planners, architects, landscape experts, sociologists,
conservationists, foresters and others.

Landscape aspects are given a prominent place in the factors considered for new
growth centres, notably in the conceptual planning of Albury-Wodonga, where
incidentally, the Chairman of the new development corporation is an engineer, as is
the head of the principal task force engaged on project formulation.

The Victorian State Rivers and Water Supply Commission, an authority largely
directed by engineers, has reaffirmed recently that its 'practice is to design its works
so that the least possible impact is made on the landscape, subject, of course, to basic
engineering requirements'.[8] This attitude is typical of other engineer-oriented public
authorities. In short, the engineer has developed 'a greater sense of social responsibility
for the quality of human life'[9] than heretofore. He has assumed a broader role in the
application of technology and this is evident in his appreciation of natural landscapes
and the need to preserve them. To quote from Sylvia Crowe again: 'The last people
who should be blamed for the loss of landscape are the engineers and scientists.
They have succeeded in their own field only too well. It is the other side of society
which has failed; the artists, the humanists and the philosophers'.[10]

THE FUTURE

The future poses new problems. Our population and our cities will continue to
grow and there will be tremendous pressures to construct new expressways, to encroach
on public open space for urban use, to build new industries, quarries, boat harbours –
in other words, to continue with large-scale technological development.

Planning will become more cumbersome and complex than it is now and there will be many attempts to 'beat the system', to break down planning controls. The money cost will keep on growing. If we are not careful the advances of the last few years will soon be lost and we will be in danger of ruining our already scarce legacy of visual satisfaction, except at great distance from our main centres of population.

The pressures of increasing numbers of people will have severe effects on our public parks and reserves, as in other countries, and new methods of public access to these lands will have to be developed if they are to be preserved for future generations. Constant vigilance and fresh efforts will therefore be needed. The engineer will play a major part in this, but he will be fully effective only as a member of a multidisciplinary team which works closely with the public and government at all levels to ensure that our unique landscape will forever be available to everybody. The cost will be great, but the aim must be achieved.

Notes and references

1. But see DAVIDSON, section two for one view of the diseconomies.
2. CROWE, S. *The landscape of power*. London, Architectural Press, 1958, p. 40.
3. PERROTT, LYON, TIMLOCK and KESA. Report for SEC(V) on Kangaroo Ground area, Hazelwood/South Morang 500kV transmission line. (Departmental report, 1965.)
4. Victoria. Parliamentary Public Works Committee. *Report on the Cranbourne-Pearcedale transmission line inquiry*. Melbourne, Govt Printer, 1970.
5. TURNER, J. S. 'Extractive industries and the landscape', in *Landscape architecture in conservation*, conference papers published by Australian Institute of Landscape Architects and the Australian Conservation Foundation, 1971, pp. 16–27.
6. Victoria. Town Planning Appeals Tribunal. Report on application by Hillview Quarries for quarrying permit at Arthur's Seat, 1973.
7. McHARG, IAN L. *Design with nature*. New York, Natural History Press, 1969.
8. LEWIS, G. W. V. State Rivers and Water Supply Commission of Victoria. (Departmental memorandum, 1974.)
9. CALDWELL, LYNTON K. *The engineers and the human environment*. International Union for Conservation of Nature and Natural Resources, Publication New Series, supplementary paper no. 30, 1971.
10. *op. cit.* CROWE, 1958, p. 42.

3. European perception of the Australian landscape: the evolution of attitudes as reflected in the arts

*Geoffrey Bolton**

The historian as artist and interpreter of the environment

Far from being a new or shallow development in Australian historical writing, concern for the environment has been evident among historians of Australia from the first half of the nineteenth century – if only because in those years there was often not much difference between history and propaganda. Two generations of writers, from John Dunmore Lang in 1834 to G. W. Rusden in 1883, aimed to present a view of Australia which would reinforce its power to attract capital, migration, or favourable political attention. Most of them wrote for British publishers and British readers. In an age of limited facilities for illustrating books, they felt obliged to sketch for their readers detailed pen portraits of the appearance and topography of Australia. In a work such as Lang's *History of New South Wales*[1], composed with only such source materials as were available to him on a long sea voyage from Sydney to London via Cape Horn, there is a long chapter given over to the geography of eastern Australia, chiefly with a view to encouraging the capitalist and migrant with information about Australia's capacity to grow wool, wheat, vines, cotton, tobacco, and practically every other crop currently in demand. Lang was the forerunner of those numerous Australian historians who have appraised the country mainly in terms of its adaptability for economic investment and primary production. He accepted Europocentric frames of reference in assessing how the environment could be transformed into social usefulness and aesthetic harmony. This was the utilitarian approach to the environment. At one time or another practically every Australian historian has been guilty of it.

To a large extent Lang reflected his contemporaries, particularly explorers and pioneer settlers. In a recent study of the attitudes of early South Australian colonists to a rural environment, Moon, a Flinders University graduate, concluded that the trees and the grasses:

> ... were mostly utilized in their natural state, little attempt being made to improve or conserve their value as a resource ... the trees were generally tried, found wanting, and consequently cleared away as much as possible.[2]

There was so much virgin bush that the need for conservation was hard to discern. But in stressing the fitness of Australia for British settlement publicists such as Lang and W. C. Wentworth followed fairly closely the literary conventions of contemporary explorers, and here they at once came up against a problem in communicating their experience to British readers. This problem has been well formulated by a modern geographer in writing of Captain James Stirling, the pioneer of the Swan River Colony:

---

* Geoffrey Bolton is Pro Vice-Chancellor and Professor of History at Murdoch University, Western Australia.

He found difficulty in translating what he had seen into meaningful terms, and had resorted to comparisons of the Swan River with Virginia and the Plains of Lombardy. Both these comparisons no doubt raised entirely different ideas in the minds of his readers than he intended. Their frame of reference was somewhat different from his.[3]

Lang was up against the same difficulty.

Consider by way of contrast John West's *History of Tasmania*[1], published in 1852 at Launceston, and doubtless better value than any book to come out of that city subsequently. West may have had propagandist motives in seeking to rehabilitate the colony from its earlier reputation as a convicts' hell, but since he published at home he was under no necessity to pad his narrative with descriptions of the scenery. His was the first significant history to address itself largely to a local audience, to those 'thousands' who 'while they venerate the land of their European ancestors, with an amiable fondness, love Tasmania as their native country'.[5] He can be taken as the ancestor of those historians who concern themselves with the impact of the environment on national character and ethos. This can be seen perhaps in a rather hopeful comment on Hobart: 'Imagination has traced in its natural outlines a resemblance to the seven-hilled Roman capital, once the mistress of the world'.[6] But it comes out more clearly in one of the few sustained topographical passages in his book, describing Norfolk Island, a place which few of his readers would have seen:

> Norfolk Island, so celebrated for its genial climate and unusual fruitfulness, is of volcanic origin, and contains about 14,000 acres . . . Its lofty cliffs, which breast the ocean, are crowned by the elegant white wood and the gigantic pine. The wild jasmine and convolvuli, which reach from tree to tree, form bowers and walks of exquisite beauty. Twice in the year the settler gathered his harvest: the lemon, the orange, and the pine, shed their fragrance in profusion and yielded the richest fruit. Though liable to occasional storms and destructive insects, the husbandman could scarcely be said to toil. Gentle showers frequently refresh the undulating soil, and pour down rivulets to the ocean. Sea breezes cool the atmosphere, and the diseases often incident to such latitudes are unknown; but no ships can anchor: it is a land unsuited to commerce.
>
> Thus it presented no incitement to exertion: it gave the indolent abundance without labour: it afforded a leisure, in which man is prone to degenerate and sink into the savage. Distillation from the cane produced spirits, more than usually deleterious: unacquainted with the process by which saccharine is crystallised, the settlers were unable to prepare sugar. They found the raw rum destructive, and attributed its fatal effects solely to the leaden worms![7]

Whether he was seeing Hobart as possibly the site of a second Rome, or Norfolk Island as lotus land, West presupposed that societies were shaped by their environment, unlike Lang who saw the environment as a *tabula rasa* on which economic man could impose his own objectives. These two stances were to be seen in much future Australian historical writing.

Sometimes both attitudes could be found in one historian. Rusden's *History of Australia*[8], completed in 1883 and published in London, still found it expedient, after sixty pages devoted to the colonisation of New South Wales and the vicissitudes of Governor Phillip's era, to break off suddenly as follows:

*The historian as artist
and interpreter of the
environment*

> And now that the young settlements are rescued from the jaws of death, we may pause
> to observe the general features of the land, and how it was tenanted by the tribes
> which studded its surface throughout its length and breadth, its plains and mountains,
> marshes and lagoons . . .[9]

And off he went with a chapter on Australian geography and anthropology, of which
it will suffice to quote this passage describing the Great Dividing Range:

> This long cordillera rises into peaks from 3000 to 5000 feet high, exhibiting abrupt,
> steep-down precipices and gorges, broken and fantastic pinnacles and crags; and,
> according to the character of the intruding rocks, and the soil derived from them, is
> clothed with dense forest, or rears its hoary shoulders in bare ruggedness intolerant
> of vegetation . . .[10]

This fine writing was still designed to arouse interest in British readers ignorant of
Australian conditions. Like the painters and lithographers among his contemporaries,
Rusden was still largely Europeanised in his sense of the picturesque. But he was an
old man when he published, and was to be practically the last Australian historian
to treat his readers to such set pieces. Already the explorers and the settlers were
altering their terms of reference in ways with which the historians would –
eventually – catch up. John Forrest, for instance, in his expeditions of 1870 and
1874 had little to say about the scenery, and as Kathleen Fitzpatrick has observed:

> The reason for the comparative dullness of his journal is simply that he was born and
> bred in the bush. The other explorers had standards of comparison; they came from
> the cool, moist green lands of the Northern Hemisphere, and to them everything
> in the Australian scene was exotic, demanded their attention, and impelled them to
> describe it to their friends and public at home in the old country. But to Forrest there
> was nothing strange about the bush or the desert; Australia was simply his home,
> which he took for granted and never thought of describing.[11]

Increasingly the next generation of historians would be journalists or academics or
civil servants whose working lives were centred on Sydney or Melbourne, those big
cities which Australians were prone to believe had few characteristics distinguishing
them from the provincial cities of the Old World.

If Rusden was in one way the last of the Old World historians of Australia, in
another respect he showed an intense contemporary interest in the effect of the
Australian environment on European man. The generation of the 1870s and 1880s,
those decades when the number of the colonial-born began to draw ahead of the
migrant population, were highly self-conscious of the emergence of a distinct
Australian type, and often sought explanations in climatic and environmental factors.
Rusden, for instance, concluded his three volumes with this prophetic flourish:

> The elements of the population indicate that they will be wanting in no excellence.
> English, Irish, Scotch, with other Europeans and some Americans, form the people
> from whose admixture future generations will spring. The exhilarating climate solicits
> enjoyment in open air, the very breath of which is pleasure . . . though pleasure may
> enervate dwellers in cities, the country cannot fail to maintain a hardy race, especially
> on the high lands which rib Australia from the snows of the Murray to the northern
> regions of Queensland.[12]

Compare his preoccupations with the north Queensland editor of 1876 who asked:
'Will this district be ultimately abandoned by its white inhabitants? Or will our
Europeans be able to accomplish the hitherto impossible feat of settling a white race

within 15° of the equator?' And he glanced at the dispiriting examples of the West
Indies and South America, where 'a parti-coloured mongrel race fills the land,
sluggish, vicious, and ignorant'.[13] Or consider Marcus Clarke, writing in 1877:

> In another hundred years the average Australian will be a tall, strong-jawed, greedy,
> pushing, talented man, excelling in swimming and horsemanship. His religion will be
> a form of Presbyterianism; his national policy a democracy tempered by the rate of
> exchange. His wife will be a thin narrow woman, very fond of dress and idleness,
> caring little for her children, but without sufficient brainpower to sin with zest.[14]

These and various other characteristics, such as longevity and bad teeth, Clarke
attributed not altogether seriously to the environment and climate of Australia. Like
the other two writers, Clarke sought the clue of the developing Australian character
in the impact of the environment.

This preoccupation with environmental determinism coincided with the closing
of the Australian frontier. In Australia as in America, the fateful date was about 1890.
After the furthest out of the cattlemen overlanding from Queensland met up with the
outermost Western Australian sheep station in 1885 the pastoral ring was closed
around Australia. After the discovery of Broken Hill, Cloncurry, and Kalgoorlie in
the decade between 1883 and 1893 there would be no further significant extension
inland of permanent settlement. The era had passed of discovering the land as
something new and deserving of examination and research, and the era had not yet
dawned of questioning the impact which European man exercised in regions settled
for more than one or two generations.

This may sound odd, because the generation after Rusden between 1883 and the
First World War is usually thought of as possessing a great awareness of the pastoral
outback, whether because of the depression and the shearers' strikes, or because of
the great drought which culminated in 1902 with its grim implication that the fertility
of the outback districts had diminished under the impact of pastoral settlement, or
simply because of the myth-making skills of the *Bulletin* school of writers. But these
developments affected the historians very little. In the first place, there seems to have
been an assumption that the real history of Australia was the history of Europeans
in Australia – understandably, since by 1890 the Aborigines were largely ousted to
the margins of Australian consciousness, and their valuable insights into the
Australian environment were almost entirely ignored. Conscious of a need to create
for Australia a history matching where possible the dignity of history as practised
in the Old World, and aware that Australia lacked many of the wars, revolutions, and
other glamorous sophistications of European history, Australians seem to have
expected from their historians a linear account of European progress, beginning with
the Portuguese and Dutch navigators and ending with contemporary politicians. In
the light of the federal movement and the impact of economic events on Australian
society in the 1890s, it was understandable that Australia's advance to nationhood
was seen predominantly in political and economic terms. The myth-making potential
of Australian history was left largely to novelists: as Brian Elliott has pointed out,
it was Marcus Clarke who crystallised Australian stereotypes of the convict era. In
like manner, it was the *Bulletin* writers who created the Australian image of the
squatting age; and probably the more optimistic among them, Paterson and Will
Ogilvie rather than the sombre images of the younger Henry Lawson. And it was not
until this pastoral myth was fully established that the historians, accepting it wholly,
ventured into the field.

*The historian as artist
and interpreter of the
environment*

Even then the universities lagged behind the journalists and the men of letters. When *The pastoral age in Australasia*[15] was published in 1911 its author proved to be James Collier, a 65-year-old Scottish graduate who after a stint as New Zealand parliamentary librarian moved to Sydney where he became a prolific and miscellaneous writer. Collier is a somewhat discursive author, but he has the great merit of a comparative dimension. Here he is on the scenery of the pastoral environment:

> The pictures of Chevalier and von Guerard are said to have no atmosphere – at least the luminous atmosphere is conspicuously absent. The trees, the mountains, the plains, even the skies are painted heavy and dark, which they seldom are. The Bush is 'stern and funereal' as it was to the first novelists and poets – Marcus Clarke and Charles Harpur – whereas in literal truth it is commonly flooded with sunshine. Homesick exiles, they had missed its characteristic note.[16]

The remarkable thing about this passage is that Collier was an exact contemporary of Marcus Clarke. He came to Sydney aged forty-nine after a lifetime spent in Scotland and New Zealand, yet he did not see himself as a homesick exile. He looked at the country through the eyes of the Heidelberg painters half a generation younger than himself. Seldom can the dependence of the historian's perspective on the creative artist have been more convincingly demonstrated.

It was not until the 1920s that academic historians ventured further into Australian subject matter. By that time the ossification of the pastoral tradition had set in thoroughly. The *Bulletin* had lapsed into a cantankerous Toryism, but still found its subject matter outback; the ghost of Streeton was still painting romanticised landscapes for the Sydney bourgeoisie; Paterson and Ogilvie had lapsed into silence. Moribund or not, the pastoral tradition still seemed the authentic Australian legend, and the wool industry the major dynamic of Australia's economic growth. The result tended to be a curious indifference to ecological detail. Stephen Roberts published in 1924 a seminal *History of Australian land settlement*[17], which in many respects has still to be supplanted; but he concentrated almost entirely on the legislative story, and almost ignored the practical environmental consequences of successive State land laws. Yet the evidence was available. State Departments of Agriculture had been in existence since the 1880s, and considerable information was accumulating to suggest the effects of stocking policies on erosion and vegetation; but the eye of the academic historian was not alerted to such considerations. It was as if these were seen as the responsibility of geographers and agricultural scientists. The dignity of history still demanded a concentration on political and legislative factors. Shann, whose *Economic history of Australia* was published in 1930, began with a promising environmental passage:

> It was not scenic beauty that attracted the [First Fleet] but the prime necessities of a seafaring people – sheltered anchorage and fresh water. Ages earlier, large streams carved out the deep valleys drowned under Port Jackson. The headwaters of those streams had been captured in some great earth change by the Nepean-Hawkesbury river system. Thus the harbour formed by their submergence had escaped silt. Deep water slept in all its hundred bays and arms.[18]

But he got no further. In particular he hardly dealt at all with the transformation which the surroundings of Sydney Harbour underwent at the hands of European man. Nobody in those years showed the least interest in the history of urban growth, though the environment in which the majority of Australians lived and breathed was of course already predominantly suburban. Almost the only comment Shann made of relevance to our theme was an aside about Macquarie's buildings in Sydney:

> Being of a generation whose fathers had seen General Wade transform the Highlands after Mar's rebellion, and which was still learning from Thomas Telford the arts of civil engineering, Macquarie naturally set high store by the civilising power of externals . . . By an emphasis on the comforts of civilisation and by the slightness of their references to colonial trade and lands [his despatches] suggest that Macquarie's mind stuck in the bark of externals and missed the inner meaning of efforts to make New South Wales a colony of self-providing and permanent homes.[19]

So much for Francis Greenway. It is only fair to say that Rusden in his time had been even more sweeping:

> Macquarie would have been the founder of a new era if the construction of ugly buildings could have conferred such a title.[20]

Those buildings are now among the holiest of holies for the National Trust. Historians have not always been allies of conservationists, and credit must be given to Malcolm Ellis for being the first to do adequate justice to Macquarie's contribution to the environment.

If we turn to W. K. Hancock's *Australia*[21], like Shann first published in 1930, it is possible to identify foreshadowings of the author of *Discovering Monaro* without leaning too much on hindsight. Hancock had the advantage of recent travel not only to England but in the Italian countryside, and a certain feel for scenery was apparent in his earliest book, a biography of the nineteenth century Italian statesman Ricasoli. He possessed standards of comparison when he approached the Australian environment. He was the reverse of the early English settler striving to interpret the Australian landscape in northern hemisphere terms; he was the Australian who, having ingested and assimilated new experiences, no longer took for granted his country's climate and scenery, but could appraise freshly the relationship of man and the environment in Australia. Nobody previously had written:

> The very soil has suffered from the ruthlessness of the invaders. The most precious possessions of Australia are her rivers, whose even flow is protected by the forests which stand around their mountain sources and the trees which line their banks. The invaders hated trees. The early Governors forbade them to clear the river-banks, but these prohibitions were soon forgotten . . . the greed of the pioneers caused them to devastate hundreds of thousands of acres of forest-land which they could not hope to till or to graze effectively. To punish their folly the land brought forth for them bracken and poor scrub and other rubbish . . . Placid low-banked rivers frequently gave place to water-channels which in rainy weather whirl along useless muddy waters threatening ruin to good alluvial lands and which in time of drought parch into hard, cracked mud. Even the River Murray (one has heard the Danube quaintly described as 'the Murray of Europe', and this phrase suggests the value which Australians ascribe to their greatest waterway) has suffered an alarming increase of its winter velocity and decrease of its summer flow through the destruction of forests around its headwaters.
>
> The advent of the white man with his ready-made civilisation has violently disturbed the delicate balance of nature established for centuries in the most isolated of continents. The Englishman eats out the Aborigine. English trout displace the native black-fish from mountain streams. And, to compensate for the rapid extinction of the native bear . . . Australia has been presented with the rabbit.[22]

*The historian as artist
and interpreter of the
environment*

There was no sequel to this indictment, no exploration of the extent to which closer analysis would vindicate this criticism of Australia's pioneers. For this there were a number of reasons. Hancock's *Australia* started so many hares that it was impossible to follow all of them up, and any prospect of his developing the themes in his book faded with his return to England in 1933. Nor was it surprising that others were slow to take up the environmental theme. The depression of the 1930s and the Second World War were inimical to large-scale historical writing. When a society is desperate for its living there is no room for environmental concern. The big issues of the day were largely political – fascism and communism, nationalism and war – and these preoccupied many young intellectuals. The best vignette of Australian environmental history published in those years was written, not by an historian or a social scientist, but by two agricultural scientists, Wadham and Wood, describing land use in Gippsland in what was almost an aside to their major theme.[23] Mainly it was once again the imaginative writers who were left to serve as myth-makers and interpreters of the environment. One example of the exploitative character of much Australian pioneering could be found in Brian Penton's *Landtakers*[24], a book whose very title was evocative. Out of several historical novels stimulated by the New South Wales sesquicentennial celebrations of 1938 *The timeless land* by Eleanor Dark stood out in its awareness of the Australian environment. The alienation of European settlers, ordering their lives by time and historical precedent, was contrasted with the finely attuned reactions of the Australian Aborigines: 'In this land, where time was only the unvarying cycle of nature, the seasons, like the trees and the animals and the men, were born and waxed to their full strength, faded, and were eternally replaced.'[25] This outlook differs interestingly from the interpretation offered some years later by Manning Clark. Like Eleanor Dark he noted the destructive effect of technological Western man on the Aborigines, but he was less concerned to stress the conflict between these cultures as a conflict between two different ways of adapting to the environment. He saw the Australian continent as a *tabula rasa* – early in his *History of Australia*[26] he characterised Aboriginal society as 'barbaric' – and his mighty theme was the fate of the three great European faiths, Catholicism, Protestantism, and the Enlightenment, after they were transported to Australia. The effect of the Australian environment on these faiths and their protagonists could be at best subtle and indirect. But Manning Clark, and all modern Australian historians with him, have learned after Eleanor Dark to recognise the harmony of the pre-settlement Aborigines with their environment.

It is necessary to stress the role of creative and imaginative writers in perpetuating an Australian sense of environment, because it was they who had to hold the field until the academic historians were at last ready to move in. Professor Jill Conway has drawn an illuminating contrast between the attitudes of Australian and Canadian writers.[27] A Canadian poet such as E. J. Pratt drawing upon an historical theme, such as the martyrdom of the seventeenth-century French Jesuit missionaries in Ontario, is apt to present the environment as hostile, unresponsive, resisting the gifts of European culture and civilisation brought by the white men. An Australian poet such as A. D. Hope – and there could be no more urbane and learned example to cite – repudiates

> . . . that chatter of cultured apes
> which is called civilisation over there.[28]

He damns the cities as five wounds on the sides of Australia, and yearns for the prophets who shall come from the desert. The same contrast can be discerned in historical myth-making. To the bulk of Canadians the heroes tend to be the men who conquered the wilderness by building the Canadian Pacific Railway, rather than Louis Riel and the *métis*; to the bulk of Australians the hero is Ned Kelly who was at home in the wilderness, rather than the railway builders. Nobody has adequately accounted for this difference of attitudes. Maybe the Canadian inland, with its ever-lasting layer of permafrost, is just perceptibly harsher than the Australian outback, so as to turn the scale from the Australians' baffled obsession with understanding the country to a feeling of outright rejection and hostility. At any rate, such is the climate of opinion within which Australian historians work and live, and it was inevitable that there should be at last those who sought to understand and interpret the environment.

During the 1950s a number of influences came to the fore which helped to create a favourable climate for environmental history. One was a substantial advance in the teaching of geography at university level, a development hindered in the past by sceptics who doubted whether there was any such subject as geography. (This doubt was raised only a dozen years ago at the University of Western Australia; today they are doubting whether there is any such subject as sociology.) Geographers were well placed to marry the insights of the historian and the ecologist, and most of the early breakthroughs in environmental history were in fact the work of historic geographers. Another factor promoting the growth of environmental history was the development after the Second World War of an outstanding school of history at the University of Melbourne and of a focus for research in the Australian National University, particularly under the aegis of Professors Sir Keith Hancock and Oskar Spate.

These sources stimulated several important developments during the late 1950s and early 1960s. There were some seminal reinterpretations of Australian history, all of which made explicit or implicit assumptions about the interaction of European man and the Australian environment. Such a work was Russel Ward's *The Australian legend*[29] (based on an A.N.U. Ph.D. thesis) which reasserted the view that the outback had exercised a transforming influence on the transplanted Europeans who roamed over its length and breadth; that the essential features of this transformation were established very early, before the gold rushes of the 1850s; and that this offered a parallel to the famous theory of Frederick Jackson Turner in the United States that the frontier was the crucible in which the new nation was formed. Australian historians had not been ignorant of the frontier theory, for Hancock, Fred Alexander, and Norman Harper had all looked at its implications for Australia; but Ward made the most systematic statement. Admittedly it was arguable that Ward's sources derived mainly from popular culture and literature, and reflected the concept of themselves which the convicts and their contemporaries brought with them from the British Isles; it could be held that these concepts flourished in Australia because of its societal makeup rather than its environment.[30] But at the very least Ward raised many significant questions about the precise inter-relation between man and the environment during the early generations of white settlement in Australia.

One obvious question was whether in fact Australia was as socially uniform as Ward sometimes seemed to suggest, or whether important regional variations could be traced. Concurrently with Ward's work a number of regional histories were brewing at the A.N.U. and the University of Melbourne, and these saw publication

*The historian as artist
and interpreter of the
environment*

between 1961 and 1965. First in point of time and artistic skill was Margaret Kiddle's
Men of yesterday.[31] Without strongly stressing environmental themes, Kiddle
nevertheless recalled Eleanor Dark in a beautiful opening chapter describing the
Western District landscape before white settlement, suggesting the easy intimacy
between the Aborigines and their landscape. Others showed less awareness of the
environmental factor in regional history, even at times hankering after the
old-fashioned setpiece of the Lang-Rusden variety. Bolton, for instance, in *A thousand
miles away*, begins thus:

> The longest coral formation in the world is the Great Barrier Reef, one of the most
> remarkable features of the Australian continent. It emerges out of the Coral Sea
> parallel to the eastern shores of the Cape York Peninsula. Stretching southward for
> 900 miles, the reef gradually swings away from the Australian shore, and at its southern
> end, in Lat. 21° South, tails off at the Swain Reefs, 150 miles out to sea from the
> Queensland coast. Inside the reef the sea lanes are interspersed by a great scatter of
> islands, most of them mountainous outliers of the coastal ranges. Sea and islands form
> a scene of memorable beauty . . .[32]

And then in 366 pages he never mentions the Great Barrier Reef again, but gets on
to the economic and social history of the European, Melanesian, and Asian settlers
of north Queensland. He is no further forward than Shann thirty years earlier.

The really important advances were made by two historical geographers, T. M.
Perry and R. L. Heathcote. Perry made a detailed study of the pattern of New South
Wales settlement between 1788 and 1829. His argument is that Russel Ward, like the
contemporary American, H. C. Allan, tended:

> . . . to underestimate both regional variations in frontier conditions and changes in
> them with the passage of time as these are reflected in the Australian social scene. Their
> 'frontier' becomes something of an abstraction undifferentiated in place and even
> (to some extent) in time. Both authors, one suspects, would assert that their interest
> lies in the processes shaping Australian society and that these processes were not
> vastly altered by the passage of time or a changed environment. But is this so?
> Frontier studies in America suggest the contrary.[33]

And he shows how, pushed from the original Cumberland plain around Sydney by
droughts, plagues of army worms, and decreasing soil fertility, settlement expanded
in a number of different directions each of which developed a different social structure.
Around Bathurst there was a big absentee landlords' sheep frontier, with a respected
managerial class 'with its Classical and Mercantile School, Literary Society, and Hunt.'
The Hunter valley was uneasily shared between smallholders and immigrant capitalists
employing large numbers of convicts. Around Goulburn there was a small men's
cattle frontier. Australian society by 1829 was already highly diversified, even within
300 kilometres of Sydney, and these diversifications represented a response to patterns
of settlement environmentally dictated. The historians' generalisations were refined
and amended by a proper attention to environmental factors.

Heathcote in *Back of Bourke*, a history of the Warrego country on either side of the
Queensland-New South Wales border, went considerably further into environmental
factors. He was probably the first regional historian systematically to explore changing
concepts about a portion of the Australian environment (in this case the inland plains
beyond the Darling) as well as charting the changing pattern of settlement. He came
to a somewhat startling conclusion about the effect of white settlement in these

districts. Denying European man the masochistic satisfaction of casting himself as
ravager and destroyer of the virgin environment, Heathcote postulated a conflict of
interests between the landholders' concern with exploitative use of pastoral resources
and official attitudes 'hoping for an extension of the intensive and conservative land
use from the more humid east on to the plains'. In Heathcote's view, opportune use of
evanescent resources paid the best dividends for those using the semi-arid plains.
The pastoralists who devised stocking practices to make maximum use of currently
available feed were probably wiser than governments who thought erroneously that
restricted use might conserve resources. Seasonal fluctuations in rainfall and
vegetation might well account for much of what had been thought of as a permanent
deterioration in land conditions. 'The concept of opportune use of resources through
controlled exploitation and flexibility in investment and techniques may have a wider
relevance than merely the semi-arid plains of Australia.'[34]

This tempered optimism about the capacity of man to learn to come to terms with
his environment was endorsed several years later by Hancock in *Discovering Monaro*.[35]
Drawing its material from an impressively multi-disciplinary variety of sources,
Discovering Monaro is subtitled 'A study of man's impact on his environment'. The
high alpine pastures of the Kosciusko National Park had been used since the 1830s
for seasonal grazing, at times crowding and damaging the pastures. In recent years
recreational groups proliferated: skiers, bushwalkers, tourists. Yet it was clearly also
essential that part of Australia's small alpine area should be left as unspoilt as possible.
That these contending conflicts of interest could be reconciled constructively by
orderly political processes was the moral of Hancock's narrative. A plan of management has been created for the Kosciusko National Park. Its success in achieving
maximum conservation of the environment may well be due in part to the sympathetic
climate of opinion which greeted the publication of *Discovering Monaro*. Methodo-
logically the book is important because it demonstrates how historians can ransack
the work of geologists, botanists, anthropologists, entomologists, and other scientists,
integrate them with the spoken and written insights of the graziers, farmers, and other
inhabitants of a region, and produce a new dimension to the historians' craft.

Others have shown the way. George Seddon's two excellent works on the Swan
coastal plain, *Swan River landscapes* and *Sense of place*[36], are masterly integrations of
material from various disciplines. The skills of the botanist and geologist are matched
by the good old-fashioned art, the Augustan art, of connoisseurship of landscape as
evidenced by some fine photography. Like Heathcote and Hancock, Seddon also
commemorates a region where the impact of European man has not so far been
inordinately blighting, though the prospects for the future are fragile. Once again the
historian, through learning to use the insights of other disciplines, may serve not only
as interpreter of the landscape, but also as prophet, if only the prophet Jeremiah.

In the present state of the historical profession several tasks for the future may be
discerned. There is a need for further regional studies of the impact of man on the
Australian environment; not forgetting Aboriginal man, whose use of fire and hunting
techniques is now thought to have had a much more profound effect on the
vegetation than has been commonly acknowledged. It would be particularly useful
if some intrepid scholar were to venture upon a history of Australians acting upon
their environment. Such a book would be bound to attract much criticism in detail,
but given the right use of written, oral, and photographic material, it would be a
stimulus and a necessity. Then we might follow the American examples and introduce

The historian as artist
and interpreter of the
environment

the teaching of Australian environmental history in a number of Australian universities. It is being planned in my own university, Murdoch, for 1976, and it could well be that in States where the Leaving curriculum is not too hidebound that secondary school students could be encouraged to undertake such projects.

Historians in the past have tended to follow a long way after the artists and creative writers in meditating upon the relationship between man and the environment in this country. As art tends towards the mythical and the abstract, it may well rest with the historians and the historical geographers to keep the tally of how Australians reacted with Australia. It is a challenging task, and well worth attempting. At the very least, nobody in future should ever dare to write economic, social, or regional history without glancing at the environmental consequences of the transactions he or she describes.

Notes and references

1. LANG, J. D. *An historical and statistical account of New South Wales . . .* London, 1834.
2. Quoted in BOLTON, G. C. and HUTCHISON, D. 'European man in south-western Australia', *Journal and Proceedings of the Royal Society of Western Australia.* 1(2): 57, 1973.
3. CAMERON, J. Perception and settlement. *Australind.* p. 52, 1970.
4. WEST, J. *History of Tasmania.* Launceston, Dowling, 1852: reproduction by Library Board of South Australia, Adelaide, 1966.
5. *op. cit.* WEST, 1852, p. 3.
6. *op. cit.* WEST, 1852, p. 34.
7. *op. cit.* WEST, 1852, pp. 36–7.
8. RUSDEN, G. W. *A history of Australia.* 3 vols., London, Chapman and Hall, 1884.
9. *op. cit.* RUSDEN, 1884, vol. 1, p. 63.
10. *op. cit.* RUSDEN, 1884, vol. 1, p. 65.
11. FITZPATRICK, K. *The Australian explorers: a selection from their writings.* Oxford, Oxford University Press, 1958, p. 24.
12. *op. cit.* RUSDEN, 1884, vol. 3, p. 672.
13. *Cooktown Courier*, 11 Nov. 1876.
14. Quoted in ELLIOTT, B. *Marcus Clarke.* Oxford, Clarendon Press, 1958, p. 215.
15. COLLIER, J. *The pastoral age in Australasia.* London, Whitcombe and Tombs, 1911.
16. *op. cit.* COLLIER, 1911, p. 284.
17. ROBERTS, Sir H. *History of Australian land settlement (1788–1820).* Melbourne, Macmillan, 1924.
18. SHANN, E. *An economic history of Australia.* Cambridge, Cambridge University Press, 1930.
19. *op. cit.* SHANN, 1930, p. 62 and 77.
20. *op. cit.* RUSDEN, 1884, vol. 1, p. 490.
21. HANCOCK, W. K. *Australia.* Brisbane, Jacaranda Press, 1964.
22. *op. cit.* HANCOCK, 1964, pp. 21–22.
23. WADHAM, S. and WOOD, G. L. *Land utilisation in Australia.* Melbourne, MUP, 1939, pp. 25–30.
24. PENTON, B. *Landtakers: the story of an epoch.* Sydney, Angus and Robertson, 1963.
25. DARK, E. *The timeless land.* London, Collins, 1941, p. 45.
26. CLARK, C. M. H. *History of Australia.* Melbourne, MUP, 1962.
27. In a paper given at the Institute of Commonwealth Studies. Duke University, Durham, North Carolina, 18 March 1974.

28. HOPE, A. D. 'Australia', in his *Collected Poems, 1930–1965*. Sydney, Angus & Robertson, 1966, p. 13.
29. WARD, R. *The Australian legend.* Melbourne, Oxford University Press, 1958.
30. At the conference where this paper was given this viewpoint was courteously advanced by Professor Bernard Smith. If I have expressed his views correctly, this might align him with Louis Hartz and the 'transplant' theory of new societies, which I am inclined to dispute. The point is worth further discussion.
31. KIDDLE, M. *Men of yesterday: a social history of the western district of Victoria, 1834–1890*. Melbourne, MUP, 1961.
32. BOLTON, G. C. *A thousand miles away: a history of north Queensland to 1920*. Brisbane, Jacaranda Press, 1963, p. 3.
33. PERRY, T. H. *Australia's first frontier: the spread of settlement in New South Wales, 1788–1829*. Melbourne, MUP, 1963, p. 2.
34. HEATHCOTE, R. L. *Back of Bourke*. Melbourne, MUP, 1965, p. 199.
35. HANCOCK, W. K. *Discovering Monaro: a study of man's impact on his environment*. Cambridge, Cambridge University Press, 1972.
36. SEDDON, G. *Swan River landscapes*. Nedlands, University of W.A. Press, 1970.
    SEDDON, G. *Sense of place: a response to an environment, the Swan coastal plain, W.A.* Nedlands, University of W.A. Press, 1972.

*Brian Elliott**

Emblematic vision: or landscape in a concave mirror

A shaving mirror concentrates the face. In it you can see little bits more clearly. I am going to talk about some literary little bits to see how they contribute to the whole face of nature.

Expression can't do without clichés. Language itself is often a stream of them. But there are clichés and clichés. They are useful building blocks. In childhood one learns to build with blocks. One can build a ziggurat, but not St Paul's.

I shall for the most part be limiting my observation to the colonial years, which were the childhood of Australia. I was told when I was very young that I must learn to walk before I could run. Most nineteenth century Australian poets walked; they hardly ran. The first Australian poet to run was Christopher Brennan, and some would say he ran so hard, he ran right out of the picture. It is a national characteristic: give a young Australian powers and techniques he is surprised to find he possesses, and he will set such a pace with them that he can annihilate his local identity in the process. But that isn't the case I am here to argue.

I shall begin with two 'little bits'; both familiar. Most of what I have to talk about will, I hope, be familiar: I am not concerned, like Bernard O'Dowd, to scour the bush for dryads and leprechauns, although I shall be looking for things that will do pretty much what he hoped those interesting exotics might. It will, I trust, emerge why I think leprechauns won't do. In the meantime here is the first of my 'little bits': I quote entire the lyric 'Australia' by James Lionel Cuthbertson:

Give us from dawn to dark
　　Blue of Australian skies,
Let there be none to mark
　　Whither our pathway lies.

Give us when noontide comes
　　Rest in the woodland free –
Fragrant breath of the gums,
　　Gold, sweet scent of the sea.

Give us the wattle's gold,
　　And the dew-laden air,
And the loveliness bold
　　Loneliest landscapes wear.

These are the haunts we love,
　　Glad with enchanted hours,
Bright as the heavens above,
　　Fresh as the wild bush flowers.

That piece contains a good sample of the landscape image-making of the later colonial years. It is perhaps a little coloured with *Bulletin*-type nationalism but not much; it isn't aggressive; we can take it to be reasonably spontaneous. It says the proper

---

* Brian Elliott is Reader in Australian Literary Studies at the University of Adelaide.

kind of things, it strings together the expected attitudes. Clear skies, remote solitudes, a heady, honey-like noonday mood. Except for the gums and the wattle the setting could be Italy, it could be Arcadia (Cuthbertson taught Latin and Greek). So it combines the local with the universal. The haunts we love, the enchanted hours, the heaven above and the wild bush flowers – that comes to something straight out of my childhood, if not out of everyone's.

Let me dwell on these things a little. The piece, as I have just said, chimes in with actual experience – mine, anyway – and has literary roots too. Some of them are old: pastoralism translated, gleaned (thinly) from Theocritus, Virgil and *hoc genus omne* (fair weather, rest in the woodland free, torrid noon and sweet recreation). This was by no means the first appearance of the pastoral spirit in an Australian context. It is a part of the *Beatus ille qui procul negotiis* syndrome which Horace (Epode 2) bequeathed, among others to Alexander Pope: 'Happy the man', and so on:

> Blest, who can unconcern'dly find
> Hours, days and years glide soft away . . .

It is nicer, certainly, according to both Horace and Pope, if you also happen to own the property; but the country sentiment is there. And it is also here in William Woolls:

> Happy the man from business free,
> As ancient mortals used to be,
> Who, far from Sydney's dusty ways,
> In sweet retirement spends his days . . .

And more particularly, here:

> Sometimes at ease supinely laid
> Beneath acacia's pleasing shade,
> Where gliding streamlets steal along
> He listens to the warbler's song;
> Or sleeps the sultry hour away
> Till soothing zephyrs cool the day.[1]

Woolls was a schoolmaster and later a clergyman, and a contemporary of both the (younger) Henry Parkes and Charles Harpur. Parkes wrote in a lyric entitled 'Solitude'[2] of 'remote gullies full of ferny plumes' and rocky places where the giant turpentines cast their mottled shade through 'groups of climbing, clustering vines':

> There I love to wander lonely
> With my dog companion only,
> There indulge unworldly moods
> In the mountain solitudes,
> Far from all the gilded strife
> Of our boasted 'social life' . . .

He probably got the little dog partly from experience and partly from a passage in Pope's *Essay on Man* (1732–4); Pope got it from an Indian source. Harpur left out the little dog but kept the solitude and pulled the local imagery and sentiments together in the well-known, 'Midsummer Noon in the Australian Forest'. There he effectively sounded the note of placid, remote, drowsy bush magic and warmth; with such music of the wildwood as a boy or a young person might recollect nostalgically in later but rarer tranquillity. Apart from the 'bright beetle' or cicada (locust, he calls it), everything in this landscape is deeply hushed:

126

*Emblematic vision: or
landscape in a
concave mirror*

> Every other thing is still,
> Save the ever wakeful rill,
> Whose cool murmur only throws
> A cooler comfort round repose;
> Or some leafy ripple of the sea
> Of leafy boughs, where, lazily,
> Tired Summer, in her forest bower
> Turning with the noontide hour,
> Heaves a slumbrous breath ere she
> Once more slumbers peacefully.

There is a modal recollection (if not a clear image) of Keats' 'drowsed' 'Autumn':
and so the slender connectives reach out. Cuthbertson may or may not be remembering
Harpur; it is not necessary to suppose he did so consciously. Moods, concepts and
images in poetry have a way of becoming common coin. They are available to be used
when required and it doesn't matter who invented them first. The same sort of tendril-
like connectives can be traced back from Cuthbertson to Keats and A. L. Gordon
(an odd couple). Through Cuthbertson's 'dew-laden air', which is faintly intoxicating,
we look over his shoulder to Gordon's

> . . . when the wattle-gold trembles
> 'Twixt shadow and shine,
> When each dew-laden air draught resembles
> A long draught of wine.

Cuthbertson's 'gold' (twice offered) also clearly stems from Gordon and as Gordon
was fond of smoking his pipe and gazing out dreamily over the seas, there is something
of that in the mood too. So allusiveness can become complex. Gordon's trembling,
dewy air recalls Keats' 'draught of vintage' and the beaded bubbles winking at the
brim (in the 'Nightingale'). Back beyond both we look to the theory of poetic *ecstasis*
in Plato. In the same way Cuthbertson's 'blue Australian skies' – a pretty phrase, by
the way, quite a good shaving-mirror image – brings back Gordon's hard blue
summer sky. The lines from Gordon continue:

> . . . A long draught of wine,
> When the skyline's blue burnished resistance
> Makes deeper the dreamiest distance,
> Some song in all hearts hath existence –
> Such songs have been mine.

I am not to be drawn about the meaning of 'resistance', burnished or plain; but we
know it has something to do with the image of sun and sky, the mood of poetical
elation and the poet's lonely and private, or intimate, vision. It is Gordon's vision, or
Cuthbertson's, or yours or mine.

Nevertheless it is all cliché. Cliché is not the enemy of perception. Once, just once,
a cliché may appear and make a brilliant and original impression: on that first
appearance it may have the effect of a startlingly new symbol. But the more successful
it is the more quickly it is absorbed into the category of automatic responses. It
becomes a banner with a powerful device. Nobody using it for a second time can ever
plant it quite so high on the alp as its first user. But on the other hand it is likely to
become a favourite decoration on the lower slopes, and to have a great sub-Parnassian
utility.

I come now to my second 'little bit' and it is a shade harder to deal with. Does this

passage, or does it not, amount to a vital, new perception of the landscape image?
Are we dealing with first-impact or second-impact cliché?

I am not planning to work this comparison hard, I only want to advance it in order
to place some sort of a check on generalisation. But if you think the Cuthbertson
lyric, however neatly pleasing, is *derived* cliché from beginning to end, what do you
make of Banjo Paterson as the poet of the 'vision splendid'?

> He sees the vision splendid of the sunlit plain extended,
> And at night the wondrous glory of the everlasting stars.

As a phrase the expression is an abysmal cliché: but *can* you ruthlessly throw out 'the
wondrous glory of the everlasting stars'? It is so naive in its mere words that one might
scarcely pause in the act of tossing it down the drain: yet though it *is* trite, what it
says is true. Let me half sidestep the issue by turning to something else of Paterson's.
What he wrote was ballad poetry, of course; that makes some difference. But I am
disposed at the moment not to stop for fine distinctions. In terms of such poetry as he
aimed at, then, what are we to make, not merely of the words but of the quality of the
vision – the capacity of the eye to see, the senses to feel – in lines like these?

> The roving breezes come and go, the reed-beds sweep and sway,
> The sleepy river murmurs low and loiters on its way.
> It is the land of lots o' time along the Castlereagh.

What sort of a landscape image *is* it? The same formula turns up again in 'Kiley's
Run': the 'sleepy river murmurs low' there, too, and the ranges sleep in the sun, which
is not very different from being in the land of lots o' time. I will defend neither
Paterson's phraseology nor his repetitiveness. Both are well enough for ballad verse
and popular ballad sentiment. But here the question is not so much the thing said as
the thing seen. How fresh is the insight? And how long can it stay fresh? I have to
admit that, when I stand by some lonely inland river, my response to its mood and its
meagre beauty is still Paterson's. The clarity of the stars on a desert night was not
unknown to others before him, but his, for all my own redundant sophistication, is the
formula I recall. I don't know if this visionary substance is sheer cliché or not; I am
not even sure what I mean by 'sheer', but I don't quarrel hotly if it is. Gordon's
dew-laden air, his blue burnished resistance – Harpur's noonday enchantment –
Paterson's roving breezes – all represent close and telling perceptions, and whether
you call them clichés or not I don't really think matters. They were new at any rate
once, and they all had too much vitality ever to grow completely stale. You can't go
on and on repeating them; that, I suppose, can make them tiresome. But their existence
reminds us of a difference between those clichés which have become simply automatic
and repetitious, and those which in their own time crystallised new and important
articulations of awareness. New articulations become clichés when they lift themselves
out of their first context to become fixed in the imagination of the community. A few –
not all – clichés develop into folk images. Some exceptions may be notable. It is
interesting to point to an example which I believe contained all the potential power
of such an articulation yet never did effectively reach the people. I am thinking of
Brennan's:

> Fire in the heavens, and fire along the hills,
> and fire made solid in the flinty stone . . .

a highly expressive image of summer which includes an encapsulated image of the
vivid fires of the opal, a suitable Australian 'flinty stone' to become a viable folk-

*Emblematic vision: or
landscape in a
concave mirror*

image. But this poetry was too calculated, too selfconscious, to do for the Australian imagination at the time (round about 1900) what ballad verse could do, and so it never established itself.

What I have just been saying, perhaps, amounts to no more than a warning that, as between one verbal cliché and another, distinction of quality, as of popularity, may be drawn, but what counts most in practice is the use to which they are put. The same can be said of wheat samples, or wool, or washing powder; so we may as well leave it at that.

I am reminded that the horizon of the present inquiry is landscape. As to what a *poetical* landscape is made of, I have already given, or implied, a partial answer: it is made of little bits. A very partial answer! But there is a sense we are all aware of, according to which, given the impression-of-the-whole which we take in at a glance, little details are what we first *consciously* notice. When, entering a room, we first suspect that something is changed, it may take us some moments to realise it is the picture on the wall that is different. That is because in practical circumstances our comprehension proceeds from the whole to the part. Since literary creativity is largely a matter of proceeding in a reverse direction – that is, of first putting together a series of images and details and then hoping they will cohere into a total effect – I think I need not labour my reasons for looking at little bits and pieces of landscapes, even if, to a logical mind, that seems like putting the cart before the horse. If you like we will think of the horizon as the properly logical landscape-container or frame. Yet from my present point of view, Cuthbertson's blue, or Gordon's burnished resistance, is just one detail, one component like any other – like Gordon's wattle blossom, or Paterson's or Lawson's reedy river, or any single one of the stars that contributes its bit of glory to the wondrous general vision. Only one detail: but one that is selected to be noticed.

With indulgence, I shall now allow myself even further to concentrate my bits and pieces. I want to look in the concentrating mirror and select among the effects not so much those which have a factual descriptive value, but those which register their impact with special commitment. I mean the more creative clichés, which I shall now proceed to dignify by calling them by another name. I will defend them as emblems. For convenience sake many of my emblems will be flowers.

So far as the spiritual or imaginative interpretation of landscape is concerned, and not merely the evocation of literal topography, I should say that the first or colonial phase of a new poetic literature must necessarily be very largely concerned with the setting up of its proper key-imagery – which is the machinery of effective suggestion in local terms. There must be selective picture-making. Most significantly there must be established an understood body or continuum of native emblems.

I spoke of banners and devices. I had in mind that what I mean by an emblem is not quite a symbol though it may be of the same order. An emblem is a kind of short cut to value. It has its current denomination but is rather paper money than gold – yet is redeemable in intellectual cash. Heraldic lions are emblems, not symbols. Emblems might be called the algebra of poetry. Your sprig of holly or mistletoe is more an emblem than a symbol. Sometimes the two may huddle close to a border and even cross it; but I should take emblems to be symbols reduced to impersonal proportions. They may be what is left of a symbol after the concentrating mirror has burned out its private allusions. Is Gordon's wattle blossom a symbol? I think it must have been when he first thought of it, but it very soon in his mind became an emblem and it was always that for those who came after. Even in Gordon's own use, the image becomes in practice rather emblematic than symbolic. Its substance is x, not $x+y$.

All mature literatures have their emblematic systems. Even in the earliest English lyric verse there already exists a firmly established range of nature emblems, as for example in the conventions relating to flowers. Roses are red, violets are blue, and so on; and there is a firm place for primroses, daffodils, buttercups and daisies. Almost as indispensable are the birds. There was a hierarchical order among these phenomena of nature which nobody questioned. Nothing ever happened to challenge it until colonial emigration introduced certain disharmonies into the widening context of poetry. It was a settled thing, for example, that in the great scale of poetic value, the prestige of the various flower emblems was established by their perfumes; and of the birds, by their singing. Roses and nightingales, by common consent, stood at the top. Colour, incidentally, was the prerogative of the flowers. Most European birds were sedate in colour, but they were excused that, since everybody expected it and after all it was their singing that counted. Similarly, all the flowers were credited with perfume, though not all (certain banks of violets, for example) had any.

Obviously I can't detail the whole stock of emblematic suggestion available to European landscape lyric; a glance at these two instances will sufficiently hint at the possibilities. We have to bear in mind, too, when it comes to developments in Australia, that new perspectives had arisen in Europe. In its earlier phases romanticism had been very closely involved with the opening up of new and unknown vistas, in America and elsewhere; and this in turn had motivated a re-examination and redis-covery of the older European landscape itself. Under industrial conditions it was tending to change and even disappear before the onward march of coal mines, potteries, machine shops and the like. This naturally added a special piquancy to the state of affairs in Australia, where there were obviously other reasons for concen-trating a good deal of attention upon description and interpretation.

One way to characterise the colonial phase in Australian landscape history, then, would be to say it was that first period of development which was preoccupied with the initiation of its emblematic system. When the emblems were set up – when they were numerous and vigorous enough for the poets to feel equipped to make independent excursions into territories of their own – then the colonial trauma was complete. We may argue a little over dates; precision is unattainable. But let us suggest that the process took up, more or less, the first century and a half, which is not really long, considering how slow a process human adaptation can be. Moreover in that time we shall not find the number of achieved, successful colonial emblems to be so very many. In any case we must confine ourselves to the most obviously major and influential instances. But what was important was not the extent of the stock, it was the fact that an emblematic system had come into operation and was functional. Detail and analysis are not at present called for; it is enough to suggest that a beginning had been made whereby not every new poetical allusion to local nature was bound to be entirely a hit-or-miss experiment. When the poets had acquired a few earlier shoulders to climb on they could themselves begin to think tall. Even a little help of the emblematic sort could serve to give them an understood impetus.

The shaping of tradition anywhere – even in old countries – depends on two elements which must work together. There must always be a continuity of fresh discovery, and there must always be a continuity of carry-over. Without both, no literature can stay alive. But clearly in a new colonial country the balance between

*Emblematic vision: or
landscape in a
concave mirror*

discovery and carry-over is disturbed, and the original European proportions cannot apply. Because of such considerations it was harder for poets in Australia to feel comfortably at home even than it had been, earlier, in America. There were two reasons for this. For one, the settlement took place at a later date and its carry-over was different. For the other, there was a much higher degree of unexpected strangeness in the Australian landscape than in the American landscape. In terms of topography, trees and flowers and the seasons, America was not so forbiddingly unlike Europe as to create difficulties. In Australia, there were radical dissimilarities which were causes of distress – including such accidents of the situation as caused Christmas to fall in midsummer, and so on; an anomaly which was artificially exaggerated to hint that even the seasons themselves seemed to follow an irrational order. That was not so very surprising. Our own contemporaries have a similarly uncomprehending disposition to question the sensibilities of their ancestors. They *ought* at once to have seen for them-selves and valued the things which so clearly distinguished Australia! They *ought* instinctively to have perceived how fruitful was the store of really expressive local nature imagery for the manufacture of poetical symbols and emblems – yet because the kangaroo and the platypus, the emu and the echidna were unlike anything they had seen before, the new settlers rejected them from poetical significance. When Barron Field, for a sort of joke, wrote poems about 'Botany Bay Flowers' and 'The Kangaroo', everybody took it that nature itself in Australia could hardly be regarded seriously. Field even suggested that this landscape had been created as a Divine afterthought, outside the statutory six days, and that is why we have animals which lay eggs, and birds which don't fly (or sing), and why the bark, but not the leaves, falls from the trees. Certainly there was emblematic material here, and poetry largely missed it. Some details were used in other ways, as for example the various heraldic emblems which the separate colonies adopted in their coats of arms and escutcheons, while the Commonwealth made a quite pretty design of the kangaroo and the emu to put on coins and over official doorways. But it is too easy to dismiss as unperceptive the difficulties, especially the *literary* difficulties, of the newcomers in settling into such a landscape. Those novelties were real, but they cut across the hard facts and the fixed attitudes of the carry-over. People can't change the habits of their thinking so fast. Even now children still expect Father Christmas to travel in a reindeer sled over winter snow to climb down chimneys and fill up stockings.

So in effect it was inevitable that the first reactions to this very un-European landscape could be a quick *practical* adaptation, but a very slow *poetical* one. This landscape, Field said, was 'unpicturesque' and 'unmusical'.[3] You need to bear in mind that where such complaints were made, they as a rule referred to the literary value of things. Life wasn't impossible in Australia. You mightn't love a gum tree, but you could cut it down and make a durable house. You could burn it and cook a good damper. But it was hard to live with it emblematically, because it wasn't an oak. Those terms 'unpicturesque' and 'unmusical' carried a specific significance for the emblematic birds and flowers, and hence invite reflection.

In the first place, of course, 'unpicturesque' is an accusation laid against the land-scape as a whole. In its primary application, the word refers to the emblemry of the eighteenth century *picturesque* in Europe, implying a combination of wild nature with human additions in the shape of ruined abbeys (like Tintern), or the sort of gloomy forest decay that Milton relished in 'L'Allegro' and 'Il Penseroso'. Salvator Rosa landscapes were not discovered in Australia, much, it must have seemed to Field, to

the country's discredit. Certainly Lieut Southwell regarded the Sydney vista with
something of a constructive sympathy:

> Nothing can be conceived more picturesque than the appearance of the country
> while running up this extraordinary harbour. The land on all sides is high, and
> covered with an exuberance of trees; towards the water, craggy rocks and vast
> declivity are everywhere to be seen.[4]

But Lieut Southwell was so charmed with the prospect that he was prepared also to
add what was not actually there: 'charming seats, superb buildings, the grand ruins of
stately edifices' – it pleased him to imagine them, in a spirit of prophecy, simply to
complete what the 'picture' lacked. Others found vistas to enjoy because they looked
more or less like the landscape they had left behind: it was high praise, for instance, to
single out some part where the trees were a little more sparsely placed than in the
crowded bushland, and describe it as resembling a gentleman's park.[5] Scrub country
was especially disliked; the vegetation was described as monotonously uniform and
drably grey, and it was regarded as a bad, untidy habit in the trees when they shed
great festoons of bark. Arthur Bowes was therefore quite an odd-man-out: not only
did he observe 'the finest terraces, lawns and grottoes, with distinct plantations of the
tallest and most stately trees I ever saw in any nobleman's grounds in England'[6] but he
was prepared to concede unthinkable praises to the birds. Far from being 'unpicturesque', he admired the *flight* (my italics) of 'the numerous parraquets, lorrequets,
cockatoos and maccaws', which he said made 'all around appear like an enchantment'.
It was there, of course, that the bone of contention was toughest: the parrot tribe
were admittedly bright, but 'unmusical', if not 'unpicturesque', did describe them.

I defy anybody to disagree. Bowes referred to some other singing birds. But in
general the gayest plumage did not go with fine voices. It was as though, having
been tantalisingly offered bright birds, the settler could now no longer be content
with drab colours even for singers. So the unhappy parrots carried the main
responsibility, over several colonial generations, for all the musical deficiencies of
the birds of Australia. Although quite early in the colonial story there developed
in the literature of prose description a spirited and sometimes minutely documented
defence of the Australian singing birds (see the writings, for example, of both the
Howitt brothers – and they were not alone), this reasonable evidence made little
impression on poetical and sentimental attitudes. What was more to the point, in
that respect, was not that there were Australian singing birds, but that all the
traditionally *accepted* bird-*emblems* were absent. The lack of nightingales, thrushes
and skylarks and all the usual poetical birds of the European repertoire was sadly
resented, and the brilliance of the parrots (there are no macaws) only aggravated
the fault. Magpies were simply not noticed in early colonial times (and no doubt
it is fair to observe that their song is so different from the nightingale's that it
could never have been considered a rival, substitute or equivalent). Quite soon the
kookaburra (called the 'settler's clock' and various other names) was a good deal
spoken of, but somehow it failed to establish itself in poetry permanently as an
emblem. It was never rated as musical in any case, but did acquire a fairly lively
local mythology; I have dim recollections from my own childhood of old-timers
telling stories of new chums who were lured to destruction (or ridicule) by the
derisive laughter of the malicious old Jack; but perhaps because the new chum
himself is no more, the bird's emblemry has sunk. I think it is a pity.

He also used to be a heroic enemy of snakes, most important to small boys;

*Emblematic vision: or
landscape in a
concave mirror*

I fancy that glory too has departed. So we may take it that not every emblem is a rock-of-ages; there is give and take even in folklore.

It is difficult to suggest why some things pass into the folk imagination and are assimilated as emblem while others fail. In the case already mentioned of Brennan's opal, the personal aloofness of the poet may sometimes be explanation enough. One other poet, Bernard O'Dowd, did after all use something like the same image. One thing is certain; it was not intellectual effort that was most fruitful in creating or in sorting out colonial emblems. A successful image had to have the common touch. Gordon's wattle blossom was the first *poetical* image to acquire emblematic status of a definite kind. It wasn't that no-one had noticed the wattle before, but nobody before Gordon had caught all the concentrated and representative impact of it. Perhaps such notions themselves were novel – that particular way of regarding the bush landscape, and the seasonal variations within it, signified native colonial feelings, only in Gordon's time.newly coming to distinct awareness. For me as a child fifty years ago the sensations of spring in the bush were a heady enchantment, even an intoxication, that remains yet as one of the most vivid and moving parts of all remembered experience. That experience seemed then axiomatic, un-questionable. The wattle was not the only native gold I knew then but it epitomised the rest. That would be about fifty years after Gordon wrote: and I don't know, truly, whether young people before his day experienced those sensations or if it was (wholly?) his initiative that defined that wonderful, fresh pleasure. I personally didn't learn it from Gordon, I hadn't read him; but others had and his emblem had gone deep into the folk consciousness. Emblems do work like that. They only function well after someone has articulated them clearly. It was an example of one wholly successful emblematisation of an image which happened just when the time was ripe (1870). (Partly the emblem had to wait on language. The word 'wattle' was used by others before Gordon, but it had often also been called 'acacia' or 'mimosa', words which had no particularly local affinities).[7] Why then, to refer back to the singing birds, did no similar new emblem arise to meet the local need? Presumably because that particular European prejudice was too deeply entrenched in the popular mind. Gordon in the same poem spoke blandly of this land 'where bright blossoms are scentless, And songless bright birds'. What those words really told the reader about Australian birds and flowers was very little, though they showed how facts could be hammered home, and the public imagination would go on rejecting change until its last shred of preconditioned resistance was exhausted. Kendall made a great thing of his forest bell-birds; we all know about them. Yet they have never become emblematic in the uninhibited way that Gordon's wattle blossom did. The first poem about magpies to make much impression was Frank Williamson's 'The Magpie's Song', which I suppose everybody knows – my generation does anyway. But I was already learning to talk when that poem came out in the only volume Williamson produced (1912). Did nobody really hear the magpie's song till then? An obvious visual image that, very strangely, never made great poetical progress as an emblem was the ubiquitous gum-tree. But one had better not be too dogmatic about that: it may be that the impression it left on people was effective enough, but too complex to be easily manageable. Australians have always had extremely mixed emotions about gum-trees, we know from the faintly derisive reaction we always experience when people use the pretentious word and call them 'eucalyptus'. That is a term for botanists and foreigners, not for you and me. But our colonial ancestors couldn't be persuaded to take the tree altogether seriously in a poetical sense. When Victor Daley wanted to make fun of the *Bulletin* editor, he offered Stephens a crown of wild gum-leaves (as though the epithet 'wild' served any purpose: – except to make a grotesque allusion to Ruskin).[8] You can't make your laurels of gum-leaves without conveying a suspicion that there are vine leaves in the garland! No, when Barron Field, in what we can only regard as the beginning of Australian time, said of the gums that they were *inhuman*, he somehow managed to poison their shadow.[9] 'All the dearest allegories of human life,' he said,

> . . . are bound up in the infant and slender green of spring, the dark redundance of summer, and the sere and yellow leaf of autumn. These are as essential to the poet as emblems, as they are to the painter as picturesque objects . . .

Oddly, his 'unpicturesque' gum-tree landscape has had a better handling from the painters than from the poets. Painters from Martens and Glover on have responded to the challenge, and if gum-trees are not fully and articulately emblematic in Heysen, I don't know what is. But in poetry, until quite recently, they required gingerly handling.

I have not, I think, said enough about the carry-over in landscape imagery. Let me digress briefly to discuss landscape art in general. As we now think of it, it is not a very ancient *genre*. Except as a necessary background to human activity it doesn't figure prominently in poetry or painting much before the seventeenth century, and it was only with Gainsborough, Constable and some others in the eighteenth, Turner in the nineteenth, that it really began to flourish. There already is a freshness of the imagination in Milton, but also a strong disposition towards formality:

> Straight mine eye hath caught new pleasures
> Whilst the landskip round it measures:
> Russet lawns, and fallows grey,
> Where the nibbling flocks do stray,
> Mountains on whose barren breast
> The labouring clouds do often rest;
> Meadows trim, with daisies pied . . .

Everybody knows the passage and can fill it out: towers and battlements, the smoking cottage chimney and Corydon and Thyrsis at their savoury meal – followed by harvest labours, dancing and fairy tales. All this amounts to a string of pretty emblems, most musically orchestrated; but there is hardly any full-bodied symbolism and no plain description. Let me come again to what I enjoy – the flowers – and move on to 'Lycidas'. The death of Edward King, who was drowned in August 1637 in the Irish channel, did not call imperatively for a landscape tribute, but there are some interesting implications in the flowers with which Milton makes his offering.

> Bring the rathe primroses that forsaken dies,
> The tufted crow-toe, and pale jessamine,
> The white pink, and the pansy freaked with jet,
> The glowing violet,
> The musk-rose and the well-attired woodbine,
> With cowslips wan that hang the pensive head,

*Emblematic vision: or
landscape in a
concave mirror*

> And every flower that sad embroidery wears,
> Bid amaranthus all his beauty shed,
> And daffadillies fill their cups with tears,
> To strew the laureate hearse where Lycid lies.

This 'catalogue of flowers' is a convention you will find in many poets, and I quote it (apart from the pleasure of the words) only to show that Milton stands here already a little liberated from the formality characteristic of earlier writing. Spenser, for example, might have done the same thing beautifully, but he wouldn't have cared about what seems very particular in Milton: they are all *spring* flowers and it would be *possible* to gather them all at the same time (more or less). They would hardly all still have been about in August, when King was drowned; but their spring-time symbolism was right for the theme of youth. Not too much violence therefore was done to nature, though some to logic.

I want to go on to quote a passage from Thomson's 'Seasons', to illustrate a changing drift. Thomson is rationally particular to get his horticultural information exact: so his details, by their very correctness, seem to lose something of poetical suggestion. His flowers are not so much emblems as mere items: he could be writing a gardener's *vade mecum*. This eighteenth century poet is an arid kind of landscapist:

> Along the blushing Borders, bright with Dew,
> And in yon mingled Wilderness of Flowers,
> Fair-handed Spring unbosoms every Grace,
> Throws out the Snow-drop and the Crocus first,
> The Daisy, Primrose, Violet darkly blue,
> And Polyanthus of unnumber'd Dyes:
> The yellow Wallflower, stain'd with iron Brown;
> From the soft Wing of vernal Breezes shed,
> Anemonies; Auriculas, enrich'd
> With shining Meal o'er all their velvet Leaves;
> And full Renunculas, of glowing Red.
> Then comes the Tulip-race, where Beauty plays
> Her idle Freaks: from Family diffus'd
> To Family, as flies the Father-Dust,
> The various Colours run . . .

This is eighteenth century precision at its coldest, perhaps – unless we choose to flutter after the birds, bees and flowers into Erasmus Darwin's *Botanick Garden*. Darwin tells us in 'The Loves of the Plants' how

> With honey'd lips enamour'd Woodbines meet,
> Clasp with fond arms, and mix their kisses sweet . . .

After this the way is prepared for Flanders and Swan and the tragedy of the left-winged bindweed: I follow this romantic path no further. *The Botanick Garden* appeared in 1789 – a revolutionary year, but *one later* than the first day of Australian creation; and so we have a plausible reason for cutting at least the poetical cable after 1788.

I am serious at any rate to the point of remarking that the main Australian literary carry-over stems more directly from the times when the earliest colonists actually migrated, than from models and influences which, though they might be better, came a little later. It was in the spirit of late eighteenth century (picturesque) landscape art that the first Australian attempts to set up standards were made. And thus, although the influence of the romantic imagination did of course penetrate to the colonies in the period of Wordsworth, Byron, Keats, Shelley, suggestion at first was taken rather less from these writers and the painters contemporary with them than from those of the earlier years. The foundations of poetry and landscape art in Australia were laid down in the closing part of the eighteenth century, and were in spirit more gothic – rational, picturesque, or gothic – than romantic, even though what was happening in the colonies was contemporary with actively revolutionary movements in European artistic, no less than political, history.

This aesthetic delay happened partly because of the lag in cultural influences caused by the change of scene, and partly, of course, because there was no great flowering of original colonial talent to assert a really fresh creative initiative. If we wish to look at what progress there was, the flowers will still serve to supply us with guidelines.

Keats was among the English poets – though he was not the first – who imputed to all colonial landscape the kind of inferiority which Gordon apparently endorsed in Australia. He said of America, in the 'Lines to Fanny',

> There flowers have no scent, birds no sweet song,
> And great unerring nature once seems wrong.

We need not suppose him humourless: the poem was part of a private letter and the lines were a joke at the expense of the portentous eighteenth century theorists who had advanced the proposition known as the 'continental degeneration of species'. That was a speculation according to which the forms of nature which flourished at home in Europe suffered an inevitable deterioration when removed to colonial situations. Experience did not bear it out (as Jefferson was at pains to argue with Buffon and certain other of the French *philosophes*); but facts had little effect on the point of view of those who were determined to believe the worst. It is possible now to suggest that in effect all such opinion, at any rate as it came to be popularly interpreted, rested upon ingrained prejudice. The grounds seem to have been mainly aesthetic and poetical. The untravelled European imagination was simply reluctant to be shaken out of its preconceived ideas. Nevertheless it has to be admitted that much that was to be seen in the new world, American and certainly Australian, *was* strange or different; and it may be that we could be inclined to look with too little sympathy on the confusions of new settlers. They must have found not merely little, but often nothing at all, to remind them of what they had grown up to think of as the norms of civilised reference.

When Australia was first settled, there was tremendous activity among the scientists, observing, classifying and naming the flowers. There was no lack of interest in the new flora and fauna. The *hortus siccus* flourished while the poetical garden drooped. It was in order to remedy this imbalance that Field set about exercising his curious rather than subtle talent in the little volume of *First Fruits of Australian Poetry* which he published in 1819. As I have already pointed out, he was not able to see Australian nature as altogether natural. But he did, all the same, direct a romantic eye to the not very promising material, and came up with the ingenious fancy that when Puck went searching for magic flowers for Oberon and 'put a girdle round the earth', he may have chosen to take in a little more

*Emblematic vision: or
landscape in a
concave mirror*

southing than anybody yet had supposed, in order to pick up in New South Wales
the mountain heath and the fringed violet that his fairy master required. These two
happened to be two local flowers that struck Field's own fancy. He could have
mentioned others. Neither of these reached emblematic status, nor did many other
native flowers, then or much later. Some almost did. There was a time when the
waratah seemed to be on the way to establishing a sort of dignified heraldic
distinction: it became a motif of formal decoration somewhere about the 1920s,
having a natural affinity for the 'art nouveau' style; but when that went, I fancy
the emblematic waratah went out with it. There is, I believe, a New South Wales
mountain boronia which is charming and has a faint perfume (and must have been
known earlier than the Western Australian variety); but it was probably too locally
limited to serve as a general symbol. The purple sarsaparilla has a wide eastern
recognition; it is to me not so familiar a flower. Some of the kennedyas are quite
widespread, and one in particular, known to my own childhood as scarlet runner
but to others by the more picturesque name of running postman, might have been
worth more emblematic acclaim. In fact as we look round us, we see great
quantities of flowers, all of which cry aloud their emblematic frustration: they
ought to have been better known and loved: but there must have been reasons. It
was not always that the flowers lacked the popular affection, rather that no poet
adored them particularly enough to celebrate them. If I look back to my own
childhood again, I can report the intensity of joy I had in early spring at making
my first discoveries of the smaller ground orchids, particularly the whole race of
grannybonnets in which I delighted, and for which, long before I had any inkling
of Latin or Greek, I painfully learned the name of *Pterostylus nana*: young prig
that I was. We children also worshipped the whole tribe of spider orchids, and
there was a beautiful blue one too, which we rather despised because it wasn't rare
enough. These bush flowers all made a grand impact on our impressionable minds.
But nature is prodigally bountiful and it was hardly expected that all the flowers
would find a Parnassian apotheosis. It wasn't as simple a matter as stringing
together a European daisy chain. There was always something secret and rather
special about the bush flowers. The meadows were never flushed with them. You
had to go and look. And that element of private revelation that remained in them
perhaps made them rather obstinate candidates for emblematical exploitation.
Their delight and beauty seemed to rest too intimately within the eye of God: they
were essentially not public flowers.

You can't make universal emblems to order, then, even out of the most promising
flowers. Emblems have to *happen*: perhaps they are just a lucky shot. Let me quote
a small, late nineteenth century poem which I personally think is about a flower
of great emblematic potentiality: but to claim that it became one would, as yet at
least, be going too far. Thomas Heney's 'Flower Everlasting':

> Shy flower that aye delights to grace
>   A desert place,
> And glorify the thankless stones
> With golden crowns and cones,
>
> While in the meads thy sisters fair
>   The bounty share
> Of wind and dew and sun, content
> With whate'er good be sent.

Some corner narrow and obscure
    Dost choose, secure
From sudden grasp of hands unkind
That oft thy sisters find.

Wouldst rather safe be than admired
    And so retired
Those charms to lovers only show
That rocks hide from a foe.

Nature denies the haunting scent
    To others lent,
Instead she gives thee longer stay
Than beauties of a day.

They ope and show their charms awhile
    Their life a smile,
Then close and gently die; but thou
Death not so swift can bow.

Heney had been reading Herrick, but it is an Australian poem, about an Australian flower, one which had the kind of intimate appeal that made it a favourite of those who knew it, while the symbolical (or emblematic) special character of its dry imperishability recommended it particularly for survival in the reader's imagination as in physical fact. Perhaps its emblemry may yet be recognised. And if that day ever comes a little of the flower's primitive glory will be bound to spill over from Heney to another short piece of Douglas Stewart's called 'Everlasting', in *The Birdsville Track*: in that way suggestion strengthens, and tradition expands and grows.

I return to Barron Field. 'What desert forests,' he exclaimed in 'Botany Bay Flowers':

        . . . and what barren plains,
Lie unexplor'd by European eye,
In what our fathers called 'the Great South Land';
Ev'n in those tracts, which we have visited,
Tho' thousands of thy [i.e. God's] vegetable works
Have, by the hands of Science (as 'tis call'd)
Been gather'd and dissected, press'd and dried,
Till all their blood and beauty are extinct;
And nam'd in barb'rous Latin . . .

Very few indeed (I abbreviate),

        (perhaps none) of all these Flowers
Have been by Poets sung. Poets are few,
And Botanists are many, and good cheap.

He was right enough, and remained right for a good many years to come. By and large, the botanists beat the poets in the race towards assimilation and adaptation (acclimatisation) over most of the first part of the nineteenth century, and we must not be surprised to see the oddly rhapsodical excitement of a Richard Howitt, who in 1840 discovered somewhere a native daisy that reminded him exactly of England and home. Equally Caroline Leakey in 1854 deeply lamented the loss of her favourite English flowers. Nothing out of England could be expected to be good:

*Emblematic vision: or
landscape in a
concave mirror*

> You may tell me of flowers bright and gay
> Blooming in Eastern lands away,
> And of climes beyond the beautiful sea,
> Where all fair things and glad may be . . .

A warm climate, she conceded, and bright colours:

> You may tell me flowers of crimson hue,
> And glorious tints of gold and blue,
> That sunnier heavens have brought to birth . . .

But it was not enough. She lacked daisies, she lacked primroses.

> Oh! dearer to me are the sweet wild flowers
> A hand unseen on England showers . . .

And that, as far as many people went, was the long and the short of it. It was from this
imaginative vacuum that Gordon's one transcendent image rescued the poetical
lethargy of the Australians. Wattle blossom was the only contestant among the
Australian flowers which was as accessible to the general imagination as were
primroses in England. But one emblem of such a glorious abundance, fragrance and
colour, was enough to save the day.

I exaggerate, of course; there were other current and emblem-like clichés and
commonplaces and Gordon used them as did other writers. But if one is making
comparisons, this one emblem clearly stands out. The poem he called 'A Dedication'
(I believe it must have been the last piece he wrote) sets out to demonstrate the basic
sources of Australian poetical inspiration, and the wattle blossom is only there as an
accompaniment to other rather more specific suggestions. But what he says
consciously seems less perceptive than that single brilliant insight which was possibly
only an accidental – if inspired – accompaniment to his general theory.

One could go on and on chasing the imagery of primroses and other futilely
nostalgic sentimentalities in Australian writing. But it wouldn't serve much purpose.
In effect, very few individual flower images ever did attain a full measure of
emblematic acceptance in Australia. This may seem a loss, but it couldn't be helped.
In the colonial range nothing as universal as the wattle blossom ever turned up again
though the *generalised* bush image (which is something quite unlike any English or
continental equivalent) does come to active expression. It is there very briefly, for
example, in Bernard O'Dowd's 'The Bush' (1912):

> When now they say 'The Bush'; I see the top
>   Delicate amber leaflings of the gum
> Flutter, or flocks of screaming green leeks drop
>   Silent, where in the shining morning hum
> The gleaning bees for honey-scented hours
> 'Mid labyrinthine leaves and white gum flowers . . .

Several images in this fragment, which is one of the few descriptively lucid passages
in a long and on the whole rather indigestible poem, have some hint of an emblematic
quality but their best effect depends on their being taken together, whereas the true
emblematic image stands alone. What the poet sees when 'they say *the bush*' is an
aggregate of new growth, early and noisy birds, and the humming of bees: this is
broad impressionism, not precise emblemry. And that seems fair enough in an age
of post-impressionist, open-air landscape art. Individual flowers did not, on the
whole, stand out, even when (like the spider orchids) they possessed a unique and

139

inexpressible local character. It never happened in colonial Australia that the 'little bits' – the small details of landscape identity – stood out in power and interest above the impact of the whole. Yet the bush was itself too large, too complex and various to bring to effective poetical subjugation. As much as had been said about it, the larger image has never been fully mastered by the Australian poets.[10] Where this leaves us at present may be hard to say. But at least there seems no reason to suppose that landscape is an exhausted interest.

A piece of writing which has never, in my view, had its full measure of critical notice, is the 'preface' by Marcus Clarke adapted to the volume of Gordon's poems published in 1876. It was not originally written for that purpose but as descriptive notes to a group of paintings; but we are justified in regarding it simply as a statement about landscape interpretation.

The statement begins by repeating, or seeming to repeat, the position taken by Field sixty years earlier: Australian poetry had no 'antiquities', the landscape lacks 'the charm which springs from association with the past'. But then Clarke goes on to say that, since as yet (it is his assertion) no poet speaks to us from the past, it is for us to look into our own hearts. And then he proceeds to examine what he calls 'the dominant note of Australian scenery', which he finds to be gloom: 'The Australian mountain forests are funereal, secret, stern. Their solitude is desolation.' Then follows a comment, like Field's, on the lack of seasonal variation. But it is somehow a fascinating monotony, an interesting desolation that he responds to; and you will feel in the emphases he selects something like a groping for emblematic focus. He is holding up the concentrating mirror:

> From the melancholy gum strips of white bark hang and rustle . . . Great grey kangaroos hop noiselessly over the coarse grass. Flocks of white cockatoos stream out, shrieking like lost souls. The sun suddenly sinks, and the mopokes burst out into horrible peals of semi-human laughter.

Rhetoric runs away with him: if he is confusing mopokes with kookaburras, that does no kindness either. But we are carried along by the spirit of the thing. The mood aroused, he enters into legend: we hear about the bunyip. Then the 'natives' dance around a fire, 'painted like skeletons'. Here we have no longer a gloomy gloom, but a pregnant and exciting one; and he carries romantic suggestion (still very gothic in tone) further by dwelling on the colour of a few names: Mount Misery, Mount Dreadful, Mount Despair. Moreover the depressive effect of those associations is immediately parried by an allusion to a cheerful passage in Kendall. Here amid sylvan scenes, he says, and in places:

> Made green with the running of rivers,
> And gracious with temperate air,

the soul is soothed and satisfied. There is a grotesque paradoxical beauty in these vistas, which will be recognised at once, he seems to be saying, as soon as their emblemry can be established. Australia, he adds, 'has rightly been named the Land of Dawning. Wrapped in mists [I emend an obvious mistake, 'midst'] of early morning, her history looms vague and gigantic,' and so on. Emblematic detail is suggested: the lonely horseman riding between the moonlight and the day, and the shadows that close him in; the strange noises he hears in the primeval forest; and (what Field had remarked on) the strangeness of the whole face of nature compared with other lands. Yet with all that, there is a fresh and captivating review of the time-context. All this

*Emblematic vision: or
landscape in a
concave mirror*

Australian grotesquery, so novel to European experience, was to the sympathetic and
visionary eye not new at all in an important poetical sense but very, very old: older
than Europe itself.

Here in every line, in every phrase almost, there is a fresh perception and a
revaluation of old expectation. 'There is a poem in every form of tree or flower, but
the poetry which lives in the trees and flowers of Australia differs from those of other
countries . . .' In this catalogue of the 'grotesque, the weird, the strange scribblings
of nature learning how to write,' the search for emblems presented itself with an eager
urgency. What Clarke saw then may not be exactly what we see now, but the character
of colonial poetic vision undoubtedly changed after this piece of writing. It served
not so much to dismiss the old rational criteria (of 1788) as to put new values on them:
'Some see no beauty in our trees without shade, our flowers without perfume, our
birds who cannot fly, and our beasts who have not yet learned to walk on all fours.
But the *dweller in the wilderness* [my italics] acknowledges the subtle charm of this
fantastic land of monstrosities . . . ' And so we come to a first manifest awareness of
the beauty and truth of our Australian loneliness as both a wilderness and a testing-
ground of the spirit. He who *dwells* in it comprehends the language of the barren
and the uncouth, the hieroglyphics of haggard gum-trees, and the like. A
phantasmagoria, Clarke calls it; but one to be treasured when it is known and
loved. (The later colonial appreciation of barren landscapes is a phenomenon related
to the increase of inland exploration and extended settlement. Clarke doesn't make
that pragmatic point, but naturally he reflects it.)

Some of Clarke's emblems became more articulate in later hands; some were
already endemic. Two nineteenth century poems which I think worth noticing in this
context if only briefly, are Brunton Stephen's 'The Dominion of Australia' (1877)
and a later one, Essex Evans's 'An Australian Symphony'.

The first (which followed just after Clarke's piece) dwells on the time image, an
image of awakening: the young nation:

> Hears in the voiceful tremors of the sky
> Auroral heralds whispering, 'She is nigh.'

This dawn-emblem or rising-sun figure was one of the most powerful of colonial
images, especially when it could be made to carry an idealistic national implication
(one may think of its later military use). Another developed emblem in the poem is
one barely yet available to Clarke and Gordon: that of artesian water, discovered in
the 1870s and at first thought to hold hopes of infinite green fertility for all the sad
outback:

> Already, like divining-rods, men's souls
> Bend down to where the unseen river rolls . . .

The poet envisaged miraculous transformations of the landscape. That never happened,
but the image was a valid symbol all the same. It was still capable of a brilliant
application in James McAuley's 'Envoi' seventy years later.

Of Evans' poem it is perhaps enough to say that, once again, it amounted to a
critical revaluation. It took a number of now standardised symbols, emblems and
clichés, and without repudiating them, pleaded for a more positive, a more
idiosyncratically national reading of them. 'Not as the song of other lands/Her song
shall be' – Clarke had already said much the same thing. He had spoken of the tone
of melancholy, which he characterised as desolate and grotesque; and he had spoken

of remoteness, loneliness, both of which Evans repeats. Evans said it was not the major mood of the country though it was a real presence:

> But undertones, weird, mournful, strong,
> Sweep like swift currents thro' the song.

The ultimate Australian melody, he suggested, was not this sad descant which the poets had been making out of the mixture of beauty with pain; it might be silence itself.

> The silence and the sunshine creep
>   With soft caress,

he said; and this put some already familiar emblems in a new light:

> The grey gums by the lonely creek,
>   The star-crowned height,
> The wind swept plain . . .

And so on; the passage is well known. You have a series of self-sustaining images like hazy blue mountains, cold white light, the campfire glowing in the evening, the sound of horsebells and:

> The curlew's melancholy note
>   Across the night.

– this last a bird new to poetry, with a shivery, melodic, weirdly atmospheric symbolism. At the end the poem comes back to its emphasis on the emblematic beauty of silence for 'Silence is the interpreter/Of deeper things.' There is poetical growth here, made not by advance into novelty, but through a new and visionary perception related to an emblemry already defined and tested.

'Almost every Englishman', said Sir Kenneth Clark, 'if asked what he meant by "beauty", would begin to describe a landscape – perhaps a lake and mountain, perhaps a cottage garden, perhaps a wood with bluebells . . . at all events, a landscape.'[11] No doubt that's right, and it isn't hard to translate into an Australian equivalent. But it wouldn't be bluebells. It's a question of values and suitability, what applies and what doesn't. And that comes down to the selection of the emblematic detail. We are reminded that when landscape develops beyond topography and into art, we are no longer looking at the face of nature merely in terms of its facts. The emblematic detail serves to concentrate and direct out attention to the human content of what we see. In the early days of landscape art it was generally thought advisable to include something in the picture which would divert the mind from mere cold fact and give it some imaginative animation – which was done by including a human figure, or group of figures; or at least something living, animals or birds. These were emblematic of the warmth of life and seemed to give purpose to the total representation. In poetry the presence of emblematic detail works similarly: it concentrates and humanises suggestion. It rationalises, epitomises and strengthens the substance of the message.

But, in a new society, a colonial culture, to find and articulate the *essential* emblemry of the national and communal mind, especially when it is necessary first to clear the way by eliminating or modifying the *false* carry-over (the chocolate-box lake, the jigsaw-puzzle cottage, the travel-folder bluebells), that is the labour of generations. It is a measure of the 'modern' conquest over the 'colonial' spirit when a firm and fresh emblematic system is at last confidently established.

142

*Emblematic vision: or
landscape in a
concave mirror*

And that, perhaps, was what was wrong in the main with Christopher Brennan.
So far as he was a landscapist (and he was in part), he wasted so much moral and
spiritual muscle in sculpting images that were *not* emblems, whether effectively of this
hemisphere or that, that he was never able to stand two-footed upon his own native
poetic ground. Our present age is one of minor rather than major lyric, yet here and
there among the landscapists you will find an independence in the use of emblematic
suggestion that is very contemporary and true to both poetical and topographical
experience. Perhaps I may be permitted to end by quoting a short piece by the brilliant
and unhappy Michael Dransfield. The poem is an emblematic Tom Tiddler's ground
but I will draw attention to only one of the items in particular: the one at the end
about loneliness and silence which he uses with an absolutely precise regard for its
Australian evolution and 'antiquity'; but like a true poet, puts his own value on it.
This is the now well known lyric, 'Minstrel'*:

> The road unravels as I go,
> walking into the sun, the anaemic
> sun that lights Van Diemens Land.
> This week I have sung for my supper in seven towns.
> I sleep in haysheds and corners
> out of the wind, wrapped in a Wagga rug.
> In the mornings pools of mist fragment the country,
> bits of field are visible higher up on ridges,
> treetops appear, the mist hangs about for hours.
> A drink at a valley river coming down
> out of Mount Ossa; climb back to the road,
> start walking, a song to warm these lips
> whitebitten with cold.
> In the hedges live tiny birds
> who sing in bright colours you would not hear
> from your fast vehicles. They sing for minstrels
> and the sheep. The wires sing, too, with the wind;
> also the leaves, it is not lonely.

A sentiment often repeated in colonial times was the tag quoted in *Richard
Mahony*: *coelum non animum mutant qui trans mare currunt.* 'The sky is different, but
not the spirit of man, at the end of the colonial voyage'. And that really was true. That
essential spirit of poetry, the intuition which must show the man how he stands in
regard to his landscape, is always the same because human nature and feeling and
need don't change. But in a colonial situation they can be pretty much thrown out of
gear. It takes a long and painful adjustment to re-establish normal relations between
the world and the spirit. That is where the mirror of poetry helps: the concentrated,
articulated perceptions it throws back are emblems by which we begin to identify
ourselves again. They are the trig-points by which the colonial imagination effects
its new triangulation, and by which it comes to discover for itself where, spiritually,
it stands.

Stout Cortez, silent upon his peak in Darien, had no trouble in his mind like to the
troubles of the Australian poets. He had the excitement of roving discovery. But the
settlers at Botany Bay also had to *live there* and draw substance and sustenance from

---

* Editor's note: First published by University of Queensland Press in *Streets of the long voyage.*

their landscape. It wasn't just a magnificent incident. It was the whole of life – they had to accept it or die.

Emblems may be insubstantial in themselves, but they are poetically solid. You can hold on to them: they are simple, necessary acts of faith.

Notes and references

1. Quoted in ELLIOTT, BRIAN and MITCHELL, ADRIAN. *Bards in the wilderness: Australian poetry to 1920*. Melbourne, Nelson, 1970, p. 32.
2. *op. cit.* ELLIOTT and MITCHELL, 1970, p. 32.
3. See 'On reading the controversy between Lord Byron and Mr. Bowles', quoted in *Bards in the wilderness, op. cit.* ELLIOTT and MITCHELL, 1970, p. 18.
4. SMITH, BERNARD. *European vision and the South Pacific, 1768–1850: a study in the history of art and ideas*. Oxford, Clarendon Press, 1960, p. 134.
5. A curiously late instance is quoted by Dorothy Green in her study of Henry Handel Richardson, *Ulysses Bound*, A.N.U. Press, Canberra, 1973, p. 331. The allusion is to a letter of Dr Walter Richardson's, dated 1855.
6. *op. cit.* SMITH, 1960, p. 134.
7. Louisa Meredith, writing in 1840, may prove this assertion wrong. *Notes and sketches of New South Wales*. Penguin Colonial Facsimiles, Melbourne, 1973.
8. RUSKIN, JOHN. *The crown of wild olive: four lectures on industry and war*. London, 1866.
9. *op. cit.* SMITH, 1960, p. 182.
10. It cannot be said that patriotic lyrics like Caroline Carleton's 'Song of Australia' or the later (and better) 'My Country' of Dorothea Mackellar master the (bush) landscape image. As for Bernard O'Dowd, he is hardly a landscapist at all in intention in 'The Bush'.
11. CLARK, SIR KENNETH. *Landscape into art*. Pelican, London, 1961 (originally published. 1949), p. 142.

*Leonie J. Kramer**

Symbolic landscapes

In October 1822, a Judge of the Supreme Court of New South Wales, Barron Field, made an excursion across the Blue Mountains to Bathurst and back. Field's poetic efforts, published as *First Fruits of Australian Poetry* (1819) were ridiculed by his contemporary Lang, and have scarcely been taken seriously by his successors. His was a minor talent, but he was sufficient of a writer to recognise that he had a problem of perception. On 7 October 1822, he saw on the banks of the Nepean what he described as 'almost the only deciduous native tree in the territory', the white cedar. This led him to reflect on the monotony of the indigenous trees, 'all as un-picturesque as the shrubs and flowers are beautiful'. He continues: 'New South Wales is a perpetual flower garden, but there is not a simple scene in it of which a painter could make a landscape, without greatly disguising the true character of the trees'. Field goes on to try to analyse the deficiencies of the native evergreens, and he comes to a conclusion which is the starting-point for this exploration of the modern Australian writer's relationship to his environment. Field continues:

> There is a dry harshness about the perennial leaf, that does not savour of humanity in my eyes. There is no flesh and blood in it: it is not of us, and nothing to us. Dryden says of the laurel:
>
> > 'From winter winds it suffers no decay;
> > For ever fresh and fair, and every month is May.'
>
> Now it may be the fault of the cold climate in which I was bred, but this is just what I complain of in an evergreen. 'For ever fresh', is a contradiction in terms; what is 'for ever fair' is never fair; and without January, in my mind, there can be no May. All the clearest allegories of human life are bound up in the infant and slender green of spring, the dark redundance of summer, and the sere and yellow leaf of autumn. These are as essential to the poet as emblems, as they are to the painter as picturesque objects; and the common consent and immemorial custom of European poetry have made the change of seasons, and its effect upon vegetation, a part, as it were, of our very nature.

And he ends this rumination by quoting Sir James Smith: 'There seems . . . to be no transition of seasons in the climate itself, to excite hope, or to expand the heart and fancy'.[1]

There are two matters of particular interest here. First, Field is right in his reference to the intimate connection in European poetry, between the seasons and human life. It is not only by such obvious examples as Spenser's 'Shepheardes Calendar', Thomson's 'Seasons', or Keats's 'Ode to Autumn' that his claim is supported. There are countless instances of the elucidation of man's experience in reference to seasonal changes – 'How like a winter hath thine absence been'; 'Now is the winter of our discontent/Made glorious summer by this sun of York'; or, to advance to T. S. Eliot, a central notion about experience *out of time* relies upon a seasonal paradox 'Mid-winter spring is its own season/Sempiternal, though sodden towards sundown'.

---

* Leonie Kramer is Professor of Australian Literature at the University of Sydney.

Field implies, in making this observation, that there is a whole area of metaphor
closed to the European poet's use by the quite different qualities of the Australian
landscape.

Second, Field expresses a problem of perception which has been of great importance
in the history of Australian writing and criticism. It is an obvious point, but it needs
to be made. No European migrant to Australia could possibly see the country as it
really was. He was conditioned by years of European experience. It was natural that
he should search for familiar analogies through which to define his new experiences.
If he were a poet, this could mean finding some familiar points of reference by which
the unfamiliar could be described. This is exactly what Field himself tries to do in his
much-ridiculed poem 'Kangaroo'. Impossible for a man of his literary education to
fit the kangaroo neatly into the great chain of being; impossible too, to write a serious
poem about so strange a creature. So Field attempts a very interesting and sensible
solution to his problem. He treats the animal as a good-natured joke on the part of
Nature – created on God's day off, as it were; and at the same time he tries to give
a reasonably accurate picture of it for his English readers:

Kangaroo, Kangaroo!
Thou Spirit of Australia,
That redeems from utter failure,
From perfect desolation,
And warrants the creation
Of this fifth part of the Earth,
Which would seem an after-birth,
Not conceiv'd in the Beginning
(For God bless'd His work at first,
        And saw that it was good),
But emerg'd at the first sinning,
When the ground was therefore curst;
        And hence this barren wood!
Kangaroo, Kangaroo!
Tho' at first sight we should say,
In thy nature that there may
Contradiction be involv'd,
Yet, like discord well resolv'd,
It is quickly harmonis'd.
Sphynx or mermaid realis'd,
Or centaur unfabulous,
Would scarce be more prodigious,
Or Pegasus poetical,
Or hippogriff – chimeras all!
But, what Nature would compile,
Nature knows to reconcile;
And Wisdom, ever at her side,
Of all her children's justified.
She had made the squirrel fragile;
She had made the bounding hart;
But a third so strong and agile
Was beyond ev'n Nature's art;
So she join'd the former two
        In thee, Kangaroo!

To describe thee, it is hard;
Converse of the camelopard,
Which beginneth camel-wise,
But endeth of the panther size,
Thy fore half, it would appear,
Had belong'd to some 'small deer',
Such as liveth in a tree;
By thy hinder, thou should'st be
A large animal of chace,
Bounding o'er the forest's space;
Join'd by some divine mistake,
None but Nature's hand can make –
Nature, in her wisdom's play,
On Creation's holiday.
For howsoe'r anomalous,
Thou yet art not incongruous,
Repugnant or preposterous.
Better-proportion'd animal,
More graceful or ethereal,
Was never follow'd by the hound,
With fifty steps to thy one bound,
Thou can'st not be amended: no;
Be as thou art; thou best art so.
When sooty swans are once more rare,
And duck-moles the Museum's care,
Be still the glory of this land,
Happiest Work of finest Hand![2]

The conditioned perception of English eyes is well illustrated by James Tucker's description of Ralph Rashleigh entering Port Jackson in late 1820s. A resident of Sydney in 1974 envies Rashleigh his view of an unspoiled scene of natural beauty. But Rashleigh had the eighteenth century civilised tradition in his immediate background; to him, nature exists to be improved by man:

> The shores of Port Jackson *then* possessed few charms, either natural or acquired; sandy bays opening to great distances inland, bordered apparently by stunted trees; rocky headlands between each inlet, crowned with similar foliage; and far away, on either hand, a background displaying dense forests of sombre green. There were *then* none of those elegant mansions or beautiful villas, with their verdant and ever blooming gardens, which *now* so plentifully meet the eye of the new colonist, affording abundant proofs of the wonted energy of the Anglo-Saxon race, who speedily rescue the most untamed soils from the barbarism of nature and bid the busy sounds of industry and art awaken the silent echoes of every primeval forest in which they are placed.[3]

That is a striking example of the conditioning of a man's perceptions. The absence of the picturesque, for Tucker as for Barron Field, is no small deprivation.

Perhaps it was easier for the scientists to rid their minds of aesthetic notions formed in another hemisphere. Perhaps they were not so prone to have their perceptions clouded by scenes from European literature, and to confuse actualities with imaginative re-creation. Charles Darwin travelled across the Blue Mountains to Bathurst in 1836. It was January, so he did not have Barron Field's problem about an inadequate spring season. He stopped at a farm on the way, which employed a large number of convict servants. He comments:

> Although the farm was well stocked with every requisite, there was an apparent lack of comfort; and not even a single woman resided here. The sunset of a fine day will generally cast an air of happy contentment on any scene; but here, at this retired farm-house, the brightest tints on the surrounding woods could not make me forget that forty hardened, profligate men were ceasing from their daily labours, like the slaves from Africa, yet without their just claim for compassion.[4]

The contrast between natural beauty and imported human degradation that troubled Darwin on this fine summer day is at the very centre of Marcus Clarke's *For the term of his natural life*. A perception such as this can be the beginning of a literary exploration which goes far beyond literal description and documentation. The smooth assertion of the lines 'Where every prospect pleases/And only man is vile', has nothing in common with the troubled and direct responses of Darwin and Clarke.

Observations such as those of Darwin and Clarke – and in the nineteenth century there are many other examples – provide the basis for the more ambitious and complex examinations of man's perception of his environment that have characterised modern Australian writing. One might describe this as the darker strand in our literature. It sometimes emerges as criticism, as in A. D. Hope's 'Australia':

> A Nation of trees, drab green and desolate grey
> In the field uniform of modern war,
> Darkens her hills, those endless, outstretched paws
> Of Sphinx demolished or stone lion worn away.
>
> They call her a young country, but they lie:
> She is the last of lands, the emptiest,
> A woman beyond her change of life, a breast
> Still tender but within the womb is dry.
>
> Without songs, architecture, history:
> The emotions and superstitions of younger lands,
> Her rivers of water drown among inland sands,
> The river of her immense stupidity
>
> Floods her monotonous tribes from Cairns to Perth,
> In them at last the ultimate man arrive
> Whose boast is not: 'we live' but 'we survive'.
> A type who will inhabit the dying earth.
>
> And her five cities, like five teeming sores,
> Each drains her: a vast parasite robber-state
> Where second-hand Europeans pullulate
> Timidly on the edge of alien shores.
>
> Yet there are some like me turn gladly home
> From the lush jungle of modern thought, to find
> The Arabian desert of the human mind,
> Hoping, if still from the deserts the prophets come,
>
> Such savage and scarlet as no green hills dare
> Springs in that waste, some spirit which escapes
> The learned doubt, the chatter of cultured apes
> Which is called civilisation over there.[5]

It is seen again in James McAuley's 'Envoi':

There the blue-green gums are a fringe of remote disorder
And the brown sheep poke at my dreams along the hillsides;
And there in the soil, in the season, in the shifting airs,
Comes the faint sterility that disheartens and derides.

Where once was a sea is now a salty sunken desert,
A futile heart within a fair periphery;
The people are hard-eyed, kindly, with nothing inside them,
The men are independent, but you could not call them free.

And I am fitted to that land as the soul is to the body,
I know its contractions, waste, and sprawling indolence;
They are in me and its triumphs are my own,
Hard-won in the thin and bitter years without pretence.

Beauty is order and good chance in the artesian heart
And does not wholly fail, though we impede;
Though the reluctant and uneasy land resent
The gush of waters, the lean plough, the fretful seed.[6]

And in the opening paragraph of Thomas Keneally's *Bring larks and heroes*:

At the world's worse end, it is Sunday afternoon in February. Through the edge of
the forest a soldier moves without any idea that he's caught in a mesh of sunlight and
shade. Corporal Halloran's this fellow's name. He's a lean boy taking long strides
through the Sabbath heat. Visibly, he has the illusion of knowing where he's going.
Let us say, without conceit, that if any of his ideas on this subject were *not* illusion,
there would be no story.[7]

Of these three examples the passage from Keneally is closest to nineteenth century
observations, mainly because *Bring larks and heroes* is an historical novel, attempting
an historical perspective. But the Hope and McAuley poems, both of which end by
modulating into a qualified affirmation, posit a much more intimate relationship
between man's perception of his landscape and his sense of his own individuality. In
Hope's 'Australia' the desert of Australia offers more challenge to the powers of mind
than does 'the lush jungle of modern thought/Which is called civilisation *over there*'.
In McAuley's 'Envoi' man does not wholly frustrate the beauty which is 'order and
good chance in the artesian heart'; and 'the gush of waters' is there in defiance almost
of the resentment of 'the reluctant and uneasy land'. In both poems, in their very
different ways, Hope and McAuley examine the contours of experience. The contours
of the land provide a defining context for that experience.

A country which can push man to the limits of human endurance can also provide
images for mental torture and despair. These are to be found in works as diverse as
Kenneth Slessor's 'Crow Country', Henry Handel Richardson's *The fortunes of
Richard Mahoney*, and Patrick White's novels. In 'Crow Country' Slessor merges the
external landscape and inner experience:

Gutted of station, noise alone,
The crow's voice trembles down the sky
As if this nitrous flange of stone
Wept suddenly with such a cry;
As if the rock found lips to sigh,
The riven earth a mouth to moan;
But we that hear them, stumbling by,
Confuse their torments with our own.

> Over the huge abraded rind,
> Crow-countries graped with dung, we go,
> Past gullies that no longer flow
> And wells that nobody can find,
> Lashed by the screaming of the crow,
> Stabbed by the needles of the mind.[8]

In the last volume of *The fortunes of Richard Mahony*, the twisted shapes of gum-trees seem like menacing madmen to the deranged Mahony; and in Patrick White's *Voss*, Laura Trevelyan offers a theory of knowledge which makes explicit the notion of the consonance of internal and external reality:

> 'I am uncomfortably aware of the very little I have seen and experienced of things in general, and of our country in particular,' Miss Trevelyan had just confessed, 'but the little I have seen is less, I like to feel than what I know. Knowledge was never a matter of geography. Quite the reverse, it overflows all maps that exist. Perhaps true knowledge only comes of death by torture in the country of the mind.'[9]

Voss is one of the many works of modern Australian writing which uses the exploration of the country as the literal base for a quasi-symbolic representation of the mental traveller, journeying into the unknown. This is not an historical novel in intention or design, but Leichhardt *is* the model for Voss and, as in Charles Darwin's account of his journey to Bathurst, so in Leichhardt's letters one can discover observations which move beyond plain description to suggest the nature of the relationship between observer and observed. Leichhardt's perceptions are interestingly free from European colouring. In March 1842, he arrived in Sydney, and wrote immediately to his friend in London, Dr Little. He tells Dr Little what he would see if they could go walking together in the Botanical Gardens in Sydney on a moonlit night:

> You'd look the full Moon in the eye; you'd hearken to the sounds of the cicadas and the crickets; your eyes would sweep over the blue mirror of the water to the dark masses of trees that frame it; in this mild weather your whole body would respond to a deep sense of well-being. You'd shout out 'Here let us build a Tabernacle!'
> And if the Moon is not shining, there's the clear vault of the sky over us, full of brilliant constellations. Every night the Centaur, the Southern Cross, the Ship Argo with Maia Placida and Canopus, Canis Major and Minor and Orion, Taurus and Gemini march across the sky; and every night the Magellan Clouds arouse my sense of wonder.[10]

Eight months later, Leichhardt was in Newcastle. Below the gaol he watched what he calls in his letter to Dr Nicholson 'a Kind of Charybdis' – a fissure in the rocks in which the water is sucked out by the tide, and comes surging back. Leichhardt writes:

> This regular falling of the water, only to come hissing back, fascinated me, and I could have watched it by the hour. There are certain impressions which are enough in themselves to engross our whole being; not because they revive old memories, or stimulate us towards more rigorous scientific observation and the possible solution of problems; but because they are intimations of power so overwhelming that we surrender to it passively in a spacious darkness of mind.[11]

In both these extracts there is a literary imagination at work, building from observations of the natural world towards an expression of a state of being induced by the experience. The phrase 'a spacious darkness of mind' comes very close to the kind of language by means of which White seeks to probe moments of special insight in those of his characters, including Voss, whom he endows with rare gifts of illumination.

The striking quality of the perceptions of Darwin, Leichhardt, and other observers of the nineteenth century must seriously qualify a widely accepted view of Australian literary history. The view is that since the early European settlers were unable to see the landscape as it really was, they were unable to understand and absorb it, and hence to write with confidence about it. The imperfections and failures of nineteenth century literature are thus symptoms of maladjustment, or evidence of the feeling of restlessness and uncertainty common to exiles and expatriates. One form of this argument is advanced by Judith Wright:

> Before one's country can become an accepted background against which the poets' and novelists' imagination can move unhindered, it must first be observed, understood, described, and as it were absorbed. The writer must be at peace with his landscape before he can turn confidently to its human figures.[12]

If one accepts this view – and it makes large assumptions – then one might well go on to argue, as Judith Wright does in relation to Charles Harpur:

> It would, of course, have been impossible for him at this time to have had the kind of appreciation of the Australian landscape that is possible nowadays. It is important for us to realise this, for it is the key to understanding all early Australian writing. Australian writers began under a hardship that no other new-world literature had had to face in the same measure. The visual, the tactile and the physical qualities of Australia are unique, and the European background of her new inhabitants singularly unfitted them to appreciate this country.[13]

The weakness in this position is the assumption that literature is critically dependent on a particular kind of familiarity with landscape. One could argue that a good writer can make literature out of the very sense of dislocation and strangeness that Judith Wright refers to. Henry Handel Richardson, Martin Boyd and Patrick White have done so. Further, Darwin and Leichhardt are only two of the many who in their journals or other writings demonstrate a fine perception of the landscape. These were, however, men of superior talents, whereas it has to be acknowledged that Harpur, Kendall, Gordon and the early novelists were not. One simply cannot assume (as Judith Wright's argument seems to require) that if they had been born later or elsewhere their literary achievement would have been significantly greater. No doubt it is too simple to suggest that the quality of literature in the nineteenth century is solely determined by the quality of its authors, but their deficiencies cannot be explained away by assumptions about their relationship to the landscape.

So far I have avoided using the phrase 'symbolic landscape' which is the title of this paper. The word 'symbolic' is one of the most abused terms in modern literary criticism. In the sense in which it was understood by the French symbolists, and by such poets as Yeats and Brennan, it is scarcely applicable to Australian writers. Few of Brennan's poems even are fully symbolist in the strict sense. Yet I would still want to distinguish between landscape and man's perception of it in the poets and novelists of the nineteenth and the first thirty or so years of the twentieth century, and the relationship proposed by certain writers of the last forty years. It is not possible to offer a detailed explanation of these differences. It would, however, be true to say that two influences have subtly changed the mode of perception of modern writers. One is the weight of accumulated history, especially the history of exploration and discovery, and the pioneering of the land. The other is the pressure of Australian experience, especially of the discrepancy between what the new heaven and new earth seemed to promise, and the severe demands made by the realities of the environment. These, and other related influences, have coincided with, on the one hand, a growing dissatisfaction with the methods of social realism in fiction; and, on the other, susceptibility to the influence of poetic methods pioneered in English by Yeats, Eliot and Pound.

In defence of my thesis that there *is* a distinction to be made I offer a few examples. One of the characters in Christina Stead's novel *Seven Poor Men of Sydney* (1934) remarks 'The sight of a large city always stirs me almost to prayer'. And the response is: 'I always feel most a man when in the city; in the country, I am almost afraid, there are no voices out there'.[14] This sentiment is particularly interesting because it is atypical. The dominant literary images of Australian reality continue to be rural rather than urban. Stead's own novels create a full and vivid picture of the life of Sydney, but not without creating at the same time a sense of its claustrophobic parochialism, its repressive control of the lives of unliberated citizens. It has to be said, however, that the claustrophobia comes from the author. It is part of her theme, and necessary to the argument of the novel. It is an interpretation given to the physical facts of city life, comparable with Barron Field's response to the Australian evergreen forest. In this novel and even more in *For Love Alone* Sydney is an ambiguous image; it is dramatically beautiful, the centre of a vigorous intellectual life, but it is also the home of poverty, deprivation and despair. The contrast with Louis Stone's *Jonah* (1911) is clear. The earlier novel attempts a realistic account of the business life of a city; the later ones press a highly personal vision of the same environment adapted to the general thesis of the novels. Both *Seven Poor Men of Sydney* and *For Love Alone* are about people who are trying to find their place in life. Their possibilities of self-realisation are restricted by political and social inequalities, and by their own emotional inhibitions. Sydney offers a setting which dramatises their struggles. Its city and inner suburbs concentrate the squalor and poverty of the underprivileged; its harbour life, by day and night, provides a sharp contrast in natural beauty, and a constant reminder of the world beyond, as ships sail in and out of the heads. And Watson's Bay, a haven for lovers on summer nights, teases the feverish imaginations of Stead's seekers, and also offers them a way to death. Her Sydney is accurate. One can trust it as one can trust James Joyce's Dublin; but its logic is that of the perceivers' state of mind, not of geography.

The same can be said of rural landscapes in modern fiction and poetry. In *The Young Desire It* (1937) Kenneth McKenzie uses the landscape of Western Australia to define his characters' modes of feeling. In *To The Islands* Randolph Stow makes the landscape of Western Australia an extended metaphor of a man's attempt to confront his own weaknesses. It is like a modern and localised *Pilgrim's Progress* in which the rough and the smooth are translated into accurate landscape images, reflecting not the eye, but the mind of the beholder. In works such as these, whether they present urban or rural images, the landscape is given meaning. It is neither a backdrop to human action, nor a decorative flourish. It is put to work as one means of exploring the subject.

Once this happens, detailed accuracy of description is not necessarily of first importance. A writer's purpose may, in fact, best be served by selected images which support general rather than specific perceptions. James McAuley's 'Wet Day' may be taken as an example. It links a natural scene with a view of man's despoliation of his world in a way that includes the ecological but goes beyond it:

Rain sweeps in as the gale begins to blow,
The water is glaucous-green and mauve and grey.
A pelican takes refuge on the bay;
Snow-white and black it rides the complex flow.

A child stands in a yellow mackintosh.
Gulls lift away and circle round about.
Cans, bottles, and junk appear as the tide runs out.
Wind cannot sweep away nor water wash

The dreck of our vulgarity. I think
The world has never been redeemed; at least
The marks it bears are mostly of the Beast –
The broken trust, the litter, and the stink.[15]

The actual setting of the poem is St Helens on the east coast of Tasmania. But the geographical identity of the scene is unimportant. It appeals to a consensus of feeling about images of ugliness and decay.

The prose writer who has most consistently made environment serve the purposes of literary intention is Patrick White, especially in the novels dealing substantially with Australian urban and suburban life – *Riders in the Chariot*, *The Solid Mandala*, *The Vivisector* and *The Eye of the Storm*. In *The Tree of Man* one sees the beginning of man's destruction of the natural environment as encroaching settlement gradually reaches out to the land that Stan Parker has tamed. Here one can see too an incipient definition of man's proper relationship to the land. Stan Parker achieves design in his surroundings instinctively. He does not plan his garden, but it takes on form under his care. Thus he accidentally creates a garden which he perceives as a unity, and which is then presented by the author as an analogue of a cosmic wholeness. An interesting paradox is detectable here, which is reflected in the formal structure of the novel. Coherence in Stan's landscape is a product of randomness, yet the novel itself is tightly structured. The result is a counterpointing of meaning and design, and a clear distinction between the imperfect understanding of the protagonist, and the larger view of his creator.

In *Riders in the Chariot* the activities of man in relation to his natural environment are wholly destructive. The crumbling mansion Xanadu is gradually being reclaimed by the bush; but this natural process of reclamation is completed by the bulldozer, which destroys the house and the bush with it:

Just before the house was completely razed, the bulldozers went into the scrub at Xanadu. The steel caterpillars mounted the rise, to say nothing of any sapling, or shrubby growth that stood in their way, and down went resistance. The wirier clumps might rise again, tremblingly, on their nerves, as it were, but would be fixed for ever on a later run. Gashes appeared upon what had been the lawns. Gaps were grinning in the shrubberies. Most savage was the carnage in the rose garden, where the clay which Norbert Hare had had carted from somewhere else, opened up in red wounds, and the screeching of metal as it ploughed and wheeled, competed with the agony of old rose-wood, torn off at the roots, and dragged briefly in rough faggots. A mobile saw was introduced to deal with those of the larger trees which offered commercial possibilities. The sound of its teeth eating into timber made the silence spin, and they were sober individuals indeed, who were able to inhale the smell of destruction without experiencing a secret drunkenness.[16]

153

> When Xanadu had been shaved right down to a bald, red, rudimentary hill, they began
> to erect the fibro homes. Two or three days, or so it seemed, and there were the
> combs of homes clinging to the bare earth. The rotary clothes-lines had risen,
> together with the Iceland poppies, and after them the glads. The privies were never
> so private that it was not possible to listen to the drone of someone else's blowflies.[17]

There is no natural order in the suburbs, only artificial uniformity, a monotonous
replication of rotary clothes-lines, galvanised garbage bins and well-drilled seasonal
gardens of imported flowers. White's account of the spread of suburbia is quite factual.
The process he describes continues on the outer fringes of every Australian city. But
where it appears in its detail to be a specific perception, it is in fact, the opposite.
What he offers as a series of observations is a carefully structured fiction. The neat
suburban barbarism of Barranugli is an essential step in White's argument. One can
see that all the houses are the same; their owners' values are the same; and if one could
see into their dreams, one would find that they, too, are the same. So it is only those
who reject, or are rejected by, the inhabitants of Australian suburbia who can enjoy
the sufferings, the privileges and triumphs of an idiosyncratic, spiritual insight. Such
people also are immune from the paralysing attractions of the synthetic world of
sterile ambitions and plastic possessions. White's thesis demands the absorption of
individual differences into a large generalisation. In his latest novel, *The Eye of the
Storm*, his imaginative re-creation of actuality is striking. Actuality is present in the
general geographical configurations of Sydney and in such details as the iron railings
of Centennial Park. But Doyle's fish restaurant at Watson's Bay becomes a squalid
nightmare of gorging faces, grotesque mounds of fish skeletons, and the swollen
corpse of a strangled dog washed up on the beach. The refinery chimney at Botany Bay
glows with hellish fire and illuminates with a ruddy glare the suicide of one of his
characters. This is a Sydney recognisable, it is true, but transmogrified as the setting
for a confrontation of spiritual forces.

This kind of imaginative fiction – like Barry Humphries's characterisation of
suburbia – is very persuasive, so persuasive that it can become our way of seeing
ourselves. It can, in short, appear to be fact. If it does, we then find ourselves in a
position not unlike that of Barron Field and Ralph Rashleigh – conditioned by *literary*
perceptions to see things through the eyes of others. There are signs that this process
has already influenced our cultural history, and, by contagion, our notion of the truth
about ourselves. The legend of egalitarianism is a case in point. It was born and
survives in spite of the evidence that should undermine its foundations. Joseph Furphy
uses that famous phrase 'Temper democratic: bias offensively Australian' to
characterise a novel which is a working-model of the social stratification of bush life
in the 1880s. The play of the writer's imagination upon his perceptions creates a
variable relationship between fact and idea in literature, and hence a truth which does
not have its exact correspondence in the actual world. This is not to say that literary
perceptions do not have a special validity. The way modern writers ask us to see ourselves is, in some sense, the way we are, or even the way we might become. But we
should perhaps recognise that if we accept a writer's view of ourselves, we may be
buying both more and a good deal less than the truth.

Fortunately, there is no generalisation to be made about the perceptions of modern
Australian writers, which are as diverse as their geographical distribution is wide.
Dr Davidson's map of the agricultural history of Australia has its literary counterpart.
The image of the dead heart captures the imagination, but it has no special prominence

among writers. The rain forests of the north, the mallee scrub, the coastal ranges, the plains and the deserts of Western Australia and the alpine country have been explored and occupied by poets and novelists. One could assemble a large naturalist's handbook from the observations which writers have made of the bird, animal and plant life of the continent. A sample would include Slessor's brilliantly sharp glimpses of Sydney and the harbour, Judith Wright's landscapes of New England and Queensland; John Blights's seascapes, and Douglas Stewart's meticulous miniatures of native animals and plants.

Though one can doubt the adequacy of Judith Wright's explanation of the failings of early Australian literature, there is clearly a sense of confidence in modern Australian writing which earlier writers only rarely display. Familiarity has bred the knowledge that the environment can be a means of expressing individual experience. Modern writers have found that even without the strong seasonal variations that Field rightly judged to be important to European poetry, the Australian landscape can reflect the common hopes, discoveries, and disappointments of human affairs in all their variety and subtlety. Thus through his exact observations of the natural world, Douglas Stewart is able to convey his perception of the philosophical questions it raises. I cannot imagine this being possible to a nineteenth century poet. The change I have been describing cannot accurately be summarised in a single example. There is no generalisation which will include the extravagant satirical and metaphoric landscapes of White on the one hand, and the direct, plain and accurate observations of Stewart on the other. One example of the modern poet's perception of his world is David Campbell's 'Night Sowing', a poem that epitomises modern Australian landscape art at its best. It amalgamates several aspects of the poet's experience – his work, his love, the creation of poetry itself, and expresses them in terms of a landscape so well understood, that it perfectly shapes the experience which is the poem:

> O gentle, gentle land
> Where the green ear shall grow,
> Now you are edged with light:
> The moon has crisped the fallow,
> The furrows run with night.
>
> This is the season's hour;
> While couples are in bed.
> I sow the paddocks late,
> Scatter like sparks the seed
> And see the dark ignite.
>
> O gentle land, I sow
> The heart's living grain,
> Stars draw their harrows over,
> Dews send their melting rain:
> I meet you as a lover.[18]

Notes and References

1. FIELD, BARRON. 'Journal of an excursion across the Blue Mountains of New South Wales, October 1822', in MACKANESS, G. (ed.) *Fourteen journeys over the Blue Mountains of New South Wales 1813–1841*. Sydney, Howitz-Grahame, 1965, p. 120. (First published 1950.)

2. ELLIOTT, B. and MITCHELL, A. (eds.) *Bards in the wilderness: Australian colonial poetry to 1920*. Melbourne, Nelson, 1970, pp. 17–18.

3. TUCKER, JAMES. *Ralph Rashleigh:* edited by C. RODERICK. Sydney, Angus and Robertson, 1952, p. 68.

4. DARWIN, CHARLES. 'Journey across the Blue Mountains to Bathurst in 1836', in MACKANESS, 1965, *op. cit.*, p. 233.

5. HOPE, A. D. *Collected Poems 1930–1970*. Sydney, Angus and Robertson, 1972, p. 13.

6. MCAULEY, JAMES. *Collected Poems 1936–1970*. Sydney, Angus and Robertson, 1971, p. 7.

7. KENEALLY, THOMAS. *Bring larks and heroes*. Melbourne, Sun Books, 1968, p. 7.

8. SLESSOR, KENNETH. *Poems*. Sydney, Angus and Robertson, 1962, p. 69. (First published as *One hundred poems* in 1944.)

9. WHITE, PATRICK. *Voss*. Ringwood, Vic., Penguin, 1960, p. 446.

10. LEICHHARDT, F. W. LUDWIG. Letter to Dr Little, 25 March 1842, in AUROUSSEAU, M. (ed.) *Letters of F. W. Ludwig Leichhardt*. Published for Hakluyt Society, Cambridge University Press, 1968, p. 457.

11. LEICHHARDT, F. W. LUDWIG. Letter to Dr William Nicholson, 31 October 1842, in AUROUSSEAU, 1968, *op. cit.* p. 568.

12. WRIGHT, JUDITH. *Preoccupations in Australian poetry*. Melbourne, Oxford University Press, 1965, p. 1.

13. *op. cit.* WRIGHT, 1965, p. 10.

14. STEAD, CHRISTINA. *Seven poor men of Sydney*. Sydney, Angus and Robertson, 1965, p. 313. (First published 1934.)

15. *op. cit.* MCAULEY, 1971, p. 222.

16. WHITE, PATRICK. *Riders in the chariot*. London, Eyre and Spottiswoode, 1961, p. 535.

17. *op. cit.* WHITE, 1961, p. 545.

18. CAMPBELL, DAVID. *Selected poems, 1942–1968*. Sydney, Angus and Robertson, 1968, p. 42.

Daniel Thomas*

Visual images

MARLBORO COUNTRY

It was suggested that I discuss visual images of Australian landscape as found in popular culture and commercial art – the popular reproductions of bad outback and mining paintings like Pro Hart's, or the photographic advertisements for Marlboro cigarettes. In fact it had never occurred to me that the Marlboro advertisements were Australian; I took them to be American for they preferred cattle to sheep and damp mountains to dry plains. I thought they were of cowboys in the Rockies. (I now know them to be Australian-made; I've even discovered the names of some of the photographers and their models.)

This would be an extremely interesting study, and I would enjoy undertaking it, but it would take many months of original research. Instead, I can only give you material with which I am already familiar: not the popular and commercial arts, but the fine arts – the art of the museums. Perceptions gained from the fine arts should in any case be subtler than those from commercial art.

Evidence from the fine arts is also reasonably comprehensive. Painters have been interested in landscape at all periods of Australian history, though inevitably less so in the twentieth century. The principal European art movements of the nineteenth century – Romanticism, Realism, Impressionism – were profoundly concerned with landscape, and their Australian extensions shared their energy.

On the other hand, in the twentieth century the principal art movements, Cubism, Abstraction, Dadaism, Abstract Expressionism, were but marginally concerned with landscape, and perhaps for that reason took shallow root in Australia. Only Surrealism, a less abstract movement, was enthusiastically embraced by Australians, and it gave 1940s landscape painting, by Drysdale, Nolan, Tucker, Boyd and others, a fresh burst of energy. Again in the late 1960s and 1970s 'Earth Art', 'Land Art', and 'Ecology Art' have been, if neither widespread nor clearly defined, at least very energetic and significant movements in America and Europe, and they helped make the Australian *landscape sculptures* at the 1973 Mildura 'Sculpturescape' exhibition perhaps the most interesting of all Australian art works in the present decade.

The above is a reminder to a largely non-art audience that visual art is generated by observation of other works of art, usually works of highest quality, as much as it is generated by observation of the life and landscape in which an artist dwells. Those other works of art are important realities in an artist's life and are part of his 'landscape'.

EXOTIC LANDSCAPE: ROMANTIC, PASTORAL, ORIENTAL

The 'Marlboro Country' of commercial art might be genuinely Australia, but there isn't much of it in Australia, and it is little visited by most Australians. It looks less characteristic of Australia than of America (and some of the Banjo Patterson – *Man from Snowy River* scenes were photographed in New Zealand).

---

* Daniel Thomas is Curator of Australian Art, Art Gallery of New South Wales, Sydney.

In the fine arts there has been a similar impulse towards what is rather remote from the daily big-city lives of most people, but although the blonde grasslands of inland Australia might be little visited by city-dwellers, they are known to be vast in area and also to be the source of much of Australia's wealth. The pastoral landscape is therefore a symbolic landscape, rightly understood to be the most characteristically Australian of landscapes.

Already in the 1820s, in Joseph Lycett's engraved *Views in Australia*[1], the pastoral landscape, embellished with homesteads, stockmen and sometimes bushrangers, is established as a theme in Australian art. The two leading colonial artists, John Glover and Conrad Martens, continue it in the 1830s and 1840s. So do the leading artists of the third quarter of the nineteenth century, Eugene von Guerard and Louis Buvelot. Yet in none of these artists do we experience Australian pastoral landscape as central to their art. It is only one of several kinds of exotica available in Australia.

In a stricter sense of the word, the uniquely Australian natural science material – the botany, zoology, geology and anthropology to which I shall return later – is the motivation for much exotic landscape art.

There is also the routine subject matter for landscape painting anywhere in the world during the romantic period – waterfalls, mountain peaks, cliffs, gorges, jungles and wilderness. Often these were available in suburban beauty spots, a mere stroll from Hobart, Sydney, Melbourne or Adelaide; sometimes they were found in more distant mountain regions, in Tasmania, the Australian Alps, the Grampians or the Blue Mountains.

The first Australian-born artist of significance, W. C. Piguenit, closes and climaxes the Australian extensions of European romantic landscape painting, in a career that runs from the 1870s well into the twentieth century, and he seldom paints anything but mountains, storms, rivers and sunsets. There is no intense light, no drought, heat nor pastoral life in his art, and since his work does not fit that stereotype of what Australian landscape is, it does not enter the consciousness of many Australians today, despite its excellence.

The most profound images of Australian pastoral landscape are Glover's and von Guerard's. Glover, however, emphasises general pastoral qualities rather than the specifically Australian.[2] A small-farmer's son from the English midlands, he had had a prosperous career in London as a conservative painter of romantic mountains and of pastoral arcadias, the latter modelled closely on those of Claude Lorrain, whose seventeenth-century Roman art remained the touchstone for all European landscape painting. Arcadia, an agricultural paradise of nymphs and shepherds in a remote, uncorrupted pre-classical Golden Age, is a timeless theme in art, and in 1830 when Glover retired to the end of the world, to Van Diemens Land, to paint and farm, he was surely acting out both personal childhood dreams and a dream embodied in many paintings and poems over many centuries. It is as if he were living in a Claude Lorrain painting. The imagery is enriched further by those paintings which include Aborigines[3] (displaced in Glover's own time), and pays them the homage of understanding Aboriginal 'agriculture' and the harmony maintained by Aboriginals with their natural landscape.

Von Guerard in the 1850s and 1860s painted a handful of even more interesting pastoral landscapes, in which energetic white settlers are juxtaposed with passive Aboriginals[4], predatory European fox with Australian kangaroo, rampant foreign blackberry with native grass.[5] They are images of immigration as aggression, but they imply destruction and regeneration as a natural cycle, to be accepted, not praised nor blamed. Like Glover's canvases, they were painted before the age of public art museums in Australia, or of popular book illustration; they disappeared into the private collections of pastoralists, remained little known and perhaps will always be too scholarly, subtle and complex to become part of Australia's common store of visual imagery. When the art museums first opened[6] it was the conventionally romantic mountains of von Guerard and Piguenit that were acquired, not their Australian pastoral subjects.

With Buvelot, who settled in Melbourne in 1865, the Romantic era is passing and Realism has arrived. Thus although his few paintings of Western District pastoral landscape emphasise the sheep[7] which were actually there rather than the cattle which were more prevalent in all European painting and in previous Australian painting, he really preferred the intimate suburban farms near Melbourne to the remoter pastoral expanses. He was almost ostentatiously concerned with the commonplace, the neglected and the humble.

Not until around 1888, when Australia had been settled a hundred years and when the centennial celebrations might have helped provoke a search for national identity, did pastoral landscapes (and figure subjects from pastoral life) become a central concern of the leading artists and the principal visual image of Australia for its predominantly urban population.

It happened quite intentionally. Although the artists – Tom Roberts, Frederick McCubbin, Arthur Streeton, Julian Ashton, Frank Mahony and G. W. Lambert – also painted many portraits, still lifes, intimate landscapes, and 'aesthetic' compositions, their small number of large, museum-scale canvases occupied most of their serious thought, and those canvases were nearly all images of pastoral life and landscape: blazing sun, heat, blonde pastures, heroic workers. They quickly entered the public collections which were their intended destinations: *The Golden Fleece*, *Fire's On*, *On the Wallaby Track*, *Across the Black Soil Plains*, *Rounding up a Straggler*, *The Prospector*[8], *The Breakaway*[9], *The Purple Noon's Transparent Might*[10], were bought by the art museums of Sydney, Melbourne and Adelaide between 1889 and 1899, and since then have been the most popular visual images in Australian art.

They were the artists' contribution to a political goal: federation of the separate British colonies into one Australian nation. Thus they were straightforward and simple in content for the benefit of their mass audience, as well as large in size.

A few more large nationalist paintings of the 1890s were bought for the art museums in the 1930s, *Bailed Up*[8], *Shearing the Rams*[9], *North Wind*[10], and by the 1940s a young generation of landscape artists, including Russell Drysdale, Sidney Nolan and Arthur Boyd, was consciously drawing nourishment from the pastoral tradition of the 1890s, but extending it with surrealist wasteland images. Later still, in the 1960s, Fred Williams would draw upon the same tradition, and it is probable that Australian landscape artists will continue to do so for ever.

Before pastoral landscape had become the dominant image, and while a wide range of romantic landscape images was still being found in Australia, there were occasional early attempts to assimilate Australia into Asia or the South Seas.

However interesting the details of natural science might be, it was generally agreed by the first artists that the Australian landscape looked dull and monotonous.

The first artists came to Australia by compulsion, as convicts, or by chance, like Augustus Earle and Conrad Martens who were travelling towards India, or else

in the hope that they could also take in some more picturesque countries. William
Westall, official landscape painter on the scientific voyage of the *Investigator* under
Captain Flinders, 1801–1803, wrote that

> '. . . the voyage to New Holland has not answered my expectations in any one way for
> although I did not expect there was much to be got in New Holland I should have
> been fully recompenced for being so long in that barren coast, by the richness of the
> South Sea Islands.'[11]

He did visit China and he tried to visit Ceylon.

Thus the Australian landscapes of Westall, Earle, Martens, Prout, and even
von Guerard, dwell on palm trees and tree-ferns, as if to assert that Australia was just
as tropically picturesque as Ceylon or Tahiti. In 1815 Governor Macquarie, on a
journey to Bathurst, noted 'a very singular and beautiful mountain . . . its summit
crowned with a large and extraordinary looking rock . . . which gives the whole very
much the appearance of a hill fort, such as are very frequent in India.'[12]

To emphasise palms and tree-ferns was also to emphasise a form that already
had a long tradition in art as an indicator of exotic landscape. Palms stood for the
ancient civilisations of Egypt and Asia. Since there was no existing tradition in art
for the eucalyptus, less interest was taken in it.

Artists continued until the 1880s[13] to roam the South Seas and the Orient in search
of romantic and exotic scenery, and to include Australia in their tours. But those
later artists who were resident in Australia only occasionally saw the place as Oriental:
Streeton in 1890s found Sydney languorous and Eastern[14], and chose an eccentrically
narrow, Japanese format for some harbour landscape panels; Hardy Wilson around
1920 linked the horizontality of Australian colonial architecture with that of Chinese
architecture; and in the 1960s Brett Whiteley could worry about Australia 'suffering
from trying to find its own identity, its identity in the Orient'.[15]

SCIENTIFIC LANDSCAPE

Most of the earliest artists, like Westall after Flinders's voyage, produced paintings
or engravings in which the landscape was only a topographical backdrop for a stage
set with a row of botanical and anthropological specimens.

Such compilations were packed with information from sources often thousands
of miles apart. Westall's *King George's Sound*[16], Western Australia, has a foreground
grass-tree, a cabbage palm, a banksia, a eucalyptus and an Aboriginal family, some
based on sketches made at King George's Sound, some at Port Lincoln, and others
on sketches made at Sydney.

To journey in the company of great scientists, Westall with Robert Brown,
Martens with Charles Darwin, was surely a great stimulus towards accurate
observation of plants, rocks or cloud-formations, and in Martens's ostensibly romantic
views there is in fact a wealth of natural-history information.

Glover likewise carefully displays a wide sample of native trees – the predominant
eucalyptus, the native cherry, the wattle, the blackwood. So does von Guerard, who
had a special fondness for tree-ferns.

Buvelot on the other hand suppresses the natural variety of vegetation, and
because the gum-tree is the commonest, he dramatises it and allows it totally to
dominate his paintings at the expense of all other trees. The botanical falsification is
psychological truth, and his public in the 1870s was surprised and delighted to find
that the common, familiar gum-tree could be so interestingly dignified by art.[17] Forty

years later Hans Heysen would complete the process of turning the gum-tree into a popular visual symbol of Australia.

The actual appearance of a particular spot was falsified by early artists in the interest of crowding scientific curiosities into the picture, by later artists in the interests of clearer symbolism.

Artists were not very interested in the actual appearance of a particular Australian spot; they never had been in Europe, and would not become so until the example of open air landscape painting of the French 'Barbizon School', and of the French impressionists, was understood. That is not to say that the earlier artists were unable to observe accurately; but that accurate observation was customary only for such minor categories of art as topographical and natural history illustration.

The first professional artist to arrive in Australia neither as a convict nor as a member of an official expedition but as a free settler was J. W. Lewin, a natural-history draughtsman who reached Sydney in 1800. He made a series of small landscape watercolours[18] in 1815 while crossing the Blue Mountains with Governor Macquarie, and they are the first landscapes to portray, straightforwardly, the casual untidiness of Australian bush vegetation and the specific colour and light of a hot, dry landscape. At that early date only a sober, scientific artist, expert in delineating birds and insects, would have wanted to paint a landscape exactly as he saw it.

INTIMATE LANDSCAPE

There is plenty of close-up detail in the earliest Australian landscapes-with-botanical-specimens; it is found in the work of Glover, once observed by a neighbour to be 'hideously faithful to nature', and of von Guerard, whose contemporaries thought his reddish pastures and hard blue skies remarkably accurate images of Australia. Buvelot's style was less detailed, and his broad paint-handling at first made his work difficult to comprehend, yet his foregrounds could dwell on humble indeterminate weeds and patches of mud.

In the 1880s the close-up detail continues but becomes different, and I think peculiarly characteristic of Australian perception of landscape. Frederick McCubbin, probably the best painter in the nationalistic generation which established the popular images of pastoral life and landscape, is also the most consistent landscape intimist, though detailed, delicate foreground close-ups of gum-leaves, wattle-blossom, tussocks and grass occur in the works of Roberts, Streeton and Conder as well.

In art there was a then currently fashionable precedent: the sprays of leaf and blossom which unexpectedly enter the picture area in Japanese prints, a device well known to the young Australian painters via the 'Aesthetic' English art of J. M. Whistler. However in Australian painting of the 1880s it seems to be the result of patient, careful scrutiny – not for botanical information but rather for familiarisation with subtleties of colour and texture. The paintings sometimes lack unity, as if their subject were the process of observation itself, the eye's jerky shift of focus from one object to the next.[19]

I would like to think that this intensely intimate, indeed affectionate involvement with close-up ground-level detail is only possible in an artist who has spent his childhood in Australia. I myself have vague childhood memories of encountering and intensely seeing minute details of Australian plant and insect life and I suspect that someone who came to Australia as an adult, someone who never crawled in Australia's dry bushland, cannot express in art this experience of surprised discovery. McCubbin and Streeton were born in Australia; Roberts and Conder who arrived as youths do not use intimate detail so often, and when they do it sometimes has more Japanese artificiality.

European and American landscape painting have nothing quite like this loving detail. They show generalised effects of light and colour, or panoramas which investigate the landform, or the colour-change of forest and pasture in autumn or spring.

Since the Australian landform was generally accepted as being characteristically flat and featureless, or else obscured by uniform eucalyptus forest, drab in colour and unchanging throughout the seasons, perhaps artists were forced to examine minute delicate things because the large-scale view was uninteresting. Perhaps, too, minute dry delicacy is especially characteristic of Australian plants; large fleshy leaves are uncommon.

The combination of intimate close-up precision with distant generalisation, as in McCubbin's *North Wind*[10] of 1890, certainly interested Arthur Boyd and Sidney Nolan two generations later, and Nolan has made a single spray of heath blossom into a startling visual event in a flat empty desert.[20]

Further, since the early twentieth century, we have been deliberately conditioned to observe native plants. I myself remember a children's picture book of wildflowers by Ida Rentoul Outhwaite, and most of us have been brought up with May Gibbs's gumnut fairies and banksia men.

But it is now necessary to introduce an opposing view of what is most characteristic in naturally occurring Australian forms. Margaret Preston, a boldly decisive artist of the 1920s to 1940s, admired the large simplifications of both modern art and primitive art, and was able to convince herself that Australia's characteristic forms were similarly bold and geometric, like the cylindrical banksia flower, or certain lilies and that large simplifications were therefore true to Australian experience.[21] Around 1940 she employed a style, based on Australian Aboriginal art, but she enlarged and coarsened its scale by comparison with the refined delicacy of linear drawing found in Aboriginal paintings on bark. She was, I think, seeing Aboriginal work as if it were the same kind of African or Melanesian work that Picasso admired.

THE COLOUR OF AUSTRALIAN LANDSCAPE

Australian landscape painting in its first hundred years is generally dark green, like European landscape painting, though Martens, Glover and von Guerard in their pastoral landscapes would indicate blonde or tawny pastures.

Buvelot's paintings shift into a generally higher key, and by the 1880s the conventional image of pastoral landscape is bleached gold. (It was already in the 1840s and 1850s a conventional Australian landscape colour in the more journalistic, illustrative art of S. T. Gill, who seldom painted in oils. The little-known Thomas Clark, later drawing master to McCubbin and Roberts, is perhaps the first to paint in the 1860s a number of pale blonde pastoral landscapes in oils). The intimate bush subjects of the 1880s are pearly grey, mauve and lavender.[23] The colour of the symbolic pastoral landscapes hardened into a harsh blue and gold convention still existing today at a low level of tourist trade art.

The colours of the accurately observed intimate landscapes on the other hand were more in tune with the *fin-de-siècle* and Edwardian taste for super-subtle, muted colour harmonies. There was an outbreak of moonrise and twilight paintings in the 1890s, pretexts for exploration of subtle colour and tone.

The most popular Australian landscape painter at the beginning of the twentieth century was the watercolourist J. J. Hilder (the earlier nationalists were nearly all in Europe at the time) and his sensitive colour harmonies were used to decorate the luxurious 1915 edition of Dorothea Mackellar's popular poem *My Country*, whose colour imagery is drawn chiefly from luxurious jewels and precious metals: 'I love a sunburnt country . . . I love her jewel-sea . . . an opal-hearted country . . . Land of the rainbow gold'.

Modernists like Grace Cossington Smith and Margaret Preston continued to observe bush landscape in complex and subtle harmonies of gold and grey and bronze.

But in the 1930s and 1940s there is a sudden shift to monochrome red landscape paintings. It probably occurs because the painters of pastoral landscape subjects began to push out further into desert country: Hans Heysen began visiting the Flinders Ranges in 1926, Arthur Murch was at Alice Springs in 1933, where the landscape is in fact red.

As a child I was aware of popular geography books like H. H. Finlayson's *The red centre: man and beast in the heart of Australia*, first published in 1935, and in 1939 I was taken to Alice Springs and Hermannsburg where Albert Namatjira's red landscape paintings were already a tourist commodity.

I don't know why Australian deserts entered popular awareness in the 1930s. Perhaps it had something to do with United States dustbowl and depression images, widely propagated in literature and photography; perhaps it was more a matter of Hollywood cowboy movies, for central Australia is mostly cattle country, not sheep. Perhaps it had something to do with surrealist painting, the period's only vital figurative art, whose landscapes were usually deserts and wastelands.

The redness, which is the real colour of central Australia, perhaps unconsciously gained popularity for its associations with the word 'heart'. Ayers Rock is a vast red monolith at the geographical heart of Australia; it stands within sight of Mount Olga, a fantastic outgrowth like monumental breasts. The two monuments attract pilgrims and I think the pilgrims might be motivated by an obscure erotic call.

It is possible that red was further popularised by the advent, around 1940, of Technicolor movie film and Kodachrome transparencies, for both processes accentuated and dramatised red.

The paintings of Russell Drysdale from 1941, but especially from the western New South Wales drought series of 1945, confirmed the new authority of red as the symbolic colour of Australia, for they were the most original new vision of Australian landscape since the 1880s. Sidney Nolan's red central Australian series followed, Fred Williams has painted a red series, and on the lowest level of furniture-store colour reproductions, Pro Hart's red landscapes might well be the most widely popular of all Australian landscape images today.

SEASCAPE

Seascape, like the intimate close-up, is I think, a landscape category which is especially meaningful for Australia. Most countries have a tradition of marine painting, concerned with ships and fishermen and naval engagements, but this scarcely exists in Australian art. Since the French Impressionists, landscapes with figures at leisure by the seaside have been common enough throughout the world, though from the 1880s they seem to be relatively more frequent in Australian art; but again this tradition is not peculiarly Australian.

The remarkable seascapes are few in number, but they indicate that for Australians an awareness of what it feels like to be caught up in the relentless thrust of surf and tide is a near-universal experience, shared by all, and of course, including Australian artists – though the artists who express it have worked in Sydney more than elsewhere.

Thus as early as the 1890s Streeton could paint *The Long Wave, Coogee*[10] in a way that communicates his knowledge of its force, and in 1901 Julian Ashton's full-frontal *The Wave*[8], is a vast nine-foot canvas surging at the spectator.

Again in the 1960s, there is a generation of Sydney artists some of whom had actually been surfies in their youth. Peter Powditch in his few paintings of waves[23] most strikingly expresses a feeling for their power; David Aspden's extended horizontal abstractions[24] can be about the flat glare of the ocean, and Michael Taylor's and Sam Fullbrook's transparent froths can be about water as an environment that is taken entirely for granted.

LANDSCAPE WITH EMOTION, DRAMA AND MYTH

Landscape art is seldom a matter of observation and information alone, and even the most deadpan, purely topographical paintings and engravings of small early settlements clinging to the edge of an empty continent at the end of the world begin to look like images of loneliness.

In Joseph Lycett's views of Newcastle[25] as it was in 1818, not only the inland wilderness is stared at, but also the sea, as if waiting for the ships which were a lifeline to the colonists' English homes.

The early topographical views of settlements more obviously express a simple colonists' pride in the achievement of civilisation in a wilderness, of laying out orderly streets and erecting solid buildings.

In fact, landscape art is deeply concerned with additions and adjustments to the landscape, not only physical but also emotional. Australia was physically empty and visually monotonous, and also empty of history, poetry and myth.

The adjustment of Australian landscape to fit nineteenth-century Romanticism by over-emphasis and exaggeration of exotic palm-trees and jungles has been mentioned. So has the crucial pastoral image, which expanded in the 1880s from a general exotic image for European consumption to become the dominant patriotic image for nationalistic Australians themselves.

Within the pastoral landscape paintings, stockmen and bushrangers operate somewhat as nature spirits. It should be remembered that Tom Roberts's bushranging subjects of the 1890s[26] were painted long after bushrangers had ceased to exist. Frank Mahony had already in 1892 painted a bushranging subject whose title *As in the days of old*[8] stressed the historical or legendary element. And in 1894 and 1897 Sydney Long's *By Tranquil Waters*[8] and *Spirit of the Plains*[27] consciously added ancient Greek nature spirits to the Australian landscape.

Conder in 1889 had painted *The Hot Wind*[28] in which a woman lies in the desert, with a serpent, and generates a drought by blowing across the embers held in an ancient Chinese bronze vessel. In 1890 McCubbin's *North Wind*[10], a dust storm subject, is unusually for him, a subject of nature in a state of violence. Around the same time there is a flood painting by Abby Alston[10] and even Piguenit in 1895 contributes a vast *Flood in the Darling*[8], which suited his dark predilections in a way that no heat or sunshine subject could.

164

A vast bushfire painting is John Longstaff's *Gippsland, Sunday Night*[10] of 1898, and the biggest of all Australian canvases, 2.7 m by 4.26 m, is Longstaff's 1907 painting[10] of Burke, Wills and King as defeated by the desert landscape in 1861. (Von Guerard painted a small canvas[29] of a sky full of flame in the 1860s and William Strutt's *Black Thursday*[30], a vast bushfire subject is of 1864, but it is more a composition of animals and figures than a landscape.)

One of the subtlest images of Australian landscape as a dangerous landscape is Frederick McCubbin's *The Lost Child*[10] of 1886. Standing in the bush a child in a blue-green dress is visually camouflaged amongst blue-gum leaves and delicately imprisoned behind a lattice of wattle twigs. The artist does however offer the hope and indeed expectation that the child will be found, for a conspicuous foreground sapling is broken, for the trackers to find. Children lost in the deceptive bush occur in the popular prints of S. T. Gill in the 1860s and David Thomas's article on McCubbin, in *Art and Australia*, points out that they were even a convention in the popular theatre.

However, despite Marcus Clarke's literary opinion, in the 1870s, that the Australian bush was sinister and melancholy (a time when Buvelot's paintings were in fact making it look familiar and intimate) and despite the 1890s outbreak of dramatic paintings of natural disasters, the majority of landscape paintings show the landscape as benign, and men perfectly at home in it.

The 1890s nature-spirits of Sydney Long are of course entirely in harmony with their environment, but perhaps a more significant turning point is a small 1887 painting by Tom Roberts, titled *The Sunny South*[10], which shows young men standing relaxed and naked in a grove of tea-trees after bathing in Port Phillip Bay. It is probably the first painting of European nudes in the Australian landscape, and it is a conspicuous indication of the fact that Australians did not feel alienated from their environment.

Sidney Nolan's Ned Kelly, and his Burke and Wills, are a revival for the 1940s of the nature-spirits of the 1880s and 1890s, just as his observation of Australian landscape is moulded by the same earlier period.

Nature-spirits are imaginary; bushrangers, explorers, fire and flood were real; historical objects begin to be sought in the 1880s and it is then that admiration of picturesque 'Old Sydney' begins, voiced earliest by Julian Ashton. Isolated paintings occur from 1889 and become numerous in 1901–1902, when much of Sydney's The Rocks was being demolished after an outbreak of bubonic plague.

Etchings and drawings by Lionel Lindsay, Sydney Ure Smith and, in Melbourne, by John Shirlow, became more characteristic of the genre than paintings. Hardy Wilson's drawings of Australian colonial architecture are scholarly, but the generally picturesque admiration of mere oldness is more common. It revives in the 1940s in the country towns of Russell Drysdale and Sidney Nolan and the cityscapes of Sali Herman.

More interesting and complex are the paintings of Lloyd Rees, produced from the 1920s to the present. He extends the school of 'Old Sydney' picturesqueness by deliberately joining Australia to the great landscapes of Europe, to the landscapes of Italy and France which are loaded with inspiration for great art. Thus, he chooses landscapes like the Illawarra, or Bathurst, whose forms are unusually hilly and interesting in their own right, but are also quite like the hills of Tuscany. Then his paintings[8] and drawings[8] improve upon these Australian landscapes by adding hill-top monasteries, fine bridges and viaducts, and other Italianate architectural and engineering features.

Finally, Arthur Boyd in the 1940s does something similar. His references to earlier Australian paintings by Streeton, McCubbin and Buvelot are clear. So are his references to the humanised agricultural landscape of Brueghel. But he sometimes offers an even more remote dimension of history to the Australian landscape by populating it with creatures not yet fully evolved into present human or animal form, or not yet fully evolved from the vegetable state.[31] He adds an awareness of prehistory to the Australian landscape.

Notes and references

1. LYCETT, JOSEPH. *Views in Australia*. London, Souter, 1824–25. Engraved from drawings of 1819–21.
2. *Patterdale farm*, c. 1840, Art Gallery of NSW, Sydney; *My harvest home*, c. 1840, Tasmanian Museum and Art Gallery, Hobart.
3. *Mills Plains*, c. 1836, Tasmanian Museum and Art Gallery, Hobart.
4. *An Australian homestead*, 1861, Rex Nan Kivell Collection, National Library of Australia, Canberra.
5. *Mount William from Mount Dryden*, 1857, Western Australian Art Gallery, Perth.
6. National Gallery of Victoria, 1864, and Art Gallery of NSW, 1876.
7. *Woolshed near Camperdown*, Australian National Gallery, Canberra.
8. Art Gallery of NSW, Sydney.
9. Art Gallery of South Australia, Adelaide.
10. National Gallery of Victoria, Melbourne.
11. SMITH, BERNARD. *European vision and the South Pacific 1768–1850*. Oxford, Clarendon Press, 1960.
12. MACKANESS, G. (ed.) *Fourteen journeys over the Blue Mountains of New South Wales, 1813–1841*. Sydney, Horwitz-Grahame, 1965.
13. Nicholas Chevalier, G. P. Nerli.
14. CROLL, R. H. (ed.) *Smike to Bulldog: letters from Sir Arthur Streeton to Tom Roberts*. Sydney, Ure Smith, 1946.
15. *Life, Australia*. Sydney, May 1968.
16. Ministry of Defence, London.
17. GRAY, JOCELYN. *Early Australian paintings*. Melbourne, Oxford University Press, 1967.
18. Mitchell Library, Sydney.
19. SPATE, VIRGINIA M. *Tom Roberts*. Melbourne, Lansdowne, 1972.
20. *The perish*, 1949, University of Western Australia, Perth.
21. *Art in Australia*. Sydney, May 1935.
22. Such as McCubbin's *The lost child*; Roberts's *Evening when the quiet earth . . .* , both in the National Gallery of Victoria, Melbourne.
23. *Seascape I*, 1969, Martin Sharp collection.
24. *Little Bay painting*, 1969, Art Gallery of South Australia, Adelaide.
25. Newcastle City Art Gallery.
26. *Bailed up*, Art Gallery of NSW, Sydney; *Bushranging*, Australian National Gallery, Canberra.
27. Queensland Art Gallery, Brisbane.
28. *Lost*; see GIBSON, FRANK. *Charles Conder, his life and work*. London, 1914.
29. Ballarat Art Gallery, Victoria.
30. State Library of Victoria, Melbourne.
31. *The Shepherd*, 1944, Art Gallery of NSW, Sydney.

Judith Wright*

Biological man

Poetry was once considered the foremost of the arts; but at present it is the least
popular art of all. There are several reasons for this, not the least being the way it is
taught in schools; but I think the basic reason is that the poet is, *par excellence*, the
speaker for natural or biological man. This is the part of us which is least under
conscious control, which feels and has emotions, rather than thinks and analyses;
which rebels against monotonous and unmeaning tasks, ugly environments and ugly
noises. These are, when you come to think of it, the chief products, as far as many
people's immediate surroundings go, of the technological revolution – of the high rate
of urbanisation and industrialisation which has been what we regard as progress.

Biological man, then, is the enemy of 'progress', and as such he has been the chief
victim of it. In its name, we have knocked him down, suppressed him and as far as
possible sat on his head. However, he is finally the most important constituent of
every one of us, whether we like him or not, and he is a man who is being robbed.

He is now starting to speak out, in various ways, about this robbery. He is imposing
'green bans', he is refusing to perform his more unpleasant and boring tasks, and he is
even starting to vote. I think he had a lot to do with the high urban vote against the
government in 1972. He is becoming a person to be reckoned with, and it might be
wise for us to listen to what he has to say. He is very ancient; his roots are in the very
beginning; but he has a wisdom denied to the financial pages of the newspapers.

His needs are simple. He has to have food, and shelter, and the employment
necessary to get these and to keep him from boredom and destructiveness; and these
are the chief needs that governments in general recognise. But in getting them, he
must not be deprived of his other needs. They are for breathable air, drinkable water,
the natural background from which he comes and which is his genetic source, and for
a way of living which will not deny everything he is and can be.

Increasingly these are disappearing and leaving him with the by-products of the
material progress that his other side, economic and technological man, has presented
him with. These, too often, are unclean air, an increasingly poisonous and poisoned
environment, a maze of traffic-loaded bitumen roads and more and more inhuman
buildings, hideous and sometimes dangerous industrial enterprises which chain him
to a job he doesn't pretend to like, and a general sense that, whatever 'progress' may
once have promised, he doesn't enjoy what it has produced. This new environment
of his was made by economic and technological man, not by biological man; or so he
feels; and it has trapped him in an ever-hastening round of demands, just to tend it,
maintain it, and keep far enough ahead of its more murderous aspects to exist at all.

This is the plight of biological man, and he responds to it by protest. This may take
the form of delinquency or criminality or simply of dropping out as far as he can.
He may seek relief in apathy, alcoholism or drugs. He may become ill, mentally or

---

* Judith Wright McKinney, poet, writer and conservationist, was a member of the Committee of
Inquiry into the National Estate during 1973–74.

physically, through sheer stress. The amount of noise, pollution, ugliness and monotony that he can stand is limited.

Since these stresses are generally treated by medical means, it seems probable that they are reflected in the cost of health services. These are soaring in the western world, at least. It is said, for instance, that in Britain the costs of the National Health Service are now increasing faster than the national GNP.[1]

Whatever method biological man chooses to express his sorrows, they make him a burden to society, financially and otherwise. The poor fellow is in a real fix. For he can't get out. He is one part of a split personality, and its other occupants include economic man, technological man, political man – the very people who are doing all these things to him. They are a great deal more articulate than he is, in fact they keep talking all the time. They rule the media, the government, the economy and the stock-market, not to mention education, and they are hell-bent on going on progressing. But they have a problem, too. They can't leave biological man behind, for he is the basis of them all.

As for his options, he can only drag them all to the doctor, the psychiatrist, or in extreme cases the judge and jury. None of these notice that he is there, for he is the only one without a voice to explain his needs. So he comes out, as a rule, with nothing better than a bottle of pills, a diagnosis that takes no account of what he really has the matter with him, or a prison sentence.

What has all this to do with poetry? Poets, or most of them, are fairly well aware of biological man. Poetry, music, painting, are rooted far back in human history and in the natural rhythms of life. Even today, when most of us have forgotten those rhythms, art still employs them – which is why music, pictures and rhythmic verse and dance often move us in ways we hardly recognise. They are based on our biological cycles, which we hardly notice now, caught as we are in the stop-go, walk-don't walk, nine-to-five, artificial timetables of our lives. But poets listen to them still, which is why biological man can get through to poets more easily than to politicians and industrialists.

It is noticeable that poets have, on the whole, a reputation for oddness, rebelliousness and nonconformity. They are among the first to cry 'Hold, enough!' when things get too tough to be put up with. As far as they can, they avoid working on assembly lines, spending their lives clipping bus-tickets, or attempting to manage banks. When, for one reason or another, they do these things, they express their feelings in verse at the dead of night, for their feelings seem to them at least as important as their need of employment to make a living. They are then the mouthpiece of biological man – or woman.

If their society can't stand this, then poets (and writers, for the two are more or less synonymous) stand to be among the first to get hurt. So Lorca did, so Neruda did, so any number of Russian and Greek and South African poets and writers have done. This has not happened yet in Australia, which is why I am able to talk to you today.

But the number of writers on the lists of Amnesty International is high, and this is a fair index of how far we occasionally go in defence of what are called the Rights of Man, i.e. biological man. Our protests are generally thought to be political, but I am of the opinion that this isn't the case. We are representing biological man, and we are protesting against the conditions made, and the terms laid down, by economic, political and technological man – our hypocrite readers, our kin, our brothers.

It has sometimes happened that poets have been temporarily misguided enough to accept the dictates and priorities of their society, and even enthusiastically support them. I am not making out a case for the lot of us. But if we are honest, we generally end up by seeing the error of our ways. Take, for instance, one of Australia's best poets, Robert FitzGerald. In the thirties, FitzGerald was a strong man for progress. His long poem, 'Essay on Memory', was a justification of the destiny of European man in the Pacific, and a plea, not for less but for more progress. He took the firm view that it was the duty of us all to 'build upwards, though we guess not to what skies'; and for this endorsement of technology, he naturally won the prize, offered in 1937, for the best poem of that year, which marked the 150th anniversary of Australian occupation of this continent. It was a perfectly good argument, if you accepted – as, after the years of the Great Depression, most people did – that economic and scientific and technological advancement held the key to the happiness and comfort of mankind and were unequivocally the best ideas produced by the human race to that end.

However, events, and the propensity of man to make a complete muck of everything he does, overtook him. In the sixties FitzGerald, an older and wiser poet, took the lead in anti-Vietnam protest and wrote bitterly of what progress, as bent awry by modern industrialism, had done to this country. It won him no prizes, but did him great honour. He was almost gaoled for his pains, and would have been so had the then Government stood by its own convictions.

Writers are not, of course, any less likely to make mistakes about the way their society is heading, or ought to head, or about what its real options are, than other people. Sometimes they have been totally off the mark, if they try. They really only know how they feel, and their functions therefore are as barometers, not computers; and since they can voice it, a lot can be deduced from poetry about the real human condition.

I happen to think that a number of the deepest hang-ups of Australians are closely related to the fact that we are, when you come down to it, still aliens in a country which we have occupied for a very brief time, compared with its original inhabitants. It is not our true background. We have spent most of our time here in trying to make it so, not by adapting ourselves to its terms, but by trying to adapt it to ours. We have attacked it with every weapon known to modern technology, and with very little regard to, or knowledge of, how it should be handled. In the process, we have set off a lot of problems, and made large parts of it even more intractable to living in than it was when we came. Its largely infertile soils have deteriorated, their highly adapted vegetation and animals have suffered sorely, forests have vanished unnecessarily, estuaries have silted, waters have been spoiled and wetlands drained, and much once useful farming and grazing land has almost gone out of production. This has happened, for the most part, in little over a century; and a people with less blind faith in the power of technology to right everything that has been done wrongly, might well be alarmed at the speed of this deterioration. However, we are not alarmed; and we are doing little or nothing to solve these problems, and little to change our ways.

To put it mildly, then, we have not loved this country, and if countries have their own *Geist* (and being a poet, I think they do) this country does not love us. I sometimes wonder whether our retreat to the cities has been a tacit recognition of this. The basic hostility between Australians and their landscape is, of course, only the background of our lives. Nor is it peculiar to Australians. But it is certainly no accident that we are, in one of the newest countries, also among the most urbanised, with more than eighty-five per cent of us living in what the Commonwealth Census classifies as 'urban areas'. Our attempts to civilise the hinterland and turn it into a place fit for Europeans to live in were brief, and in the main we have retreated in some disorder, leaving some disorder behind us. It will be less and less populated in comparison with the cities as the machines increasingly take over.

This history of our confrontation with a landscape we did not understand or enjoy is fairly clearly set out in our poetry. This began, for all intents and purposes, with Charles Harpur, himself a man of the land, son of convicts, and an idealist and radical. He was born at Windsor and spent most of his life in the districts near it, and in the Hunter Valley, where he cleared forests, farmed sheep (which he disliked) and ended his days on the South Coast. A few sporadic raids on Sydney, attempting to make his name as playwright and poet, failed; but much of his verse was published in the radical and country newspapers.

Harpur's dream was of an Australia which would be the home of a regenerated egalitarian race, purified of the class-consciousness and injustices of England. As such, he saw, it would have to be a loved country, and at that time it was no more than a distant and despised place of exile, from which most people longed to escape back to their original homelands. He used the Wordsworthian tenets of Early Romanticism to try to convey a vision of the landscapes he lived in. It was still largely an English vision, but to this the mountains and forests lent themselves fairly easily. In a few poems he managed to express some of their beauty and the beauty of the light around them – a light we have largely dimmed today. But he knew its differences too, and tried to convey these as well; and he saw, too, the plight of the Aboriginals. Being a compassionate man, he wrote indignantly of what was happening to them; but being also a European, he could not help seeing them as mere savages, so that his sympathy did not go far.

His optimistic utopianism did not last long. It was less Australia that he wrote of, than a Wordsworthian landscape inhabited by supposedly perfectible man. During his lifetime, the main explorations were carried out and it became clear that Australia was a great deal more inhospitable than the Lakes country; and its population was not interested in being perfected, but in making as much money as possible. He died a disappointed and neglected man, and though his dreams were to crop up again and again in later poets, they were never again the rosy early vision he had tried to convey.

Kendall, who as a young man had accepted something of those dreams, soon came up against the same realities. His landscape, of the coastal rivers and forests, was also a romantic one, but it was sentimentalised into a backdrop for his own increasing sorrow and failures, while the arid landscape of which the explorations brought increasing reports symbolised in his poetry the bitterness he felt.

By the end of the century, Lawson was scolding the bush for its monotony and hardships, and the city for its cruelty. The more optimistic school of bush balladist-influenced writers generally took the view that these hardships were just what was turning Australians into tough, pioneering, materialistic types able to make us an equally tough nation; and the smug nationalist poets on the whole felt that the landscape was something to be conquered and made to pay up in the interests of progress and the national spirit.

The most important poet of the turn of the century, however, was Christopher Brennan, a Europocentric scholar and man of the city. Brennan simply disregarded the problems of the landscape, and declared that his poetry might as well have been

written anywhere else, in China for example. This solved the problem of how to be
a writer in a country far distant from the centres of European thought and culture, but
only a poet of Brennan's stature could carry it off, and it still did nothing to give him
an audience, either here or overseas. It was Brennan's tragedy that Australia was not,
in fact, Europe; and he too died a neglected and disappointed man.

Biological man, who had been kept hard at work by the conditions of the country,
and on the whole in a background which at least did not contradict his needs, had so
far had little to say. He found his best voice in the work of John Shaw Neilson, a
gentle countryman. Neilson simply accepted the landscape he grew up in and loved
it for its own sake, finding nothing in it either strange or hostile. It was the city he
hated, for its stony conformity to 'the straight line and the square' and its materialism.
He finally had to leave the country where he had worked for many years at labouring
jobs of every kind, but he was never able to accept the conditions the city made.
Few poets have voiced so clearly the discomfort of natural man under the conditions
made by technological urban man.

Slessor, Neilson's contemporary, was on the other hand a city man first and
foremost, and most of his poems have Sydney and its harbour as their background.
'You find this ugly, I find it lovely', he wrote of the teeming life of William Street,
though he knew that it was also Cannibal Street where man ate man – and woman for
that matter. But Slessor was a victim of the city too, of its fragmentation of human
relationships, of its loss of real communication, and I think this theme was increasingly
the underlying subject of his poetry, as in that splendid evocation of Sydney Harbour,
'Five Bells'. He had spasms of a rather light-hearted nostalgia for some simpler way
of living, as in 'Country Towns'; and his poem 'South Country' is a bleak picture of
the dying ring-barked forests of the south coast, butchered to make way for farmland
to feed the ever-growing cities. Slessor is one of the most brilliant of our poets,
but he was not a happy man.

After the war, the pace of urbanisation, industrialisation and the retreat from the
country increased more rapidly than ever. It was argued that since most Australians
now lived in cities, city poetry was the only kind worth while. Most poets were also
now university-educated – a new thing in Australian poetry; and for the first time, also,
Australian poetry was being set in school and university syllabuses. Clearly, poetry
must become more sophisticated, more scholarly, more urban and urbane; and
accordingly it did so. The Jindyworobak movement, which had in a rather muddled
way espoused the cause of the landscape, and demanded that Australians should try
to make some concessions to the terms of natural man as exemplified by the
Aboriginals and their culture, wavered and fell back in disorder. The bush was still
seen as little more than the habitat of Dad and Dave and Wayback Dan; and the
Aboriginals had nothing we could use. Urbanisation, technology and progress were
the thing, and not many poets stood out against this powerful movement.

Not until the sixties did anyone begin to wonder where all this was leading us.
Slowly a reaction began. The young, sickened by Vietnam, that most technological
and indefensible of wars, joined the international revolt against universities and the
established verities. The academicism of poetry began to crumble at the edges, and
poetry went into the cafés, becoming instant communication, the assertion of personal
relationship. Gradually environmentalism, the whole-earth movement, any number
of small cults and communes of varying views, began springing up; muddled versions
of Asian philosophies were popular. In the attempt to do one's own thing, rather than

171

the things that industrial technological society demanded, the movement sometimes took art, too, and wrung its neck in the interests of the direct experience. But perhaps more people were writing, painting, making music than ever before. For art, like the landscape itself, was becoming a kind of refuge from the more appalling aspects of urbanised man.

How long this movement will last, in the face of all the forces against it, I don't intend to predict. But biological man is behind it, and his needs are urgent. He may turn out to be stronger than we think. The trouble is that he is not a rational creature, and his methods may be too crude to work well. Driven too far, he reacts with violence and despair, and he may drag everything into irrecoverable chaos, before society has begun to revise its terms in his favour.

The tragedy, of course, is that those who are most aware of the tyranny we now live under, and which we have made for ourselves, are the first to go under. The Aboriginals are, and always have been, the most obvious instance. Knowing so deeply the real needs of biological man, which include as a first condition a unity with nature and the landscape, and a kinship of feeling and co-operation with others, they have never been able to understand, let alone adapt themselves to, the terms of our society. So they suffer, for our society cannot afford to give into their needs, while they cannot make the concessions it demands. Yet the biological man in all of us can understand and sympathise with them, if we let him.

I keep saying 'him'; but here, of course, there should be a pronoun including women in humankind. Women, too, are capable of knowing what it is to be influenced by one's biological needs. At present, we are trying to adapt ourselves to the demands of technological industrial society and play a bigger part in it. Except so far as the question of equality of opportunity goes, I don't agree with this particular aim. Women have the sense to know that our present society is a killer and needs curbing in all our interests. Who wants to be liberated into it, on its present terms? I would rather try to adapt it to the needs of biological humanity. There isn't much time left for us, otherwise.

Reference

1. GOLDSMITH, EDWARD (ed.) 'Blueprint for survival', *Ecologist*. 2(1) December 1972.

Frank Moorhouse*

The bush against
the laundromat

I want to outline impressions and information I have about how people are
reorganising themselves both in the city and the country and to look analytically at the
back-to-the-earth movement.

If we had the beatniks of the fifties, the hippies of the sixties, then we have the
Greenies of the seventies – the back-to-the-earth movement, the ecological action
groups, and those people campaigning against modern city development.

Hooked up to the Greenies are movements of social reorganisation within the big
cities, especially in Melbourne and Sydney, with internal migration, a sorting out into
cohesive homogeneous groupings, and a weak, but related, emotional communalist
movement both in the city and the country.

To identify the back-to-the-earth movement as a radical fashion is to give it
perspective, but not necessarily to denigrate it. To classify it as symbolic behaviour
still leaves it valuable as a sign or signal of perhaps permanent changes ahead for
society. Neurotic radicalism, 'youth rebellion' or 'novelty radicalism' is often a
dramatisation of valid issues or ills which in the wider society are either accommodated
or unarticulated. It is true that neurotic radicalism also carries anxiety – unjustified
fear –'along with perhaps a higher sensitivity to real threats, that maybe some people
see things earlier, or have an earlier breaking point under growing city stress, which
others will respond to at a later point.

The city against the country is, of course, one of the great polarities of civilised
times. Just about every thinker has stated a position on it, in literature and in politics.
A friend pointed out that Juvenal nearly 2000 years ago wrote about it. In his Satire III
he says, 'myself, I would value a barren offshore island more than Rome's urban
heart.'[1] Juvenal then listed the problems of living in Rome – traffic, bad planning and
corruption (which has also been a recurring item in Australian political history).

Symbolically, the country has been mother, 'mother nature', and the city has been
a denial of nature, at variance with the natural order. The country has symbolised
innocence and purity; the city artificiality, decadence and pestilence. The country is
claimed as organically the true community, the small village, while the city is
described as anonymous, the lonely crowd.

The values can be reversed in literature and song, with the city being the heartbeat,
the pulse of civilisation and the arts, while the country is stagnant, a backwater
of hicks and yokels. As Johnson said, 'No, sir, when a man is tired of London, he is
tired of life: for there is in London all that life can afford'.[2]

The bohemian fashion of the fifties and sixties and of other decades was to boast
that one had never left the city limits – to be the ultimate city man with a distaste for
the rural life. But the fashion is now anti-urban, anti-city. The songs don't sing 'How
you going to keep them down on the farm now that they've seen Paree?' They sing,
'People call me country but I don't care'. In Thoreau's formulation the city was

---

* Frank Moorhouse is a writer working in both fiction and journalism. He is a frequent contributor
to *The Bulletin*.

mindless and conformist while the country was individualist, meditative, philosophical – deep, a dialogue with nature, a seminar with God.

I dug out my adolescent copy of *Walden* – one of those cult books which in a complicated and mysterious way you find your way to when young, the books that seem to come to your attention at just the right time. I dug out my old copy and found that as a seventeen-year-old I'd marked sentences which I considered terribly important.

I had heavily underlined, 'If a man does not keep pace with his companions, perhaps it is because he hears a different drummer'.[3] In the margin I'd written 'very true'.

Our society lives out the city-country polarity both ritualistically and earnestly. At its strongest we have Thoreaus in the outskirts of our cities and in the bush – hermits whom as a child in the country I remember watching and persecuting. I remember with others stoning their camps and it remains a humiliating guilt. I guess we were instruments of the town's own restrained fear of deviation.

Again, at its strongest we have the current phenomenon of rural communalism and the flight from the city. At its weakest, mildest, we have the symbolic return to nature – the weekend drive, the Sunday driver, drinking a thermos of tea around a forty-four gallon drum of rubbish at a roadside rest stop.

THE WEEKENDER DREAM

The five and five-and-a-half-day week created a new leisure period known as the 'weekend' – an expanded Sunday – towards the end of the last century, and the railways promoted the trip to the country. In Australia, popular motoring in the thirties, abundant land, and the urge to be with nature produced the dream of having a 'weekender', a second dwelling. Weekend pioneers cut roads and found virgin beaches, built huts known as a 'place'. The newly-found areas were known as 'spots', a good fishing spot, a good camping spot. You or a real estate agent shared the dream with others and soon, imperceptibly, a township sprang up, with a milkbar-general store, a petrol pump, then a hall, and then a camping ground, and then by gradual 'improvement', a replica of a city suburb with mown lawns. The escapees rebuilt the prison around them – they were back in the city. The weekenders often become 'life enders' – retirement houses – and the retirement is seen as an extended weekend.

The pioneers soon had to share the beaches with vacationers who came in tents and caravans. This was resolved by creating 'camping grounds'. The campers, shooters, and fishermen acted out the polarity and in the twenties and thirties and even through to present times, treated the farmlands and bushlands as a public domain. Before the War, especially, farmers often complained of city people who used the paddocks and farm land for camping and picnicking. Chambers of Commerce sometimes urged the farmers to permit this because the city people spent money in the towns. But the signs went up, 'Private Property,' 'No Campers', 'Keep Out', 'No Shooters', and the towns provided camping grounds where the city people were herded and policed by local government by-laws.

But the shooters were not accommodated, and today the farmers and shooters are still in conflict over land rights. The shooters continue to use the land. It is almost a carryover from the poaching of the working class. I share the sense of wrongful exclusion, which must go back to the land enclosure acts.

The weekender people and the towns are today in conflict with the transients who won't be put in the camping grounds and don't want to be restricted by regulations, by-laws, ad-hoc rules of managers and rangers. They are bikies and surfers. As one distressed coastal newspaper said, 'they use the beaches as bedrooms'. It has come close to violence along the New South Wales coast, a fight over who 'owns' the beaches, territorial rights and personal space.

THE ALIENATION OF THE NATIONAL PARKS

The National Parks were another way society tried to accommodate the need for urban man to have something of a rural existence.

But the parks to not 'belong to the people', they belong to those who control them, the rangers. The National Parks and Wildlife Service in New South Wales is a highly attenuated delegation stretching from the State Parliament through the Cabinet to the Minister of Lands, to the Director of the Service, down to Park Superintendents, and eventually to the rangers and their forbidding signs.

In talking to people in the·National Parks Service I was told that the signs can't say 'please' because this implies an option. The legal staff want them to be legally precise so as to secure convictions and carry authority. The parks provoke remarkable vandalism and aggression. The weekenders, the Sunday drivers, the campers, the shooters, and the fishermen are acting out simple and psychological urges. The simple need for variation in the pattern of life, the recreational value of physical activity and change of scene, together with a need to 'touch base'. There is the practice of the primitive skills of fishing, hunting, and survival.

I suppose there is also the imperative of technology – railways, cars demand to be used. Possessions employ their owners. There is the flight from stress; the city is the family and work arena, so the bush becomes a refuge. As Lewis Mumford points out, early suburbia and the 'place in the country', represent the masses taking over the practices of the well-to-do. 'They proposed in effect to create an asylum, in which they could, as individuals, overcome the chronic defects of civilisation while still commanding at will the privileges and benefits of urban society'.[4] Once it became a mass movement most of the benefits were lost.

SCHEMES OF CLOSER SETTLEMENT

In Australian political life, we had anti-urban movements which agreed on the virtues of the country and the dangers of the city but were of little success. Closer settlement policies, including the settlement schemes aiming to put returned soldiers on the land, were seen as having virtues beyond economics (they seem now to have had little economic virtue at all). Supporting closer settlement in 1905, Holman (Labour M.L.A., New South Wales State Parliament) said

> Get the bulk of our people away from the towns and give them such conditions
> that young fellows can make homes for themselves and settle down in comfort as
> soon as they arrive at a marriageable age and there will be no real difficulty then
> about the declining birth rate. It is the town life and the greater or lesser degree
> of degeneracy – in the physical and well as moral sense that attends it . . .[5]

Since the economic disasters from the miscalculation of economic viability, the virtues of closer settlement schemes have been under-stressed in recent years, although the War Service Settlement Scheme formally terminated only in 1970. Under the Rural Reconstruction Scheme the policies are in fact reversed. The number of rural holdings has been declining as the government now pays to amalgamate small uneconomic farms.

THE CRY OF DECENTRALISATION

There are still policies for getting people out of the city, but the reason given for doing so changes from party to party and decade to decade. It would be generous to attribute decentralisation plans to the thinking of the English nineteenth century town planner Ebenezer Howard, who argued that every city, community, or organisation had a limit of physical growth, an optimum size.

Don Aitkin (Professor of Politics, Macquarie University), thinks that decentralisation began with the Royal Commission of 1911 into the drift to the cities. 'This word, a cliché of Australian political rhetoric, has become a modern Country Party's rallying cry. As a policy . . . invested with a certain mysticism . . . a cure for most of Australia's ills, a panacea for problems of defence, industry, education, health and morals'.[6] Almost certainly, decentralisation and closer settlement schemes have some roots in historic anti-city emotion.

THE BACK-TO-THE-EARTH MOVEMENT

There has been a spectacular revival of rural romanticism in the seventies. It is in contradiction to present government policies of farm amalgamation and is occurring now when small farmers are giving up. It is a non-commercial 'new peasantry' with a communalist and co-operative ideology running through it. I'm not aware of any significant earlier movement like it in Australian history, although it has been a recurring theme in American history. Depressions, especially that of the thirties, caused evicted tenants and unemployed persons in some places to form 'happy valley' shanty and tent communities along the New South Wales coast, in Queensland, and around Sydney at La Perouse, Lidcombe and Sutherland. There were people who tried subsistence and backyard farming. In the United States there was something of a subsistence farming movement with Ralph Borsodi as one of the main proponents in his books *The ugly civilisation*[7] and *Flight from the city*[8] which is one of the cult books of the new back-to-the-earth movement both here and in America.

But economically unmotivated middle-class city dwellers turning to experiments in subsistence farming, barter, mutual aid, and communalism is new. Although statistical accuracy is difficult, the editors of *Earth Garden*, one of the magazines of the movement, estimate that 30 000 people have left the cities to 'return to the earth' since 1970, for a combination of motives other than commercial farming.

In talking with some of the people involved in this movement and analysing written material I found motives more elaborate than those of countryside recreation. The back-to-the-earth movements breaks into:
   (a) people who've bought small farms and go to them at weekends, working in the city, and who intend to, or dream of, living on the farm eventually for non-commercial purposes.
   (b) families living on small farms from one hectare upwards, trying for a degree of self-sufficiency.
   (c) more than one family living together on a farm with a variety of communal arrangements.
   (d) clusters of families in one area with a similar ideological approach for farm and country living – as at Kangaroo Ground and Castlemaine, Victoria.
   (e) Loners, hermits, vegetarians and others with a nature ideology and self-sufficiency ideals.
   (f) communes of individuals and families, and sometimes joint purchase of land,

with pooling of resources and labour, as at Cairns, Nambour, Atherton, and Cedar Bay in Queensland, Bega and Nimbin in New South Wales, and Shalam in Western Australia.

The *Alternate Pink Pages* lists about a dozen communes, but the editors of *Earth Garden* said the number is unknown. I've heard of about thirty communes, some with up to fifty members. Two publications, now established for about two years, give the movement some cohesion and visibility. Both still receive letters from new readers which express surprise that other people are doing the same thing as they are, that is, leaving the city. *Earth Garden* has published eight issues since 1972, going from a sale of 2000 to 10 000 and still climbing. *Grass Roots* – 'a magazine for down-to-earth people' has a smaller circulation. Organisations have formed in the movement, but are for service and information rather than political purposes, e.g. Organic Gardening and Farming Society of Tasmania, The Consumers Co-operative Society, and the Communal Living Information Centre.

MOTIVATION

The back-to-the-earth movement is self-motivating; that is, it is not a result of government policy or economic pressure. Often those involved in it are trained for work other than farming, and voluntarily give up their jobs or transfer their work to the country. As far as I can detect, there is no classical anarchism, or socialism apart from simple 'co-operativism'. There are some purist Christian and eastern religious (Hare Krishna and Meher Baba) communes. The Israeli kibbutzim schemes have influenced some people. I can't find political theories or a political vocabulary in the conventional sense, and except for Nimbin and the religious groups, the movement does not proselytise.

There is mysticism in the movement. It goes from the formalised mysticism of Hare Krishna and Meher Baba to a low key, non-doctrinaire form of Australian transcendentalism. This is not as total or as fierce as, say, that of Thoreau: 'What after all does the practicalness of life amount to. The things immediate to be done are very trivial. I could postpone them all to hear this locust sing'.[9] But there is a recoil from the 'artificiality' of city life, a stress on the primary intuitions, and a belief in beneficial psychological changes from being close to plants and animals. There are trades of pantheism, belief in illimitable human potential, and anti-materialism. And basic anti-city emotion.

But the Australian back-to-the-earth movement keeps mysticism well supported with 'functional' justifications for the leaving of the cities – health, advantages for the rearing of children, escape from psychological or physical dangers of city life, e.g. pollution, stress. The statement of aims of the magazine *Earth Garden* has the functional-mystical balance: '*Earth Garden* presents a range of natural life-styles. It is intended as a key to sources, practical ideas and alternatives to the nine-to-five drag. *Earth Garden* is concerned with the back-to-the-earth movement, surviving in the city, living in the country, organic gardening, community, outdoors, food and diet, living more with less, and the inner changes which follow when you are in tune with nature. Let us lead you up Earth's Garden-path to the good life'.

Earth Garden, *Grass Roots*, and the newspapers produced for the Nimbin Festival use systems jargon – input, output, resources, data, tools, hardware, software, soft technology, structures – but will mix in articles on theosophy, yoga, fasting, and eastern religions.

Apart from mystical justifications and functional advantage, an ideology of self-reliance, self-improvement, is also present. Although the context is fashionable and radical, its ideas are from small business and individualism – 'making do with less', 'testing yourself', 'independence', 'being your own boss', 'regaining control of your own life'.

Finally, ecological theories and data are probably the strongest single intellectual spur to the movement. This is probably the explanation for the appearance, the revival of rural romanticism. There has been an accumulation and wide communication of data about resource deficiencies and ecological threats. The accumulation of data is probably critical enough to produce reaction and changes in people's behaviour.

Some of the utterances of the back-to-the-earth movement make it sound like a premature acting out of the forecasted ecological disaster. Some talk and behave as if the breakdown of the system has occurred. 'Very shortly the corner store mightn't have any milk'. 'The four foods of survival are wheat, powdered milk, honey and salt. You can pack a month's supply for one person into a five-gallon can and bury it. It will keep for fifteen years or more . . .' (The word survival occurs frequently throughout the publications). The spectrum of 'natural' ways as opposed to 'artificial' ways runs through organic food, special diets, vegetarianism, natural healing, anti-psychiatry, and avoidance of some manufactured items.

Swirling around these specific motivations are the suggestions of others, disowner-ship of one's culture (self?), the technological, rationalist culture as 'spoiling' the natural world; the earlier mentioned symbolic dramatisation of a yearning to return to the mother (earth) purity, innocence of maternal relationship; search for, or return to, family in the commune structure, which often has a guru or father-figure.

In a complicated society with decision making without consultation and often at a great distance from those affected, the new movements are sometimes a concrete attempt to regain control of the life system – to see where the food is coming from, what is happening, how the system affects the person. A group of individuals tries to be a 'whole world'.

As for the farming life, I'd like to quote from Henry Lawson's story *Settling on the Land*, written at the turn of the century:

> The worst bore in Australia just now is the man who raves about getting the people on the land, and button-holes you in the street with a little scheme of his own. He generally does not know what he is talking about.
>
> There is in Sydney a man named Tom Hopkins who settled on the land once, and sometimes you can get him to talk about it . . .
>
> Tom was discharged a few years since . . . He says his one great regret is that he wasn't found to be of unsound mind before he went up-country.[10]

Meanwhile back in the city there are other manifestations of the anti-urban movement by those who for whatever reason can't go 'up-country'. It is expressed through the 'natural living' spectrum and through some anti-city protest movements such as anti-high-rise, anti-motor car, anti-expressway (all symbols of modern city). These have bona-fide social problems within them but I think they also have an emotional link with the anti-urban revival.

There is a city commune movement, the size of which I cannot estimate, where families and individuals live in the same dwelling and experiment in living arrange-ments, food buying co-operatives, with the symbolic return to nature at the markets every Friday. Some of it is good old traditional bohemian and student living presented in a new vocabulary. Probably more substantial is the grouping of like-minded people in the same suburb, or in fraternal precincts. But to conclude, here is a fictional illustration of an urban commune taken from a book I am writing:

THE COMMUNE DOES NOT WANT YOU: A SHORT STORY

At the door of the commune I hesitated. What ectoplasmic shapes and indistinguishable bearded faces and mumbling cabalism throbbed here, Oh Lord.

I knocked. Do you knock at a commune (too unflowing? does it pre-empt their attention?) or does one just go in, pacifically smiling. Or is it by initiation.

A young man who looked as fresh as a police constable, no beard, came to the door, opened it, and went back in.

'Hey', I called, 'is this Milton's commune?'

'It's not *Milton's* commune but he lives here, yes', the fresh face said to me over his shoulder.

'Is he in?' I asked the receding back but the man disappeared into a dark hole at the end of the dark corridor.

Don't they have any caution. I could be an enemy of the commune.

Any remnants of bygone manners.

Any guidelines.

I groped my way into the commune.

There appeared in the dim light, amid the raga music, to be a person in every room or the shape of a person. Were they the residents or were they callers. Or were they too, answering the advertisement for the room. In a commune there is always this group sitting around the kitchen table reading, or picking at themselves, toes or noses, drinking tea and you don't know if any of them live there or whether you can sit in that chair or is it Big Paddy's chair or is that where Milton always sits.

I'm too carefully dressed. I reprimand my bow tie with a twist, a sharp yank.
No one looked up when I came in.

'Hullo there.'

I gave a small, but positive, wave.

Someone dragged phlegm a mile along their nasal passage.

They had their heads down, reading upside down newspapers, drinking tea from enamel army mugs.

'Is Milton in?'

'I think he's in his room.'

I could not see who said this, I could not see their lips move.

'Which is his room?'

'Just bang on the wall and shout.'

I was not going to bang on the wall and shout.

'I think he's with some chick', someone else said.

Milton has been beguiled by post-World War II girls.

I moved into the other room. It was not so much that I 'moved' more that the unreceptivity of the kitchen poked me out, through a huge circular hole in the wall into yet another even darker room. They had knocked this huge circular hole in the wall. I sat down on a lopsided bean bag chair, keeping one of my feet outriggered so that I wouldn't fall over. The beans always move away from me, seem to push me rather than *receive* me.

A pig squealed out from under me. A pig.

In the dimness I saw a girl with long suffocating hair about her face, who said:
'Come here Pushkin, did the nasty man sit upon you?'

'It wasn't my intention', I told her, 'I like . . . pigs.'

'Do you have a pig?' she asked.

'I did have a cat but it decamped. It went away. Greener pastures. World travels.'

'Cats only do that to people who illtreat them.'

'Oh no – it just went.'

'You must have illtreated it.'

'No, cats just go sometimes.'

'That's the only reason they run away.'

'No, I like cats.'

'You hurt Pushkin.'

'I didn't mean to hurt Pushkin. I want to see Milton about the vacant room. Is
he with a chick?'

'Don't use the word "chick" with me if you want an answer.'

But I was going to say to her that the Kitchen Klutch used it, but oh well. I let
it go.

'The herbs look good – the watercress is growing well.'

'Anyone can grow watercress.'

I was going to tell her that in the story *The Girl Who Met Simone De Beauvoir in
Paris* the male is based on me. That I have agonised over the questions of liberation.
I am not very good at liberation. I wanted to reconstruct my personality but some
parts were missing.

I suppose you import the missing parts.

I told her instead that I went to a commune once in Phoenix, Arizona, where everyone was smoking dope and I was drinking Lone Star beer and they had a prize pet
Red Indian who noticed this and came over to me and said wow man, you drinking
Lone Star beer, give me some man, I love beer, I can't smoke this shit. Where you
from? I told him Australia and he said he'd heard great things about Australia, like
everyone drinks. I said yes everyone drinks, almost everyone. He said that sounded like
the place for him.

At first she made no comment.

Then she said, 'Do you always talk so much – you're not a very "still" person are
you?'

How long, I thought, should I give Milton if he's with a girl.

'How is the commune coming along – nicely?' I asked.

'Look man, this is a house we all share, if you want to call it a commune, you call it
a commune, but for us it is a simple experiment in shared living with a poly-functional
endo-space.'

Ah! The huge circular holes knocked in the walls.

I had been told, that as for sharing it was Milton who paid.

'Why do you wear a bow tie?'

'Oh that', I looked down as if it had grown there unnoticed by me, 'Oh . . . a bit of
a lark . . . a bit of a giggle . . . a bit of a scream . . . a sort of a joke. For gaiety?'

I thought she was staring severely at me.

'Oh, about clothes – I don't give a damn. A lark. Dress never worries me. I've got
some jeans at home, actually.'

'Oh', she said, 'I thought for a moment that at least we'd have one male here who
presented himself with style. Men think that caring about clothes is a female thing.
And therefore beneath consideration. See, another way of putting down women.
Dress, for me, is a way of speaking to others.'

'I like the idea of a sharing experience', I said, 'learning to share Milton's money.'

'I find that offensive', she said.

'Oh come on', I said, 'it was a joke. I lived with Milton before in the Gatsby House and he paid then. I mean it wasn't a moral statement. Far be it for me . . .'

'I didn't know Milton then,' she said. She was, I could tell, not interested in knowing about anything which happened before her existence.

Don't blame her.

I began to hum.

Then I thought of something chattily pertinent to say, knowing about brown rice and communes and such, 'In Chinese restaurants it was always sophisticated to order boiled rice instead of fried rice. I always like fried rice best but ordered boiled rice to be sophisticated. Now I read Ted Moloney and he says ordering fried rice is gastronomically daring and he does it and it is perfectly sophisticated'.

Again she made no comment. I think she was being 'still'.

She spoke. 'I don't find that in any way interesting – getting hung up about sophistication and all that.'

'But I thought it showed . . .·never mind . . . have you read the latest Rolling Stone?' I asked.

'I don't read newspapers,' she said.

'Oh. I read every newspaper.'

'You must have a very messed up head.'

'I read the manifest content and I read the non-manifest content. I read the archetypes, the osmotypes and the leadertypes.'

'I don't read any newspapers,' she repeated.

'Oh I really just read the manifest content. Once I used to classify news into Merry Tales, Fairy Tales, Animal Tales, Migratory Legends, Prose Sagas, and Cosmogonic Legends . . . but I gave up doing that. I just read the paper now.'

'I'm a dancer.'

'Oh yes?'

'I'm learning Theatre of the Noh.'

'It's a rich world. I'm learning Theatre of the Maybe.'

'Is that some sort of put-down?' she said aggressively.

'I wonder if he's finished yet', I said, nodding upwards.

'Do you know Lance Ferguson?'

'No.'

'Do you know Sheena Petrie?'

'Sheena Petrie? No.'

'Are you Australian?'

'Of course, I'm from Sydney.'

'Strange that you don't know anyone.'

'It's a big city.'

'Where do you live?'

'Here, here in Balmain.'

'No . . .!!!'

'Yep – for ten years.'

'Incredible, and you don't know Lance Ferguson or Sheena Petrie?'

'Never heard of them.'

'Wow,' she shook her head to herself and made a sort of coughing laugh, 'hoh wow – you must live in a hole in the ground or something.'

'I guess,' I said glumly, 'they're Milton's other scene. I'm from his first scene.'

As I said it I felt like a character who had been killed off in the first Act and had accidentally drifted on stage in Act Two.

'And you say you know Milton.'

'Yes, of course.'

'You mustn't know him very well if you don't know Lance Ferguson or Sheena Petrie.'

'Ten years – I've known him for ten years – he's my closet friend.' I meant of course, *closest* friend, but it came out that way. Its homosexual implications do not have to be explained. She did not register the slip.

'Are you part of the Balmain Bourgeoisie?'

'No. Not a part of the Balmain Bourgeoisie.'

'Who do you know?'

'Adrian Heber.'

'Everyone knows Adrian Heber. He's a spy.'

'He isn't a spy. I wonder if Milton's finished yet.'

I heard a lavatory flushing. 'Maybe that's him', I said.

'No, that's Harvey.'

'How do you know.'

'He has a weak bladder.'

I hummed again.

Then I said: 'Perhaps I should go up or something.'

She then left the room, without saying where she was going, but she took the pig with her – as if I couldn't be trusted with it.

I fancied that I could still hear the bed squeaking above me.

I looked through the huge circular hole in the wall at the people still sitting around the kitchen table.

I gave up. I went to the wall and banged and shouted, 'Milton.'

No one answered.

I went back into the dim endo-space and fought my way back on top of the bean bag chair.

I heard then a voice above me somewhere call out imperiously, 'You!'

I looked up and saw a girl's face at a manhole-size break in the ceiling. I had not hitherto noticed this ragged hole, perhaps a communications hole or something like that. She was not the girl with the pig but another girl and she wore, as far as I could see, nothing more than a man's shirt.

Maybe a committee had been watching me from the room above, the whole time. Saw me sit on the pig.

'Here's a note from Milton and your book.' She dropped the book and a note wrapped around a stone.

I picked up the note. It read: 'Go away, the commune does not want you.'

The book he returned was Olive Schreiner's *Stories, Dreams and Allegories*.

'Did he like it?' I called up to her, pretending the note was of little consequence, that I was not deeply wounded.

'He said he didn't even open it. If you gave it to him he says it must have a malign intent. He said you are always tearing at his equilibrium.'

He fears I will scratch his duco.

The girl said, 'Milton said to tell you that applying for the room under the name of Buckminster Fuller was not considered a good joke and the commune was not fooled.'

And, consequently, the commune did not laugh?

'Are you Sheena Petrie?'

'No.'

'Do you know her?'

'Of course, everyone in Balmain knows Sheena. She's Milton's best friend.'

'Is there a commune for people who do not fit very well into communes?'

'I was instructed not to talk with you any further. You must go now.'

References

1. JUVENAL. *The sixteen satires*. Harmondsworth, Penguin, 1967, p. 87.
2. BOSWELL, JAMES. *The life of Dr Johnson*. London, Everyman, 1906, vol. 2, p. 131.
3. THOREAU, HENRY DAVID. *Walden*. New York, Mentor Books, 1953.
4. MUMFORD, LEWIS. *The city in history*. Harmondsworth, Penguin, 1966, p. 553
5. CROWLEY, F. K. comp. *Modern Australia in documents*. Melbourne, Wren, 1973, v. 1: 1901–1939, p. 84.
6. MAYER, HENRY and NELSON, HELEN (eds.) *Australian politics: a third reader*. Melbourne, Cheshire, 1973, p. 418.
7. BORSODI, RALPH. *The ugly civilisation*. New York, Simon and Schuster, 1939.
8. BORSODI, RALPH. *Flight from the city: an experiment in creative living on the land*. New York, Harper, 1972. (First published 1933.)
9. THOREAU, HENRY DAVID. *A week on the Concord and Merrimac Rivers*. London, Scott, 1889.
10. LAWSON, HENRY. *Prose works*. Sydney, Angus and Robertson, 1948, pp. 6, 9.

Other pertinent publications

Alternate Pink Pages, Stephen and Phil, P.O. Box 8, Surry Hills, N.S.W. 2010, Australia.
Cosmos, P.O. Box 249, Cremorne, N.S.W. 2090, Australia.
Earth Garden, P.O. Box 111, Balmain, N.S.W. 2041, Australia.
Grass Roots, P.O. Box 900, Shepparton, Victoria 3630, Australia.
Moving and Living, 3 Cardigan Street, Glebe, N.S.W. 2073, Australia.
Nimbin Good Times, one edition only for 1973 Nimbin Festival. A.U.S., 95 Drummond Street, Carlton, Victoria 3053, Australia.
Scrounge, P.O. Box 161, Glebe, N.S.W. 2073, Australia.
The City Squatter, Sydney, Australia.
The Last Whole Earth Catalogue, 558 Santa Cruz Avenue, Menlo Park, Ca., U.S.A.
The Mother Earth News, P.O. Box 70, Hendersonville, NC., U.S.A.

4. The built environment, buildings, towns and cities

*Denis Winston**

Nineteenth century sources of twentieth century theories: 1800-1939

THE COLONIAL HERITAGE:
1788-1850

Australia was founded in the Georgian Age, the age of good taste, transportation and the gallows: the age when the architecture of reason could be recreated from well known copy books by even the most reluctant convict labourers and craftsmen. But it was also a time when the old formalities were fighting a rearguard action against those new Romantic enthusiasms expressed earlier by writers like Rousseau, which had their first material expression in such things as the rustic Hermitage of Marie Antoinette at Versailles and the great English landscape parks and gardens. It was the latter which, with the famous Royal Parks of London, Paris, Berlin and Vienna, inspired the newly settled countries like Australia to endow their main cities with a Domain, a Botanic Gardens, or an Adelaide Parklands.

Almost all the large central area parks in Australia were provided by the early Governors, since whose time few significant additions have been made. In those early days, European trees were usually planted, followed by exotics domesticated in South Africa or the Americas: native trees and shrubs were too forceful a reminder of the harshness of the untamed Australia still so near at hand.

Today we are discovering with pride the natural beauties of Australia: its unique animals, its multitude of birds, its wildflowers, its rain-forests; even its deserts have a new fascination in the age of air travel and air conditioned hotels! But for the first settlers in Australia the prevailing atmosphere was of hostility and fear: fear of famine, flood and epidemics; fear of the Aborigines whose numbers were unknown, and of the convicts and possible revolution, fear of the bush and the trees whose timber blunted English axes. Like Dr Johnson suffering in the Scottish wilderness, but with more reason, the early settlers found the Australian bush by no means loveable or beautiful; and there was a veritable 'rage against the trees', so hard were they to fell or build with.

Nevertheless, as in India before Queen Victoria's time, there seems to have been a more imaginative interest in, and a better understanding of, the human and geographical characteristics of the newly settled country than at a later date, so that Mrs Charles Meredith[1] could write of Sydney in 1839, 'The bright white villas . . . and the universal adjunct of a verandah or piazza served to remind us that we were in a more sunny clime than dear, dull Old England where such permanent sunshades would be as intolerable as they are here necessary'. For a hundred years this was forgotten and a series of more and more unsuitable architectural styles was imported from the cool countries of the northern hemisphere. Leslie Wilkinson, Professor of Architecture at the University of Sydney, was one of the first influential voices to draw attention to the relevance of the

* Denis Winston was Foundation Professor and Head of the Department of Town and Country Planning at the University of Sydney until his retirement at the end of 1974.

187

architecture of the Mediterranean to the temperate zones of Australia; but that was after the First World War.[2]

Our inheritance from this colonial, pre-industrial period in Australia includes the wide streets of Melbourne and Adelaide and nearly all the country towns laid out by surveyors like Thomas Mitchell in New South Wales. These were un-European things, until Louis Napoleon cut the avenues through Paris – which Vienna and Berlin soon copied – to ventilate them and mitigate their stench. These wide streets were also safety measures for the quick movement of troops in an emergency, and were a reminder of those Roman camps and colonial towns whose plans each nation in Europe copied when they began to develop their own colonies fifteen hundred years later. New Orleans, Philadelphia, Adelaide, Melbourne and Bathurst were the direct descendants of Roman Chester, York and Timgad.

With wide streets went large building plots; even the town-lands in Adelaide had originally one acre plots: horses, cattle, hens and pigs had to be provided for, so that good yard space and extensive out-buildings were general. Even today Australians expect that a family home should accommodate the two cars, with trailer or caravan, and have room for the children's tent as a summer sleepout; and many home sites relatively close to the centres of the main cities are still big enough for this.

Finally there was the uniform Georgian architecture, necessarily simple, often of timber instead of brick or stone, with wooden shingles instead of tiles, and generally painted white in the Regency manner of Brighton and Cheltenham: the first and last time, so far, that a coherent building style could be seen in Australia.

GOLD, INDUSTRIALISM AND GROWTH:
1850-1890

The colonial world, the world of Governor Macquarie, Francis Greenway and Captain Piper[3] with his villas and his entertainments in the grand manner, was ended by the discovery of gold and the successive 'rushes' in New South Wales and Victoria which led to a new age of rapid, unmanageable growth and the coming of the railroad and the factory, quick wealth, scarce labour, democracy and materialism. The building speculator took the place of the Government Surveyor, and the resulting chaos has continued to our own time.

Rugged individualism in business, laissez-faire in politics, and the enormous energies for good and evil that these released, mark the period of Australia's most spectacular urban growth before the last great ferment of the 1950s and 1960s. We know from writers like Dickens and Zola what conditions were like earlier in England and on the continent of Europe, and if we want to visualise nineteenth century Manchester, we have only to visit Calcutta or Bombay to experience the same conditions today on a larger and more terrible scale. Melbourne in the 1850s to which immigrants came from China to California at the rate of 2000 per week, living in tents beside the Yarra and doubling the population in a single year, was not very different.[4]

All this was part of the Industrial Revolution which changed the face of cities everywhere: and they all changed, or are changing, in the same way. Sydney and Melbourne grew at an even greater rate than Manchester and Birmingham and they are no 'newer' than most of the industrial towns of Europe, except for the

ancient centres of the latter, with their medieval street patterns and the handful
of old buildings which are all that is left of the original city.

In Australia, as elsewhere, the growing numbers of factory 'hands' were
accommodated in hovels or shanty towns within the necessary walking distance of
their work. To finance the large scale harbour installations, the iron foundries,
the gas works and other utility undertakings, a larger scale capitalism arose,
symbolised by the bank buildings and insurance offices which in their Victorian
exuberance were among the most important monuments of their day.

And, as each State became self governing, its Parliament Houses and government buildings, usually in a free classic style like those of Victoria and Queensland,
added to the interest of the architectural scene. Increasing wealth made possible
the employment of European, especially Italian craftsmen, and much of our
appreciation of these Victorian buildings springs not so much from the quality
of their overall design, as from an admiration for their rich decoration and expert
workmanship, so far beyond the skills and resources of today.

But the architects were principally engaged in that 'battle of the styles' which
ended in a complete breakdown of established standards and an eclecticism that
made a 'Byzantine' bank, a 'Venetian' post office, a 'Gothic' school or an 'Egyptian'
church seem equally appropriate. Alan Moorehead[5] has written of the 'fatal
impact' of western civilisation on the islanders of the Pacific area but in Manchester
or Melbourne the collapse of cultural traditions, the loosening of social controls
and the loss of standards of design were almost as disastrous: and the process is
still continuing.

This was the age of Telford, Brunel, Paxton and the Crystal Palace, when the
engineer displaced the architect as the practical builder, and engineering structures
began to dominate the sky lines: railway stations, covered markets, gas tanks,
aqueducts, bridges and later power lines, telegraph and telephone wires with their
supporting forests of poles and pylons became a major part of the urban prospect.
From 1870, advertisements in the form of posters and hoardings added their note
of untidy commercialism to the already chaotic scene, while the air was filled with
coal-dust and soot, and those black fumes which only the more anti-social breweries,
power stations and hospitals belch from their chimney stacks today.

Cast and galvanised iron were appropriate materials for this industrial age.
Cast iron in all its mass-produced floridity was a practical decoration for the new
hotels, the wealthy homes and the terraced houses of Sydney and Melbourne
during the last half of the century, and its use spread throughout Australia.
Galvanised iron in the form of corrugated sheets was a heaven-sent answer to the
problem of speedy roofing and, together with cast iron balconies and valances,
changed the urban scene, making possible the arcades and street awnings so
appropriate in the land of fierce sun and sudden storms and, until recently, so
eagerly demolished.

FEDERATION AND THE END OF THE VICTORIAN AGE:
1890-1918

The booming gold rush years were followed by their aftermath of financial
disasters, strikes and unemployment. After the Bank Crisis of 1893 building work
almost came to a halt and there was time for thought, followed by new resolution
and the growth of a national spirit that culminated in Federation.

189

In 1896, Archdeacon Boyce was proclaiming that: 'Sydney's slums were as bad
as anything in London'. But it took an outbreak of bubonic plague in 1900 to
impel action. The epidemic affected most Australian ports, as well as Glasgow
in Scotland; but only in Sydney did it take a serious hold, with over 300 recorded
cases and 103 deaths. The plague spread from the rat-infested warehouses and
overcrowded slums behind the wharfs of the old 'Rocks' area west of Sydney Cove:
State Parliament quickly approved large scale resumptions and demolitions,
vesting control in a board which subsequently became the Sydney Harbour Trust,
whose rehousing activities were among the earliest of their kind in Australia.

Industrial cities were meeting similar problems everywhere, and the disclosure
of horrible conditions of dirt and squalor led to the reforms which, in England
for example, emerged from such varied activities as Joseph Chamberlain's great
municipal enterprises in Birmingham, the work of Sydney and Beatrice Webb,
the creation of the London County Council, and the enlightened housing activities
of industrialists like Lever and Cadbury at Port Sunlight and Bourneville.

England was the acknowledged leader in Europe for her domestic architecture,
and a number of influences, including the work of William Morris, the Arts and
Crafts Movement, and the writings and buildings of such architects as Lethaby,
Voysey and Baillie Scott culminated in the idea of the Satellite Town or Garden
City, brilliantly promoted through Ebenezer Howard's influential book *Tomorrow*,
a peaceful path to real reform,[6] which appeared in 1898 and was followed by the
building of Letchworth Garden City, Hampstead Garden Suburb, and eventually
the English New Cities Programme and, in 1954, Elizabeth in South Australia.

Since whaling ships from New Bedford first called at her ports, Australia has
always been influenced by fashion, invention and enterprise from America – from
Cobb and Company's coaches to the balloon-frame timber house, and from the
Californian bungalow to the skyscraper. During the early years of this century
the 'City Beautiful' movement, a product of the 1893 World's Fair in Chicago
and the proselytising vigour of Daniel Burnham led to the rehabilitation of the
L'Enfant plan for Washington and a general enthusiasm for civic improvements.
The latter took the form of parks, avenues and vistas, monuments and civic
centres, and although some earnest planners claimed that such luxuries merely
attracted people's attention from more serious matters like housing and public
health, it was as a result of Burnham's work, followed by Sir John Sulman among
others in Australia, that we can today enjoy St Kilda Road in Melbourne with the
parks along the Yarra, the extension of Martin Place, Sydney, the improvements
to North Terrace and the Adelaide Park Lands, and many similar benefits.[7]

The more comprehensive landscape skills and architectural discipline of America
and the social concern which resulted in the English Town Planning Act of 1909
were combined in the design for Canberra by the Chicago architect Walter Burley
Griffin, whose strong control of the city's structure within its landscape framework
was balanced by the tree planted residential areas with their liveable bungalows
and gardens.

Chicago was also the home of the skyscraper, made possible by the steel frame
and the elevator. Larger scale business operations, serving greater areas, and the
railways, which brought so many more people within reach of the city centres,
created new demands for hotel rooms and office space. Buildings began to go higher
and so did land values. Thus began that snowball process that we are still trying

ineffectually to deal with today. Australian towns were changing from fairly compact, two and three-storey, white and grey settlements to cities with higher, more tightly packed, central areas surrounded by belts of industrial activities, and then the ever spreading suburbs where the most popular building style was known as 'Queen Anne', associated with Home, Respectability and Sound Investment!

These new suburbs which were soon to occupy the major part of every Australian city were encouraged by State Governments concerned by the evils of the inner city slums and anxious to provide low cost homes on cheap land. Daceyville Garden Suburb in Sydney, started in 1914, is an early example of the policy which later developed into the Australia-wide War Service Home Schemes.

Following at a distance the architectural fashion introduced by Norman Shaw in England and later copying details of continental *Art Nouveau*, the new homes, which made use of machine-made bricks and imported Marseilles tiles, were of a prevailing orange, red or purple colour, startling to many people today. But either in imagination or reality, the new suburbs were 'Garden Suburbs': streets were beginning to curve with the contours and there were shrubs, if not trees, to soften the effect of the materials.

PROGRESS, DEPRESSION AND WORLD WAR II:
1918-1939

Even before the peace of November 1918, two extraordinary Town Planning Conferences took place in Adelaide and Brisbane attended by representative and influential people from all Australian States, and New Zealand. The main concerns were clearly: homes for the men soon to be returning from France and the Middle East; clearance of inner city slums; garden city ideals for the new suburbs; and civic beautification, especially by means of parks and open spaces. A further subject of discussion was the matter of 'zoning' to control the use, height and density of new building developments. These ideas and their results in practice dominated city development between the wars.

The motor car was perhaps the most revolutionary addition to life after 1920, the latest of the inventions which, like the railway and the steamship, increased the mobility of man and left its mark upon his civilisation and his cities. With better roads the carriage-folk had for long driven to the city from their homes and gardens in the suburbs; the tram, the electric train and, after World War I, the bus and the motor car, brought the suburbs within reach of nearly everyone.

And so the period between the wars saw an accelerated growth of suburbia, where the American timber frame cottage with white painted timber or fibrous asbestos cladding, joined the red and orange of the older brick and tiled dwellings. It was hard to discern a prevailing style; there developed a whole gamut of styles, though none more fanciful or inappropriate than those of the same period in England so engagingly described and illustrated by Osbert Lancaster.[8]

Living conditions in the terraces, courts and tenement flats of Leeds, Liverpool or Glasgow, and perhaps even more significantly, relationships between English landlords and their Irish tenants, make the Australian's demand for his free standing home on his own plot of land easy to understand. But this aspiration for the security and privacy of a freehold home and land is equally evident in the latest arrivals from Italy and Greece, Spain and Holland: it is no unique 'Australian' characteristic, but a universal one which new-found affluence and mobility has brought within reach of a greater proportion of Australians than of most other people.

Generally the architectural interest of the inter-war years lies in the painfully slow struggle to gain acceptance for contemporary design. This was the case for all buildings, but especially so for the domestic dwelling — the sacred home.

As early as 1917, the Sydney architects James Peddle and S. G. Thorp were experimenting with adaptations of the bungalow style made famous by Charles and Henry Greene in California: low pitched, overhanging roofs, dark timber and rough stone were a foretaste of much later developments which attempted to establish a sympathetic relationship with the environment and a new concern for climatic suitability. Meanwhile echoes of the work of the great continental pioneers such as Adolf Loos, Walter Gropius and le Corbusier were reaching Australia, chiefly via English architectural journals, and isolated Australian experiments began to appear from the 1920s.[9]

Both in his planning and his architecture Walter Burley Griffin was perhaps the most influential of the pioneers of this period in Australia, combining a feeling for the natural landscape with a strong sense of overall design, and an inventiveness which was always stimulating, even when imagination outpaced technique. The Castlecrag estate, in Sydney, with its careful contour planning and its homes merging with the Hawkesbury Sandstone bushland was far ahead of most current thinking, while his Capitol Cinema and Newman College in Melbourne were among the first accomplished architectural breaks with the past on a significant scale in Australia.

Structural steel became plentiful after 1915 when the first blast furnace was established at Newcastle, and this encouraged ever bigger and higher city buildings, though fire safety considerations normally limited their height to 45 metres. Most of these new buildings were in a simplified, though gigantic, classic or renaissance style, but there were still flavourings from all past periods while, for the more venturesome, there was the exciting choice between a strongly vertical 'modern' effect as in the Myer Emporium in Melbourne or a horizontal 'modern', stemming from the work of the Dutch architect Dudok, and used for many of the new hotels with their hygienic tiled fronts.

The cinema, of which hundreds were built, might well be the symbol of the 1920s when the celluloid world of make-believe was transmitted to the buildings themselves. Glass, chromium plate, grilles and plaster decoration of every kind added to the confusion of the city scene which well expressed the confusion of a society drifting towards the Great Depression and the Second World War.

CONCLUSION:

NOT A COLONY, BUT STILL A PROVINCIAL OUTPOST

We often hear it said that Australia is the most highly urbanised country in the world, and it is true that a large proportion of the population lives in what are defined as urban areas for statistical purposes. Beyond the coastal fringe the vast areas of the continent are empty, not 'highly urbanised'. The latter expression arises mainly from the dominance of the capital city in each State, and the size of the combined population of these State capitals compared with the total population of Australia.

Sydney illustrates most clearly the way in which these capital cities attained their dominant position. While still a settlement of tents and bark shelters on Sydney Cove, and before the settlement had even proved its ability to survive, the Government, with Phillip as 'Captain General and Governor in Chief', was firmly established; and Government with its Administration became the most important element of Sydney, and of each new State capital as it was founded. Professional and financial activities revolved around the Administration, and communications by land or sea, and later by air, radiated from the cities into the interior and overseas.

Since survival was at first dependent upon provisions brought by ship, each city was a port-city on the seaboard of a virtually unknown hinterland. When wool and wheat became available for export they were naturally funnelled through these established ports, to the advantage of the growing commercial interests in them. It was inevitable that manufacturers should locate themselves chiefly in these same cities in which raw materials from Australia and overseas were most accessible, from which finished goods could be most easily distributed, and around which the biggest labour pools were established.

When mechanised farming began to push people off the land in search of employment, higher education and a greater variety of cultural opportunities, the capital cities had more to offer of all these things, and were moreover the centres of regions which provided the best all round living conditions in their State. They were magnets for settlement for overseas immigrants and equally for Australian migrants from rural areas – as they are today.

Apart from the small number and large size of her main settlements, the conclusion of any study of the development of Australian cities and towns before 1939 must be that the urban landscape here has differed little in any fundamental way from that of Europe or America during the same period. The streets were wider than in Europe and the densities lower; the suburbs spread further, generally with one-storey bungalows, and by contrast the central business districts began to develop, from 1900 onwards, with American type multi-storey office buildings.

There was as yet little feeling for external tidiness or polish, and country towns had often that 'High Noon' look of an American film set with false wooden fronts along the main street hiding one-storey iron roofed buildings. Many roads were still unsealed, and the lack of main sewerage meant dependence on septic tanks or night soil collection from an outside privy, often mercifully hidden beneath a choko vine or bougainvillea. The architectural situation has been well summed up by the Sydney architect William Laurie who, writing in the *Australian Encyclopedia* of 1958,[10] pointed out that an indigenous Australian style of architecture never emerged because at the period when serious building was first undertaken, the organic and unanimous development of European architecture was breaking up, under the influence of the Industrial Revolution, into a state of eclectic confusion from which it has hardly yet emerged.

Most of us still hope that Australian geographical and cultural influences will lead to practical, interesting, and even beautiful regional distinctions in building which will acknowledge varying climates, make use of indigenous materials and develop new structural techniques. There are of course already important differences between the architecture of the different States: the wooden homes of tropical Queensland, for example, offer a characteristic contrast to the neat stone dwellings of Adelaide; but the dominance of European and American methods of construction, the ease and speed of travel and transport, and the glamour of whatever was happening in London or Paris, New York or Los Angeles, kept Australia, before the Second World War, if no longer a British Colony, still a provincial outpost of western industrial civilisation.

Notes

1. MEREDITH, MRS CHARLES. *Notes and sketches of New South Wales*. Sydney, Ure Smith, 1973, p. 35. (First published 1844).
2. FREELAND, J. M. *Architecture in Australia: a history*. Melbourne, Cheshire, 1968, p. 233.
3. BARNARD ELDERSHAW, M. *The life and times of Captain John Piper*. Sydney, Australian Limited, Editor's Society, 1939.
4. Commonwealth Bureau of Census and Statistics: *Commonwealth Year Books, 1850-60*.
5. MOOREHEAD, ALAN. *The fatal impact: an account of the invasion of the South Pacific, 1767-1840*. London, Hamish Hamilton, 1966.
6. HOWARD, SIR EBENEZER. *Tomorrow, a peaceful path to real reform*. First published 1898, republished as *Garden Cities of tomorrow*, OSBORN, F. J. (ed.) London, Faber, 1965.
7. WINSTON, DENIS. *Sydney's great experiment: the progress of the Cumberland County Plan*. Sydney, Angus and Robertson, 1957, p. 26.
8. LANCASTER, OSBERT. *Homes sweet homes*. London, John Murray, 1939.
   LANCASTER, OSBERT. *Pillar to post*. London, John Murray, 1938.
9. TANNER, HOWARD. 'Stylistic influences on Australian architecture: selective simplification 1868–1934', *Architecture in Australia*, 63(2): 57, 1974.
10. LAURIE, WILLIAM. 'Architecture', in *Australian Encyclopedia*. Sydney, Angus and Robertson, 1958, p. 233.

References

Australian Town Planning Conference and Exhibition. *Proceedings of the first Town Planning and Housing Conference and Exhibition, Adelaide, 1917*.
Australian Town Planning Conference and Exhibition. *Proceedings of the second Australian Town Planning Conference and Exhibition, Brisbane, 1918*.
CANNON, MICHAEL. *The land boomers*. Melbourne, Melbourne University Press, 1966.
FOWLES, JOSEPH. *Sydney in 1848*. Annotated facsimile edition, Sydney, Ure Smith, 1962.
LAWRENCE, D. H. *Kangaroo*. London, Heinemann, 1923.
MOOREHEAD, ALAN. *The fatal impact: an account of the invasion of the South Pacific, 1767–1840*. London, Hamish Hamilton, 1966.

*Fred Ledgar**

Planning theory in the twentieth century: a story of successive imports

The development of theory and practice depends on the extent and nature of accumulated knowledge and experience and to understand why we do what we now do in town and regional planning it is necessary to trace back the threads and to identify major influences.

The history of the impact of western man on the Australian environment is short. In architecture and in town and regional planning we are still trying to adapt practice and theory, developed elsewhere, to our somewhat unusual circumstances. That we fumble and proceed cautiously is not surprising. The ground is relatively unknown and the need to plan has been forced upon us by rapid population increase in urban areas. The task we face is a new one not only here but throughout the world. Under these conditions, as Constantinos Doxiadis points out, 'man tends to shrink into the dimensions of the past'.

As far as we know, the first plan in Australia was prepared by Governor Phillip for the city of Sydney in 1792. Characteristically, it was largely disregarded in the initial stages of growth; but a plan prepared in 1807 by James Meehan, a government surveyor working under Governor Bligh, provided a firm base for the present city centre. Perth, in Western Australia, was founded in 1829 but the first official plan for it did not emerge until 1838. Melbourne was established in 1835, in accordance with a simple gridiron plan set out on the ground by Robert Hoddle from a tent pitched on the site. Brisbane, established in 1824 as the administrative centre of a penal establishment, owed its location to the remoteness of its site from the main centre of population in Sydney. A plan of Brisbane Town, Moreton Bay, was published in 1839 and the site was subdivided into the customary rectangles for sale in 1842. Until that date, because of the nature of the settlement, a Government decree forbade anyone to approach within 80 kilometres of Brisbane without permission.

Colonel Light's famous plan for Adelaide emerged in 1836 (Figure 42) and may, in fact, have been prepared in London as were so many of the plans for Australian towns, often with slight regard for the contours of the site. Colonel Light was a soldier. He liked order and discipline and one is tempted to speculate that the green girdle around the old city centre was a defence device rather than an aesthetic feature. It is not always appreciated that fears of invasion of Australia persisted right up to Federation in 1901 and there are still gun emplacements on the seaward approaches to all our State Capitals. Baron Haussmann's much praised replanning of Paris in which he cut vast swathes through the mediaeval muddle of houses and streets was certainly not motivated by a desire to adhere to the principles of civic design. He was more concerned with triumphal marches, mob control and making the crooked places straight. A 'whiff of grape shot' is much more effective down a boulevard than in a tangle of narrow alleys. Canberra is not designed for guerilla

* Fred Ledgar is Professor of Town and Regional Planning at the University of Melbourne.

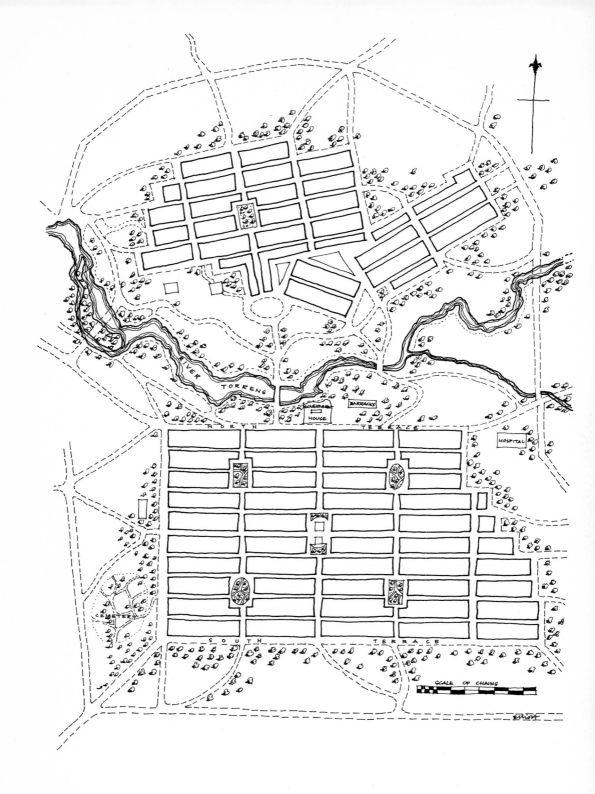

Figure 42. Colonel Light's plan of the city of Adelaide, 1836–7

196

Planning theories in the
twentieth century: a story
of successive imports

warfare. Nor is Chandigarh or Brazilia and all are seats of Government – which provides interesting food for thought (Figures 43, 44, 45).

The use of the gridiron plan in the design of early Australian towns was universal and not surprising. The surveyor was the planner of the first Australian towns. The gridiron is a form which is quick and easy to lay out and read and the blocks are easily identified and measured. It is a plan form that has been used by all colonial powers throughout history. It is not an organic form of growth and, as a result, it tends to be departed from under extreme pressure of development. Thus, each capital city in Australia, as its 'boom time' came, created its bottlenecks and converted its radial cattle droving tracks into main arterials focussing on the heart of the city where the market traditionally lay.

Interest and concern about town planning emerged early in Australia. Perhaps the contrast between the spacious base of all the plans – wide streets, large blocks, and ample open areas – and the squalor and muddle of the infilling and fringe development may, in part, have been responsible for an awakening of concern amongst responsible citizens about the state of the cities. This seems to have occurred about the turn of the century and was given impetus by a savage outbreak of bubonic plague in 1909 in the wharfside slums of Sydney. Between 1910 and 1912 Sydney spent over $4 million on widening streets and removing insanitary development. There is no doubt that the first Housing and Town Planning Act of 1909 in the United Kingdom was carefully studied here. John Burns, the president of the Local Government Board which was the predecessor of the Ministry of Health and responsible for Town Planning at that time, in introducing the Bill to Parliament said:

> What is our modest object? Comfort in the house, health in the home; dignity in our streets; space in our roads; and a lessening of the noises, the smoke, the smells, the advertisements, the nuisances that accompany a city that is without a plan, because its rulers are Governors without ideas, and its citizens without hopeful outlook and imagination. Industry is the condition of a city's being; health, convenience and beauty the conditions of its well-being.

This was simple, stirring stuff of universal appeal and suitable for export. The Garden Cities and Town Planning Association was one of the organisations behind the promotion of the Housing and Town Planning Act of 1909 and its 'modest object'. This organisation arranged a lecture tour of Australia in 1914. It seems to have focussed on South Australia, perhaps because Adelaide was always talked of as a garden city – a city in a garden.

One of the members of the team that toured Australia, propagating the garden city gospel, was the assistant secretary of the Garden Cities Association, Charles C. Reade. He had the grandiloquent title of Honorary Lecturer and Organiser, Australasian Town Planning Tour. He was also the Honorary Organising Director of the first Australian Town Planning Conference and Exhibition held in Adelaide in 1917. When the rest of the team went home he remained behind to become the first Government Town Planner in South Australia. In a report on the planning and development of towns and cities in Australia[1] to the South Australian Government, on the occasion of the promotion of the Planning and Development Bill of 1919, Reade extolled the virtues of town planning and said:

197

> It is being increasingly recognised that if . . . the drift of population from the country districts to the cities is to be checked it is essential that they either be economically planned and laid out or improved and developed in the interest of productive conveniences and rural welfare generally.

Here is one of the roots of a policy of decentralisation in Australia. Decentralisation, involving the support of existing centres and the filling up of the interstices in a sparse pattern of settlement has lain right at the heart of much of Australian planning policy. One of the many interesting illustrations in Reade's report (Figure 46) to the South Australian Government shows the Township of Alawoona in South Australia indicating the type of standardised plan apparently usually adopted for new towns at that time in South Australia. It is a perfect mini-Adelaide – the town centre, of fixed size, being made up of quarter-acre blocks and enclosed by park lands. Reade provides a suggested alternative, giving a sketch design for town of 'limited size and uncertain future' (Figure 47). He reproduces a basic garden city with park belts, avenues, boulevards, vistas, crescents, parks and civic centre. The only apparent concession to Australian conditions was the conscious orientation of the principal streets with necessary changes in direction to avoid hot, northerly winds and to minimise dust nuisance. Charles Reade was also the designer of Mitcham Garden suburb which is illustrated in the report (Figure 48). It is a very British place contained within the gridiron legacy of Light's original plan.

Mention must be made of John Sulman in this brief look at the antecedents of our planning theory and practice. He visited and was impressed by Paris in 1873. His work as a professional valuer took him into the slums of London. Arriving in Australia in 1885 and visiting all the major cities and some of the larger towns he saw a need for planning and quickly espoused the cause. His roots were in Europe and his book *Town planning in Australia*[2] is full of nostalgic comparisons between here and there. Some of his schemes for remodelling Sydney are reminiscent of Hausmann's work in Paris. His residential subdivisions are clearly modelled on Letchworth.

Walter Burley Griffin, a strange and sensitive Chicago architect with a feeling for landscape, is another man who has had a profound and lasting effect on our planning heritage. In many ways his contribution in Australia has been as significant as was the influence of Frank Lloyd Wright in America. Griffin visited and admired the gardens in Versailles and this can be clearly seen in his design for Canberra (Figure 43). His wife – a superb draughtsman – loved to play with compasses; so Canberra is a city of circuits. Griffin also left his mark in Sydney and Melbourne in both buildings and housing layout. His plan for the town of Griffith in New South Wales is a collector's gem (Figure 49).

Tertiary education always has a great influence on the development of a profession. It is interesting to note that until recently the Professors of Architecture in Sydney, Melbourne, Adelaide and Perth were all products of the University of Liverpool and were contemporaries. The recently retired Professor of Town Planning from the University of Sydney was of the same vintage and from the same University. There was one brief period when the three major planning schools in Australia were under the control of men who had worked together in the University of Manchester where undergraduate study in town and regional planning began as early as 1949. The leaders in education in architecture and town planning

Figure 43. Canberra

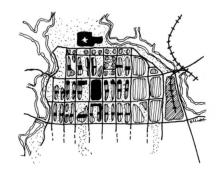

Figure 44. Chandigarh, India

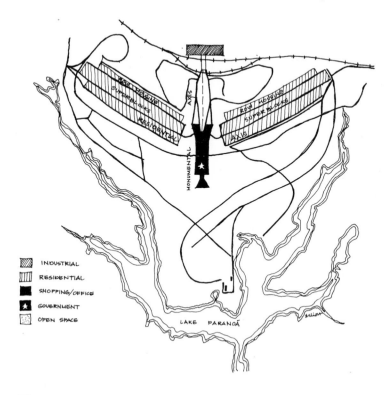

Figure 45. Brasilia, Brazil

199

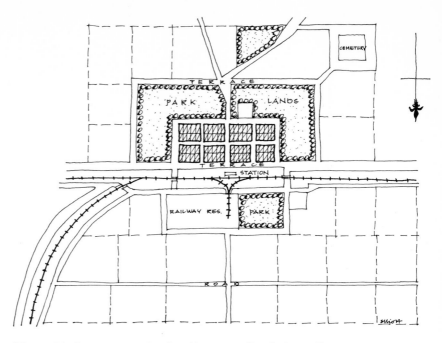

Figure 46. Government plan for Alawoona, South Australia

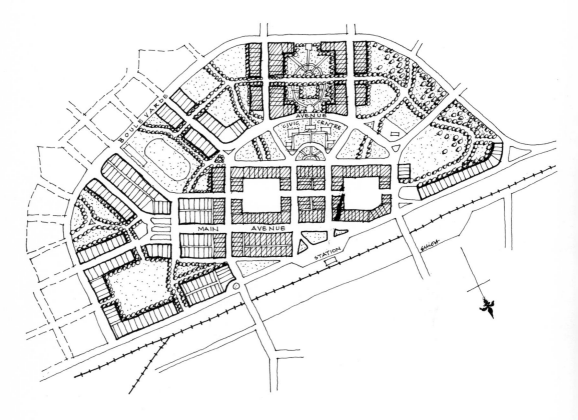

Figure 47. Charles Reade: alternative design for Alawoona, South Australia

200

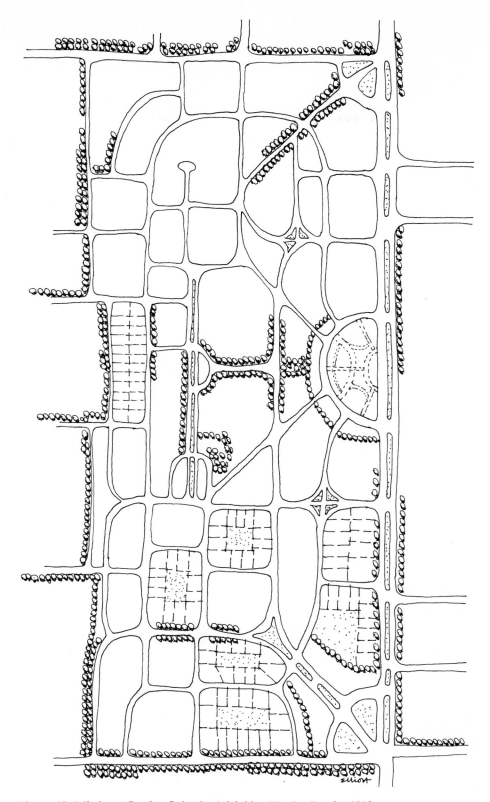

Figure 48. Mitcham Garden Suburb, Adelaide, Charles Reade, 1919

201

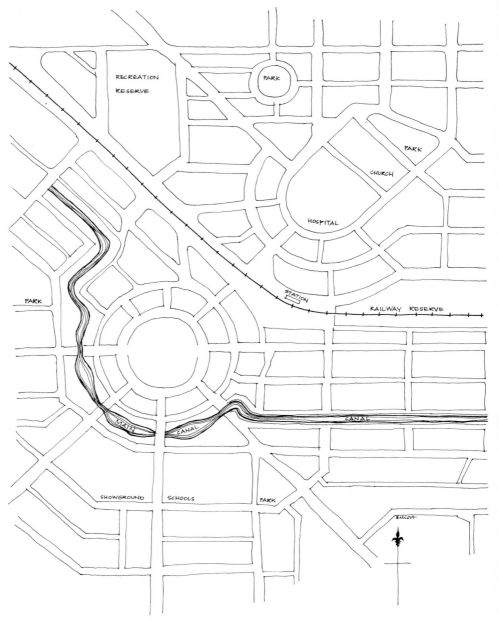

Figure 49. Plan of Griffith, New South Wales, Walter Burley Griffin

*Planning theories in the
twentieth century: a story
of successive imports*

in Australia over the past quarter of a century all came under the influence of
Reilly, Abercrombie, Adams and Osborne. It is only in the past two years that
academics of other than British origin have been appointed to head the architecture
and planning schools in Australia.

The acceptance of land use planning as a function of State Government
began with the promotion of Bills of various kinds in each of the states between
1916 and 1920. Particularly good progress was made in Victoria, at least in the
Metropolitan area. A Metropolitan Town Planning Commission was established
in 1922 and produced an admirable report in 1929.[3] The contents of the foreword
to the report are timeless and worthy of reproduction.

> The unmistakable tendency of cities to increase rapidly in population and
> expansiveness should forcibly impress upon all legislators and administrators the
> desirability of taking steps in due time to provide for the necessities of the future.
> The lessons to be learnt from the absence of such a policy may be found in the
> extensive and costly reconstruction schemes which have taken place in many cities.
> It is now generally realised that if a city is to serve best its true functions it must
> have guidance and control in development according to a well-considered plan. In
> this way only can economy in public expenditure as well as efficiency and comfort
> be enjoyed by the various classes of people who constitute its population. Prudent
> expenditure at an opportune time will obviate much larger expenditure in days to
> come. Wise planning in relation to constructive developmental works can provide
> for many future public needs, and, if not exercised, the result is that impassable
> barriers are created which will make it impracticable except at huge cost to furnish
> the community with facilities that can now be predicted as future necessities. The
> endeavours of the Commission have been directed to the formulation of proposals
> which, if carried out gradually, it believes will ensure that the requirements of a
> rapidly growing population are provided for in the most economical manner, and
> with a view to the welfare of people generally. Melbourne, it is believed, is destined
> to become a really great city. It has many noble proportions and outstanding
> advantages, but if the foundations already laid are to have a worthy superstructure
> its future must ever be kept in mind. These considerations have been always before
> the Commission in its work.

It is also interesting to note that the introduction to the Report contained the
extract from John Burns' speech to Parliament already quoted.

Many of the recommendations in the Report, labelled then as urgent, still
await attention. The widening of Bridge Road between Church Street and Hoddle
Street is a good example. Some, like the improvement of Kew junction and the
widening of High Street, St Kilda, have just been completed. An underground
rail loop, now being dug and scheduled for completion by 1980 was proposed in
more or less the same location as now chosen. In the fifty or so years that have
passed since the report was commissioned many desirable projects have become
incapable of implementation or will eventually cost many millions of dollars more
than they would have, had the contents of the report been heeded. The dark clouds
of the depression years drove thoughts of city planning from the minds of politicians
who had more urgent day to day problems to cope with, and by the time prosperity
returned we were on the brink of involvement in another World War. The
Metropolitan Town Planning Commission Report of 1929 was shelved and not
taken down again until after 1940.

During the war years in Britain a number of reports were produced that had a far-reaching effect on the growth and development of planning activity there. The Town and Country Planning Act of 1932 was a solid, conservative measure, reasonably well attuned to the climate of its time, but, during the war, as so often happens in times of stress, the people raised their sights and started to look for a better urban environment. The blitz highlighted the extent of blight. There is little that is so visually sad and sorbid as an area of 19th century industrial housing with its entrails showing. The word 'overspill' crept into planning vocabulary accompanied by thoughts of new cities and a brave new world.

Between 1940 and 1942 the Barlow,[4] Scott[5] and Uthwatt Reports[6] were produced and dealt with the distribution of industrial population, the use of land in rural areas and the problems of compensation and betterment. The New Towns Committee, under Lord Reith, produced reports that set the scene for an accelerated New Towns program carried out under the New Towns Act of 1946. A spate of new Planning Acts emerged, culminating in the Town and Country Planning Act of 1947. As in earlier days, the effect was felt in Australia and even the Commonwealth Government was impelled to participate. In 1944 the State Premiers met with Prime Minister Chifley and resolved to attack the problem of planning and development on a regional basis. It is not insignificant that a Labour Government was in power at Federal level at the time. A concentration of power in Federal Government hands combined with a system of regional instead of State control has deep roots in Labour policy.

In Victoria, a State Regional Boundaries Committee recommended that 'to facilitate the investigation of resources and the planning of future development' the State be divided into thirteen regions. Reports were eventually prepared for all except the most difficult and important one based on Port Phillip Bay, but unfortunately no regional plans emerged and the reports have not been updated.

Obviously the States saw the threat to their position in developing the regional concept. Even today we do not develop regional capitals. Instead we call them 'growth centres'.

As a further development in Victoria, the Town and Country Planning Act of 1944 was made law. Comparable legislation was enacted in the other States about the same time or a little later.

Generally speaking the early post war legislation to regulate planning in Australia was sound but it was permissive – it required no authority to do anything – it only enabled them to do so if they wished. The result, as one might expect, was patchy. Yet the stage was set and the post-war years have seen steady but assured progress in the area of town and regional planning and an increasing sophistication in techniques. We have progressed from the planning scheme era, characterised here as in the United Kingdom by two-dimensional zoning plans, to the level of Strategy Plans, Action Plans and Statements of Planning Policy. There have been some splendid achievements on the way. The nettle of Canberra, a mockery of a National Capital with a resident population of 15 156 in 1947, was grasped by Prime Minister Robert Menzies who created the National Capital Development Commission in 1957 and gave it the power and the assurance of funds on a continuing basis to plan, develop and construct the city of Canberra as the National Capital of the Commonwealth. In less than 20 years, under the control of the National Capital Development Commission, driven by Sir John Overall, Canberra lost its media-promoted image of a 'good sheep station spoiled' and has

*Planning theories in the
twentieth century: a story
of successive imports*

become a thriving regional 'growth centre' with a population of 140 966 in 1971.
It is undoubtedly one of the most outstanding examples of planned development
in the world. Its principal exports – administration and education – are sure-fire
bases for growth. The problem now with Canberra is not to promote its growth
but to regulate it. As the urban area of the National Capital spreads towards its
statutory boundaries, the vultures sit in the paddocks and on the fences over the
border in New South Wales awaiting the feast of unearned increment.

All the planning authorities responsible for the major metropolitan regions
in Australia have, in recent years looked at the various alternatives for their
future growth. The work done by the Melbourne and Metropolitan Board of
Works, the Town and Country Planning Board of Victoria and the State Planning
Authority in South Australia are typical of the sort of exercise carried out by
Metropolitan Regional Planning Authorities in Australia during the past ten years.
The recent work done in Melbourne by the Town and Country Planning Board of
Victoria and the Melbourne and Metropolitan Board of Works arose out of a
letter addressed by the Minister for Local Government, the Hon. R. G. Hamer,
to the Town and Country Planning Board on 3 May 1966. The Minister forwarded
a copy of his letter to the Town and Country Planning Board to the Melbourne
and Metropolitan Board of Works asking them to consider the same matter and
to furnish considered views. Basically the Minister was seeking answers to three
questions. Firstly, what was the most desirable shape and nature of the urban
community of Melbourne in the future; secondly, what was the most suitable
method of planning and regulating the future growth of the metropolis; and thirdly,
what was the most suitable authority or authorities to carry out such planning
supervision?

In the present context, two paragraphs from the Minister's letter are of
particular interest. Having said that the metropolis of Melbourne was tending
to grow in an easterly and south easterly direction the Minister went on to say:

> Such a widely dispersed metropolis, unless carefully planned, at once raises a threat
> to the surrounding countryside. This will require special attention. In addition,
> nobody could happily contemplate a future metropolis of seemingly endless
> suburbia spreading outwards indifferently. It must be strongly emphasised that future
> planning should take full account of the surrounding countryside as a vital part of
> the metropolitan environment.

> Accordingly, I would urge the Board to give particular attention to the possibility
> of urban decentralisation with provision for 'satellite' towns of, say, 100 000 or
> even greater population, each based on a sizeable industrial and commercial area
> and separated from the existing metropolis, and from each other, by broad tracts
> of open country, natural parkland and recreation space.

Here, indeed, is a clear indication of the way in which the mind of the
responsible Minister was working in relation to the future shape and growth of
Melbourne. The basic concept was the development of garden suburbs, new towns
and green belts but with no apparent awareness of potential conflict with the then
current policy of State-wide decentralisation.

In response to the Minister's letter the Town and Country Planning Board,
as one might have expected, quite properly devoted the major part of its work
to a consideration of the organisation and administration under which effective

planning could be carried out. The results of their work are contained in a document entitled 'Organisation for strategic planning'.[7] The Melbourne and Metropolitan Board of Works, on the other hand, again quite understandably, were far
more concerned with the actual physical form the city might take and in particular
were concerned to indicate the extent of the area over which they thought planning
control ought to be extended, presumably under their direction. On this latter issue
they failed to achieve their objective. They determined a reasonable and potentially
acceptable extension of the metropolitan regional planning boundaries and when
consulted sensibly influenced the determination of the boundary of the Melbourne
Statistical Division to make both co-incidental. The State Government promptly
removed many of the benefits that would have resulted from this co-operative
action between the Board and the responsible Federal authority by creating the
Western Port Regional Planning Authority to control the Mornington Peninsula.
Further undesirable fragmentation of control over land use is at present being
contemplated by the State Government through the creation of a separate regional
authority for the Yarra Valley and the Dandenong Ranges. At the present time,
in the metropolitan region around Melbourne, planning control is shared by the
Melbourne and Metropolitan Board of Works, the Western Port Regional Planning
Authority, the Geelong Regional Planning Authority and a host of municipal
councils. Many other organisations like the Environment Protection Authority and
the Land Conservation Council have their fingers in the planning pie.

The Town and Country Planning Board and the State Planning Council have
the task of co-ordinating activity by a large number of competing and often
conflicting authorities. With the emergence of strong initiatives at Federal level it
seems very necessary that a strong and outward looking organisation at State level
should exist and that there should be a unified, not fragmented control at regional
level. A unified regional policy and a sensible use of scarce, skilled manpower
both seem essential if we are to maintain and improve the environment in our
spreading urban areas.

The Melbourne and Metropolitan Board of Works in the document *The
future growth of Melbourne*[8] considered three main methods of coping with future
development. These were: controlled outward growth (Figure 50); metropolitan
satellite city growth (Figure 51); and the development of growth corridors (Figure
52). They also looked at the effect of redirected growth to the north and the west
and the satellite growth in combination with controlled peripheral growth. In the
event the Board's preferred solution was a combination of growth corridors,
redirected growth and some limited satellite town development (Figure 53). This
was described as the most reasonable and practicable solution. Growth corridors
were seen as being the most flexible and adaptable to a situation where minimum
redevelopment occurred. The Board certainly kept its options open. The whole
exercise was a salutary illustration of the need to be aware that sound professional
advice is sometimes distorted or even discarded for political reasons.

The South Australian State Planning Authority in a brief pamphlet entitled
Adelaide 2000 – the alternatives,[9] in October 1969, looked at six alternatives. The
first (Figure 54) was to let the city sprawl and scatter. That they should have even
considered that this was a viable alternative which needed to be paraded before the
public is, in itself, interesting. It is perhaps indicative of how shallow are the roots
of the idea that land use in Australia should be controlled at all by government.

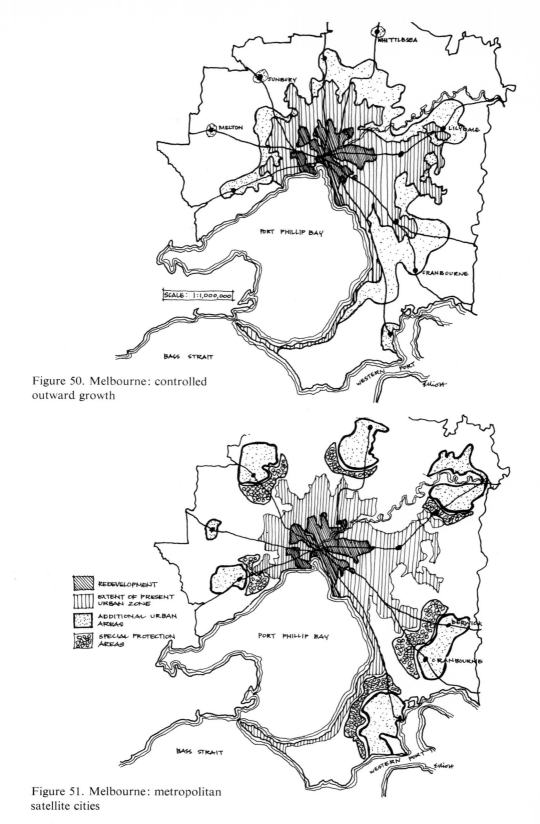

Figure 50. Melbourne: controlled
outward growth

REDEVELOPMENT
EXTENT OF PRESENT
URBAN ZONE
ADDITIONAL URBAN
AREAS
SPECIAL PROTECTION
AREAS

Figure 51. Melbourne: metropolitan
satellite cities

207

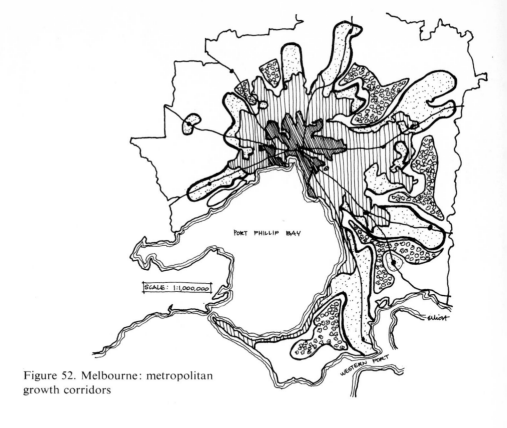

Figure 52. Melbourne: metropolitan
growth corridors

The second alternative (Figure 55) considered was decentralisation on a State-wide basis with substantial towns being developed as far afield as Ceduna, Port Lincoln, Port Pirie, Port Augusta, Renmark and Mount Gambier. The third alternative (Figure 56) was a more familiar one involving a series of satellite towns developed in locations separate from the metropolitan area; each town having its own residential, industrial and shopping areas and designed for a population of at least 100 000. Seven such towns were considered. One was in the mid-north, two in the Barossa Valley, two on the River Murray, one on Lake Alexandrina and one at Victor Harbour, south of Adelaide. The fourth alternative (Figure 57) was to convert Adelaide to a compact multi-storey city. As a practical solution to the problem of growth in metropolitan Adelaide this seemed no more acceptable than the idea of letting the city sprawl and scatter in a formless way. The State Planning Authority next looked at the possibility of creating twin cities (Figure 58) with a new one of lesser order to the south of Adelaide. In the final analysis the preferred solution was an extension of Adelaide by way of the addition of 'districts' each of which would be comparable to Elizabeth New Town or larger (Figure 59). The hope was that there would be a combination of the advantages of living in a small town and of living in close contact with a highly centralised and highly specialised city centre. This eminently sensible decision has since been diluted by the decision to develop one of the satellite cities away from the metropolitan complex. Throughout the development of planning theory and practice in Australia the main failing has been to spread manpower and material resources too thinly.

208

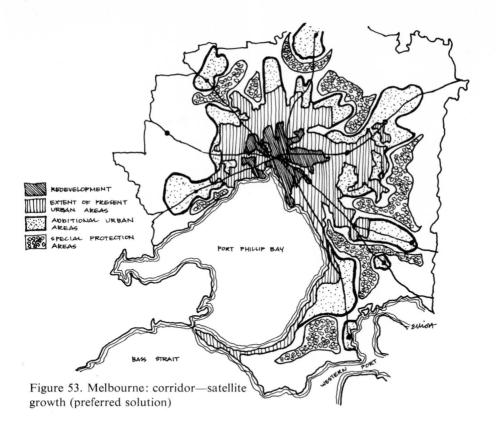

Figure 53. Melbourne: corridor—satellite
growth (preferred solution)

One of the purposes of the pamphlet was to stimulate public debate on the
issue of the future of Adelaide. This it did and it provoked some very interesting
reactions. The first was a feeling that urgent action ought to be taken to control
continued population growth in Adelaide because there was evidence that growth
on the scale envisaged – a doubling of city population in 30 years – would be
harmful not only to the environment but also to the economy. It was suggested
quite strongly that, as an alternative, Adelaide should be limited in size to 1 500 000
and that additional cities of at least 250 000 population should be built sufficiently
far from Adelaide to ensure their separate existence and development. In response
to this suggestion the new town of Monarto, near Murray Bridge, has been
commenced. It may yet prove to be too ambitious a project when put into a
national context and ranged side by side with other growth centres like Canberra
and Albury-Wodonga.

All the capital cities in Australia seem to have opted for corridors or linear
growth as a means of coping with urban expansion. It is seriously to be hoped that
the concept has not been seized upon by the decision makers as a rationalisation
of the present land use chaos that exists along every arterial route leading into
our capital cities.

All the plans for the various capital cities, when analysed, look good and
interesting. Yet, somehow, there is no joy or excitement in them.

Perhaps the task of remodelling our existing cities is too hard. Certain it is
that the job is difficult, often tedious and frustrating and far less satisfying than
work on new towns on virgin sites. However, the greatest challenge and most

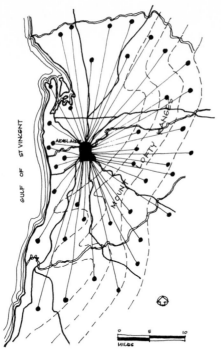

Figure 54. Adelaide 2000—sprawl
and scatter

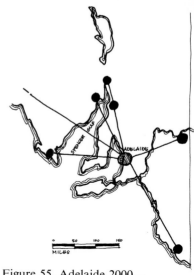

Figure 55. Adelaide 2000—
decentralised

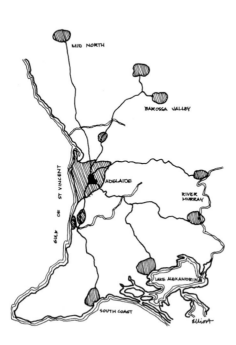

Figure 56. Adelaide 2000—satellite towns

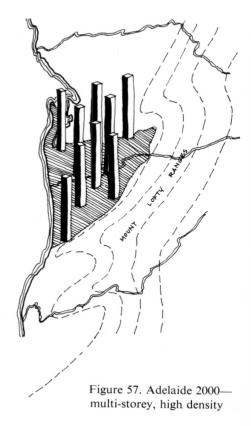

Figure 57. Adelaide 2000—
multi-storey, high density

210

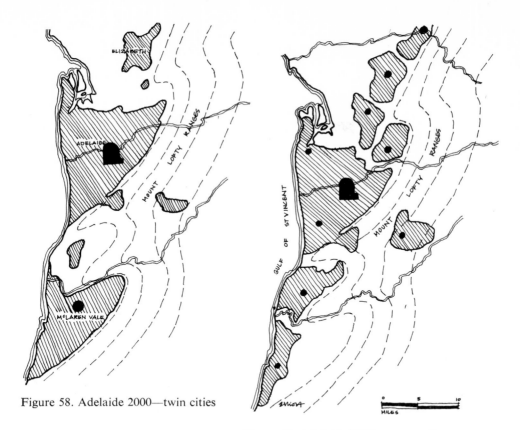

Figure 58. Adelaide 2000—twin cities

Figure 59. Adelaide 2000—metropolitan districts (preferred solution)

important task that faces us today is not to create more Canberras, desirable though that may be. It is to make our existing urban areas more satisfying and desirable places to live in. It is wrong for all the interest to focus on the new growth centres in New South Wales, at Albury-Wodonga on the border of Victoria and New South Wales, at Geelong some 60 kilometres from Melbourne and at Monarto in South Australia at the expense of our present cities.

I suspect one can trace the reason for this interest in new centres and in decentralisation to a deep feeling that city growth is evil and that instead we should seek to decentralise and to spread our industry and population. The desire to decentralise is a clear reflection of a feeling of guilt about the conditions in the urban concentrations that we have created in the south-eastern corner of the continent and about the vastness of the land we control and its relative emptiness. For long there has been a nagging feeling that we must populate or perish, tame the bush and fill the space with towns and people. Even when we embark on a worthwhile exercise of planning and building additions to the urban complex in a metropolitan region it seems necessary – or is deemed so to be by those concerned – to dub them as satellite cities or new towns. Melton and Sunbury in Victoria are good examples. They are 23 kilometres and 37 kilometres respectively from Melbourne. When and if built, they will be integral parts of the metropolitan complex. Elizabeth New Town, 27 kilometres north of Adelaide is as much a part of Adelaide as Frankston is of Melbourne. Melton and Sunbury, when completed will be artificially fostered extensions of the urban concentration of Melbourne.

211

Decentralisation has been a talisman to which the politicians have long held but, despite all the protestations, the statistics speak their message loud and clear. Between 1961 and 1966 the population of Australia and Victoria grew by just under 10.0 per cent. Between 1966 and 1971 the population of Australia grew by 10.0 per cent and that of Victoria by 8.8 per cent. Between 1961 and 1966 the population of New South Wales grew by 8.1 per cent. During the same period the population of Sydney grew by 12.0 per cent. Between 1966 and 1971 the population of New South Wales grew by 8.6 per cent and the population of Sydney grew by 11.0 per cent. Between 1961 and 1966 the population of the capitals of all the States and Territories grew by 14.0 per cent whereas in the rest of Australia the population increased by only 4.7 per cent. In Victoria the contrast was equally noticeable: Melbourne increased by 13.5 per cent, the rest of the State by 3.5 per cent. In Victoria, between 1961 and 1966, only 4 provincial centres with a population of more than 10 000 in 1961 grew faster than Melbourne: these were Geelong with 14.5 per cent increase in the 5 years, Morwell and Traralgon with a 14.0 per cent increase and Shepparton with a surprising and exciting figure of 28.9 per cent. However to put these figures and places in perspective we must remember that for every new face these growing places share there were over 10 new faces in Melbourne. The situation between the census years of 1966 and 1971 in Victoria was that Victoria's population increased by 8.8 per cent and Melbourne's population increased by 13.3 per cent. During this period not one provincial centre in Victoria with a population of over 10 000 in 1966 grew faster than Melbourne.

In New South Wales between 1966 and 1971 a few places grew faster than Sydney. They were Albury (17.1 per cent increase in the 5 years), Armidale (18.1 per cent), Dubbo (13.7 per cent), Gosford-Wyong (36.7 per cent), Tamworth (19.7 per cent), Taree (12.5 per cent), and Wollongong (14.6 per cent) and of these, Gosford and Wollongong are essentially a part of the Sydney megalopolis.

In 1966, 82.9 per cent of Australians lived in towns and cities. By 1971 this figure had increased to 85.6 per cent. In Victoria 82.6 per cent of the total population lives in places with the population in excess of 5000 people. The trend is towards increasing urbanisation. The fundamental fact underlying the present situation is that the capital cities are taking an ever increasing share of the population of the States and the degree of unbalance in the distribution of the population is increasing. In 1954 Melbourne had 62.1 per cent of Victoria's population; in 1961 it had 63.4 per cent, in 1966 over 65.5 per cent and by 1971 this figure had risen to 68.2 per cent. At this pattern Melbourne will have 80 per cent of the State population by the end of the century and it has been forecast that by then the population of the metropolitan region could be between 4.9 and 5.6 million people. Should this total not be reached, and currently there are reasons to assume that it may not be, it is unlikely materially to affect the proportion opting to live in Melbourne.

If we are trying, by a decentralisation policy, to avoid having six out of every eight Australians consciously choosing the advantages of metropolitan living by the year 2000 then we are seeking the impossible. No matter how vigorously a decentralisation policy is pursued throughout Australia, if past records and trends are any guide, it will have little effect on the growth of the capital cities. To cope with the anticipated growth of Melbourne alone would require the equivalent of a British New Town to be built each 3-5 years. Apart from the magnitude of

Planning theories in the
twentieth century: a story
of successive imports

the task there is every reason why people should wish to come and live in metropolitan regions. Young people leave provincial centres because they will lack
opportunities if they stay there. Fundamentally the people who leave the provincial
centres go to the metropolitan centres in order to provide themselves with a
wider choice of some kind. Many country towns find themselves in a descending
spiral. A reduction in country population lowers the standards of services capable
of being maintained for the smaller number of people remaining. The development
of larger and more sophisticated machinery on farms reduces the need not only for
farm labour but also for the handyman in the country town. If a part breaks
on a machine, the specialised services of a city based organisation are often necessary. Improvements in transport further reduce dependence on local services. In
England, in the 18th and 19th century during the transport revolution, the market
village at eight kilometre intervals was replaced by the market town at 30 kilometre
intervals. Now the city is sucking the heart out of the market towns and the market
town in Australia is much more vulnerable than its counterpart in the United
Kingdom.

Each new resident establishing in a city enlarges the choice of goods and services
available to his neighbours and increases the magnetism of the city for the friends
whose life in the country is the poorer for his departure. Generally speaking the
larger the city the more rapid its sustained growth is likely to continue and the
more certain it is that – given a free choice – most people will continue to find
that the growth of freedom in the cities more than compensates for the almost
universal growth of congestion and confusion and pollution with size.

Fundamentally the problem is one of unbalanced development; the metropolis
is congested and inefficient, and the people living outside the cities are deprived
of many facilities regarded as essential to a full life in the modern world. Decentralisation of the kind that involved the artificial support of a large number of small
places has not worked and we are therefore turning our efforts towards a policy
of recentralisation under which it is hoped to devise a pattern of settlement so that
everyone, everywhere has reasonable access to centres providing for a wide range
of interests. Such cities will need to be substantial in size, probably between a
quarter and a half-million, if they are to offer an adequate choice of goods and
services to support anything like what has come to be thought of as a full life
in a complex modern society. The problem is that to create such centres takes great
investment, enormous effort and the use of scarce skills. The result may well
be that our existing cities where most people live will continue to be neglected.
Australia's metropolitan centres, especially Melbourne and Sydney, are at present
growing so fast that is extremely difficult and expensive to solve their backlog
of physical and social problems while providing at the same time for the demands
of growth. That is why the easing of the pressure of growth by diverting some of
it to other potentially large centres would be sound policy. Yet we must not neglect
the replanning and redevelopment of our existing centres, slow and tedious though
it may be. It is relatively easy to divert attention from pressing circulation and land-
use problems to glamorous 'new town' projects in Berwick, Sunbury, Melton,
etc. These are not new towns in the accepted sense – they are planned extensions
of the metropolitan regions and their establishment should have an appopriate
infra-structure including a conscious assessment of their impact on the pattern of
movement and on the form and growth of the central business district. To establish

a Melton or a Sunbury without an expressed regional policy on such fundamental matters as these is not good planning. It is window dressing.

We should consider carefully, too, before we embark on a policy of expanded provincial towns. It should not be forgotten that a resident in a new town eighty kilometres or so from London has a highly sophisticated public transport system available to him. Also, although a town may be a satellite of London, a resident of it only has to look over his shoulder and Birmingham is not far away. The residents of the expanded towns of Runcorn and Warrington have a choice of Liverpool or Manchester. A resident in an expanded town on the fringe of a metropolitan region in Australia is in a very different situation.

As an observer of town planning affairs over a period of some forty years in various parts of the world I form the view that the basic dislike of the big city relates to the change in its texture and grain as it grows. Big cities tend to become impersonal because their component parts become too large for comprehension and too coarse to include those elements which relate directly to individuals – the smaller shop that gives a personal service and the small-scale specialised service trade. Their disappearance from the city, where they traditionally belong, is due to rents being forced up by competition from large, highly capitalised, high turnover and high profit organisations. The effect on the appearance of the city is equally disastrous. Magnificent cathedrals are dwarfed by monstrous slabs; impersonal stores which are little more than massive vending machines replace establishments where a delicate interchange between proprietor and customers used to occur.

I believe that people will continue to congregate together in cities, but somehow we must devise monetary and physical controls which will ensure that large numbers and great extent do not destroy the human scale of cities. The cities will spread in linear or in cellular pattern but we should seek to avoid gigantism in any component part. City centres, for example should be compact, accessible, comprehensible and on a pedestrian scale. City parks should be urban and intimate, shopping centres should not be a huddle of buildings amidst vast car parks. Residential areas should not be so big that mono-cultures develop. We should assist the expansion of those provincial centres that have or can be given a basis for future survival before contemplating the establishment of new growth centres and, finally, we should develop a national planning strategy that transcends and, if need be, disregards State boundaries.

Notes

1. READE, CHARLES C. *Report by the Government Town Planner: planning and development of towns, cities in South Australia*. Adelaide, Government Printer, 1919, p. 12.
2. SULMAN, JOHN. *Town planning in Australia*. Sydney, Government Printer of New South Wales, 1921.
3. Victoria. Metropolitan Town Planning Commission. *Report*, 1929, p. 13.
4. Great Britain. Committee on Land Utilisation in Rural Areas. Chairman: Sir Leslie Scott. *Report*. London, HMSO, 1942, Cmd 6378.
5. Great Britain. Royal Commissions. Distribution of the industrial population. Chairman: Sir Montague Barlow. *Report*. London, HMSO, 1940, Cmd 6153.
6. Great Britain. Ministry of Works. Expert Committee on Compensation and Betterment. Chairman: Sir Augustus A. Uthwatt. *Final Report* London, HMSO, 1942, Cmd 6386.

Planning theories in the
twentieth century: a story
of successive imports

7. Victoria. Town and Country Planning Board. *Organisation for strategic planning: a report to the Minister for Local Government in response to his letter of 3 May 1966 on future growth of Melbourne.* Melbourne, 1967.
8. Melbourne and Metropolitan Board of Works. *The future growth of Melbourne: a report to the Minister for Local Government on Melbourne's future growth and its planning administration.* Melbourne, 1967.
9. South Australian State Planning Authority. *Adelaide 2000 – the alternatives.* Adelaide, Government Printer, October 1969.

Further reading

Australia. National Capital Development Commission. *Tomorrow's Canberra: growth and change.* Canberra, Australian National University Press, 1970.

Encylopedia of urban planning. New York, McGraw-Hill, 1974.

HARRISON, PETER. Approach to a metropolitan plan. *Architecture in Australia.* 57(4):630–34, August 1968.

KEEBLE, LEWIS. *Principles and practice of town and country planning.* London, Estates Gazette Limited, 4th edn. 1969, 1972.

KUZELKA, ROBERT D. *The tiger's back: a report on Australian organisations for metropolitan planning administration.* [Sydney], Planning Research Centre, University of Sydney, 1969.

LEDGAR, FREDERICK W. Town and country planning in Victoria. *Law Review.* 2(3):283–302, 1960.

Melbourne and Metropolitan Board of Works. *Planning policies for the Melbourne metropolitan region.* Melbourne, 1971.

MORRISON, IAN. Linear growth planning. *A.P.I. Journal.* 8(1), 1970.

STRETTON, HUGH. *Ideas for Australian cities.* North Adelaide, The Author, 1970.

*Philip Cox**

The growth and decay
of an Australian
vernacular architecture

'The vernacular' is defined in the *Oxford Dictionary*[1] as 'that which writes, uses or speaks the native or indigenous language of a country or district'. The word was first applied to architecture in 1857, when Sir George Gilbert Scott used it in his work *Secular and domestic architecture* in reference to rural buildings.[2] Since then, the word has come into general use to describe the whole sphere of architecture other than what is called 'high style' architecture. In this paper, the word will be used for buildings and art forms directly related to a European-based culture influenced by Asia, rather than by the indigenous Aboriginal culture of Australia, although some techniques used by the Aboriginals were adopted by the Europeans.

Vernacular architecture has not been recognised as a distinct field of study until recently. Older books and articles on vernacular architecture generally are widely scattered and this condition exists to a marked extent today. The houses and other buildings of the farmer, cottager, rancher or craftsman do not figure in the histories of architecture. This lack of literary, and therefore official, recognition has made them especially vulnerable, likely to disappear or be destroyed by alteration: this condition is world wide. Architectural history has been mainly concerned with the study of monuments and monumental buildings. It has followed the rise and fall of one civilisation after another through the study of conscious works of art and architecture, created by men of design talent, sometimes by men of genius, who have captured the spirit of their times. It is this architecture that is commonly referred to as 'high style' architecture, and it represents a very small part of the built environment. Most buildings have been vernacular buildings.

The bulk of the built environment has always been made up of the houses and buildings that service common people. In the past, the building of vernacular structures was a synthesis between man and the environment, where the occupier or user was very much a part of the design process, and not as he is today in most circumstances, a consumer. The vernacular process was the projection of common ideals within a community, expressed in physical terms, through a profound physical and aesthetic understanding of the materials; and the assemblage of those materials into a basic architecture providing shelter according to local need (Figure 60).

The basic need for the first Europeans for building in Australia was shelter from, what was for them, a hostile climate. These settlers were used to a more temperate European climate, in marked contrast with the Aboriginal tribes who saw no need for established settlement or built form, excepting a bark shelter or leafy mia-mia which gave them all the protection they needed. To them, the climate was mild; except for some skins in the winter months, little clothing was used at all.

* Philip Cox, architect, planner and author is in private practice with Philip Cox, Storey and Partners Pty Ltd.

The need for shelter was the first part of the process: the next was the establishment of a house form and this was generally made by the use of existing models,
varied to suit the particular situation. The model used in Australia was the English
Georgian farmhouse as evolved after centuries of refinement, coupled with the
imagery and experience gained by the adaptation of native architecture in India
and other British colonies in the more tropical zones. The builder and client held
a shared image of the house and the form of structure, and the question of size
was governed by availability of materials and money. In the examples of vernacular
architecture of the early part of the 19th century, there was little striving for
conscious aesthetic results; rather, the Georgian model was adopted for reasons of
familiarity, climate, economy and building technique. The original English Georgian
model was the result of many generations of work; it was clear and concise, easy
to build, flexible in its arrangement and was a synthesis between the requirements of
the proprietor and the technology of the people who built it.

When the first settlers arrived, the building materials to hand at first seemed
limited. There was clay in abundance for the moulding of bricks, or for the use in
pisé or adobe construction. There was plenty of timber, but the hardwoods were
hard and difficult to work. There was stone, which had to be quarried and worked,
and this was too difficult. There were the inferior materials such as sticks, bark,
leaves, straw, palm fronds and reeds, which the Aboriginals used in their temporary
structures. On the ships there were sail cloth, canvas and paper. These were the
ingredients of the first Australian vernacular buildings.

Captain Arthur Phillip arrived with Sydney's first prefabricated building[3] – one
designed by Jeffrey Wyatt, later to become Sir Jeffrey Wyatville, decorator and
architect to George IV. It was a five-roomed timber house using panel construction,
built by a contractor called Smith in St George Field, London and was similar to
the standard prefabricated cottages used in India. It proved most unsatisfactory,
as it leaked and let the wind in; however it had been easy to obtain and was
quickly erected without much skill. Apart from this, the first houses were an array
of wattle and bark huts covered with bark roofs or split timber shingles from the
casuarina, or with the reed which grew along the river banks. The word 'wattle'
was soon attached to the acacia because its flexible branches and twigs could be
wattled or woven for wall construction and then covered with clay pug for water-
proofing.

Timber was not used initially to the extent that it was used in the colonisation
of the Americas, mainly because the most common tree around Port Jackson was
the Sydney Apple or red gum (*Angophora costata*), one of whose peculiarities is
that the centre or heart of the log is usually decayed, leaving only a shell of usable
timber.

However, huts were erected from the she-oak (*Casuarina*), so called because of
its resemblance to the American live-oak. The early timber huts were 4m x 3m in
plan and four posts about three metres long were set directly into the ground to the
depth of about a metre. The posts were squared above the ground. A groove
about 25 mm deep was chiselled into the length of each flat face, and the tops
of the posts were tenoned to fit into mortices cut in a plate running around the
top. Trimming pieces for the heads of doorways and the tops and bottoms of
window openings were morticed and tenoned, and then pegged with wooden
dowels into the posts. The roof was pitched and usually hipped and formed from

217

Figure 60. The country towns in Australia with their wide verandahs gave a distinctively national character as well as forming the functional aspect of shelter from sun and tropical downpours of rain.

Figure 61. Vernacular timber cottage.

sapling rafters in pairs leaning against each other onto a ridge piece at the apex, checked and pegged to the plate at the eaves. Having established the central roof frames, slimmer saplings were run transversely across the rafters and either lashed with cord, or pegged to them, to support the thatching or bark which formed the roof cover. The infill of the structural wall frames was an array of materials, commonly cabbage-tree palm cut to appropriate lengths, or saplings with their ends adzed and shaped so that they slipped horizontally into the grooves between the posts. The hut could be left in this condition, but as this was draughty, clay was pugged between the cracks. The doors to the huts were framed and ledged and hung sometimes on leather hinges, with a lock constructed from a timber latch-piece. The windows lacked glass, and were shuttered with a series of vertical timbers or with casement shutters made like doors, or with thin wattles woven into a lattice.

The floor of this building was clay trampled to a smooth finish, and the walls were whitewashed with a mixture of white pipe-clay. In many cases the buildings were even cruder affairs – especially the convict shelters. Few casuarina trees grew in areas to which they were given access, and so their huts were usually wattle and daub.

One of the reasons for founding the colony was the hope of supplying timber suitable for naval purposes. Univeral disappointment was experienced, as revealed in the writings of members of the First Fleet '. . . the timber well described in Captain Cook's voyage', said Phillip '. . . but unfortunately it has one very bad quality, which puts it to great inconvenience; I mean the large gum tree which splits and warps'. Surgeon White added his experience with timber '. . . how any kind of house . . . can be raised up, the timber being so very bad, it is impossible to determine'. The first buildings were therefore rude affairs; from the early illustrations of Sydney Cove, they had the appearance of crude rural buildings resembling the English model. They were all rectangular structures, with simple fenestration patterns arranged in the way children do when they draw houses: central door with flanking windows. Because of the scarcity of limestone and the laborious collection of oyster shells for lime burning, bricks were bedded in mud, with grass or reed reinforcement. The sudden torrential downpours of rain in Sydney required their mud walls to be extra thick, so that when the mud was washed out structural failure would not follow.

As new lands and better timber were discovered in the Pennant Hills district, on the North Shore and in the Hawkesbury Valley, timber was more universally used, especially after the discovery of cedar in 1790 by Watkin Tench. Timber was cheaper to use in construction than wet materials, so structures could be built quickly without much expert labour.

Bush or slab huts were built entirely of wood in the following manner: four posts were sunk into the ground to a depth varying with the height and size of the building. These supported long beams and wall plates grooved on the underside; immediately below them wood sleepers were laid on the ground a little below the surface, grooved like the wall plates on their top surface, forming the main foundations of the building. The sides, wooden walls, were formed of slabs, the ends of which fitted into the grooved plates, the sides were smoothed off at the edge to make them fit close together. On the wall plates, a simple roof was fixed in the usual manner, the covering of which consisted of shingles or of the wiry

grass of the country or the bark of trees, usually of the 'stringy bark'. The bark
was stripped from the trunks in sheets of about two metres by one, and was
fastened to the roof by means of a wooden frame, so constructed as to clasp every
sheet, and thus keep down the whole. The chimneys, which were placed outside
at either end, were also built of wood, and were fortified on the inside with stone,
which was carried sufficiently high to prevent the flames from reaching the outer
slab (Figure 61).

The construction of these primitive buildings varied according to location and
especially the availability of materials (Figures 62, 63). The interiors of some huts
were lathed and plastered for extra comfort; in others, sail-cloth was stretched
across the ceiling or across the battens against the wall.

The English Georgian farmhouse existed for the most part as a plain rectangular building, two storeys high with symmetrically placed chimneys and regular
fenestration pattern. This model was amended in Australia by the addition of a
verandah and the incorporation of a central breezeway from the front door to
the back, providing access to the principal rooms. The fear of fire, the generation
of heat from an open cooking fire in a hot climate, and the use of convict servants
generally caused the kitchen and servant block to be detached and connected to the
house by a covered way. This pattern or model was largely adopted by the more
affluent land-holders; however, it also became the pattern of hotels and way-side
inns, when the tap-room was located on the ground floor and the accommodation
upstairs. This type of building was widely used in Tasmania, but many examples
can also be seen around Sydney, such as *Robin Hood Farm*, Minto, or the *Settlers
Arms* at St Albans.

By 1815, changes were coming over the penal settlement at Port Jackson.
The town had begun to grow; houses were strung along the bullock lanes and
around the sandstone ridges. The town was acquiring streets cleared of tree stumps,
warehouses, inns, hotels, churches and hospitals and a school – much of this due
to the energy and determination of Macquarie. The early architects, such as
Greenway, Kitchen and Bloodsworth, began to have an impact upon the primitive
architecture which had evolved from the first week of settlement. Theirs was a simple
and noble architecture. *The Rum Hospital* in Macquarie Street has more to do with
British architecture in India and America than it has with the English source model.
Its wide verandahed colonnade is reminiscent of many other 'colonial' examples,
and yet through this influence and in its response to local climate and its use of
local materials, an Australian architecture was evolving. It was simple in plan,
and relied on its materials for its total effect. The adoption of the verandah created
an architecture of high contrast, with deep shadows and sharp accents, where total
form and silhouette were important against the steel blue, almost white Australian
sky.

The bungalow was introduced into Australia at an early stage by the officers
of the army who had served in India, where Macquarie's regiment, for example,
had been stationed. The typical Australian vernacular expanded from this model.
The bungalow was devised in Bengal in India (the word 'Bangla' meaning 'belong-
ing to Bengal' as in 'Bangla-desh'), and generally denoted a single storied dwelling
complete with verandahs and breezeways designed to combat the humid conditions
of that country. The word was often used to refer to a garden pavilion. The
Oxford Dictionary records first use in 1676, in a diary written by Master

Figure 62. Many materials were used in the construction of the rural
vernacular giving rise to a variety of forms.

Figure 63. The vernacular is untaught—it is the natural use of materials
joined together in the simplest possible way.

Streynsham on 25 November of that year when he recorded, 'It was thought fitt . . .
to sett up Bungalls or Hovells . . . for all rich English in the Company's Service as
belong to their Sloops and Vessells'. In 1847, a Mrs Sherwood commented, 'The
Bungalows in India . . . are for the most part . . . built of unbaked bricks and covered
with thatch, having in the centre a hall . . . the whole thing being encompassed by a
verandah'.[4] The word, by this time, was in wide use referring to a single storey
dwelling with pitch hip roof with verandahs and porches. *Horsely Park* in New
South Wales is a direct translation of the Indian bungalow and early photographs
of the interior show the dining-room complete with punkas. The plan of *Horsely
Park* is essentially open – something which the Chicago School and Frank Lloyd
Wright took up – with principal rooms accessible to front and rear verandahs,
providing a spacious central living space. Where windows were vulnerable to the
sun, they were equipped with ventilating shutters and additional solid panel
shutters were built within the reveals of the window internally to give extra security
from attacks from natives or bushrangers.

The late examples of Colonial domestic architecture derive from the low squat
bungalow form rather than the two-storey English form direct, although there are
many early examples of bungalow form such as *Elizabeth Farm* (1793-1794),
Claremont Cottage (1822), *Kelvin* (1820), *Glenfield* (1817), which are all verandah
forms. However in the more high style architectural works such as *Rouse Hill*
(1818-1822), *Camden Park* (1833-1835), an official residence such as Government
House, Parramatta (1816), and the city townhouses built by members of the
merchant or land-holding elite, the two-storey English Georgian model was used.

The country homestead became the main stream of the vernacular process
by its very nature, and included all craft activities which are exclusively associated
with Australian culture. The outbuildings of the country homestead became the
vehicle of bush ingenuity and craft, where feats of workmanship and mastery over
materials were achieved with full understanding of a hostile environment. Throughout Australia one can find the testimony of these structures: they are as important
to an Australian culture as the Gothic cathedrals are to Europe. The great barns
at *Tocal*, Paterson, New South Wales, are some of the finest examples of timber
vernacular to be erected in this country – they are simple in form, reflecting the
hipped roof homestead and supported on giant timber columns (Figure 64).
From the columns, timber elbows for truss supports were attached, carefully
chosen from the branches of trees where the grain followed the required stress
lines. Throughout these buildings there is a display of craftsmanship, ingenuity
and skill. It is possible to see carefully constructed tenoned joints, and timber
pegged to timber. No nails were used in the construction other than in fixing
the shingles and their battens (Figure 65).

Woolsheds were given construction priority in the development of the Australian
grazing property (Figures 66, 67, 68, 69). They take a variety of forms, generally
simple rectangles forming a nave so that a simple roof truss could be repeated.
Sometimes a transept was introduced to allow a wool sorting room, a dispatch
office and sometimes a circular or octagonal building constructed as at *Gostwick*,
Uralla, New South Wales, where the full genius of the bush carpenter was realised
on what must be Australia's most unusual woolshed.

The Australian vernacular was open-ended in its plan; it had to be flexible
in its arrangement and capable of addition. The domestic plan generally resulted

Figure 64. Some of the most important timber vernacular buildings can be seen at *Tocal*, Paterson, New South Wales.

Figure 65. The honed timber usage of framework in this shelter can easily be appreciated.

Figure 66. Woolshed, western New South Wales. The hip-roof form which became the usual vocabulary homestead architecture was also used in outbuildings. These unite with the landscape and give the appearance of forming man-made hills.

Figure 67. Woolshed, *Kinchega*, New South Wales, near Menindee.

Figure 68. Woolsheds, *Midkin*, Moree, New South Wales. The vernacular architecture is low-lying organic with stony horizontal emphasis. The early woolsheds were mostly constructed of timber generally using round timber construction.

Figure 69. Woolshed, *Tottinglon*, Victoria. The internal spaces of the woolsheds express structural honesty and create the same mood as many Gothic structures.

in a four-room cottage with central hall, with a verandah on at least three sides. When more rooms were required, the verandah form was extended. *Nindooinbah* in Queensland is a good example of continuous growth from an original four-room cell, developed into a multitude of rooms connected by verandahs of varying dimensions to form a semi-enclosed courtyard space.

In Queensland, the vernacular took on a different appearance with the development of the stilt form. Why this was so nobody is sure. Certainly the Melanesian Islands home of the indentured Kanaka labour was customarily built in this form, and the same type of house can be seen from Papua New Guinea to Japan in traditional house forms. Perhaps the excessive humidity, the fear of white ants which like dark foundations, and the need for drying areas in a climate which is unpredictable, forced the early Queensland builders to build up in the air. The first buildings in Queensland were the typical verandahed bungalow types on ground. The elevated house does not appear until the 1860s, after which time it became common. Few other variations took place in Australia. The Georgian high-style architecture took a more 'Italianate' or Mediterranean overtone in South Australia by adopting solid brick arcades in lieu of the more slender verandah. Cellar rooms provided alternative summer-time accommodation. These features are attributable to the hot dry climate of that State.

The vernacular architecture of Australia became universally accepted by the 1860s; it was the model observed by all. It has that quality to which Amos Rapoport refers in *House Form and Culture*:

> Another characterstic of vernacular is its additive quality, its specialised, open ended nature, so different from the closed, final form typical of most high style design. It is this quality that enables vernacular buildings to accept changes and additions which would visually and conceptually destroy a high style design.[5]

This is essentially true of Australian homesteads, which in many cases have been progressively built over a century, starting from a rude timber hut, adding extra rooms as necessity arose with increased children or staff, often reflecting ecomonic conditions through materials. Homesteads like *Lowlands* in Western Australia show this development clearly, and *Coochin* in Queensland, where a series of hip roof pavilions are linked with verandahs to form an amazing homestead complex almost like a village. Each addition is characterised by its period and yet submerged by the heavy discipline of structural knowledge and availability of materials to form part of a totality.

The products of the industrial revolution had little effect in the Australian vernacular type except for the more obvious trappings of cast iron columns or verandah railings. Some attempts were made again in the importation of cast iron houses from Europe and prefabricated timber houses from Germany and America, but these were not successful and had little effect on the main stream of thought. The cast iron trappings were added to the old form which had been evolved from Georgian times. Essentially it was the same house, perhaps lighter, more typical in expression.

The kitchen was the area where innovation was first apparent. At *Marwood* in Victoria, the lady of the house wrote in the 1860s:

The kitchen is in the house and fitted up with every convenience, a sink, plate rack, a
complete dresser, clean water led inside with a pipe and a tap, and I intend having
another pipe to carry away the dirty water into a covered drain, and we have
likewise a very complete American cooking stove, which Mr Buckmall has kindly
presented to us, so that the kitchen labour is abridged as much as it can well be.
Perhaps this may seem curious to you writing about such a simple thing as this,
but you must recollect there is scarce a place in the bush that has anything else but
the old fashioned hut kitchen with its great yawning fireplace that will scorch you
to go near it, iron tripods and camp oven to cook in, and water in a dish outside
or standing in a pail, so that our kitchen is an uncommon affair.

The vernacular architecture did not change. The wealthy grazier adopted the
high-style architecture of the city where eclecticism was rampant: Italian architectural style raged with Gothic forms.

As one architect remarked:

We live in an era of Omnium Gatherum, all the world is a museum. To design any
building nowadays is therefore to work under the eye, so to speak, of the Society
of Antiquaries – and all the while their very critics demand, not without contempt,
why it is that our age has not 'a style of its own' like all other ages. How could it
have a style of its own under such circumstances? Or otherwise, let us answer,
it has no style of its own in one sense and has in another a very notable style of
its own, and a very novel one – the style of this miscellaneous connoisseurship –
the style of instinct, superseded by knowledge.

Yet Victorian eclecticism was influenced by the vernacular, especially in the
verandah forms, where great cast iron verandahs surrounded the masonry box
and Italian or Gothic arcades were extended to shade the walls.

Within the century the basic vernacular architecture continued with the same
vocabulary. It is even now difficult to date some of these buildings – they employ
the same vocabulary devised in the first thirty years of settlement (Figure 70).
Homesteads of great size were constructed in Victorian and Edwardian times in
the vernacular manner, almost small villages which included schools, a store, and
housing for the outriders. The First World War saw the destruction of the
vernacular in Australia. The soldiers who fought in the First World War had
fought with the vision of *Australia Felix*, the Australian tradition of owning one's
piece of dirt, and the Government obliged. After the war the big stations were
cut up for soldier settlements and the homesteads which then sprang up had less
to do with the vernacular heritage.

There are many reasons why the vernacular faded. Firstly, the tradition was
broken by the First World War which was an unprecedented opportunity to see
other lands. Tradition was also broken by specialisation in the building industry,
especially with the rise of trade unionism in Australia, which led to the segregation
of house building into trade items of specialist nature, replacing the traditional
home builder who was 'jack of all trades', and versed in the vernacular tradition.
The third reason was the striving for originality for its own sake rather than
expression within the vernacular exercise. When a society becomes dissatisfied with
traditional forms, the vernacular process can no longer work. After the First
World War, traditional forms were jettisoned in Europe and schools such as the
Bauhaus were especially devised to think afresh. Its philosophy was to break with
traditional forms of building. The building industry generally was reorganising

Figure 70. Some of the early pioneer cottages using slab timber have been preserved to remind us of the simplified form of dwelling house which finally evolved into the more sophisticated hip-roof form of the Australian vernacular.

itself, especially with the introduction of new materials such as steel, iron and glass. A new architecture was being created as a result and the image of the world as previously seen before the First World War was shattered. Originality and progress became key words to the new generation, sounding the death-knell of architectural co-ordination, the vernacular and the respect for adjoining people and rights. Codes and restrictions devised by Government took their place.

The problem seems to be that our society has created so much that there is excessive choice, yet in any art or architectural exercise, the limitation and economy of material is an essential ingredient of that art. Today there are too many alternatives, which causes the breakdown of craft, art and tradition. Our architecture generally shows an assorted array of new materials, each competing for dominance with the architectural framework. It is the 'featurism' Robin Boyd described in *The Australian ugliness*. 'Featurism is not directly related to taste, style or fashion... it is the evasion of the bold, realistic, self-evident, straight-forward, honest answer to all questions of design and appearance in man's artificial environment'.[6]

During the period between the two World Wars and after, attempts were made at rationalising the ordinary cottages with luxury images. The simple vernacular forms were abandoned for more complicated plans. In lieu of the simple rectangle with gable, hip roof and verandah, more complicated forms arose, such as 'double fronted' and 'triple fronted' bungalows. Because the plan was complex so was the roof; hip forms and gables were used in a variety of ways – complexity was the required effect which ultimately destroyed the urban form, particularly the street as it had been designed in former times.

For the last twenty years, architects, planners, and sociologists have been concerned with the image and the visual aspects of the urban and suburban environment – its sprawl, its lack of amenity, its lack of urban creation, its complete visual poverty. Yet nothing has been done. There is not a glimmer of hope that our urban sprawl will abate or even modify. Our once well-mannered streets in the western suburbs of Sydney, which were graced with cottages of Queen Anne or Victorian design, of asymmetrical front with verandah and picket fence, are quickly disappearing – and in their place are three-storey walk-ups, built to mini-mum council requirements. This goes on uncontrolled.

The bulk of the built environment is the work of people other than architects and therefore the total blame cannot rest solely with the latter. Society must look at itself, reassess its values, determine what is worthwhile environmentally, and preserve it. In the last ten years, after the first impact of contemporary architectural thought had swept the country, giving rise to many fine buildings of international standard, a group of younger architects were concerned at the loss of the Australian image as they understood it. They were worried by the steel and glass boxes which appeared unsatisfactory from a climatic and visual point of view. They were con-cerned with the Australian heritage, and the loss of that heritage through neglect or destruction – it was about that time the National Trust movement started in Australia. These architects were concerned with a more organic architecture than the international school offered – they were interested in using timber and bricks in an unconscious way so the materials could be appreciated for their own sake. They were influenced by the vernacular forms of Australian architecture, particularly the honest simple structural expressions of barns and farm buildings in which

229

the structure was clearly expressed and formed the space. Frank Lloyd Wright, Charles Rennie Macintosh, Richard Neutra and others who were concerned with an architecture related more closely to the soil and yet using the spatial and open space manipulations of the modern movement, provided inspiration. Architects such as Sydney Ancher in New South Wales adopted the single vernacular house form and translated the trabeated style into contemporary terms. Roy Grounds and Robin Boyd of Melbourne had been experimenting with verandah forms particularly in the construction of the Black Dolphin Motel at Merimbula on the south coast of New South Wales. Here timber was used freely again without embarrassment or concealment. On the west coast of America the same thing happened in more sophisticated and slicker ways. Joe Esherick, Drake, Charles Moore, began designing buildings in brick and timber which reflected the bold masses and forms of the American vernacular, particularly the clap-board farms and barns (for example, at Sea Ranch in northern California). Each country has developed through the vernacular an architecture which is more genial in its character than that of the 'international style'. The vernacular style here does not compete with the international school, for its principles are towards an Australian architecture. Sometimes the issues are clouded. The critics of the 'Sydney' school as Ancher and his colleagues are now called, often confuse its superficial similarities with a past architecture, whether it be a verandah or a pitched roof, and so accuse it of sentimentality. Yet both are more functional than a flat metal deck with unprotected plate glass picture windows.

From such indigenous elements, an Australian architecture may again rise. Max Freeland says in *Architecture in Australia: a history* – 'Because it contained much that was Australian generated, it seemed to hold a promise that after a century and a quarter Australian architecture might at last be going Australian'.[7]

Notes and references

1. *Oxford English Dictionary*, 1933 edn., p. 137.
2. SCOTT, SIR GEORGE GILBERT. *Remarks on secular and domestic architecture, present and future*. London, John Murray, 1857.
3. The first prefabricated building arrived with the First Fleet in 1788.
4. *op. cit. Oxford English Dictionary*, 1933 edn.
5. RAPOPORT, AMOS. *House form and culture*. Englewood Cliffs, N.J., Prentice-Hill, 1969, pp. 5–6.
6. BOYD, ROBIN. *The Australian ugliness*. Melbourne, Cheshire, 1969, p. 26.
7. FREELAND, JOHN MAXWELL. *Architecture in Australia: a history*. Melbourne, Cheshire, 1959, p. 311.

*Stuart Murray**

Contemporary architecture and environmental impact

Philip Cox has dealt with the vernacular architecture in Australia before World War I; Robin Boyd[1] has been unsurpassed in his critical appraisal of the Australian environmental heritage from then up to the fifties; I propose in this paper to examine the effect on the Australian environment of the architecture of the fifties to the present day.

Environs is described by the *Oxford Dictionary* as 'the outskirts of a city, districts surrounding a town' – *environment:* 'surroundings, region, conditions and influences'. The traditional Australian environment existed not only in groups of vernacular buildings in the form of early homesteads and historic country towns, but in the streetscapes of Sydney and the other capitals, Victorian terraces, and institutional precincts such as the Victoria Barracks.

J.M. Freeland in his history of architecture in Australia[2] describes the cities' growth in buildings both in size and quantity in the 1960s; and the architectural profession's dilemma and desperate efforts to fit itself into a high pressure business world. Philip Cox has explained the effect of the problems of excessive choice and abundance of alternatives, and how this brought forth a variety of styles competing for dominance; these factors, combined with Australia's sparse heritage of older buildings, have often tended to work against the creation of a stable, and therefore, psychologically reassuring, environment for our cities and suburbs.

The growth of Australian contemporary domestic architecture in the 1950s began with a re-examination of the house-to-site relationship; a rediscovery of the physical attraction of the Australian bushland suburb, first with a tentative extension of the house into landscape by the use of glass walls, and terraces with a linear enclosure of pergolas. Sydney Ancher's houses used slates the colour of eucalypt leaves, flat roofs with natural gravel, and walls lime-washed with colour to match the trunks of gum trees. The full glass walls made the floor levels of the house seem to extend to the terrace and bush beyond.

A vigorous natural movement in architecture, (well known as the 'Sydney School') combining the use of natural materials both inside and outside, in an often bewildering complexity of levels following rocky sites, with terraces and decks level with tree tops, rediscovering those values that Freeland attributes to Walter Burley Griffin's buildings 'at home with their environment from the day they were finished'.[3] They embraced and merged with the native landscape in superlative confidence (Figure 71, 72). The embrace evolved into an extension of the house walls into courtyards – outdoor rooms in the bush (Figure 73).

It was not until the late fifties that any large buildings began to be built in Australian cities since before World War II. High-rise apartments and office buildings which were then built had little to add to their surroundings, and the adverse environmental effects of tall buildings were soon felt – the microclimates

* Stuart Murray is in private practice with Ancher, Mortlock, Murray & Woolley Pty Ltd, Architects and Planners, North Sydney.

231

Figure 71. Merged with the bush in superlative confidence.
Woolley House, Mosman, Sydney, 1962

Figure 72. Terraces and decks level with the tree tops, Woolley House

232

Figure 73. House extension into bush. Glass walls and the terrace.
Ancher House, Killara, Sydney, 1945

Figure 74. Consumer architecture—new vernacular of merchant builders' suburban
environment. Pettit and Sevitt houses, St Ives, Sydney, 1967

Figure 75. Townhouses—
entries with privacy similar
to the single house.
Wollestoncraft, 1969

Figure 76. Townhouse—inner city living with increased densities.
Penthouses, Rushcutters Bay, Sydney, 1968

of shade and wind problems, the invasion of privacy by overlooking, noise of increased densities and the visual obtrusion of elements of violently contrasting scale into urban and neighbourhood precincts. The urban environment was being re-formed, in part by design, but more by the accident of an uncritical demand, plus the crude forces of population pressure and economic growth.

These pressures had two polarising effects: a rapid decline in the aesthetic qualities of hitherto relatively stable environments and a gradual growth in social appreciation of the physical environment and building forms. The architects who, up until then had been working at domestic scale, found themselves faced with the task of creating a physical framework to provide for a rapid growth in urban society. What had been discovered was that the behavioural response of people to their physical surroundings is fundamental to their attitude to life; the role of architecture was changing from the expression of the individual to that of a formative environmental factor of social growth. The problems which the architects of the sixties had to meet were the influences that urban form has on the control of one's individual privacy and the provision of a public environment that is at once evocative of social values and facilitates social activities.

Parallel to this there was the anomaly of consumer-architecture, where the person to build was not the user; architecture became a product or design process and the users were its consumers.

In the early sixties the preoccupation with single-house design was transferred to merchant built houses. This broke new ground in Australia, where the speculative builder had hitherto been a necessary evil. This unlikely, but long-needed, marriage between architect and builder, albeit a consumer architecture, created a new, although somewhat forced vernacular – forced, because of its very aptitude to be stylish: a new vernacular, because it pursued some of the sound architectural values of the fifties. Natural material, good house-to-site relationship, even the courtyard – the outdoor room was used. These merchant built houses, now competing in public housing developments, have played a major part in raising the environmental standards of Australian suburbia (Figure 74).

Australian domestic architecture then developed into what was known as town-housing, in reality a variation of the old terrace house; it was an answer to near and inner city living that provided privacy like that of a single house (Figure 75), at the same time increasing densities to a level close to three-storey flats (Figure 76), in an environment of neighbourhood intimacy and scale (Figure 77). The house-to-house relationship is as adaptable to uneven topography as the terrace house (Figure 78), landscaped private courts (Figure 79) and entry areas provide varied spatial complexity and interest as well as privacy. Both Federal and State housing agencies have now entered into the field of town houses for public housing.

Australian architects in the mid-sixties were then becoming aware of the importance of the treatment of the space around a building; the relationship of building to building. They began to regard the space between buildings as an outdoor room (Figure 80), to be treated as spatial sculpture, its walls the adjoining buildings or its doors the gaps between them, its floor the paving or landscaping, its ceiling the open sky, its furniture, trees, seats, lights, and other equipment necessary for social activities (Figure 81).

The first large building complexes to hit the Australian cities, apart from the city office building, were regional shopping centres; in reality these are the direct

235

Figure 77. Townhouses—neighbourhood intimacy and scale. Cremorne, 1969

Figure 78. Townhouses—adaptable to uneven topography—spatial complexity.
Mosman, Sydney, 1972

236

Figure 79. Townhouses—
landscaped private courts.
Penthouses, Rushcutters
Bay, Sydney, 1968

Figure 80. The outdoor
room, Badham House,
Cronulla, Sydney, 1959

237

Figure 81. Outdoor rooms in the city, Town Hall Square, Sydney

Figure 82. The outdoor room in the city—MLC Plaza Model, Sydney

238

descendants of city arcades, but on a scale to handle large suburban populations
in controlled internal environments. The external environment of such complexes
had an unfortunate impact on the neighbourhood precincts into which they were
inserted. No amount of architectural input could disguise their scale in contrast
with adjoining single-storey housing separated by several hundred metres of
carpark. A spatial relationship such as this between buildings defied environmental
control, except for ivy on the shopping centres and trees in the carpark. Architecture
perforce had accepted the combined pressures of private transport, location theory,
and the economic market.

The cities in the sixties had begun to rebuild themselves with no clear idea of
what sort of environment was called for. As a result, high index, high rise, high
profit office buildings won the day. In terms of open space and environment for
buildings, the private commercial sector was slow to show response, with little or
no guidance from the authorities of the day. Except for notable exceptions such as
Australia Square in Sydney, private developers in Australian cities gave away
precious little space to the public (Figure 82).

Government developments used spaces around and between buildings with little
understanding and a great deal of dull public taste. Of course there are notable
exceptions to that rule, such as the Government Architect of New South Wales.
The State schools, courthouses and office complexes which the New South Wales
Government has produced over the last decade are notable for the design of the
buildings and their spatial complexes. Using a rationale of the suitability of
structure and materials for the particular scale of problem with restrained stylish-
ness, and a limited palette of materials, it set an example in good public taste
for environmental design, architecture which could truly be called vernacular.

Public authorities in the seventies finally began to legislate for environmental
codes for open space, but have found it as difficult to analyse environmental qualities
of spaces, as they have found it to dictate architectural aesthetics. The impact of
new building complexes in the existing environment, upon microclimates of shade
and wind, topographical and geological features, noise factors, traffic generation,
increased pollution, amplified services, visual effects of scale, materials, building
shape, streetscape and skyline considerations are now being included in planning
and design codes as factors to be considered by private development. Public space
between buildings probably meets its nemesis in that environmental no mans' land,
the street. Except for city closures which are increasing in Australia to provide
unplanned plazas and pedestrian space, the Australian suburban street continues
to remain an environmental receptacle between the boundaries of private property
for every service authority; a proliferation of signs and oddments of street furniture.
Except for Canberra and new town developments and housing estates, the traditional Australian suburban street environment is the origin of that old adage,
'private wealth and public squalor'.

Conscious attempts to design buildings as various elements within precincts
came first from the Australian universities during the sixties. With growing
numbers of students and a control over large land areas, they began building
programs which suddenly revealed the necessity for controlled development and
the conservation of land by its most efficient use.

Analysis of briefs and future projections of student growth showed the real
need for the space between the buildings to be planned as efficiently as the archi-

tecture itself. The 'outdoor rooms' were analysed as closely as the building briefs themselves and spatial systems evolved representing the types of space based on function (Figure 83, 84).

The classification of spatial systems in the university precincts are two major types, movement spaces and 'places', or static spaces. The first caters to through movement of pedestrian and wheeled traffic (Figure 85), the second to activities which take place within the static space itself (Figures 86, 87, 88). Different function space types have certain landscape elements, such as paving, lighting, signs, planting, etc. associated with them; and so on. Thus has been evolved a vernacular for the treatment of vehicle roads, pedestrian routes, courts and recreation spaces, as outdoor environment, using the existing or future buildings, and topographical or landscape features, as walls, paving or planting as floors etc. Next, by analysing the building requirements and giving them building forms, structure and materials, connecting them into the spatial systems with climatic and microclimatic considerations, it is possible to produce a design for a university with a diverse population of up to 15 000 people per day.

During the late sixties, Australian architects found themselves involved in the design of large scale urban environments, both for government and private agencies with control over large areas of land in cities or precincts, who are interested in the now recognised benefits of comprehensively designed environment (Figure 89). Working with social, economic and transport planners, architects are able to create conceptual physical designs of neighbourhoods or town centres, of populations from 10 000 to 20 000 people, in three dimensions at a scale which will result in an identifiable environmental image. Such projects can be conceived down to the detail of the public spaces and buildings forms, with a precise idea of the building type and content. The periphery of such precincts is where architect meets planner, and the physical precinct fits into a framework of urban and regional planning (Figures 90, 91, 92).

Let us examine the economics of this type of environment. Everyone is aware of the primary capital cost of good built environments. Budget-conscious clients require cheap, efficient, beautiful buildings; the architect's dilemma lies in the conflict between his client's requirements and his responsibility to society at large, whose concern with the environment is with the urban and rural landscape at large. The client's budget allowance for environmental input generally is what is left over after his basic requirements have been met. It is no wonder that it is seldom achieved.

The built-environment of today could be described as consisting of high-energy, purpose built, short life buildings. The first two terms, high-energy and purpose built are readily understandable, high-energy because of their high consumption of materials and energy, purpose built because of the specialist use buildings that the individual user demands. Short life is the inevitable end of such special purpose buildings. They generally do not adapt to the changing needs of society.

The rapidly growing demand for urban buildings and spaces has a tremendous impact on the natural environment. No other activity of man, except perhaps war, literally removes whole blocks of natural landscape as the extraction of building materials. It is the ultimate destruction of a national estate. The effect of iron ore extraction on the Western Australian landscape is well known; and yet a Western Australian mining leader advocates nuclear explosives to blast out iron ore! Exploration leases are established in the adjoining Hamersley National Park.

Figure 83. The outdoor room— 'static space', Shortland University Union court

Figure 84. Indoor square—pedestrian circulation, Plant laboratory, CSIRO, Canberra

Figure 85. Pedestrian route bridge connection to Sydney University Wentworth Union

Figure 86. Outdoor room—'static space'—pedestrian square,
Sydney University Engineering School

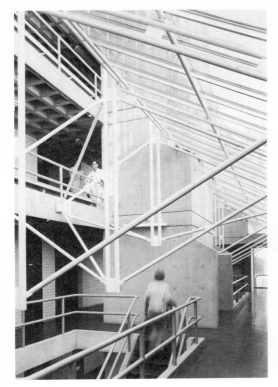

Figure 87. Internal street environment, Sydney University, Aeronautics and Mechanical Engineering School

Figure 88. Indoor street. Pedestrian and student spaces through Sydney University Union

Mining companies have spent $225 million in the past 15 years, and will spend $205 million in the next five years, on environmental control measures, rehabilitatating 7900 hectares of mined land. Its exploitation implies that the land has only one use, because of its destructive nature. Mining, despite rehabilitation, has a dominance as a form of land use. The problem of extraction of limestone for cement and marble in New South Wales at Bungonia, Colong and Wombeyan is well known. There are inexhaustible supplies at Yass, but accessibility and road tax concessions are the major location factors. Limestone extraction at South Marulan and Bungonia has resulted in the occupation of natural reserves for waste dumps and the destruction of natural caves. One of the most unfortunate aesthetic effects of building material extraction is the stone quarrying on the west face of the Mt Lofty range, visible from the city of Adelaide. Beach mining claims to affect only 8 km² of natural coastline per year in New South Wales but these leases are in long thin strips; adding for roads, dredge lines and power it comes to approximately 130 km² of natural recreational coast areas affected per year. Rutile is used for white pigment in paint.

Bauxite leases near Perth are 20 800 km² in extent. This will leave a heritage of a giant land use problem. The open cut extraction will go as deep as 24 metres; replacement of the overburden and pine reafforestation may meet salt water table problems and result in the pollution of adjoining agricultural lands. The red residue mud ponds will be held in clay lined silt pits of 2000 hectares in extent, with caustic soda effluents.

243

Figure 89. Urban environment. Physical design of town centre, Campbelltown, N.S.W.

looking west along Bland St, at Forbes

Forbes Street, looking south at Harmer street

Figures 90, 91, 92. Design of urban spaces—Woolloomooloo redevelopment

Another major building material problem is the supply of timber. Australian forestry authorities have estimated a target for pine plantations of 1.2 million hectares by the year 2000, one third of which are under production already. Their projected population/demand-estimates maximise population forecasts. Pine plantations, it is claimed by Australian Government forestry authorities, improve the environment; their main effect in New South Wales will be to eliminate, by destruction, a major proportion of wet sclerophyll forests, the richest habitat for flora and fauna and the richest eucalypt forest type. It is mistakenly assumed that wood is a renewable resource: this requires qualification – a forest as a natural ecological unit is only renewable under limited methods of management. Pine plantations are not among them. They are intensive forestry which suffers from almost all the disadvantages of intensive high yield agriculture, including soil erosion, river silting, deterioration of soils and fertility.[4]

The woodchip industry also, is indirectly related to buildings (the uses of chipboards have increased rapidly as a substitute for timber in interior fitments and furniture) but has been based on an export economy philosophy without regard to environmental economics. Environmental costs cannot be adequately assessed because the extent and location of areas and the programs have not been released. The disadvantages are even more drastic than plantations, with a disastrous effect on animal and plant life, watershed properties and soils. Huge concessions are proposed for the future in Tasmania, whose forest area is regarded as one of the last great forest wildernesses of the world. Soon it will cease to be. The south coast of New South Wales, the Northern Territory and eastern Victoria have similarly destroyed areas which were previously wildernesses.

The hidden costs of such environmental economics as mining and forestry are primary ones; secondary effects include the processing of building materials. Factories and plants are located adjacent to labour supplies with immediate and obvious effects on residential environments. Fallout and air pollution from Port Kembla steelworks has reached intolerable conditions. The increasing use of synthetics in building results in growing petro-chemical industries and others with noticeable pollution problems in urban areas.

But the most critical unseen cost of the man-made environment is the enormous consumption of energy in our society. Here I will not go deeply into the limits of supplies of energy or building materials, other than to refer to the exponential rates of exhaustion of non-renewable resources summarised in *The limits to growth*[5] and, of course, to the current awareness of the energy crisis. Even assuming all such projections and statistics are excessively pessimistic, the underlying message is clear – some decided change will be necessary in our basic approach to buildings.

Approximately 25 per cent to 30 per cent of all energy used today results from previous architectural and building decisions. This includes the processing of materials such as aluminium, the construction industry, and the maintenance and operation of buildings. To date such consumption has been predicated on a cheap, inexhaustible supply; the supply is now known to be exhaustible, nor will it remain cheap.

Of this energy used in architecture and building decisions, about one quarter of it is wasted in the following ways: in the last thirty years, increased mechanisation in the building industry has replaced human labour. Techniques of production discourage repair of fittings and equipment, and replacement requires a large investment of materials and energy. It is often more economical for speculators

246

to demolish old, perfectly sound buildings than to renovate. Real estate values
based on maximum profits encourage the premature demolition of sound structures
with a useful anticipated life. It is difficult to evaluate the decision to replace such
a building with one serving the same or another purpose, especially when the
decision will require energy to demolish, energy to rebuild, and probably a higher
consumption of energy in maintaining the new space. Demolition, often of historic
buildings, often destroys irreplaceable acquired characteristics of environments of
diverse style and scale.

Another area of wasteful energy and material use is the over-use of materials
and over-design of structure. It is a fact of the building economy that the over-use
of material comes from current economic pressures to reduce labour time *even
at the expense of more material*. The tendency over the last five or ten years to
use tower cranes and large precast panels in lieu of smaller elements and more
labour is obvious. The design criteria for the thickness of such panels are almost
inevitably based on their structural sufficiency for lifting, and not for their performance as a wall. Any structural engineer will confirm (with provisos that the
codes be rewritten, and that a budget allowance for increased labour in formwork
and specific erection precautions be taken) that structural concrete and steel can
be designed safely with half the material. The further cumulative weight of
buildings may be reduced and foundation savings made. The saving in cement
production alone can result in large economies in energy consumption.

Wood too is used excessively; every member is designed as if disconnected
from the rest of the structure. Timber structures, considered integrally with their
floor, wall and roof linings, could effect consequential material and energy savings.
Not enough use is made of precast and prefabricated elements such as gang-nail
hardwood trusses.

Over-design of systems, too, is obvious. The over-design of lighting is seen
dramatically in the lighting of office buildings; one switch which turns on a whole
floor. Consider the immense heat exchange of an air conditioned building which
dumps its waste heat outside.

Frankly, it seems to me that sometimes, although the architectural profession
is nominally committed to efficient planning, too many structures are wastefully
designed, often under influences of current social values of image, prestige and power.
Energy utilisation and efficiency have little bearing on the proposed solution to
many building problems. At times it also seems that, simply, the wrong building
has been built; one suspects that many new buildings will not be suitable for the
functions for which they were designed for more than a comparatively short time.
In many of our cities, permanent reinforced concrete multi-storey carparks are being
built, including basements. They have low headroom, are deep in plan, and have
almost no services. They are unsuitable for almost any other use, yet there is a
real possibility that in the future either the private car will be severely curtailed
or banned from the locations where the carparks are built. With little more
financial outlay they may be built to allow future adaptation. Otherwise they will
be derelict, until their expensive demolition. Hence the description, 'high-energy,
purpose built, short life'.

The two basic approaches to achieve energy savings will produce two diametrically opposed environments. One stabilises the internal environment by a
tight skin, with nominal thermal transfer, and a nominal surface area to contain

the required volume. Here, the greatest efficiency is achieved by refining mechanical performance and taking advantage of the interdependency of its systems. The BHP building in Melbourne is probably the best example of this type in Australia, with a total energy system, using natural gas for power, heating and cooling, making a net saving in operation power.

The second approach assumes that the outside environment is not hostile at all times; allowing the natural elements to be understood and used when they contribute to inside comfort and performance quality, and excluded when they are undesirable. These include solar heating, cooling with outside air, natural light, wind energy and water. Advanced work on solar ventilation and heat exchange is being carried out by the CSIRO in Melbourne, and environmental sciences have been established in most architectural schools in Australia. A younger generation of architects is examining possibilities of future buildings with their own energy support systems based on natural environments. To put such theories into practical use in the near future, Australia will need measures such as the creation of a national energy and resource conservation system; techniques of evaluating the energy rating of a new building based on the energy required in the operation over a long-life span; new techniques of re-use, modification and upgrading existing buildings (recycling). Based on these criteria, building priorities may then be re-established.

We need a research policy to reinvestigate building elements to re-define their functions; and to re-evaluate physical requirements (such as optimum and variable lighting and heating levels). In redetermining these physical requirements, we will again realise that we live in a natural environment which can be used; reliance on mechanical systems is so complete that the performance possibilities of the building as a whole have been downgraded. The basic principles of performance possibilities of a building may be seen in practice everywhere man has had to live without the benefit of cheap and readily available power, taking advantage of sun, shade, wind and utilising waste products to environmental advantage.

Certain vernacular building types have achieved delicate environmental balance, through determining mass, material and openings. Highly technological societies often substitute new materials which may seem more convenient or readily available, even cheaper, than traditional ones, but which tend to destroy such natural balance. This is a short term economic decision. The natural approach to buildings has been termed 'low energy, loose fit, long life'. If architects do not begin to design more 'loose fit' buildings offering greater adaptability there will be, as I see it, in addition to the enormous impact on natural landscapes, at least four adverse consequences in the urban environment.

First, there will be a direct economic waste as a result of the unavoidable write-off of buildings after a comparatively short period. Second, there will be reduced functional efficiency, and indirect economic loss as a result, quite early in the life of a building. Third, there will be environmental degeneration when buildings have become functionally and economically unsound. And fourth, further environmental problems will be created by frequent rebuilding. There is nothing more disturbing to amenity than an accelerating of functional obsolescence and the rebuilding that follows. The public, you and I, find derelict buildings, demolition and continuous new construction work an unpleasant and disturbing environment.

Five years ago, it was possible to advocate the national, controlled use of resources and materials in a building as a matter of choice. For the immediate future it is a matter of necessity. Like Philip Cox, I believe that a consciously limited, precise use of available energy and materials would bring architecture back into the historic stream of the great architecture of the past.

References

1. BOYD, ROBIN. *The Australian ugliness.* Rev. edn. Harmondsworth, Penguin, 1972. (First published 1960).
2. FREELAND, J. M. *Architecture in Australia: a history.* Melbourne, Cheshire, 1968.
3. *op. cit.* FREELAND, 1968, p. 247.
4. ROUTLEY, R. and ROUTLEY, V. *The fight for the forests: the takeover of Australian forests for pines, wood chips and intensive forestry.* Canberra, ANU Research School of Social Sciences, 1973.
5. MEADOWS, D. L. *et al. The limits to growth: a global challenge.* New York, Universe Books, 1972.

*Ian Burnley**

The suburban metropolis in Australia: some demographic forces at work

Writing in 1925, the social ecologist Ernest W. Burgess commented that the outstanding fact of modern society is the growth of great cities. He outlined several features distinguishing urban from rural populations and discussed the urbanisation process with particular reference to United States cities at the early stages of the twentieth century:

> . . . the larger proportion of women to men in the cities than in the open country, the greater percentage of youth and middle-aged; the higher ratio of the foreign-born, the increased heterogeneity of occupation, increase with the growth of the city and profoundly alter its social structure. These variations in the composition of population are indicative of all the changes going on in the social organisation of the community. In fact, these changes are a part of the growth of the city and suggest the nature of the processes of growth.[1]

Most of these comments apply equally well to the Australian metropolis and society in 1974. In common with the large industrial cities (notably Chicago) which Burgess was considering, and which at a later stage of America's industrial revolution had experienced a very heavy immigration of persons of diverse cultural origins, Australia's post-World War II urbanisation witnessed, and was profoundly affected by the development of heavy industry and a large-scale international immigration program. The metropolitan State capitals in Australia, however, displayed dynamic growth throughout most of the nineteenth and early twentieth century, growth being significantly slowed only by the severe depression of the 1890s and the Great Depression of the 1930s. Furthermore, the role of international migration was also dominant in the 19th century as a factor in metropolitan growth although it began to be rivalled closely by natural increase after 1860. Thus migration and mobility have been of considerable importance in the growth of Australia's large cities, and international migration has at almost all times been more important than internal migration in metropolitan growth. A task of this paper then is to review the impact of migration in suburban development and differentiation, but against a background of general population change within the cities. This means a consideration of birth and death rates and in some instances fertility change, along with the migration factor. The internal population structure of Australian large cities (and in fact component analysis of city population growth) has been a much neglected field of research in Australian urban studies. It might even be useful to ask whether the massive suburbanisation trend so typical of metropolitan Australia was a consequence of rapid population growth or whether other factors were equally important.

THE PATTERN OF METROPOLITAN GROWTH

Before discussing population change in the large cities of Australia, it might be prudent to consider the trend of metropolitan growth from the 19th century

---

* Ian Burnley is a lecturer in the School of Geography at the University of New South Wales.

*The suburban metropolis in
Australia: some
demographic forces at work*

through to the present. To an extent this means the consideration of population growth rates and also the rate of increase in population centralisation in the respective States. One must be careful with population growth rates, however, because at the earlier stages of population growth from a small population base, more rapid increases commonly occur relative to later periods of growth yet the later increases, because of the much larger population base, represent more massive population numbers and may have more urgent economic and social implications.

Prior to 1860, natural increase was limited because of ill-balanced sex ratios in Australia arising from convict settlement, although because of immigration, population growth rates were quite high. After 1860, the rate of population growth was slower, but it remained very high by international standards. Population growth rates averaged 3-4 per cent per annum between 1860 and 1890[2] and for metropolitan Sydney and Melbourne they averaged between 4-6 per cent per annum. The higher rates in Sydney and Melbourne reflected the population centralisation process so ubiquitous in the contemporary era but which was well under way in this period as the figures in Table 1 indicate.

Table 1. Percentage of colonial population in the respective capitals, 1871-1901

| | Year | | | |
	1871	1881	1891	1901
Sydney	27	30	34	36
Melbourne	28	33	43	41
Adelaide	23	37	42	45
Brisbane	13	15	24	24
Perth	21	20	17	20
Hobart	19	18	23	20

Source: GLYNN, S. *Urbanisation in Australian history*, 1788-1900. Melbourne, Nelson, 1970, p. 29.

Metropolitan growth in the latter third of the nineteenth century was far from being regular or uniform. Melbourne grew rapidly in the 1850s and 1880s, more slowly in the 1860s and 1870s, and hardly at all in the 1890s because of the recession in the latter decade of the century. Sydney's growth, overall, was much more consistent, apart from a relatively small increase in the 1860s. Adelaide grew very rapidly in the 1860-1880 period, and very slowly in other decades. Apart from Perth, all cities showed a much reduced growth rate in the 1890s. The rates of growth of metropolitan Sydney and Melbourne in the latter half of the nineteenth century are evident in Table 2, although it will be remembered that these have been inflated by the expansion of peripheral boundaries.

Table 2. Annual rates of growth for Sydney and Melbourne, 1851-1901[1]

| | Year | | | | |
	1851-1861	1861-1871	1871-1881	1881-1891	1891-1901
Sydney	7.7	4.8	6.3	7.0	2.7
Melbourne	50.0[2]	4.7	3.6	7.4	0.8

Note:
(1) No adjustment at this stage has been made for boundary adjustments.
(2) This inflated figure reflects the Victorian gold rushes.

After this period of very high rates of growth (except for the economic recessions) due to high levels of rural-urban migration, international migration (especially from Britain) and large family sizes, there was a marked fall in growth rates due to a declining birth rate and fall in average size of family and a diminishing rural-urban migration. Indeed, studies by Lincoln Day indicate that the fall in family size with the demographic transition took place first in metropolitan areas (from late 1880s) and last in rural areas (from late 1890s).[3,4]

By the 1930s, the birth rate of Australia's cities had fallen to very low levels so that even with the limited immigration of the period, the growth of Sydney and Melbourne did not exceed one per cent per annum. In the post-war era, their annual rates of population growth ranged between 2 and 2.7 per cent per annum, rates not too much greater than that of the total population of Australia, but much greater than between 1930-39, or during the War years. The reason for their growth in recent times being not much greater than Australia's total population was in part their large share of Australia's population, and also because of the minimal importance of internal migration in their growth. Considerable in and out migration did take place to metropolitan Sydney and Melbourne but the net gain was insignificant. For example, between 1966-71, 152 000 persons aged over five years moved into metropolitan Sydney and were resident there at the 1971 census while 161 600 moved out, indicating a high turnover internal migration although there was in fact a net loss of internal migrants. And in Melbourne, turnover internal migration rates were high, indicating high population mobility although the net gain in population from this source was minimal. In Brisbane, Perth and Adelaide, however, population growth rates were near 3 per cent per annum in the contemporary era, and an important part of this growth was a strong net gain in internal migration. Thus between 1966-71, there was an inflow of 92 200 persons to Brisbane through internal migration of persons over five years and an out-migration of 73 500 giving rise to a net gain of 18 700 persons, equalling 21 per cent of intercensal population increases. Similarly, in Perth, internal migration accounted for over 17 per cent of the intercensal population increase. Generally this means that while population mobility was high in Sydney and Melbourne, the internal migration impact on intra-urban population mobility, and population structure was almost certainly greater in recent times in Brisbane, Perth and Adelaide than in Sydney and Melbourne. The same applies to Wollongong, Geelong and Canberra as lesser, but significant rapid growth points. In some cities, then there may be greater problems in some residential areas because of the lack of supportive kinfolk in the neighbourhood or city because internal migration often separates movers from kin.

But with the major southern cities of Sydney, Melbourne and Adelaide, immigration was the main demographic component in growth throughout the 1947-1971 period, more important than natural increase or internal migration in aggregate. Thus whereas the net gain in foreign-born to Australia between 1947-1966 accounted for 38 per cent of population growth, the net gain of foreign-born in Melbourne accounted for 59 per cent of that city's growth, and in Sydney, 55 per cent.[5] Thus where natural increase was responsible for 58 per cent of Australia's population growth in the period, natural increase constituted only 42 per cent of growth in Melbourne and 45 per cent of that in Sydney. And in Adelaide, like Wollongong, natural increase was only 29 per cent of total growth. Adelaide

*The suburban metropolis in
Australia: some
demographic forces at work*

became par excellence a migration city with 71 per cent of its population growth
the direct result of migration – 56.5 foreign-born migration; and 14.5 per cent
Australian-born, predominantly internal, migration. Between 1966-1971, the net gain
in foreign-born through migration to Melbourne accounted for over 50 per cent
of intercensal growth, natural increase 46 per cent and 4 per cent from internal
migration. In Sydney, foreign-born migration accounted for almost 60 per cent
of 1966-1971 intercensal population increase. Clearly immigration has been critical
in the major south-eastern cities of Australia in the population dynamics of these
cities, and in internal population and social differentiation of the cities.

SUBURBAN VARIATIONS IN POPULATION STRUCTURE
AND DEMOGRAPHIC PROCESSES

In the modern industrial metropolis, inter-area contrasts in population structure
and processes have often been more profound than those between rural and urban
areas, or cities of different sizes. This has almost certainly been the case in Australia.

Even in the nineteenth century, before suburbanisation was massively under way,
intra-urban variations reflecting a sifting and sorting of metropolitan populations
were readily apparent. In considering mortality it can first be said that mortality
levels in Australian cities in the nineteenth century were generally lower than in
their European counterparts. In Europe, mortality rates were often higher in urban
than in rural areas – the cities there were often called 'killers of men'. In Australia
the pattern was quite different. The cities, when compared with rural areas, offered
a reasonably healthy environment, and much better prospects of medical attention
when needed.

However, between 1875-1885, death rates were over 10 per 1000 mean population
higher in metropolitan Sydney than in the remainder of New South Wales,
indicating the spread of disease in more crowded conditions in the metropolis.
After 1900, death rates remained only one or two points per 1000 higher in the
metropolis than outside, and age structure variations may have accounted for the
difference. Nevertheless, some Australian mortality figures reveal surprisingly
high death rates in urban areas. In part this can be accounted for by heavy infant
mortality, retirement to urban from rural areas, and the location of hospitals in
urban areas. Nevertheless, epidemic diseases (including typhoid and cholera)
were by no means absent from Australian cities in the nineteenth and early
twentieth centuries. The fight for public health was waged in Australia as well
as in Britain and declining urban mortality was in part associated with progressive
improvements in water supply, sewerage, drainage and other facilities. The cost
of providing these facilities varied with the density of the settlement and in
the outermost suburbs costs tended to be prohibitive. Perhaps largely because
of the lack of facilities and public health supervision in outer residential areas,
death rates were quite often higher in suburbs than in central city areas. It can
be seen in Table 3, however, that in the contemporary era, death rates have been
highest in the inner suburbs of Sydney, a trend also followed in Melbourne.

In contemporary times, infant and neo-natal mortality rates have varied
considerably between Local Government Areas (LGAs) within both Sydney and
Melbourne, from 29 per 1000 live births within Richmond and Collingwood in
1970 to only seven in many outer municipalities, while in Sydney rates varied from

between 25-30 in Sydney, South Sydney and Marrickville to only 6-10 in Warringah, Ku-Ring-Gai and Sutherland. While lack of comparability of relevant social services between suburbs may be of some importance in these differences, other factors are clearly of importance. M.G.A. Wilson found that density of housing, occupation, the incidence of working mothers and proportion of migrants in the population were all of importance in incidence of infant mortality within cities.[6] In other words, levels of infant mortality were highest in areas of low socio-economic status, higher density of housing, higher incidence of working mothers and higher proportions of southern and non-European migrants. These associations were correlative or associational, rather than necessarily causal. Adequacy of social and medical services in paticular areas is important, as well as the awareness among the population of service availability. It has been found in the United States that medical facilities are located by factors such as accessibility, which in turn are influenced by the personal perceptions of the services available. Religious, ethnic and socio-economic status can limit a patient's choice to inadequate medical care.[7,8] Demands and supplies of services are distorted by the cultural and economic characteristics of an area, and by the medical profession's responses to them. Medical services are often spatially unevenly distributed, of varying quantity and quality, and particularly oriented to the demands of higher socio-economic groups in large cities.

In Table 3, intra-metropolitan variations between suburbs in crude death rates which have as yet not been age-standardised are listed for Sydney for the period 1952-1970. It will be noted that the highest rates were in the inner-ring suburbs and the lowest were in outermost and newer suburbs. Most of the variation recorded in the Table is accounted for by variations of age-sex structure, the inner suburbs being characterised by an ageing population with out-migration in younger and intermediate ages and the outermost suburbs of expansion being characterised by younger married couples with children, fewer elderly persons and thus low crude death rates. Preliminary age standardisation for some LGAs indicates, however, that higher mortality levels existed in South Sydney, Botany in the inner suburbs, and Auburn in the middle-distance western suburbs. Environmental factors may have been involved here.

In contrast to the pattern of crude death rates, birth rates were highest in general in the outer suburbs and lowest towards the inner city although the variation by 1970 was not as great as with death rates. Thus in nine out of ten outer industrial-residential municipalities, birth rates were over 20 per 1000 in 1970, while in middle-distance areas there were no LGAs with birth rates over 20 and in the older residential inner suburbs of Sydney, crude birth rates were over 20 in five out of eleven municipalities. The average birth rate was 15 in the older middle-distance suburbs, 18 in the inner suburbs and over 22 in the outer industrial and residential suburbs. Earlier in the post-war era, the birth rate differential between inner and outer suburbs had been much greater as Table 4 indicates, but through time, birth rates tended to increase in some inner suburbs, most notably Marrickville, in which the birth rate increased from 17.5 in 1952 to 21.1 in 1962 and 27.1 in 1970 compared to the metropolitan rate of 19.1 in 1970. Marrickville, along with South Sydney, Leichhardt, Ashfield and Botany underwent a form of 'demographic rejuvenation' with the inflow of a foreign-born population, predominantly southern Europeans, and the starting of their families. Southern

254

*The suburban metropolis in
Australia: some
demographic forces at work*

Table 3. Intra-metropolitan variations in crude death rates in metropolitan Sydney, 1952-1970

	Year							
	1952	1956	1960	1962	1964	1966	1968	1970
Older residential inner suburbs								
South Sydney-City of Sydney	13.9	14.4	12.4	15.0	15.9	15.4	15.5	16.2
Leichhardt	11.1	13.0	13.0	12.3	13.0	14.2	13.7	14.1
Drummoyne	12.0	11.8	11.6	13.3	12.8	13.4	13.9	13.0
Ashfield	14.1	14.0	15.0	14.1	15.6	15.7	17.7	15.8
Strathfield	11.3	11.6	11.1	13.6	15.3	13.9	13.7	15.5
Canterbury	8.4	8.7	8.4	9.6	9.1	9.4	10.3	9.4
Burwood	10.7	14.7	12.7	13.1	14.0	15.2	12.6	12.3
Marrickville	11.9	12.4	12.2	13.2	13.3	12.7	12.5	12.5
North Sydney	11.9	13.0	12.6	13.0	14.0	13.7	12.6	13.6
Woollahra	11.9	13.5	13.4	12.6	12.2	13.5	12.5	12.7
Botany	7.6	9.6	10.7	12.1	11.2	9.4	11.2	10.1
Older middle-distance LGAs								
Mosman	14.4	16.4	18.0	15.9	15.4	16.3	17.1	15.7
Willoughby	10.8	11.0	10.4	10.3	11.4	13.6	11.9	11.6
Lane Cove	8.9	9.4	9.9	10.6	11.3	12.6	11.5	11.3
Concord	7.9	9.7	9.0	11.2	12.3	13.2	11.3	11.9
Hunters Hill	8.0	7.6	12.2	11.3	12.8	15.3	10.8	11.6
Rockdale	8.3	7.7	9.0	10.2	10.8	11.2	11.6	11.4
Parramatta	10.9	10.4	8.4	8.7	8.4	9.4	8.9	9.2
Waverley	10.1	12.6	12.4	12.6	13.1	13.3	13.2	12.9
Newer middle-distance LGAs								
Kogarah-Hurstville	8.8	10.7	11.8	8.2	9.4	10.4	9.5	9.8
Ryde	9.7	10.1	7.6	8.2	8.4	9.0	10.0	9.6
Bankstown	5.6	5.6	5.3	5.7	6.7	6.7	6.6	7.7
Auburn	11.8	11.4	11.5	11.7	13.7	12.9	12.5	12.7
Manly	11.1	13.5	12.0	12.2	13.4	13.0	11.4	13.9
Outer industrial-residential								
Fairfield	7.0	7.0	5.8	5.4	5.4	5.6	5.1	5.6
Holroyd	6.3	3.9	4.9	5.4	4.5	6.8	6.0	6.4
Blacktown-Penrith	7.2	6.1	5.5	5.6	4.9	5.0	5.2	5.2
Liverpool	8.5	6.5	5.6	6.1	7.4	4.6	4.8	5.6
Ku-Ring-Gai	10.6	10.1	9.0	9.2	8.9	8.5	9.8	9.2
Hornsby	9.9	8.0	7.6	6.9	7.4	7.5	7.1	7.9
Warringah	8.7	8.4	7.7	7.9	7.9	7.6	7.6	7.3
Baulkham Hills	6.0	6.1	6.2	5.8	4.8	5.4	5.0	5.2
Sutherland	7.2	6.7	5.6	6.7	6.3	6.3	6.7	6.4
Campbelltown	5.6	7.3	7.6	8.0	6.6	8.5	6.1	7.7
Total metropolitan	10.6	10.8	9.6	9.8	10.1	9.9	9.6	9.5

Source: New South Wales Statistical Register, Australian Bureau of Statistics, Sydney.

European settlers tended to migrate as single persons or young marrieds, or marry soon after arrival and begin family formation in Australia rather than migrate with children.

The interaction of the birth and death rate differentials, reflecting widely different age structures and life cycle stages in different parts of the cities gave rise to sharp differences in natural increase rates between suburbs. Excepting Botany and Marrickville, rates were generally low in the inner LGAs of Sydney (under 0.6

255

Table 4. Intra-metropolitan variations in crude birth rates in metropolitan Sydney, 1952-1970

	Year							
	1952	1956	1960	1962	1964	1966	1968	1970
Older residential inner suburbs								
South Sydney-City of Sydney	19.1	17.9	18.9	19.8	19.6	21.2	20.1	22.8
Leichhardt	18.4	18.1	18.9	21.4	20.6	21.0	20.7	21.0
Drummoyne	15.5	14.7	15.3	14.6	14.9	14.9	15.1	17.0
Ashfield	17.0	14.3	18.2	17.8	18.8	20.1	20.9	21.8
Strathfield	15.6	12.9	11.1	13.9	13.5	12.4	12.2	14.5
Canterbury	18.7	16.6	16.8	17.1	16.2	16.1	18.0	19.7
Burwood	14.7	15.5	17.5	15.3	14.9	15.5	14.4	14.9
Marrickville	17.5	17.0	19.9	21.1	23.0	24.2	26.0	27.1
North Sydney	16.6	15.6	14.8	14.9	14.9	13.2	13.7	14.4
Woollahra	12.7	14.1	13.0	11.2	11.7	11.4	11.9	12.5
Botany	17.4	15.9	20.5	19.3	14.6	18.0	21.9	20.6
Older middle-distance LGAs								
Mosman	15.8	15.2	13.5	13.8	14.0	13.2	13.5	14.8
Willoughby	16.0	13.5	11.6	12.9	11.7	12.5	13.0	15.1
Lane Cove	18.1	17.3	15.0	16.0	14.8	13.4	13.4	15.6
Concord	14.5	11.7	11.3	12.1	11.8	12.8	14.0	17.2
Hunters Hill	10.6	9.9	17.5	13.5	11.4	13.4	11.8	10.5
Rockdale	16.1	11.0	13.2	14.6	13.7	13.9	13.6	15.4
Parramatta	22.2	19.9	18.6	19.5	17.8	17.1	15.9	17.8
Waverley	15.0	14.4	13.3	13.9	13.3	13.2	15.1	16.4
Newer middle-distance LGAs								
Kogarah-Hurstville	23.0	21.1	16.8	15.1	14.4	13.7	15.1	15.6
Ryde	23.0	22.8	19.6	20.7	17.8	16.4	14.8	16.3
Bankstown	28.4	26.2	26.9	21.9	19.3	17.3	17.2	19.1
Auburn	19.8	18.0	17.2	17.1	14.9	16.3	15.3	17.8
Manly	17.0	19.9	16.5	15.1	13.6	12.4	12.3	14.1
Outer industrial-residential								
Fairfield	27.2	27.6	25.3	25.9	24.4	21.3	20.6	22.2
Holroyd	18.9	25.4	22.2	23.8	19.8	21.4	20.6	24.8
Blacktown-Penrith	30.3	24.0	31.7	31.4	27.1	23.4	24.2	24.9
Liverpool	26.9	25.0	27.3	28.2	31.8	22.4	21.9	21.5
Ku-Ring-Gai	17.9	19.4	18.4	18.9	16.3	14.7	14.7	15.1
Hornsby	25.3	21.2	21.1	23.3	22.0	19.7	20.5	20.0
Warringah	28.1	22.4	23.9	24.8	20.5	20.1	21.9	22.4
Baulkham Hills	17.1	17.1	20.1	22.1	18.7	20.1	23.2	27.6
Sutherland	31.2	28.4	27.3	26.6	22.3	20.2	19.8	20.1
Campbelltown	22.7	22.7	27.5	28.3	22.5	22.1	21.4	23.9
Total metropolitan	18.5	18.9	19.1	19.6	18.3	17.9	18.1	19.1

Source: New South Wales Statistical Register, Australian Bureau of Statistics, Sydney.

per cent per annum). In Woollahra, Strathfield, Mosman, Hunters Hill, natural decrease often occurred, i.e. death rates exceeded birth rates in old prestigious suburbs with ageing populations and low familism. But in the outer suburbs where for age-structural and life cycle stage reasons birth rates greatly exceeded death rates, natural increase was between 1.5-2.0 per cent per annum. These differences, not considering for the moment migration, gave rise to widely differing growth rates in various ecological zones of the metropolis. Such variations have implications

The suburban metropolis in
Australia: some
demographic forces at work

Table 5. Intra-metropolitan variations in natural increase rates in metropolitan Sydney, 1952-1970

	Year							
	1952	1956	1960	1962	1964	1966	1968	1970
Older residential inner suburbs								
South Sydney-City of Sydney	5.2	3.5	4.5	4.9	3.7	5.8	4.5	4.5
Leichhardt	7.3	5.1	5.9	9.1	7.6	6.8	7.0	6.9
Drummoyne	3.5	2.9	3.7	1.2	2.0	1.6	1.2	4.0
Ashfield	2.9	0.3	3.3	3.7	3.3	4.4	3.2	6.0
Strathfield	4.3	1.3	−0.1	0.2	−1.8	−1.5	−1.6	−1.0
Canterbury	10.4	7.9	8.5	7.5	7.1	6.7	7.8	10.3
Burwood	4.0	0.8	4.8	2.1	0.9	0.2	1.8	2.6
Marrickville	5.6	4.6	7.8	7.9	9.6	11.4	13.5	14.6
North Sydney	4.7	2.6	2.2	1.9	0.9	0.5	1.1	0.8
Woollahra	0.7	−0.1	−2.5	−1.4	−0.5	−2.2	−0.5	−0.2
Botany	9.9	6.3	9.7	7.3	3.3	8.6	10.7	10.5
Older middle-distance LGAs								
Mosman	1.5	−1.2	−4.5	−2.1	−1.4	−3.2	−3.6	−1.0
Willoughby	5.2	2.5	1.2	2.6	0.3	−1.0	1.2	3.5
Lane Cove	9.3	8.0	5.1	5.4	3.5	0.8	1.9	4.3
Concord	6.5	2.0	2.3	0.9	−0.5	−0.5	2.6	5.3
Hunters Hill	2.7	2.3	5.3	2.2	−1.4	−2.0	1.0	−1.0
Rockdale	7.7	3.3	4.2	4.4	2.3	2.7	2.1	4.1
Parramatta	11.2	9.5	10.2	10.7	9.4	7.8	7.0	8.5
Waverley	4.9	1.8	0.9	1.4	0.2	−0.1	1.9	3.6
Newer middle-distance LGAs								
Kogarah-Hurstville	13.2	9.2	6.0	6.7	4.9	4.1	4.7	5.1
Ryde	13.4	12.7	12.0	12.5	9.5	7.3	4.5	6.7
Bankstown	22.8	21.0	19.1	16.2	13.0	10.6	10.5	11.4
Auburn	8.0	6.6	5.7	5.4	1.3	3.4	2.9	5.2
Manly	5.9	6.4	4.5	2.9	0.2	−0.7	1.0	0.2
Outer industrial-residential								
Fairfield	20.2	20.9	19.5	20.5	19.0	15.7	15.5	16.5
Holroyd	12.6	21.4	17.3	18.4	15.3	14.6	15.0	18.4
Blacktown-Penrith	23.1	18.5	26.0	26.5	22.1	18.4	19.0	19.7
Liverpool	18.5	18.5	21.6	22.1	24.5	17.8	17.1	15.9
Ku-Ring-Gai	7.3	9.3	9.4	9.8	7.5	6.2	4.9	5.9
Hornsby	15.3	13.1	13.5	16.4	14.7	12.2	13.3	11.9
Warringah	19.4	15.3	15.3	15.7	12.6	12.5	14.3	15.1
Baulkham Hills	11.2	11.1	13.9	16.3	13.8	14.7	18.2	22.5
Sutherland	23.9	21.8	21.7	19.9	16.0	13.9	13.1	13.6
Campbelltown	17.2	15.4	19.9	20.3	16.0	13.6	15.3	16.3
Total metropolitan	7.9	8.6	9.5	9.8	8.2	8.0	8.5	9.7

Note: Rate per 1000 mean population.
Source: New South Wales Statistical Register, Australian Bureau of Statistics, Sydney.

for planning for creches, pre-schools, class room numbers, aged accommodation, specialised medical services and the like on an intra-suburban basis.

The other major demographic component in intra-urban population change has of course been migration, both international movement as well as the more local inter-suburban residential mobility and internal migration generally. A major factor in change has been international migration as Table 6 testifies. Generally

Table 6. The role of immigration in population change within broad ecological areas and selected LGAs in metropolitan Sydney, 1947-66

	Australian-born & other population decrease	Overseas-born increase as % Australian-born decline	Total population decrease %	Overseas-born increase	Southern Europeans as % overseas-born increase	Australian-born increase	Total population increase
Older residential inner suburbs							
Sydney	−84 474	35.2	−25.6	29 762	56.3		
Leichhardt	−22 098	50.5	−15.6	11 167	71.9		
Drummoyne	−6 860	65.6	−7.2	4 505	74.2		
Ashfield	−19 106	72.0	−6.3	7 278	43.4		
Strathfield	−3 899	70.2	−4.2	2 737	28.3		
Canterbury				12 777	49.2	3 629	16 410
Burwood	−3 750			5 244	34.3		1 494
Marrickville	−31 808	62.4	−13.5	19 852	67.2		
North Sydney	−13 395	35.6	−14.3	4 765	15.1		
Woollahra	−11 453	39.5	−12.8	4 519	10.6		
Botany	−1 862	351.1		6 548	41.6		4 586
Randwick	−3 401	473.5		16 104	31.0		12 703
Older middle-distance LGAs							
Mosman	−1 669	133.8		2 233	10.0		564
Lane Cove				2 204	10.3	3 088	5 292
Concord	−5 514		−8.0	3 230	44.2		
Hunters Hill				976	20.4	1 760	2 736
Rockdale				7 076	47.5	235	7 311
Parramatta				11 252	22.1	37 053	48 305
Waverley	−20 143	44.4	−15.0	8 950	17.2		
Newer middle-distance LGAs							
Ryde				7 235	29.2	33 460	40 695
Bankstown				23 739	16.6	93 546	117 285
Auburn				3 794	40.1	2 704	6 498
Manly				3 175	9.1	1 511	4 686
Outer industrial-residential							
Fairfield				25 400	24.9	45 579	70 979
Holroyd				10 237	44.6	31 457	41 694
Blacktown				19 813	20.1	63 520	83 333
Remainder metropolitan area:				85 408	11.6	341 452	426 860

Source: Censuses of the Commonwealth of Australia, 30 June 1947, 1966.

the inner suburbs of all Australia's capital cities, but particularly Sydney, Melbourne and Adelaide, have lost population considerably in the last quarter century, the decline in some cases becoming evident as early as the 1921 and 1933 censuses.

Between 1947-1966, the Australian-born and other residual immigrant populations in the inner and older middle-distance suburbs declined by 229 500 in metropolitan Sydney. This declining population situation was the result of

*The suburban metropolis in
Australia: some
demographic forces at work*

invasion of non-residential land uses, mortality of an ageing population, low birth
rates, but above all a heavy out-migration of the Australian-born population
especially between ages 20-45. The out-migration was partly a life-cycle stage
phenomenon as persons moved from relict housing areas to the metropolitan
periphery of middle-distance suburbs. This reflected in part increasing affluence so
that a wider range of housing choices became available for a larger segment of
the inner metropolitan population than hitherto. At the same time, towards the
end of the 1960s and in the early 1970s, there was a selective return migration to
certain refurbished inner suburbs of professional and white-collar workers, notably
to Glebe, Balmain, Annandale and Paddington. This return movement was not
strong enough, however, to seriously off-set the heavy net migration loss
of the Australian-born in the inner suburbs. The trend towards depopulation
of the inner suburbs and some older middle-ring LGAs was substantially off-set,
however, by the massive impact of foreign-born immigration which slowed the total
population loss in all inner suburbs and actually arrested it in some, bringing about
a total population increase of modest dimensions. Thus in this area of Australian-
born population loss within inner Sydney, there was an increase of over 112 000
overseas-born, or over 48 per cent of the Australian-born loss. Table 6 indicates
that the southern European birthplace groups constituted the greater part of the
overseas-born increase in the inner LGAs of Sydney, Marrickville, Leichhardt and
Drummoyne compared with 32 per cent of the overseas-born increase in metropolitan Sydney. Greeks, Italians and Maltese together accounted for 67 per cent,
72 per cent and 74 per cent of the foreign-born increase in Marrickville, Leichhardt
and Drummoyne respectively. But in Waverley and Woollahra, which were much
higher in social status than those LGAs, the southern European contribution to
the overseas-born increase was well below the metropolitan average. The foreign-
born increase in these areas of more moderate Australian-born decline consisted
of migrants from many areas of Europe, more especially persons of Jewish origin
from central and east Europe. Population succession was the main population
change process operating in these suburbs.

Fringing the innermost suburbs of Australian-born decrease and ecological
succession were areas of moderately declining Australian-born population but with
immigrant succession resulting in total population increase. These areas were
Mosman, Burwood, Randwick and Botany. Many factors were involved, such as
partitioning of older homes into smaller units and possibly a higher density due
to larger family size, including extended families with recently arrived southern
Europeans in Botany, Randwick and Burwood. Certainly Greek, Italian and
Maltese heads of households had more persons per dwelling unit in metropolitan
Sydney (4.80, 4.09 and 4.66 respectively) than the Australian-born (3.29) in 1966.
In contrast to the inner suburbs of total population decline, the United Kingdom
and Irish-born were significant in the overseas-born increase, especially in Randwick
and the North Shore LGA, Mosman.

Many of the middle-distance suburbs were areas of pre-war housing of moderate
total population (and Australian-born) growth where immigration contributed
strongly to growth. These areas tended to surround the inner suburbs concentrically.
Population increases were generally below 40 per cent between 1947-1966 implying
that while Australian-born and natural increase occurred, there was an Australian-
born net migration loss along with an inflow of overseas migrants. In Canterbury,

Rockdale and Auburn, all southern LGAs, southern Europeans were important in the overseas-born increase but in the North Shore LGAs of Manly and Lane Cove, United Kingdom and Irish-born were important whereas the role of the southern European groups was insignificant. The movement of southern Europeans into Canterbury, Rockdale and Auburn occurred mainly in the 1961-1966 and 1966-1971 periods and reflects in part a movement out from core areas of initial settlement into contiguous areas of better housing.

In the outer areas near the urban periphery where the housing was built in the post-war era in the main, total population growth was greater than 80 per cent between 1947-1966 and the overseas-born contributed 24 per cent of the 872 000 total increase, only half their impact on metropolitan Sydney as a whole. The impact was stronger, however, on the outer industrial LGAs of Blacktown, Holroyd and especially Fairfield. In Fairfield, United Kingdom, German, Polish, and Italian-born were important in growth, while in neighbouring Holroyd, United Kingdom, Italian and Maltese-born contributed substantially to the overseas-born increase.

Differential inter-urban age-sex structures resulted from age-sex selectivity in intra-urban mobility and migration. In the inner suburbs, as mentioned, there was

Table 7. The impact of Australian-born children aged 0-24 of foreign-born parentage on the child and young adult age structures of selected inner suburban municipalities, Sydney & Melbourne, 1971

LGA	Australian-born children aged 0-24 of overseas-born or mixed parents	Australian-born children aged 0-24 of southern European-born parents	All Australian-born aged 0-24	Australian-born children 0-24 of overseas-born and mixed parents as % of all Australian-born aged 0-24	Australian-born children of southern European-born parents as % of all Australian-born aged 0-24
Sydney					
City of Sydney	3 625	1 088	14 121	25.7	7.7
South Sydney	3 951	1 909	11 007	35.9	17.3
Marrickville	11 957	6 868	26 187	45.7	26.2
Leichhardt	6 559	2 997	21 518	30.5	13.9
Drummoyne	2 979	1 813	9 108	32.7	20.0
Botany	3 520	1 340	10 948	32.2	12.2
Randwick	9 325	2 738	38 304	24.3	7.1
Melbourne					
Melbourne	8 286	3 514	25 102	33.0	14.0
Fitzroy	3 741	2 517	6 810	54.9	37.0
Collingwood	3 125	2 199	6 032	51.8	36.5
Richmond	3 879	2 716	8 010	48.4	33.9
Brunswick	8 009	6 079	15 360	52.1	39.6
Northcote	8 164	5 839	19 536	48.8	29.9
Prahran	5 263	2 383	16 328	32.2	14.6

Note: In the first column, children with one parent born overseas and one in Australia were summated and the total number halved.
Source: Census of the Commonwealth of Australia, 30 June 1971.

The suburban metropolis in
Australia: some
demographic forces at work

a net out-migration of Australian-born in the 20-45 age group (the reproductive years) and an in-migration of foreign-born, especially southern Europeans. Migration to Australia has tended to be heavily age selective with a strong concentration in the 'twenties and thirties' on arrival. Because of this selectivity in the in- and out-migration to central city suburbs, and residential concentration of southern European (and more latterly west Asian migrants), the immigrant population disproportionately contributed to the young and early-middle-age adult age structures in these areas. Ultimately, therefore a high proportion of children born in the inner suburbs have been children of foreign-born and especially southern European parents. The implications of this are fairly obvious as far as pressures on schools, language difficulties and the like are concerned. In Table 7, the children of foreign-born parentage are computed as components of the child and the young adult age structures in selected inner Sydney LGAs at the 1971 census. Melbourne data are included for comparative purposes.

Table 8. Variations in population density and mobility attributes between selected Sydney LGAs, 1971

		Density			Mobility-Migration		
Ecological area and LGA	Persons per sq mile	Persons per acre of zoned residential land	0-14 yr olds per acre of zoned educational land	Overseas -born	Overseas -born % of total population	Persons still resident in same dwelling as in 1966 Number	%
Older residential inner suburbs							
Ashfield	14034	28	196	15901	35.4	16900	37.6
Strathfield	5063	17	63	6992	25.7	13203	48.6
Canterbury	10120	21	223	35739	27.4	55400	43.7
Burwood	11389	24	117	10253	32.2	13830	43.4
Marrickville	15119	40	441	40618	42.0	35795	36.9
South Sydney	9562	55	493	14338	36.8	15614	40.1
Botany	5533	34	144	14325	37.5	16767	43.8
Randwick	9334	34	89	35678	28.8	52623	42.5
Older middle-distance LGAs							
Rockdale	7441	22	142	20505	24.3	44845	53.2
Waverley	18887	40	335	23337	35.6	25698	39.2
Newer middle-distance LGAs							
Bankstown	5419	18	108	32045	19.7	102078	62.7
Kogarah	6268	15	133	8169	17.3	27244	57.7
Hurstville	7023	18	216	9601	14.1	40181	59.8
Outer industrial-residential							
Fairfield	3042	18	124	37819	33.5	60001	53.1
Holroyd	5100	18	106	17683	22.9	40301	52.1
Campbelltown	285	15	72	7874	23.0	62818	48.2
Liverpool	680	24	147	19467	23.6	39977	48.5
Sutherland	1060	15	134	22974	15.2	81488	53.8

Source: Census of the Commonwealth of Australia, 30 June 1971.

261

Finally, intra-metropolitan variations in population density and mobility as at the 1971 census are tabulated for metropolitan Sydney (Table 8). Clearly the highest densities were in the inner suburbs often in areas of nineteenth century terrace or row houses except that in Waverley, modern apartments and units accounted for the very high levels. With the exception of Waverley and Strathfield which were higher status areas, densities of children per acre of educational land were generally higher in the older, poorer, lower status inner suburbs, notably Marrickville and South Sydney, which were also areas of migrant concentration. Migrant concentrations here tended to reinforce social segregation because of their higher concentration in unskilled occupations than the Australian-born in the same residential areas.

It will be noted that in common with many large cities, population turnover and mobility rates varied considerably, being in general highest in the inner suburbs and outer suburbs and lowest in more stable middle-distance suburbs. This has implications for notions of community stability or instability and neighbourhood cohesion, or otherwise, in different parts of the metropolis.

It can be seen, then, through the simple description of intra-urban demographic processes operating in Australia's largest metropolis, that very considerable demographic variations have emerged which are part and parcel of the scale of urban development. These have implications for different life styles, and possibly, life chances in areas that differ in their urban ecology. In understanding what Vernon and Hoover have called the 'anatomy of a metropolis'[9] – which emphasises process and change over time, rather than variations at one point in time, we can perhaps understand more of the dynamics involved in Australian societal change. Too often, perhaps, demographic change has been ignored in the study of urban society and economic structure over emphasised, whereas what is needed is an integration of the two, set against the historical development of the city. This would contribute greatly towards sharpening our perception of the urban environment, which forms so great a part of the human environment in Australia.

Notes and references

1. BURGESS, ERNEST W. 'The growth of the city: an introduction to a research project', in PARK, R. E., BURGESS, E. W. and MCKENZIE, R. D. (eds.) *The city*. Chicago, University of Chicago Press, 1925, p. 47.
2. GLYNN, SEAN. *Urbanisation in Australian history, 1788–1900*. Melbourne, Nelson, 1970, pp. 28–29.
3. DAY, LINCOLN H. 'Family size and fertility', in DAVIES, A. F. and ENCEL, S. (eds.). *Australian society: a sociological introduction*. 2nd edn. Melbourne, Cheshire, 1970, Chapter Two.
4. DAY, LINCOLN H. Differential fertility in Australia: paper presented at biennial meeting of the International Union for the Scientific Study of Population, London 3–11 September 1969.
5. The net gain of the foreign-born in metropolitan statistical divisions was calculated by surviving the foreign-born population forward from each census, and the Australian-born populations by use of the appropriate Life Table. Where the survived populations overlapped, the differences were halved and apportional between the two populations. It should be noted that the foreign figures would be inflated by internal migration.
6. WILSON, M. G. A. Patterns of infant mortality in Australian cities: paper presented to the Institute of Australian Geographers' Conference, Adelaide, 1973.

*The suburban metropolis in
Australia: some
demographic forces at work*

7. MORRILL, R. L., EARICKSON, R. J. and REES, P. 'Factors influencing distances travelled to hospitals', *Economic Geography*, 46:161–171, 1970.
8. DE VISE, PIERRE. *Slum medicine: Chicago style. How the medical needs of the city's negro poor are met*. Chicago Regional Hospital Study Working Paper no. 4.8, 1968.
9. HOOVER, EDGAR M. and VERNON, RAYMOND. *Anatomy of a metropolis: the changing distribution of people and jobs within the New York Metropolitan region*. New York, Doubleday, Anchor, 1962.

*Maris Buchanan**

Evaluating the urban environment:
a Melbourne study

INTRODUCTION

Much of the work in human geography may be described in broad terms as the study of the relationships between man and the environment – both the natural environment and the built environment. We study these relationships to identify existing and potential areas of stress, conflict and pressure on the resources of the environment. In the cities, conflict has arisen in residential suburbs subjected to water and air pollution from industrial activities or noise pollution from transport networks. There is pressure on resources where welfare services, schools and other facilities are inadequate to meet the requirements of the population, and where population and dwelling density per unit of zoned residential land are high. There is stress in areas inadequately served by public transport, particularly in the new suburbs in urban fringe locations. Ward and Dubos, in their book *Only one earth*[1] have discussed the diseconomies of long periods of daily commuting and the stresses which can arise in family life when young wives are virtually isolated in the suburbs for long periods of the day.

An integral part of the study of man-environment interaction is the examination of processes which are altering the character of the urban environment. In population terms, these processes include the expansion of outer suburbs, and the renewal of inner suburbs by ethnic rejuvenation, Housing Commission development or the replacement of the single family dwelling with high rise flats and home units. These processes are increasing in variety and in complexity, they are intensifying and they are spreading geographically – in short, the per capita impact on the environment is increasing, especially in urban areas.

Australia is a country in which an extremely high proportion of the population lives in several large metropolitan areas – the proportion was just over 60 per cent in the State capitals in 1971.[2] New towns and cities are being planned to house future population increases, and there is a continuing drift from the country to the city.[3] Most recent overseas immigrants are also to be found in Australia's big cities, where they can get jobs. Many of the problems encountered in large urban centres are becoming urgent matters for concern and it seems essential that some attempt be made to study these problems and to evaluate the quality of the urban environment from the point of view of those who live there but who are not normally involved in planning decisions. Questions must be asked relating to prevailing attitudes towards and opinions about life in urban centres with a view to tackling some of the social problems of the areas, as well as the economic problems, transport congestion and pollution.

The authors of *Human ecology: problems and solutions*[4] have suggested that the quality of life may be measured in terms of the number of alternatives and opportunities available. These 'personal options' consist of access to different

* Maris Buchanan is a Research Fellow with the Botany Bay Project at the Australian National University.

landscapes and choice of residential environment, of place and type of work
and of cultural and recreational facilities. Population growth and the increasing
exploitation of resources to satisfy basic human needs means that this range of
options may be gradually diminishing – that is, the quality of life is being reduced.
It has been pointed out that if zero population growth is achieved, most of our
energies could be redirected towards improving the quality of the environment.
Even for those who do not accept the concept of zero population growth, there is a
need to establish and maintain population numbers suited, first, to the resources of
an area at any one time or level of technology and, secondly, to the range of options
available to the population in the area. These options must cover every major
aspect of life – work, leisure-time activities, travelling and shopping – and the
relationships of these activities to environmental factors must be examined in
terms of stress, conflict and pressure on resources.

ASSESSING THE QUALITY OF THE URBAN ENVIRONMENT

There are many different approaches to assessing not only the quality but also
the problems of the urban environment, and in recent years geographers and
planners have emphasised the need for a systematic study of the relationships
between the physical and social environments of urban areas.[5-11] Behavioural
geography, the recognised term for the study of human activities in a spatial
context, now encompasses a broad range of interrelated themes, but the main
topic of concern is with man-environment interaction processes which are responsible for generating observed, spatial patterns and which are of considerable value
in explaining and predicting the outcome of environmental planning and management issues.[12] There are now many studies in geography and planning of the ways
in which people make use of their environment, that is, their activity patterns in
the broadest sense – movement to work and to shop are two examples. These
studies, which rely heavily on analysing frequency of movement, distance, direction,
purpose, method and cost have provided many useful insights into life in urban
areas.

Despite the large number of such studies carried out to date, there is still room
for more investigation of activity patterns within urban areas. One field which has
remained largely untouched until very recently is the study of recreation activities.
(Walmsley and Day,[13] in their review of the literature on man-environment
interaction, include a short section dealing with recreation studies.) With the
increasing amounts of leisure time now commonplace in the community and the
increasing affluence throughout society, it is becoming more important to know
what people are doing and what they want to do with their recreation time and
with the other resources which they now have for recreation activities. There has
been much work on recreation in the United States and Great Britain, and this
can provide guidelines for investigations in Australia. Several writers have discussed
the opportunities for recreation within urban areas and the need to make the
best use of relatively small pockets of land.[14,15] Studies of shoreline and river
recreation facilities and green belt facilities are also relevant to the Australian
urban situation.

Another approach to assessing the quality of the urban environment is to
question people about their attitudes towards the areas in which they are living,
the housing they are occupying, the facilities which are available to them in that

area and their preferences relating to these factors. It is only recently (within the last ten years) that geographers, sociologists and planners have turned their attention to studies of this nature and a whole new field of inquiry has opened up. Geographical studies of environmental perception range from theoretical issues such as the precise measurement of perception[16] and attempts to model perception,[17] to studies of the various factors which impinge on the perception process and on the learning and decision-making stages involved.[18-20] Much of the work on perception is interdisciplinary, being the concern of environmental psychologists, sociologists and planners as well as geographers. Because attitudes and opinions are extremely difficult to measure, it is necessary to exercise caution in analysing them. Merely taking the techniques used by psychologists to analyse attitudes and opinions may not solve the problems of how to assess attitudes towards urban environments, and may overlook some essential components of the environmental perception problem. Psychologists would be amongst the first to point out that the phenomena of the mind are never entirely quantifiable,[21] and geographers and planners have an additional dimension to consider – the spatial dimension.

THE MELBOURNE STUDY: DATA AND METHODS

One essential component of the study of attitudes and opinions must be a consideration of those factors which are proving influential in producing a variety of patterns of perception. The factors may range from purely economic criteria to less easily measured but equally vital impressionistic factors. Despite its fundamental importance, this is one area which has received little attention, a situation which has prompted a number of writers to emphasise the need for a closer investigation of the factors which are important in different perceptual situations.[22,23] The Melbourne Family Survey (currently being undertaken by the Department of Demography, Australian National University), is a broad investigation covering many aspects of urban life in Australia. With emphasis on the family and on family planning, the Survey included several questions relating to the residence location preferences of the Melbourne housewives and to their perceived advantages and disadvantages of living in Melbourne. Analysis of the responses to these questions together with the considerable amount of background information available from the survey provided the opportunity for a relatively detailed examination of the factors which were relevant in the perception process. The analysis has revealed some interesting points concerning attitudes towards life in Melbourne, some of which may be of significance for future planning decisions.

The sample included women aged between 15 and 60 years who had been married once and who were still living with their husband. Thus the viewpoints analysed are those of women in a family situation and various stages in the family life cycle are represented. Encel,[24] in his study of Australian families, noted the increasingly active role of the mother in the social aspects of family life, which would suggest that her views on the urban environment should be relevant to planning policy. The Melbourne sample was a locationally-based stratified random-sample with the probability of selection being equal throughout the metropolitan area. As such, it was representative of different socio-economic groups and also of the many immigrant groups which are a feature of Melbourne society. A comparison of the attitudes of the Australian-born group with those of some of the immigrant groups was one of the focal points of the study and was particularly important in view of the large numbers of overseas migrants in Australia's urban and metropolitan areas.[25]

RESULTS AND DISCUSSION

An appendix with several tables of results is at the end of this Chapter. The figures in the first table indicate a strong preference for the present address, while the numbers selecting alternative locations decreased rapidly with increasing distance from the present address and decreasing familiarity with the environment. This pattern accords with the findings of other studies of residence location preferences, all of which have shown a strong desire to remain at the current place of residence.[26-30]

Over 30 percent of the women mentioned the employment opportunities for their husbands as the best thing about Melbourne (Table 2). Next most important were the fact that they had always lived in Melbourne and the presence of friends and relatives in the city. The most frequently mentioned worst aspect of Melbourne was the weather (Table 3). Next most important were the pollution and noise of the city, while smaller numbers considered that Melbourne was too expensive, too crowded, or that travelling within the city created problems for them. Features representing more specifically the built environment – namely, the beauty of Melbourne or the ugliness of the city – were scarcely mentioned as the best or worst aspects of living in Melbourne. Perceived advantages of Melbourne appeared to be related more to the material benefits to be derived from living in the city and to familiarity with the physical and social surroundings. Over 60 per cent of the housewives agreed that life in the country is more pleasant than life in the city (Table 4a), while less than 30 per cent agreed that Melbourne is a lonely place (Table 4b).

Also as a preliminary stage in the investigation, the relationships between the residence location preferences and the perceived best and worst aspects of Melbourne were examined. Emphasis on the employment opportunities for the husband was higher in the groups preferring not to live in Melbourne than in the groups preferring to live at their present address or elsewhere in Melbourne. For the last two groups the fact that they had always lived in Melbourne was more important than for other groups. Those who wished to live elsewhere in Victoria favoured the shopping facilities in Melbourne but tended to think that the city was polluted, noisy or too crowded. Those who would elect to live somewhere in Australia other than in Victoria disliked the weather in Melbourne more than all the other groups.

The next stage in the analysis was to examine the relationships between the preferences and attitudes and a range of characteristics of the Melbourne house-wives. The various characteristics used fell essentially into two groups – those describing the housewife's background and those describing her present situation. On the whole, the results (which are summarised in the appendix, Tables 5 to 10) showed that some of the characteristics were more important than others in explaining variations in preferences and attitudes. For example, certain contrasts were apparent in the attitudes of the younger and older sections of the community (Table 5). The oldest age groups contained the highest proportions of those preferring to remain at their present address, while those in the youngest age groups had the highest expectations of moving, particularly within Melbourne.

The youngest immigrants were those with the greatest desire to return to the home country. The older women placed less emphasis on employment for their husbands as the best aspect of Melbourne, and more of them mentioned the beauty of the city and the fact that they had always lived there as best aspects. The proportions mentioning the presence of friends and relatives, one of the most important best aspects, did not vary in the different age groups.

Level of education, one of the background characteristics, also produced some interesting differences in preferences and attitudes (Table 6). More full-time education was equated with a greater desire to live elsewhere in Melbourne, Victoria or Australia and overseas. However, in the case of the immigrants in the sample, the proportions desiring to return to the home country decreased markedly with increasing level of education. Emphasis on the employment opportunities for the husband was less amongst those in the more educated groups. Reference to the entertainment and cultural activities in Melbourne, to the beauty of the city and to the unhealthiness, pollution and noise were all associated with a high level of education. Respondents who thought that Melbourne was too expensive tended to belong to the groups with low levels of education, while those who thought the city too crowded were mainly in the more educated groups. Travelling problems appeared greater to those with higher levels of education and this, plus the reference to the beauty of the city by the more highly educated groups, probably reflected the tendency for these groups to be living in the outer suburbs.[31]

As mentioned earlier, one of the main points of note was a comparison of the preferences and attitudes of the Australians and the immigrants in the sample (Table 7). The British group had the smallest proportion wanting to stay where they were, while the Italian and Greek groups had the highest. This could be an indication of greater overall dissatisfaction on the part of British immigrants in Australia and also reflects the tendency for Southern European immigrants to form close-knit groups in urban areas.[32] Satisfaction with the current place of residence is also associated with length of residence in Australia, although the relationships were not always clear-cut. On the whole, the proportions of immigrants desiring to return to their home countries were small (less than 10 per cent). The presence of friends and/or relatives in Melbourne was a favourable aspect of the city for quite large numbers of the immigrants with the exception of the Dutch. Nevertheless, the proportions of all immigrant groups who mentioned that they were lonely in Melbourne were higher than the proportion of Australians. The immigrants placed greater emphasis on the employment opportunities for their husbands in Melbourne than did the Australians, and much of their desire to remain in the same place in Australia may be due to this. It was also of note that the Greeks and Italians comprised a large proportion of those who considered Melbourne an expensive place to live.

Length of residence in Melbourne and the presence of friends and relatives in the city were also important influences on preferences and attitudes. Overall, the proportions desiring an alternative location decreased with increasing length of residence in Melbourne and the increase in the proportions preferring their present address was particularly marked (Table 8). Amongst the immigrants, the decrease in desire to return to the home country with increasing length of residence was also noted. The frequency with which the weather was mentioned as the worst thing about living in Melbourne increased the longer the respondents had lived in the city. Conversely, the importance of employment for the husband decreased with increasing length of residence in Melbourne, which would suggest that many of the more recent arrivals had come to Melbourne largely because of the employment opportunities available there for the husband. As anticipated, the importance of the presence of friends and relatives in the city increased with increasing length of residence of the respondent.

These points were reinforced by a comparison of the residence location preferences and attitudes of the Australian-born women in the sample who had always lived in Melbourne and those who had not always lived there (Table 9). Slightly higher proportions of those who had always lived in Melbourne would prefer to remain at the present address or to live elsewhere in Melbourne and slightly higher proportions of the incomers to Melbourne would prefer to live elsewhere in Australia. The fact that a higher proportion of those who had not always lived in Melbourne mentioned the employment opportunities for their husbands as the best thing about living in Melbourne supported the suggestion that those who have moved to Melbourne had done so largely to get work.

The respondent's current place of residence in Melbourne was also taken into consideration and was found to be associated with quite marked variations in preferences and attitudes. The Melbourne Local Government Areas (LGAs) have been grouped by Stimson[33] into eight socio-economic areas on the basis of 1966 census data and these eight areas formed the basis for this analysis. It became clear that location within the city was a surrogate for many of the other variables measuring the socio-economic status of the respondents. For example, area 3, which comprised Fitzroy, Collingwood and Richmond had the highest proportion of respondents who would like to return to their home country (Table 10) and this was a reflection of the large number of Greeks in that area.[34] This was also the area where greatest emphasis was placed on employment opportunities for the husband, where the presence of friends and relatives in the city and the fact that they had always lived there were of least importance and where the proportion of respondents who thought Melbourne too expensive was highest. The third area, and also the fourth, comprising Melbourne City, South Melbourne, St Kilda and Prahran, contained the highest proportions mentioning the employment opportunities for the wife as the best thing about living in Melbourne.

The area with the highest proportion of respondents who considered the pollution and noise of the city its most undesirable features was the first one, the western suburbs, where much of the city's industry is located. Areas 6, 7 and 8, the outer eastern and north-eastern suburbs, had the highest proportions who said that Melbourne is too crowded. As these are not areas of high population density,[35] the views expressed by the residents in this instance must reflect their overall impressions of Melbourne rather than their attitudes to the particular district in which they are living. The majority of those who thought that travelling within the city constituted a problem lived in area 8, the outer eastern suburbs. However, a considerable proportion of the residents in that area considered the beauty of the city to be its best aspect.

Probably the most interesting point of note in relation to the spatial variations in residence location preferences was the increasing desire to remain at the present address with increasing distance from the central city area. The desire to move to another part of Melbourne also declined with increasing distance from the centre of the city. This strong preference for the suburban locations was noted by Johnston[36] in a study of Christchurch and by Pryor[37] and Troy[38] in studies of certain Melbourne suburbs. The desire amongst the immigrants in Melbourne to return to their home country was strongest in the inner city areas and relatively evenly spread throughout the remainder of the city. This would suggest that, as immigrants become established in the city and move out to 'more desirable' areas, a process described by Lee[39] in relation to Italians in Melbourne, the wish to return to the home country became less. This pattern of movement is, of course, also associated with length of residence in Melbourne.

CONCLUSION

The characteristics which have been discussed in detail do not represent an exhaustive list of all relevant criteria influencing preference and attitudes. One additional aspect which could be important is the amount of movement by an individual within the city area both for work and social purposes. Interaction within cities has been discussed at length by Beshers[40] in his work on urban social structure. Movement influences an individual's ideas about and impressions of different parts of the city, brings him into contact with a broad cross-section of the city's population and enables him to make comparisons of different areas. In short, movement widens the knowledge of the city and increases awareness and understanding of the city's advantages and disadvantages. Some data were available relating to the movements of Melbourne housewives to visit their parents and other relations. An examination of the frequency and distance of movement and of the type of contact (whether by telephone or by visiting) showed that the proximity of relations did contribute significantly to the desire to remain at the same address. Martin[41] has commented on the closeness of family ties in certain Adelaide suburbs and it would be interesting to test her hypotheses further in relation to the Melbourne data. Another factor which could be of importance and which was not included in the Melbourne study is the rural or urban background of the respondent. City life may appear more or less attractive to rural-urban migrants once they are settled in the cities than it does to those who have always lived there.

A number of writers have commented on the role of inertia in inducing acceptance of the current place of residence.[42-44] An attempt was made to assess the importance of inertia amongst the Melbourne housewives by examining the residence location preferences and the number of times that the family had moved to a new home. Those who had moved once had the highest proportion (70 per cent) who would prefer to remain at the present address and this proportion declined only slightly with an increase in the number of moves (to 63 per cent for those who had moved eight times). These results appear to indicate that satisfaction was not necessarily greater amongst those who had moved seldom or never and that a considerable amount of movement in search of satisfaction was taking place. The results also indicated that higher levels of education, which may be equated with higher socio-economic status, were likely to result in greater expectations of moving and more sophisticated housing requirements.

In this chapter, attention has been focused on the attributes of the respondents in an effort to outline some of the factors which influence preferences and attitudes in an urban community. The analysis has relied on relatively simple methods of examining the relationships between the preferences and attitudes and the various

characteristics of the respondents, and each factor has essentially been considered
in isolation. However, to disregard the interplay amongst the many factors which
are involved considerably limits our understanding of the observed variations
in preferences and attitudes. The use of appropriate multivariate statistical techniques,
which are equipped to deal with the complex interrelationships amongst the large
sets of variables commonly found in behavioural studies, could provide a more
detailed insight into the manner in which preferences and attitudes are formed and
also into the relative importance of a range of factors in different behavioural
situations.

To conclude, therefore, this study has attempted to outline certain characteristic
preferences and attitudes of different socio-economic and ethnic groups within the
city. Both the characteristics describing the backgrounds of the respondents and
those describing their present situations were associated with the different preferences
and attitudes towards the urban environment. It was interesting to note that one of
the most important factors affecting an individual's liking or disliking for her
present surroundings was the proximity of and contact with friends and relatives.
If there are planning implications to be drawn from this study, possibly the major
one is that in decisions to establish new urban communities, no matter how many
amenities and attractions are planned, people will not be fully content unless their
social environment is congenial and they are not isolated from family and friends.

The responses also pointed to a general awareness of environmental issues,
heightened by the frequent references to the pollution, noise and unhealthiness
of the city. This is an encouraging sign for future campaigns to improve the quality
of life in Australia's urban areas.

References

1. WARD, BARBARA and DUBOS, R. *Only one earth: the care and maintenance of a small
   planet.* London, Andre Deutsch, 1972, p. 156.
2. ROWLAND, D. T. and BURNLEY, I. H. 'The urbanisation of the Australian population'.
   Paper delivered to Joint Urbanisation Seminar, Australian National University,
   Canberra, 1973, p. 2.
3. BURNLEY, I. H. and CHOI, C. Y. 'Population components in the growth of cities'.
   Paper delivered to Joint Urbanisation Seminar, Australian National University,
   Canberra, 1973, pp. 4–12.
4. EHRLICH, P. R., EHRLICH, ANNE H. and HOLDREN, J. P. *Human ecology: problems
   and solutions.* San Francisco, Freeman, 1973, pp. 261–2.
5. MICHELSON, W. 'An empirical analysis of environmental preferences'. *Journal of the
   American Institute of Planners.* 32:355–360, 1966.
6. MICHELSON, W. 'Urban sociology as an aid to physical development: some research
   strategies', *Journal of the American Institute of Planners.* 34:105–108, 1968.
7. KAIN, J. F. and QUIGLEY, H. M. 'Evaluating the quality of the residential
   environment', *Environment and Planning.* 2:23–32, 1970.
8. VANDERMARK, E. H. 'Measuring the quality of urban environment', *Australian
   Journal of Social Issues.* 5:179–200, 1970.
9. HOINVILLE, G. 'Evaluating community preferences', *Environment and Planning*
   3:33–50, 1971.
10. PARKES, D. N. 'Scalogram analysis in planning for urban renewal', *Royal
    Australian Institute Planning Journal.* 9:27–32, 1971.
11. MENCHIK, M. 'Residential environmental preferences and choice: empirical validating
    preference measures', *Environment and planning.* 4:445–458, 1972

12. WALMSLEY, D. J. and DAY, R. A. *Perception and man-environment interaction: a bibliography and guide to the literature.* Occasional Papers in Geography no. 2, Geographical Society of New South Wales, New England Branch, 1972, pp. 74–75.

13. *op. cit.* WALMSLEY and DAY, 1972, pp. 74–75.

14. FAIRBROTHER, NAN. *New lives, new landscapes.* Harmondsworth, Penguin, 1970, pp. 211–2.

15. PATMORE, A. J. *Land and leisure in England and Wales.* London, Newton Abbot, 1970, pp. 74–111.

16. DOWNS, R. M. 'Approaches to, and problems in, the measurement of geographic space perception', Seminar Paper series A, no. 9, Department of Geography, University of Bristol, 1967, pp. 2–6.

17. STEA, D. 'The measurement of mental maps: an experimental model for studying conceptual spaces', in Cox, K. R. and GOLLEDGE, R. G. (eds.). *Behavioural problems in geography: a symposium.* Studies in Geography 17, Department of Geography, Northwestern University, Illinois, 1969, pp. 228–253.

18. GOLLEDGE, R. G. 'The geographical relevance of some learning theories', in COX AND GOLLEDGE, 1969, *op. cit.* pp. 101–145.

19. WOLPERT, J. 'The decision process in a spatial context' *Annals of the Association of American Geographers.* 54:537–558, 1964.

20. WOLPERT, J. 'Behavioural aspects of the decision to migrate', *Papers and Proceedings of the Regional Science Association.* 15:159–169, 1965.

21. CHEIN, I. 'The environment as a determinant of behaviour', *Journal of Social Psychology.* 39:115–127, 1954.

22. DAVIES, W. K. D. (ed.). *The conceptual revolution in geography.* London, University of London Press, 1972, p. 332.

23. GOLLEDGE, R. G., BROWN, L. A. and WILLIAMSON, F. 'Behavioural approaches in geography: an overview', *Australian Geographer.* 12:59–79, 1972.

24. ENCEL, S. 'The family', in DAVIES, A. F. and ENCEL, S. (eds.). *Australian society: a sociological introduction.* 2nd edn. Melbourne, Cheshire, 1970, pp. 273–300. (First published 1965.)

25. *op. cit.* BURNLEY and CHOI, 1973, pp. 12–16.

26. GOULD, P. R. 'Structuring information on spatio-temporal preferences', *Journal of Regional Science.* 7:259–274, 1967.

27. GOULD, P. R. and WHITE, R. R. 'The mental maps of British school leavers', *Regional Studies.* 2:161–182, 1968.

28. JOHNSTON, R. J. 'The residential preferences of New Zealand school students: some tests of the economic and ecological man concepts', *New Zealand Journal of Geography.* 50:13–24, 1971.

29. HARTMAN, C. W. 'Social values and housing orientations', in BELL, GWEN, and TYRWHITT, JAQUELINE (eds.). *Human identity in the urban environment.* Harmondsworth, Penguin, 1972, pp. 304–315.

30. GIBBINGS, M. J. *Housing preferences in the Brisbane area.* Australian Institute of Urban Studies, Queensland Division, 1973, pp. 66–69.

31. JOHNSTON, R. J. 'The population characteristics of the urban fringe: a review and example', *Australian and New Zealand Journal of Sociology.* 2:79–93, 1966.

32. JONES, F. L. *Dimensions of urban social structure: the social areas of Melbourne, Australia.* Canberra, ANU Press, 1969, pp. 66–86.

33. STIMSON, R. J. 'Hierarchical classificatory methods: an application of Melbourne population data', *Australian Geographical Studies.* 8:149–172, 1970.

34. BURNLEY, J. H. 'The ecology of Greek settlement in Melbourne', *International Migration.* 10(4):161–177, 1972.

35. *op. cit.* STIMSON, 1970.

36. JOHNSTON, R. J. 'Mental maps of the city: surburban preference patterns , *Environment and Planning.* 3:63–72, 1971.

37. PRYOR, R. J. 'Urban fringe residence: motivation and satisfaction in Melbourne', *Australian Geographer.* 11:148–156, 1969.

38. TROY, P. N. *Environmental quality in four Melbourne suburbs.* Canberra, ANU Urban Research Unit, 1972, p. 148.

39. LEE, T. R. 'The role of the ethnic community as a reception area for Italian immigrants in Melbourne, Australia'. *International Migration.* 8(1–2):50–63, 1970.

40. BESHERS, J. M. *Urban social structure.* New York, Free Press, 1962, pp. 109–126.

41. MARTIN, JEAN I. 'Suburbia, community and network', in DAVIES and ENCEL, 1965, *op. cit.* pp. 301–339.

42. BESHERS, J. M. and NISHIURA, E. N. 'A theory of internal migration differentials, *Social Forces.* 39:214–218, 1961.

43. MYERS, G. L., McGINNIS, R. and MASNICK, G. 'The duration of residence approach to a dynamic stochastic model of internal migration: a test of the axiom of cumulative inertia'. *Eugenics Quarterly.* 14:121–126, 1967.

44. NEUTZE, M. 'The process of urban development', in *Analysis of urban development,* Tewksbury Symposium, University of Melbourne, 1970, pp. I.63–I.71.

APPENDIX

Table 1. Residence location preferences*

	Number	Per cent
Present address	1732	65.3
Elsewhere in Melbourne	431	16.3
Elsewhere in Victoria	171	6.4
Elsewhere in Australia	195	7.3
Abroad (home country)	73	2.7
Abroad (elsewhere)	30	1.3
Uncertain	20	0.7
Total	2652	100.0

Table 2. Best aspects of Melbourne*

	Number	Per cent
Employment for husband	857	32.3
Employment for wife	31	1.2
Schools	126	4.8
Friends/relatives here	487	18.4
Entertainment/culture	84	3.2
Shopping facilities	135	5.1
Housing	33	1.2
Born here/always lived here since arrival in Australia	491	18.5
Excitement of city life	64	2.4
Beauty of Melbourne	95	3.6
Good weather	61	2.3
Life style—preferable to Sydney	69	2.6
No response/other	119	4.5
Total	2652	100.0

* The responses are coded as a series of nominal variables indicating presence or absence of each preference and best and worst aspect of the city in the respondent's subjective assessment.

Table 3. Worst aspects of Melbourne*

	Number	Per cent
Unhealthy/pollution/noise	367	13.8
Too expensive	180	6.8
Too much travelling	163	6.2
Too crowded	202	7.6
Relatives/friends elsewhere	89	3.4
Unfriendly/lonely place	94	3.5
Housing problems	37	1.4
Crime/violence	67	2.5
Weather	743	28.0
Lack of culture/entertainment	55	2.0
No response/other	655	25.5
Total	2652	100.0

* The responses are coded as a series of nominal variables indicating presence or absence of each preference and best and worst aspect of the city in the respondent's subjective assessment.

Table 4. [a] Responses to statement: Melbourne is a lonely place†

Response	Number	Per cent
Agree	732	27.5
Uncertain/no response	73	2.8
Disagree	1847	69.7
Total	2652	100.0

Table 4· [b] Responses to statement: Life in the country is more pleasant than life in the city†

Response	Number	Per cent
Agree	1737	65.5
Uncertain/no response	60	2.3
Disagree	855	32.2
Total	2652	100.0

† The responses to these statements were coded +1 for 'agree' and —1 for 'disagree' with a zero designating 'uncertain' or 'no response'.

Table 5. Preferences and attitudes of different age groups (column percentages)

Birth Year	1910-14	1915-19	1920-24	1925-29	1930-34	1935-39	1940-44	1945-49	1950-54	Total
n =	104	164	288	367	359	384	432	427	125	2652
Residence location preference										
Present address	77.9	73.8	71.2	71.2	68.0	70.0	60.0	56.4	40.0	65.3
Elsewhere in Melbourne	11.5	11.6	12.2	8.5	14.8	14.6	20.6	21.1	36.8	16.3
Elsewhere in Victoria	2.9	7.3	6.0	6.5	6.1	3.7	6.3	8.7	11.2	6.5
Elsewhere in Australia	6.7	5.5	6.9	9.3	7.2	7.0	6.5	8.0	8.0	7.4
Overseas (home country)	1.0	0.6	1.7	3.0	2.0	3.7	3.9	3.0	3.2	2.8
Overseas (elsewhere)	0.0	0.6	1.0	0.8	1.1	0.5	2.1	1.9	0.0	1.1
Uncertain	0.0	0.6	1.0	0.8	0.8	0.5	0.7	0.9	0.8	0.0
Total	100.0	100.0	100.0	100.0	100.0	100.0	100.0	100.0	100.0	100.0
*Best aspect of Melbourne**										
Employment for husband	14.4	24.4	29.9	26.7	35.9	38.0	35.7	35.8	27.2	32.3
Friends/relatives	18.3	22.0	20.5	15.8	15.9	14.8	19.2	21.1	22.4	18.4
Born/always lived here	27.9	23.8	18.4	21.3	15.6	17.7	16.4	15.9	23.2	18.5
Beauty of Melbourne	5.8	4.3	4.5	4.6	3.6	3.9	2.8	2.6	0.8	3.6

* Selected items only.

275

Table 6. Preferences and attitudes according to level of education (column percentages)

	Years of full-time education				
	< 7	7-9	10-12	> 12	Total
Residence location preference					
n =	396	905	1023	296	2652
Present address	78.5	67.0	60.0	59.8	65.3
Elsewhere in Melbourne	11.1	15.6	18.7	17.6	16.3
Elsewhere in Victoria	1.5	7.7	7.0	7.8	6.5
Elsewhere in Australia	1.8	6.4	10.2	8.8	7.4
Overseas (home country)	6.6	1.8	2.1	1.7	2.8
Overseas (elsewhere)	0.3	0.6	1.3	3.7	1.1
Uncertain	0.3	1.0	0.8	0.7	0.0
Total	100.0	100.0	100.0	100.0	100.0
Best aspect of Melbourne					
Employment for husband	56.6	25.2	28.5	31.1	32.3
Entertainment/culture	1.5	2.7	2.8	8.5	3.0
Beauty of Melbourne	0.8	3.0	5.0	4.7	3.6
Worst aspect of Melbourne					
Unhealthy/pollution/noise	5.6	15.8	14.4	18.2	13.8
Too expensive	18.7	6.3	3.4	1.7	6.8
Too much travelling	1.3	5.8	7.8	8.8	6.2
Too crowded	2.0	7.0	8.7	14.2	7.6

Table 7. Birth place and variations in preferences and attitudes (column percentages)

	Birth Place					
	Australia	Britain	Netherlands	Italy	Greece	Total
Residence location preference n =	1632	244	35	200	177	2652
Present address	65.6	48.8	57.1	79.5	75.1	65.3
Elsewhere in Melbourne	16.1	21.3	17.1	6.5	17.0	16.3
Elsewhere in Victoria	7.9	7.8	14.3	1.0	0.6	6.4
Elsewhere in Australia	8.6	11.1	2.9	2.0	1.1	7.3
Abroad (home country)	0.1	6.6	8.6	10.0	6.2	2.7
Abroad (elsewhere)	0.8	4.1	0.0	0.0	0.0	1.3
Uncertain	0.9	0.4	0.0	1.0	0.0	0.7
Total	100.0	100.0	100.0	100.0	100.0	100.0
Best aspect of Melbourne						
Employment for husband	22.7	39.3	43.5	52.5	62.2	32.3
Friends/relatives	22.3	11.9	2.9	12.0	10.2	18.4
Worst aspect of Melbourne						
Too expensive	3.6	5.3	11.4	20.5	20.0	6.8
Unfriendly/lonely	2.4	4.1	5.7	8.0	5.7	3.5

Table 8. Length of residence in Melbourne and preferences and attitudes (column percentages)

| | Number of years | | | | | | |
	< 1	1-2	3-5	6-10	11-20	> 20	Total
Residence location							
preference n =	75	138	209	353	543	1330	2652
Present address	46.7	47.1	57.4	64.0	66.1	69.6	65.3
Elsewhere in Melbourne	24.0	17.4	16.3	15.6	16.0	15.9	16.3
Elsewhere in Victoria	6.7	7.3	5.3	6.2	6.6	6.5	6.4
Elsewhere in Australia	14.7	10.9	10.5	7.7	7.2	6.1	7.3
Overseas (home country)	8.0	11.6	7.2	4.8	2.6	0.4	2.7
Overseas (elsewhere)	0.0	5.1	2.9	0.9	0.9	0.7	1.3
Uncertain	0.0	0.7	0.5	0.9	0.6	0.9	0.7
Total	100.0	100.0	100.0	100.0	100.0	100.0	100.0
Best aspect of Melbourne							
Employment for husband	44.0	60.1	58.4	43.9	38.1	19.3	32.3
Friends/relatives	9.3	8.7	8.6	11.9	16.9	23.7	18.4
Worst aspect of Melbourne							
Weather	16.0	21.7	22.5	25.2	27.8	31.1	28.0

Table 9. Residence in Melbourne (Australian-born only) and preferences and attitudes (column percentages)

| | | Always lived in Melbourne | | |
		Yes	No	Total
Residence location preference n =		949	683	2652
Present address		68.4	61.4	65.3
Elsewhere in Melbourne		18.4	12.9	16.3
Elsewhere in Victoria		6.0	10.5	6.4
Elsewhere in Australia		5.6	12.9	7.3
Overseas (home country)		0.2	0.0	2.7
Overseas (elsewhere)		0.5	1 2	1.3
Uncertain		0.8	0.9	0.7
Total		100.0	100.0	100.0
Best aspect of Melbourne				
Employment for husband		17.2	30.5	32.3
Born/always lived here		32.4	11.1	18.5

Table 10. Variations in preferences and attitudes by location in Melbourne: socio-economic areas (column percentages)

	Area								
	1	2	3	4	5	6	7	8	Total
Residence location									
preference n =	283	405	101	255	282	839	239	248	2652
Present address	69.6	64.9	47.5	55.3	64.2	67.7	66.1	71.0	65.3
Elsewhere in Melbourne	16.6	16.5	26.7	22.0	17.7	15.4	10.0	12.5	16.3
Elsewhere in Victoria	5.3	7.2	5.9	8.2	5.3	5.8	10.9	4.0	6.4
Elsewhere in Australia	5.3	6.7	5.9	7.1	7.8	8.0	8.8	7.7	7.3
Abroad (home country)	2.5	3.7	10.9	2.4	2.1	1.7	3.4	2.4	2.7
Abroad (elsewhere)	0.4	0.5	2.0	2.4	2.8	0.7	0.4	1.6	1.3
Uncertain	0.4	0.5	1.0	2.8	0.0	0.7	0.4	0.8	0.7
Total	100.0	100.0	100.0	100.0	100.0	100.0	100.0	100.0	100.0
Best aspect of Melbourne									
Employment for husband	39.2	38.8	51.5	33.7	28.4	27.7	30.1	27.0	32.3
Employment for wife	0.4	0.7	4.0	4.7	0.4	0.7	0.8	0.8	1.2
Friends/relatives	17.0	15.3	9.9	18.0	22.7	20.9	15.1	18.6	18.4
Born/always lived here	21.6	19.8	10.9	14.5	20.6	20.4	15.5	14.5	18.5
Beauty of Melbourne	1.1	0.7	2.0	0.8	2.8	5.1	3.4	10.5	3.6
Worst aspect of Melbourne									
Unhealthy/pollution/noise	20.9	14.3	8.9	16.1	14.9	12.0	11.3	12.1	13.8
Too expensive	10.6	12.6	16.8	5.9	3.9	3.6	5.9	4.8	6.8
Too much travelling	2.8	4.7	1.0	3.5	5.7	8.1	6.3	10.9	6.2
Too crowded	4.6	4.7	4.0	7.1	7.8	9.5	10.5	8.5	7.6
Unfriendly/lonely	0.4	1.2	0.0	0.4	0.0	2.5	2.9	2.8	3.5

*5. Changing perception
of the Australian
environment: current
attitudes and future
trends*

*Donald Horne**

A social history of
Mrs Edna Everage

NOTE:

Barry Humphries's great archetypal creation Mrs Edna Everage crystallises a group of characteristics that can help order discussion of Australian social issues, and be useful in observing Australian society. In sketching in here a possible history of Mrs Everage, it is no more intended to suggest that this is an overall sketch of Australian social history than Humphries intends us to imagine that Mrs Everage represents all Australians. There are as many Australian social histories as there are types of Australians.

I

To understand Mrs Edna Everage one must go back to her great-grandfather, who had been born in one of the new industrial towns of England and had emigrated to Australia in 1849. *His* grandfather had been a country boy, and in the industrial slum where they lived there had already matured a legend of the pleasant rural arcady existing before there were great manufacturing towns. (In fact his grandfather had moved from a worse to a better slum when he moved from country to city.) When this arcadian dreamtime was created in the imagination of the industrial poor, sturdy yeoman farmers were cast as the backbone of rural life, and it was the sober and civilising virtues of agriculture that were believed to have sustained society. The hope that he could 'return' to this utopia of a past that had never existed but that legend now gave him as a birthright, caused Mrs Everage's great-grandfather to come to Australia. In this new land he believed he might be able to set up as a farmer and so recover his natural rights as an Englishman.

In Sydney he found the rhetoric of his dream flourishing: there were speeches about the need for 'a numerous, industrious and virtuous agricultural population', hopes that 'within a few years the deserted interior of the colony will present a beautiful scene – a thousand cottages along each creek, gardens full of flowers'. However, there was no land policy that made it possible for this to happen; and even if there had been it wouldn't have worked, because Australia wasn't that kind of country.

So Mrs Everage's great-grandfather simply got a job in town. Even if it was a better job than he had in England, and with more money to it, this was not what he had intended. He did, however, gain several important and sustaining victories. The first was that he was able to rent one of the 'humble cottages springing up in thick clusters', and, with the new softening of leisure pursuits which was seen as a debrutalising of the lower classes, he could then set up in his backyard a garden of imported flowers and vegetables. He may not have become a sturdy yeoman, but at least he now commanded the broad square feet of his own backyard, among plants as exotic as he was.

He began to hope for even more. Building societies were developing; there were

---

* Donald Horne, author, is presently Research Fellow at the University of New South Wales. He was Editor of *The Bulletin* from 1967-72.

281

banks for workmen's savings; and he had his own two hands. When he could
afford it he bought a block of land and on it he built a small wooden house in one
of those areas described by W.S. Jevons as resembling 'the wooden huts of a
military encampment . . . Unpretentious as it is to any conveniences or beauties, it
yet satisfies [the labourer or mechanic] better than the brick built, closely packed,
and rented houses of English towns'.

It was here that he spent the rest of his life, extending his house, improving it,
maintaining his garden. He sometimes still had dreams of a farm of his own;
but when the land reform policies came he stayed where he was, which was just
as well, because he knew nothing about farming and didn't have enough capital
to learn through experience – although there were still times when he would imagine
that perhaps where so many have failed he might really have made a success of it.
He had a framed certificate of his building society membership on his walls and of
his friendly society membership. For a while there was also a certificate of his temperance society membership. (In one of the great ideological divisions of the age he
had for a while declared himself for temperance although never, as he often pointed
out, for total abstinence. Even in his moderation he was always moderate.)

It was in this wooden house that Mrs Everage's grandfather was born, but
when it came to his turn to set up house it was, because of his marriage, to Melbourne that he turned, in one of the suburbs, advertised as a 'rural arcady', that
were being opened up along the new railways. To buy his block of land he went
to a land sale carnival, with free travel and free luncheons, where some paddocks
had been pegged out into rectangular grids of streets. For the rest of his life he
was fairly sure that some of the bidders had been working for the auctioneer and
that if it hadn't been for their bidding-up he might have got the land more cheaply;
but then he couldn't be certain.

The paddocks filled out with houses. Shops began to form along the railway
line, near the station. Footpaths were cleared. Gas and water pipes were dug in.
Schools and churches, and a mechanics institute went up. They laid out a racecourse
not far away. There was an oval for cricket and football, bowling greens, public
tennis courts. But there was still a market garden and a dairy farm in the district
and since the new settlement clung fairly close to the railway line there was open
country not far off, even some bush. A second generation suburbanite, Mrs
Everage's grandfather tended his garden with great assiduity and skill and, with
his wife and rather large family, made of his home something that expressed the
greater part of the meaning of his life. Several people came to Australia to write
books about such a new phenomenon. By one of them he was seen as the 'petty
suburban proprietor' who would sit 'on his veranda on sunny Sunday mornings,
smoking and discussing things with his fellow workmen'. He felt himself a 'unit in
the community, a somebody'.

Now it is time to record the birth of Mrs Everage's father. At the time of his
birth there were many favourable omens. The new ice chests had come in, and the
new vegetable cutters, jelly strainers and egg beaters. The sewing machine had
arrived and the small iron-frame piano, available on time payment. Of particular
significance to her grandfather, there was also in the invention of the mechanical
lawn mower, a most significant technological revolution.

A third generation suburbanite, as he took the schooling they offered him and
went up the social ladder a bit by becoming a white collar worker, Mrs Everage's

father had finally discarded that dream of a yeoman's arcady that had risen and then declined in the preceding four generations of his family. In fact he scorned the cocky farmers, as the yeomen had now become, and was soon to laugh at them as 'Dad and Dave'. To be master of his own backyard was good enough for him. Besides, if he wanted a bit more fresh air, there was fishing nearby, plenty of places for picnics, and plenty of opportunities for sport. A country where, as the English saw it, there was 'no class too poor to play, as at home', could seem 'a genuine Democracy, the people really wanting what it wishes to get'.

There was some celebration of this democracy, and even of the fact that 'Australia, perhaps for the first time in history, has presented the spectacle of magnificent cities growing with marvellous rapidity and embracing within their limits a third of the population of the States of which they are the seats of government'. But a more usual view (which still sought the traditional idea of rural virtue) saw in Mrs Everage's suburbanite father and grandfather examples of the greatest peril of the age. 'The civilisation in the Australian cities is not new, but an old, hoary-headed, decrepit European civilisation, which appears half the world over to be tottering to its grave. Any stranger can see . . . the luxury and refinement of the old world gnawing at the heart of the new . . . As soon as a nation shuts itself up in cities it begins to decay.' There was only one hope: 'The Anglo-Saxon devotion to sport and athletics might save the people'.

So even if the suburbanites were now contented to cultivate their gardens, reformers still wanted to hustle them out of the cities and set them up on the land. 'Sydney, Melbourne and Adelaide are like huge cancers whose ramifications of disease spread far into national life. The city tribe of clerks and similar employees [are] carried on the back of some struggling farmer or miner or stock-raiser. If our cancers are not extirpated, they may yet destroy the nation.'

In the late nineteenth century there was already talk of how 'the overflow of bricks and mortar has spread like a lava flow'. As one late nineteenth century observer put it: 'The houses are all as like one another as peas in a box – four-roomed squares or six-roomed oblongs built of red brick, and with every detail exactly the same'. In the new century distaste for the externals of houses extended to distaste for their inhabitants. 'Barebrick habitations . . . unrelieved by trees or greens . . . shrivel up every poor little instinct and aspiration towards natural purity and beauty.'

However these black moods, ranging from aesthetic distaste to a sense of social and moral catastrophe, are no way of setting the scene for the birth of Mrs Edna Everage herself, the archetype of suburban optimism and homelover's progress. More bustle and belief is needed for this event. To prepare for her birth we should contemplate the kinds of miracles that augured it: the building in Melbourne and Sydney of 'skyscrapers' of up to 12 storeys; the installation of elevators; the spread of department shores; the installation of the new wireless service in Australia by the Marconi company; the appearance of horseless carriages; of flying machines; and the invention of office life – cash registers, telephones, typewriters, typists.

In this mood we can now record the event itself: Mrs Everage was born in the romantic profusion of her father's Queen Anne house, with its confident assertion of taste and respectability. As token of its up-to-dateness, beneath its red tile roof there had been introduced novelties even later than the Queen Anne style of which the house itself was composed: leadlight windows had been put in as an improvement to the facade; an art nouveau kookaburra was to be seen in the drawing room; a sleepout had been added at the back; and at one side of the house her father had installed a fernery.

When, with the spread of the motor bus, suburbs began to expand away from the railway lines into the bushland, Mrs Everage's family moved with them: their Queen Anne house now seemed unbearably old-fashioned so they went off to one of the new bus suburbs, where they had bought one of the new Californian bungalows, 'set low and close to the ground as a fortress'. By this time the six capital cities, which held half the total population, were uniquely suburbanised, covering a greater area for their population than any other cities in the world.

Mrs Everage grew to maturity and marriage in the age of the hiking craze, of the spread of golf courses and the beginning of their democratisation, of the first council swimming pools, of the 'spin' in the motor car to look at 'views' or enjoy the pleasures of a 'chop picnic' and of the slight softening of the idea of the typical Australian from that of the bronzed Anzac to that of the bronzed surf lifesaver. In some terms this seemed to represent continuing success, but some pleasures, in particular gregariousness, seemed to be lost. Perhaps this didn't matter so much for Mrs Everage herself who was part of a big family that knew how 'to make its own fun', but hotels had ceased to be meeting places, the cities were deserted at night, the new suburban centres provided no meeting points. There was a remarkable shrivelling of the opportunity for men and women to enjoy themselves together in public places other than at sporting events or beaches. Within many households there were conditions of almost siege-like isolation.

However critics found something more than that. While in most other countries it was usually the elites who were considered to blame for whatever seemed wrong, in Australia, because the suburbanites seemed arrogantly above their station, or because there was a new social situation for which the old culture had no appropriate concepts, the people were held responsible for almost all of what were seen as Australia's inadequacies. The idea of a uniquely destructive class jealousy was invented by Lord Bryce and others, and had a long silly season; for other commentators suburbanites were seen as uniquely frivolous, their attention 'divided between beauty competitions, the racing and betting news, and the latest of inane reviews'. D.H. Lawrence, who would have been unlikely to blame the state of England on its ordinary people, without any hesitation blamed the state of Australia on its suburbanites, when he was confronted with the unfamiliarities of Australia. He complained of a concern with 'the mere vulgar level of wages and prices, electric light and water closets and nothing else. You *never* knew anything so nothing... They are healthy, and to my thinking almost imbecile'. He did add, as one might say of a domestic animal: 'Yet they are very trustful and kind and quite competent in their jobs'.

Of such criticisms Mrs Everage, as she got on with her married life, of course knew nothing. There were too many new things to think about: new ideas such as breakfast room suites and built-in furniture; new machines such as electric cookers, hot water jugs, electric irons, electric toasters, carpet sweepers and then electric vacuum cleaners. New visions of the future at electrical and radio exhibitions. New diversions in the wireless and the talkies. As soon as they could manage it she and her husband moved to a new house, done in Spanish Mission.

After the Second World War both Mrs Everage and her critics accelerated in activity. For a start, to brighten things up, Mrs Everage went mad with cans of paint and feature walls. The result was that while her predecessors had earlier been attacked for the dull uniformity of their housing, she was now attacked for her excessive individualism. Mrs Everage was seen as the prime prompting for what became known as 'the Australian Ugliness'. Fundamentally she was the one to blame for all those advertising hoardings and telephone wires, and for that matter the state of the Australian novel, the Menzies government and the censoring of *Lady Chatterley's Lover*.

Unaware of these responsibilities, she reached great triumphs in her new home. Dreams of rationality were made manifest in her planned kitchen and in the open space, but there were even more significant changes in her backyard. She stopped running the hens and growing the vegetables that to her great-grandfather had been symbols of his new freedom. Clothes props went out with the Hills hoist and quiet Sunday mornings with the electric mower. There was a moment of sincere nationalism when she planted her first lemon-scented gum. Then the new relaxed style was epitomised in a most significant act: Mrs Everage extended her house into the garden: she put in a patio. But her sense of fulfilment was disturbed by the new criticism: it was now evident that the answer to Australia's problems was to sweep away backyards altogether. Apart from the immigrants, the backyard was what was most wrong with our cities. Among their critics the backyard had become the hated symbol of the Everage family's well-known individualism and conformity.

And when the Everages got out of their house they behaved just as badly. Their new motor-car-given mobility merely produced what were seen as new vulgarities – motels, drive-ins, the esky – or new despoliations of the countryside. And the new relaxed and more vicarious styles – all those suburban pizzerias, take-away Chinese food cafes, and provincial French restaurants – could also be derided. To some, that successful answer to suburban isolation, the N.S.W. poker-machine club was seen as the final failure of suburbanism, although it might be more usefully compared to the democratisation of rich men's games in the nineteenth century.

II

Now it is time to put to Mrs Everage the straightforward question: *Mrs Everage, what is your role in moving towards a community landscape responsibility in a pluralist society?*[1]

She might be rather pleased to be asked the question. Not that she would answer it very intelligibly. We could all have a good laugh as she confidently tapped at her glasses and compulsively repeated the phrase 'Excuse I' until, at last deciding she knew what we were talking about, she brought us to a climax of laughter by pointing with satisfaction to the nature strip in the front of her home. But it would be nice for someone to ask her something. There is no great record of anyone asking her any questions before.

Even if we didn't listen to her answer as such, it might be illuminating to listen to some of the words she used and in general to get some idea of what might be going on in her head. In the same way an efficient advertising agency before working up a campaign gets some idea of how consumers see things and how they express themselves. This helps the agency settle on the key words and phrases of advertisements designed to influence consumers towards making what we then describe as their decisions.

I am assuming that when we speak of a 'community landscape responsibility' we are not really imagining that this is a matter in which we would expect any initiatives from Edna Everage; we would be even less likely to expect them from her nephew Bazza Mackenzie or from her neighbour Sandy Stone. (The 'we' here can be interpreted variously, but in general we should imagine that 'we' are Mrs Everage's 'they'.) I take it that what we mean is something ranging between trying to arrange things so that if there is anything she wants that doesn't interfere with what we want we might let her have it, to not taking her into account in any way at all, except instrumentally, viz. how do we get her to do everything we want her to do and practically nothing she herself wants to do – for, it should, in fairness, be added, her own good.

I am not, for the sake of this particular argument, quarrelling with this kind of attitude: these are the kinds of ways things usually happen. What I wanted to point to was that if we take this kind of course we should at least be careful not to blame Mrs Everage individually for what we now consider to be the follies of the past; and that when we are in the saddle, we perhaps might blame ourselves rather than Mrs Everage for what no doubt will be the many things that will go wrong in the future.

Now, if I might speak up on her behalf somewhat more positively: we should acknowledge that if we are looking for principal villains, we will find them, of course, on the farms, not in the suburbs. As we all know, the principal despoliation of Australian landscapes was carried out by farmers – who were the heroes of our predecessors. It is true that all those backyards gave our cities an unusually large spread for the size of the population and this made the provision of services more costly per unit. But in estimating overall landscape-despoliation, compared with farms, the cities didn't take up much space. Farms were a cheaper, more efficient way of despoiling the landscape than cities.

One might also point out on behalf of the Everage family that they would have been delighted if the cities had been planned so that it was still easy to find large leisure spaces, including wilderness areas, close to their suburban homes. And outside the cities, while they wanted to enjoy their drives and their holidays, it was not necessary to their enjoyment that the countryside should be as messed up as it has been; in fact it would have better suited the holiday interests of the Everages if there had been better earlier planning of recreation areas and national parks.

It wasn't their fault that until yesterday prevailing opinions, including those of nearly all intellectuals, writers and artists, were concerned with extirpating the great cancer of the cities: and that it was rare for anyone to see certain quite distinctive characteristics in the Australian cities that, if they had been given sensitive and intelligent protection, might have been turned into policies that could have helped show much of the rest of the affluent world how it really wanted to live. (Mrs Everage may be a more trans-national figure than we imagine.)

One hears a great deal about our foreignness as intruders in the Australian landscape. Quite true. But one might also draw attention to the unfamiliarity of the Australian *social* landscape, our long intellectual disdain for any study of it, and the way in which, instead of seeking to give them meaning, we have frequently been simply repelled by those sections of the Australian social landscape which seem distinctive. We all have weaknesses, which are related to our strengths. One of the potential weaknesses of the special concern of people who speak of themselves as environmentalists is that they might tend to restrict their concern with humanity to the things it makes – its buildings, roads, farms, dams, artefacts and so forth – without being concerned with its social nature: there is a danger that they might see humans as the tool-bearing animals but not as the culture-bearing animals. To this, in Australia, can be added a disdain for the characteristically Australian. Since until recently the reactions of many Australian intellectuals have tended to be as alien to the Australian social landscape as the reactions to the physical environment were of William Dampier or James Cook, this means that Australia's environmentalists must be doubly careful: like other environmentalists they must not forget the social landscape, but even if they remember it, as Australian environmentalists they must not forget the *Australian* social landscape.

This wouldn't matter if concern with landscapes were merely a technical or expert matter. But of course it isn't. As we know, landscapes are entirely a human concept, a creation of the conventions of our senses and of our cultural history. There are no landscapes in nature. No other living thing perceives in the same way as human beings and how humans simplify their perceptions into meaning varies with their cultural experience. It is not only that we live in a pluralist society: there is also a plurality of landscapes. In this sense, to speak of 'a community landscape responsibility' may be to demand that this plurality of landscapes should be replaced by one idea of what a landscape is: if this is so, acknowledging in the same sentence as we speak of 'a community landscape responsibility' that society is 'pluralist' may mean little more than wondering what we should do about those people in Australia who do not agree with our beliefs about what a landscape is or should be.

But in this connection we may not have quite the difficulties with Mrs Everage that we fear. Of course we must give her needs a certain widening of vision; we will have to teach her that mangroves are as good as river red gums, that lizards can be as nice as wallabies, and that the Coorong is really as beautiful as Lakes Entrance. But ever since she planted that lemon-scented gum in her backyard she has been very willing to learn. Perhaps we should be learning how to speak to her.

And she would be the first to remind you that she likes to leave things as she found them. It's true, she will confess, that there were two occasions in her youth when she stole some gum tips from a national park, but it's her nephew Bazza you have to watch in this regard, not Edna Everage: if you put signs up clearly telling her what not to do, she won't do it. She is, for example, very much against the French causing all that pollution in the Pacific. She supported Mr Whitlam for putting up signs telling them not to do it.

The very bounciness of her optimism, her faith in the possibility of endless improvement, her appetite for change, her continuing new delight in each new gadget and each new idea, and her very materialism all make her liable to respond to our bidding. We are in effect still offering her the old prospect that great new improvements can be achieved. It is an idea she is thoroughly used to: look at the patio and the Hills hoist.

But is there not here something of which to beware: seen from the right distance might not our own approaches be in certain ways much the same as Mrs Everage's? Are we not all of us – both the Everages and we, the 'we' people –

taking an affluent suburban view of how easy things are and what the priorities should be?

Perhaps I could make my point by going back a few paragraphs to where I was talking about how the principal despoilers of Australian landscapes were, of course, the farmers. At that stage, I might have added that the farmers' despoliation was, on balance, a good thing. Not of course the inefficient parts of it, but overall: because it made it possible for human beings to eat and to clothe themselves. It is true that if we were going to do the whole thing over again, we could do it more neatly, with less ruining of resources and with better preservation of wilderness areas, and more of them. But if we were going to do it all over again we would still despoil the wilderness, or as we used to say, develop it: because if we didn't there would be less food and less clothing.

Mrs Everage's potential willingness to see a large part of Australia as one big nature strip may not be all that different from those views of potential landscapes that we ourselves clothe in bigger words. We have all stopped seeing rural landscapes as simply something to 'develop'; instead landscapes become, for some, pantheist, divine; for others, symbols of innocence; or reminders of the goodness of everything except man; or guarantees of stability, states of equilibrium in which nothing much changes; or patterns of beauty; or items of observation, whether for science or for colour slides; or just nice places where we can relax, feel we're away from it all and get some fresh air.

If we think of the great crises of diminishing resources and excessive population of the future our views tend to be comfortably blurred in the middle but after that, at the end, as far as the eye can see, we reach a new stage of equilibrium in which we lead frugal lives in natural landscapes and feel all the better for it. As Mrs Everage might say life will be one long bush picnic.

In the meantime, since we are a rich country, we imagine that we will be able to guard our resources and cultivate our landscapes with our new sensitivity. But even if we are to reach this new equilibrium it can only be through intermediate disasters.

Given the catastrophes that await us from the calamities of overpopulation and pollution and a realisation of a future of depleted resources and the subsequent 'storm of crises' that will burst on us, taking us by surprise even though we think we know all about what will happen next, how long will we be able to continue to view landscapes with our present satisfied eyes? How soon will it be before we are again forced to see them as suppliers of food and clothing, tools and shelter?

Notes and References

1. 'Towards a community landscape responsibility in a pluralist society' was the title originally given to this section. We changed it to 'changing perceptions of the Australian environment', partly because of changing perceptions (Editor).
The first part of this paper owes a debt to the following:
HORNE, DONALD. *The Australian people: biography of a nation.* Angus and Robertson, Sydney, 1972.
HORNE, DONALD. *The education of young Donald.* Angus and Robertson, Sydney, 1967.
FREELAND, J. M. *Architecture in Australia: a history.* Cheshire, Melbourne, 1968.
BOYD, ROBIN. *Australia's home: its origins, builders and occupiers.* Melbourne University Press, Melbourne, 1961.

*Bernard Smith**

On perceiving the Australian suburb

In his *Introduction*, George Seddon noticed that 'Australians are still learning to see where it is they live'. His observation provides me with the theme for my own paper.

How *do* those of us who live in suburbs – and most Australians do – relate to our neighbourhoods? Are they places which, physically and mentally, we are trying to get away from? Do we drive through them each morning and evening, to and from work, our eyes fixed upon the car in front, upon straying pedestrians and traffic lights? Have we seen where we live? Has it entered our imagination?

It is a problem, of course, in perception; and as Sir Otto Frankel has already remarked: 'Perception is, in one sense, a personal and private matter'. Perhaps I may be forgiven therefore if I begin on a personal note.

It was my good fortune, many years ago, to become a friend of the first person, so far as I know, to see the Australian suburb. Years later I made the acquaintance of that strange man who first heard the suburban voices. What Sali Herman saw and Barry Humphries heard is today a part of the history of Australian self-awareness. They have taught a new generation of Australians to take more notice of what is around them.

Let me tell you a story about Herman to illustrate my point. It was 1943, during World War II. Herman and his wife lived in Wylde Street, Potts Point, Sydney in the same block of flats as my wife and I and our two children. One evening Sali and I were returning home together when he stopped me, as we arrived at the foot of the McElhone Stairs, which led from lower Woolloomooloo to Victoria Street, Kings Cross. He tugged at my arm and exclaimed with delight 'That will make a good painting'. It did; and some months later Herman entered the painting in the Wynne Art Prize (Figure 93). The Wynne was the oldest art prize in Australia, established by Richard Wynne, who pioneered residential settlement at Mount Wilson, that fine rural retreat in the Blue Mountains. The conditions of the prize stated that the Trustees of the Art Gallery of New South Wales should award it to 'the Australian producing the best landscape of Australian scenery in oils or watercolours or the best example of figure sculpture, executed by an Australian sculptor'. But Herman, who had spent the first half of his life in the cities of Zurich and Paris, submitted this suburban scene of a street stairway and terrace houses. The Trustees of the Art Gallery of New South Wales were sharply divided as to its eligibility for the prize. Was the scene a landscape? I recall the discussion well for, by a curious set of circumstances which need not detain us here, I was acting Director of the Gallery at that time and it fell to me to conduct the vote for the award. As soon as the award was announced in favour of Herman, one highly respected member of the Trust left hurriedly in great vexation, exclaiming loudly 'the painting is not a landscape and the man is not an Australian'.

---

*Bernard Smith is Power Professor of Contemporary Art and Director of the Power Institute of Fine Arts at the University of Sydney.

Figure 93. *McElhone Stairs*. Sali Herman, 1944 (Canvas 26½″ × 22″)

When Herman painted McElhone Stairs most of the neighbourhood was regarded as a slum. The *Bulletin* critic described the painting as 'a melancholy account of one of Sydney's slummiest aspects', and four years later a group exhibition, the Strath Group, was criticised as 'mostly slums under the influence of Sali Herman'. Practically everyone agreed in those days, whatever their political persuasion, that the inner suburbs of Sydney were slums and that after the war, with post-war reconstruction, the slums must go. But Herman did not see the inner suburbs in that way at all, and went on painting in the neighbourhood where

he lived: Kings Cross, Darlinghurst, Paddington, Woolloomooloo. He painted·
these suburbs with a new warmth and affection, and in defence of his art he wrote:
'houses are a part of life as it is, just as human beings are. An old man or an old
women may not be attractive but may have beauty in their character. So it is with
houses. When I paint them I look for the character, regardless of prettiness or dirty
walls'.

Herman certainly understood the character of McElhone Stairs. They were a
part of his daily life and must have revived memories of stone stairways in
Montmartre and the life he had left in Europe. But it was not all memory. On that
fine, clear winter afternoon he saw the stairs as if for the first time: the brown
sandstone, the rust-red tin, the wall of the terrace against the blue sky. Art, of
course, is like that. Half-way up the steps there is a seat set into the face of the
cliff, a popular place for sitting in the sun. Paulette Herman, Sali's wife, often
sat there, dreaming at times I suppose of her native Brittany. At the bottom of
the steps he painted two American sailors with their girl-friend (the Woolloomooloo
Docks nearby were a great place for a pick-up) and higher up he put children
and dogs, and pensioners clinging to the rails. Right at the top is a mother with
her child – which reminds me how we taught our own two children to count by
counting the same steps as we walked them every day between our flat and the
Woolloomooloo free kindergarten.

Today, of course, Herman's paintings are justly admired for their aesthetic
qualities. But they also occupy an important place in the historical perception of
the Australian suburb. Prior to 1945 no Australian artist had identified himself
so completely as Herman with the suburb, with the exception of Danila Vassilieff,
another migrant artist, and Vassilieff worked largely within the more limited
vision of the slum syndrome. Before Vassilieff and Herman, Australian artists were
not inspired by suburbs. The suburbs were a place where one might be born and
reared in, and might have to work in, but not a place to be experienced for the
purposes of art. The suburbs existed, in the words of Robert Rauschenberg, in
the gap 'between life and art'.

I do not want to suggest that Australian towns, cities and suburbs were not
drawn and painted before 1945. Of course they were. But they were not experienced
as a personal environment. They were used rather to justify stock concepts, provide
evidence of prevailing ideas and attitudes. The suburb as a slum is but one of these
stock concepts. The earliest drawings and paintings of Australian towns were made
to justify a different point of view altogether; to provide evidence of civil progress
and good government. Governor Macquarie encouraged Joseph Lycett, the convict
artist, to paint townscapes for such purposes and they came up clean and precise;
tokens of British order in a southern wilderness (Figure 94). I wonder what they
really looked like? Most of our early colonial townscapes are rendered from this
point of view. Later, during the second half of the century, it is the social life rather
than the building fabric of the towns that is given prominence, but the point of
view is similar. Evidence of the Britishness of colonial life is being provided for
the information of friends and relatives back home.

Towards the end of the century, Australian artists became more emotionally
involved with their subject matter. For a moment in our history it seemed that
we might achieve a vision of the city at least comparable, if not equal, to the urban
scenes of the French impressionists. But Tom Robert's *Bourke Street* (Figure 95),

Figure 94. *Parramatta, N.S.W.* Joseph Lycett. Lithograph from *Views in Australia*, 1824.
National Library, Canberra

Arthur Streeton's *Redfern Station* (Figure 96) and Girolamo Nerli's *Wet Evening*
are brilliant exceptions. The pull was all the other way to the blue hills, the giant
gums and the manliness of bush life. From the 1860s to the 1960s the history of
the Australian city is one of vigorous, continuous growth; a growth the beneficence
of which was rarely questioned. But it was also a century during which landscape
painting was the dominant artistic genre. The story of that pre-dominance from
Buvelot to Nolan and his contemporaries has often been told, and I do not propose
to recount it, even briefly, here. I propose instead to advance the view that this
pre-occupation with landscape has been largely responsible for the creation and
maintenance of a false consciousness of what it is to be an Australian. For most
Australians, including Australian artists, are born and reared in the suburbs. The
suburb is their environmental reality; a reality which few, if any, have chosen to
describe. As a young man (for he is usually male) the Australian artist lives with his
wife (or whoever) and children in a rented house in an 18 x 36 metre suburban
allotment (give or take a metre) until his work becomes known and sells well
enough for him to contemplate a change of residence. He then moves out, like any
other successful member of the middle classes, to a more attractive suburb on the
rural fringe of the city, or perhaps into the nearby bush itself. He participates
that is to say, in a demographic trend typical of our cities until fairly recent times.
And to this physical movement of residence from the old to the new, from the
central to the fringe suburbs, we may compare a parallel movement in the artist's
imagination. If he paints suburban scenes at all, they usually belong to his early
years as an artist when he is more securely tied to his suburban environment.

Figure 95. *Bourke Street*, *Melbourne*. Tom Roberts (oil)

Figure 96. *Redfern Station*, *Sydney*. Arthur Streeton, 1893

But this youthful phase does not last. The typical Australian painter, until quite
recently, has identified with the bush or the desert as he grew older, and from the
1940s onwards the image of man appears less frequently in the Australian
landscape. Our artists, from their suburban allotments, had begun to penetrate
imaginatively into the arid regions ruled by the *Deus ex machina*, that technological
god who permits only symbols of space, form and power into his impersonal
kingdom; they had entered, you might say, the Simpson's desert of significant form.

The strong preference for up-country imagery has not been, of course, entirely
without value. It has helped to unify the Australian tribe, by providing an emotional
iconography to which our own particular bourgeoisie might respond: for of them
too it may fairly be said that their work is in the city but their hearts are in the
bush and the suburbs are the best compromise. The bush landscape has also
performed an important sociological role. It has taught us to appreciate Australia
in its natural state: to see the beauty of the wilderness. This is so normal with us
today that it is difficult to imagine a time when men thought differently. Yet as
late as 1777 the great Scottish historian, William Robertson, could still write:

> The labour and operations of man not only improve and embellish the earth, but
> render it more wholesome, and friendly to life. When any region lies neglected and
> destitute of cultivation, the air stagnates in the woods; putrid exhalations arise
> from the waters; the surface of the earth, laden with rank vegetation, feels not the
> purifying influence of the sun; the malignity of the distempers natural to the
> climate and new maladies no less noxious are engendered. Accordingly, all the
> provinces of America, when first discovered, were found to be remarkable unhealthy.

Early settlers in Australia had similar unkind remarks to make about our
wilderness. But our landscape artists succeeded in imposing an aesthetic order upon
the wilderness which has been as compelling and as influential in its own fashion
as the pastoral and agricultural orders imposed (as Dr Davidson has demonstrated
to us) by human settlement. Indeed many landscape artists such as Sir Arthur
Streeton have been vigorous and influential conservationists. Their deep love of
natural landscape has greatly assisted the movement for nature conservation, a
movement which began more than a century ahead of the corresponding movement
to conserve urban environments. Our first national park was gazetted in 1879; but
we still await Acts of Parliament which will give legal protection to urban environments. Finally, one must concede that the landscape painters won an audience
for art from a rugged, pragmatic, philistine society. In this they have been civilisers.
Now I am prepared to concede all this and still maintain that the overwhelming
predominance of landscape painting has created a false consciousness of what it is to
be an Australian. These images created by suburban artists for suburban man were
at best recreational images and at worst images of escape; they testify to a flight from
environmental actuality. True, much art is like that, and some great art is like that.
But such art at its best comes to us with a sense of personal and inner urgency that
most of our bush-motivated arts lacks. And there is another way in which such paintings develop a false consciousness. They are presented as emblematic of Australia, but
in fact they disguise an old European romanticism – the view of Australia as a
wilderness inhabited by wild men of the woods – some black, some white – a view
of us which has its origin in Rousseau, and has long prevailed, let it be stressed,
in the great metropolitan centres of Europe, Asia and North America. It is a
misleading view, because it is a view which we have taken from others, proceeded

to touch up a little, and then cherished as our own. Unfortunately, it is also a view
which encourages the belief that the Australian is mindless: a man of nature,
distrustful of theory, of intellect, and of those qualities of life traditionally
associated with cities and with civilisation. It is a view that has helped to create a
mythical Australian; a creature who lives on the other side of history.

There is however, I believe, an alternative available to Australians which will
help to redress the imbalance brought to our self-awareness by this obsession
with Rousseau's noble savage. That alternative draws its respect from man as
fabricator and artificer rather than from his condition as a natural man of the
woods: from *homo faber* rather than *homo naturalis*. It replaces mythical man by
historical man; and it emerges from a growing awareness that Australians possess
a history. Little has been done to trace the emergence of this alternative image of
the Australian; and all I can hope to do here is to provide a few pointers that may
help to identify some of its sources. In order to appreciate the emergence of historical man in Australia we must, it seems to me, take account of the difference of
history for the historian and of history for the man in the street. For the historian,
history is a picture of the past which he fashions in a personal struggle with words
and documents. But for the man in the street, history is something that he can see,
here and now in the present, something which has happened to survive from the
past. It is a kind of perception, an ability to see the past as one of the qualities
of presently existing things. This historical perception, as distinct from book
history, often begins with an awakened respect for the fabric of old buildings.
Little, it seems to me, is really known about the psychological sources of historical
perception; but it can arise with dramatic suddenness in a society and affect radical
changes in the priorities given to popular values.

Something of this kind happened to Italy in the fifteenth and sixteenth
centuries when it discovered its classical past, and to Britain in the eighteenth
century when it discovered its Gothic past. In Australia the primitive beginnings
of historical perception make an appearance not surprisingly as we approach the
centenary of European settlement. *The Picturesque Atlas of Australasia*, published
in 1886 to celebrate the approaching centenary, is a relevant document here.
For example, it describes the Rocks area of Sydney as follows: 'it has a quaint,
old-fashioned air about it. It has a suggestion of old Folkestone, with a touch of
Wapping, and a reminiscence of Poplar. Those in search of primitive Sydney will
find more of it here than anywhere else'. The comparisons are admittedly English,
but the search is for a *primitive* Sydney. Here, surely, we have the beginnings of a
tradition at once popular, antiquarian, and somewhat sentimental. With a new
warmth of feeling and a measure of personal identification, artists began to draw
the old streets and houses of the city. Etching was fashionable at the time and this
newly-discovered awareness of history may best be seen in the etchings of Lionel
Lindsay, Sid Long, Sydney Ure Smith and others. In 1902 the New South Wales
Government commissioned a group of local artists to paint the buildings of Old
Sydney, mostly in the Rocks area. It is not surprising that it was around the oldest
area of close human settlement in Australia that a popular consciousness of the
historic past began to grow.

At this time too, a few Australian writers began to turn their attention to
suburban life. The first suburban factories had begun to appear; and Edward
Dyson, born in Ballarat, had worked in one of them. His characters 'Feathers' and

'Benno' introduce a new character, a suburban character, the larrikin, into Australian writing. Louis Stone in his fine novel *Jonah* gave the larrikin to us once, and once only, realistically and in the round before C.J. Dennis proceeded to sentimentalise him out of existence.

The larrikin was an urban product, but his characterisation grimly supported Rousseau's bucolic dream. He is the victim of the cultural impoverishment of the

Figure 97. *Strike's aftermath.* Dattilo Rubbo, 1913

inner suburbs. The city is a mad mother who produces schizoid children. The few
artists who turned to life in the cities have a somewhat similar tale to tell. In his
picture *Strike's aftermath* (Figure 97) painted in 1913, Dattilo Rubbo contemplates
the direful consequences that may befall those who, by listening to evil counsel,
vainly try to rise above their station in life. This is the view of the city which is
adopted by the social realist painters of the 1930s and early 1940s. When Danila
Vassilieff began painting street scenes in Sydney in 1935, a critic wrote: 'the drab-
ness, dirtiness and squalor of these regions as they strike a stranger is pungently
expressed[1] (Figure 98). In 1939 Harry de Hartog sees the inner suburbs as an

Figure 98. *Little sisters, Fitzroy.* Danila Vassilieff, circa 1936–1943 (25″ × 22″)

Figure 99. *Night Image*. Albert Tucker, March 1945 (Oil on hardboard 28″ × 22″)

impoverished environment (Figure 100). During the war years Albert Tucker was even capable of seeing the Melbourne tram car as, of all things, a symbol of evil. A whole series of his tram car paintings are called *Images of evil* (Figure 99). Eventually the town planners succumbed to the image of the evil city. In the years immediately after the war they planned huge radial freeways capable, it was then believed, of bringing the workers daily to and from the dormitory suburbs on the edge of the bush where everyone, it seems, wanted to live.

It is not surprising that seen as a product of industrial society the city was not a place to be loved: from William Blake to Friedrich Engels a powerful, forbidding picture had been drawn; and it was precisely that picture which our social realists proceeded to copy. They polished the dark side of Rousseau's coin. It was not from that source, but the gentler vision of architects and antiquaries that a less

Figure 100. *Saturday evening*. Harry de Hartog, 1941

hostile vision of the city gradually began to take shape. It began, so far as
Australia is concerned and as far as I know, in the 1870s in the office of James
Barnet, the Government Architect of New South Wales. When he designed a new
Court House for Bathurst his work quite consciously reflected the work of
Greenway some fifty or more years before. The central portico at Bathurst echoes
Greenway's Convict Barracks, the wings, his Court House at Windsor, and the
extremities of the wings remind one of a colonial homestead like 'Bungaribee'
(Figures 101, 102). This retrospective admiration for early colonial architecture is
also reflected in Barnet's decision in 1883 to rebuild the Macquarie Lighthouse at
South Head of Sydney Harbour in the same style as Greenway's original (Figure
103). Admiration for colonial work continued on into the present century to
culminate in the work of Hardy Wilson. For ten years, from 1912 to 1922 Wilson,
with love and affection, sought out old colonial buildings and made magnificent
drawings of them. His great work of *Old colonial architecture* is not architectural
history: 'I am no historian', he wrote. But he possessed what I have called
historical perception. 'Years ago', he wrote in his introduction to *Old colonial
architecture*, 'when I returned to Australia from the study of architecture in Europe
and America, my enthusiasm for ancient buildings was immense. Immediately,
I began to search for early architecture, and found a few beautiful old houses in
the neighbourhood of Sydney, where they were hidden away and unknown because
of the apathy which is felt in new lands towards a past not far enough removed
from the present to awaken veneration, or to stir the spirit of romance. Thereafter
I spent my leisure hours in looking for more, and with each new discovery my
eagerness grew, and I learnt to love these simple structures'.

From Wilson's love of old buildings, and the pioneering efforts of a few of his
friends such as Sydney Ure Smith, a new image of the Australian as a man with

Figure 101. Right wing, Bathurst Court House, New South Wales, 1878

Figure 102. *Bungarribbe on Eastern Creek, New South Wales.* Drawing by Hardy Wilson, 1921

Figure 103. F. H. Greenway's original Macquarie lighthouse, outer South Head, Sydney (1817, later demolished) beside James Barnett's existing lighthouse (1883). Reproduced by courtesy of the Mitchell Library, Sydney.

a history gradually began to emerge. We may gain a glimpse of it in Wilson's great book:

> In pioneering days these homesteads resembled small villages. Each provided its own necessary commodities. The grape furnished wine and the wheat bread. On the pasturage grazed sheep and cattle, and grey olive trees gave a fruit which has become distasteful now that salad is taken without oil [he was writing in 1923]. In the kitchen gardens flourished artichokes and luscious lemons, and bountiful crops of commoner nourishment. Blacksmiths, carpenters, shepherds and vignerons, dwelling in out-buildings, were employed in welding iron and turning wood, tending flocks and vineyards, in short performing all those tasks necessary to sustain a village in the wilderness.

It is, of course, a highly-coloured, pastoral and patrician image that Wilson draws for us. But it is a vision drawn, even if idealistically, from history; of men at work, of *homo faber*, not of the Australian as a beautiful wild man of the woods, or a hero sticking it out in the dead heart.

When the National Trusts came into existence in the years after World War II they inherited from Wilson and his generation both their enthusiasms and their somewhat exclusively patrician point of view. Their sense of history did not extend much beyond Georgian and Regency monuments. But in recent years a more liberal view of what is historic has begun to come into favour. This popular historical perception has now spread to many styles and from the protection of individual historic buildings to the protection of whole historic environments.

It is perhaps worth considering the nature of this historic perception in more detail. It is a mode of vision by which the past is perceived in the present; the past is apprehended as a sensuous quality of things presently observed. In this it is closely related to aesthetic perception and may be seen, I believe, as a kind of fourth or temporal dimension of aesthetic perception; so that things are seen not only as spatial but also as temporal constructs. When we say that one new building fits well into its environment and another fits badly we are, in a sense, aware of agreeable or disagreeable shapes and forms imposed, as it were, not upon space, but upon time. In some degree the temporal element is present in all perception, since perception is a complex physiological process which involves both pure sensation and memory, or as Bergson put it, 'In the end, to perceive is no more than an opportunity to remember'. But historical perception deepens the temporal perspective: things that were once seen as merely old and obsolescent are seen in a new light as human heritage. In Herman's phrase, we see into 'the character of things' (Figure 104).

It is quite remarkable how quickly an awareness of local history can arise in a community. In Glebe, the area in which I live, and know best, the Australian Government recently bought some nineteen hectares of Church Land in order to preserve both the traditional community and the historic environment. Yet as recently as 1970, the State Planning Authority of New South Wales made an official study of the area which took them a number of months to prepare, the result of which was to advise us all that the only buildings in Glebe in its view worth preserving were a group of bungalows built in the 1930s on the edge of the suburb. That study was prepared, surprisingly enough, by young officers of the Authority who were regarded at the time as being reasonably enlightened in these matters. However, an active community unwilling to have its suburb destroyed by two enormous freeways and indiscriminate high-rise developments, flatly rejected the Authority's opinion. It developed opinions of its own about the quality of its environment, and gained a new awareness of local history as a by-product of community participation. Although the threats to Glebe remain, the new sense of historical values which the residents have discovered for themselves and transmitted to others should do much towards making the suburb a more neighbourly place to live in and preserve the environmental fabric of traditional buildings for those who come after them.

The new awareness of local history at a popular level that is now emerging in many suburban communities in inner-city areas has come about as a response to the challenge of those who wish to demolish the material envionment and disrupt the social environment for various reasons, the best known of which are industrial development, high-rise apartments, and freeways. The response has met with some measure of success; and is now strong enough to be recognised as a continuing issue in local, State and national politics. But it requires a much broader base if it is to survive and develop. In particular it must direct its attention to the acquisition of exact knowledge and the involvement of wider sections of the community.

A broader concept of history must be developed in the public mind so that there is a wider recognition that all environments whether urban, suburban or rural are in some measure historic environments. Each area should possess an active historical society, and that society should be concerned with collecting verbal and written documents from old residents. It should develop an inventory of the

Figure 104. *Governor Bourke Hotel*. Etching by Lionel Lindsay

material fabric of the area. A local photographic society, if one exists, should be
encouraged to untertake a visual inventory of the area. Local art groups should
be encouraged to make topographical drawings and paintings of buildings and
precincts. As Ruskin pointed out many years ago, drawing is one of the best
ways of seeing. Sketching in the open air, a practice which has been discouraged by
the passionate devotees of abstract art, should be encouraged again. The artist
should be seen in the streets again. Some communities may possess a potential
archaeological site, an old pottery, a glass factory, which may provide grounds for

303

an archaeological study. The recent creation of a Society for Historical Archaeology
in Australia is a highly important indication of the new awareness. So too is the
growth and spread of local historical journals. In the area in which I live, the
Leichhardt Historical Journal, while maintaining a good professional standard,
seeks out information from all sections of the local community. The provision of
a museum of local antiquities, even if it begins only with a room in the local
library, should be encouraged. We desperately need exact knowledge about local
building techniques so that conservation and restoration may proceed intelligently.
Such knowledge is directly connected with the quality of the perception which we
bring to an environment. The psychologists tell us that we do not see that which we
do not know. It follows therefore that in order to preceive our own environment
as an historical and contemporary reality, we need much more exact knowledge about
it. And since we are in part moulded by our environments, a knowledge of one's
environment is an aspect of self-knowledge; and conversely an incapacity to perceive
one's environment becomes an incapacity to perceive an aspect of personal being.
So that these matters should not be thought of merely as pleasant ways of filling
in leisure time, for those who possess leisure time. No matter how active people are,
how wide their obligations to their businesses, their professions, their trade
and callings, they should be encouraged to give a tithe of their personal time
towards improving the quality of life in their own communities. This is a question
of no small importance. For the daily activities of many highly important and very
busy people frequently involve them in the spoliation and destruction of communities wherein they themselves do not live. This may help to explain their
relative lack of interest in their own communities. But we all have to live somewhere. A better understanding of our own neighbourhoods may possibly help us
to respect or at least not destroy those of others.

Editor's Note:

Professor Smith has recently published a book on Glebe, which he was too modest to
list as a reference:
Smith, B., & Smith, K. *The architectural character of Glebe, Sydney.* Sydney, University
Co-operative Bookshop, 1973.

*Bruce Mackenzie**

Design with people

I was born in Paddington in inner Sydney, and have since lived in Sydney in
Bondi Junction, Bankstown, Annandale, Bondi Junction again, Bankstown again,
Greenacre, Petersham, Darlinghurst and Thornleigh. During World War II, I was
evacuated from Bankstown to Goulburn, 208 kilometres from Sydney, to escape
the threat of wartime bombardment, and came back to Annandale.

While I was in my teens, I began an abortive career in photo-engraving as a
craftsman, and threw myself into bicycle racing, competition tennis, surfing,
underwater spearfishing, bushwalking, rock-climbing, canoeing and motor cycling.
None of this is intended to glorify my youthful exploits: it is submitted as evidence
of my experience of metropolitan Sydney, life in a rural city, and association with
many forms of recreation including an intensive involvement in the natural
environment. Although I was very mobile locally, my living and working life-style
was never confused by extensive travel overseas and personal association with other
ways of life. For ten long years the house in which we now live was built bit by bit,
and in the meantime, we lived in inner-city tenements, inner-suburban terrace
houses and fringe-suburban single-family dwellings, including the one we built.

Humble beginnings in landscape construction work led to landscape design,
and eventually a serious commitment to landscape planning. I have worked with
the poorest and the best of the commercial enterprises engaged in land development, and with the least and the most enlightened government development
agencies. At no stage was I influenced by the doctrines of a formal school of
landscape teaching.

I therefore justify any stand I take on the issues before us, on the basis of
personal experience living in, and working seriously with, our environment,
influenced by a persistently questioning mind.

THE AUSTRALIAN URBAN 'TRADITION'

Intimate personal knowledge of one metropolis need not normally give an
understanding of the ways of life and urban structuring to be found throughout
a nation. But relatively simple historical, evolutionary processes, taken together
with this country's physical configuration, have produced a man-made environment which is remarkably consistent throughout the nation.

Physically, the coastline of the island continent has represented the first line
of contact with the communication corridors to the rest of the world. It has always
been, and still is, a far more attractive magnet for people than the intimidating
vastness and comparative harshness of the interior. The forbidding distances
and oppressive climate of the undeveloped interior, might in other circumstances
have been moderated in their impact by the growth of rural settlements, with a
subsequent expansion of services and amenities. However, this prospect could hardly

* Bruce Mackenzie is in private practice as a landscape consultant.

become a reality when in the first instance the immigrants came from a world already retreating from rural incentives to those of the urbanised society.

Thus the initial rural settlers of even the more favoured districts were too few to sustain the debilitating effects of the pull to the urban communities of the coast, which continued to increase their drawing capacity under the influence of industrial expansion. A more equitable distribution of the nation's population through a network of rural cities and towns never became a reality.

The large cities themselves were subjected to patterns of growth related to a combination of transport development and rampant commercial land exploitation, politically sponsored. Initially the pedestrian-oriented community moved from its essentially compact confines through thin corridors served by the new railways. Introduction of the more flexible web of transport provided by public buses enabled a gradual infilling of the expanses between rail routes.

After the depression of the 1890s and at the time of Federation of the States and of the growth of the trade union movement, governments began to initiate large-scale cheap-housing programs. In the tradition of the already established speculative building of the individual low-cost house on its own block of cheap land, sprawling suburbia became firmly entrenched. More recently, the ability of an affluent society to acquire personal transport, the individual motor car, has expanded suburban sprawl to the extent with which we are now familiar. In view of these circumstances, hardly controlled or promoted by the demands of the ordinary citizens, the term 'traditional' applied to his way of life seems unfair and misleading. It over-glamorises the nature of his limited choice. Fundamental influences – historical, political, economic and physical – have shaped the big cities. The blindly adopted 'tradition' of the cities had also effectively moulded the structures of the country towns, so that a monotonous consistency prevails, hardly affected by the regional qualities of natural or cultural characteristics.

CONSEQUENCES OF TRADITION

The elements of the typical Australian-built environment are a low-density sprawl, consuming and squandering large parcels of land, without cohesion between the scattered parts, and no clear definition between town and country. Generally, an identifiable heart is missing, as the town's centre is as loosely structured as the sprawling dormitory of its suburbs. The visual quality of these physical components is generally mundane, and made poorer by the failure to provide adequate services and facilities to such a far-flung suburbia.

One consequence is the loss of diverse regional traits and their replacement with a series of indistinguishable grey urban blobs. Let us consider, as examples, two very different places, to illustrate our ability to replace the highly distinctive with the barely distinguishable.

The first is Katoomba-Leura in the Blue Mountains of New South Wales and the second, Tuggerah – Lakes Entrance on the coast of New South Wales. The first site is a rugged plateau about 900 metres high overlooking deep canyons of great grandeur. The latter was a natural complex of visual subtlety typical of our coast.

Two more extreme manifestations of nature in fairly close proximity could hardly be imagined. Explore the streets of each township and the only significant environmental difference will be the general gradients of the road pavements.

To recognise any impact from their diverse natures one would need to fall over the cliff at Echo Point or into the seas at Toowoon Bay. (The deep canyons and sea still persist.)

The drab homogeneity extends over most of the wide range of land types where we have built towns and cities. Sydney, with its hills, and based on its harbour is an exception to some degree, but it is important to recognise that this is by no means to the credit of comprehensive planning. Sydney on its waterways is beautiful in spite of all that we have done. It is sobering to acknowledge, moreover, that most of the urban population is quite remote from the harbour and has little access to it.

Sydney was also lucky in having land useless for agriculture to north and south. As a consequence, it now has two great parks – the Royal National Park and Ku-ring-gai Chase National Park – which have become integral parts of the expanded metropolis. These must be rare examples of natural near-wilderness reserves so close to a large city. One wonders if their dedication would have been possible had they not then appeared so remote and ruggedly inaccessible to the speculative entrepreneur.

Some planners and politicians assume that Australians like quarter-acre blocks, because they have chosen to live like this, but there is little real choice, and the new outer-suburban home-owner faces real disabilities:

(a)   anonymity behind a superficial thin expression of identity;
(b)   unreasonable distances (by city standards) between his home and place of work, places of entertainment and recreation, homes of friends and schools, shops and services;
(c)   inadequate or no public transport, making car ownership essential;
(d)   a strong possibility of there being no mains sewerage, and a lack of amenities such as libraries, community centres, swimming pools and parks.

The costs to the community and subsequently to the individual, in providing and maintaining long lines of services and utilities are disproportionately high related to population numbers. The cost to the individual, of his land, his home and his share of road pavement and stormwater drainage is also high.

Despite all the foregoing comment, the traditional norms must always be important influences on any next step in planning future growth and cannot be ignored. At the same time, the assumptions that may be falsely exaggerated, can deny all participants the opportunity to assess the financial and social costs of the norm and the opportunity to evaluate alternative processes with differing cost/benefit implications.

Out of the same analysis of the individual's apparently limited desires arises another damaging misconception. This is to preclude his ability to appreciate aesthetic standards beyond the inherent qualities of his adopted suburban life-style. If it can be accepted that his urban environment is the result of a set of circumstances and dynamic processes beyond his personal control, then it must be acknowledged that his choice has been artificially determined.

To presume his lack of interest or favourable response to alternatives ignores the fact that there has been no real opportunity for him to observe and judge other ways on their own merits. The premise is a denial of the integrity and dignity of the average man.

307

A CHANGE IN ATTITUDE – A CHANGE TO LEADERSHIP

It is easy to observe an apparent built-in community apathy and inertia, a resigned tolerance of anything and everything – and mistakenly describe all of it as indifference. However, if such an unhappy assessment of Australian culture prevails in the future the fault will lie with the country's leaders, its development policies and the planning tools it employs.

The results of the past can be condemned by the critical observer, and more or less rationalised by the impartial student. Ugly though so much of them are, our cities and towns have been fairly comfortable places to live in, at least physically. The compensations for a lack of enlightened planning came strangely enough from the very sparseness and immaturity that we lament.

There used to be unoccupied lands of all sorts, vacant quarries, deserted orchards, strangely attractive stormwater canals, a multitude of ways to go to school, the pictures, the football field. A brief Friday night journey could transport you to a primitive idyllic beach environment for a weekend camp. The abundance of space and attractive places, and the quick convenience of their access made planning for recreation, for escape, partly redundant – at the time. We escaped so easily.

Now, with the explosion of post-war development those places are mostly taken up in some sort of despoiled or alienated way. The quick Friday night journey is a thing of the past. To get to a place of simple natural excellence will demand a planned and somewhat desperate, lengthy journey and probably a crowded one. As a consequence, it will be a much less frequent or attractive venture.

Population growth ensures that vacant spaces within the urban fabric of new growth areas will disappear rapidly unless we insist that they stay.

The same speed of expansion renders past practice inadequate and potentially disastrous – far beyond anything we have recognised to date. Immediate past practice means commercially motivated unco-ordinated annexing of land parcels on-to an ever-spreading fringe, in response to market demand and profit opportunities.

The ordinary citizen might appear to have suffered a loss of integrity and personal dignity in the mire of contemporary suburbia. But his loss can't be compared with the mediocrity of the country's institutions that promote and condone such irresponsibility in the name of progress.

There is an awakening now and it is fortunate that the present Australian population is still fairly small. Regrets about past practice and present inadequacy can be readily diminished in the face of development prospects which will double a population in thirty years. The quick doubling process will no doubt proceed and this expectancy awakens urgent concern.

A RATIONAL EVALUATION OF PROGRESS

After basic human needs such as food, air, water, safety and health what else is there that is important for people? The phrase *quality of life* is now commonly used to indicate all the reasons for surviving beyond creature level. Unless the quality of our existence can be maintained or improved there would seem to be little incentive in working for the future. Progress in quality is the only progress that should matter to us. If all progress is evaluated within the framework of this

simple philosophy, then of the intrinsic resources of the land, the resources tied
up in the human spirit must assume greatest importance. This belief is too easily
devalued as being idealistic, unrealistic, or romantic beyond reason.

The depressing ramifications of under-privilege may contaminate the life-quality
of all parts of the community. However, such a doomsday assessment of our
future is hardly what I would predict. Instead, I recognise an irrepressible spirit
and suggest that the forces of development and progress should get right behind it.

WAYS AND MEANS

A very small business needs to balance its books week by week. As the scale
of the business operation increases it can plan for, and gauge its successful progress
monthly, yearly and so on according to the magnitude of its investment and returns.
The giant corporations in industry and commerce can plan decades into the future
and sustain calculated losses for years in anticipation of long term profits.

The giants of business must make sure that their planning energies will make
money. They must look forward to optimum results over the long term, or suffer
deprivations in the face of competitors. At this scale of operation, guidance may
be drawn from past experience, but success will depend upon their abilities to
foresee and predict the future. The process demands inspiration and hard work.

The nation's commitment to the best possible community standards of accommodation and function surely must be the biggest business operation of all. Despite
the fact that this huge undertaking has an assured market, (or perhaps, because of
it) we look back to the past for our guidance with barely more than a nervous
glance ahead. My comment applies even to the best of our planning activities
which are so far, sparsely distributed throughout the country.

Lack of planning, and growth resulting from speculative enterprise, are still
the rule, both in fact and in attitude. Our planning philosophy and planning
energies must be brought into line with the scale of the task – both the demographic
scale and the time scale.

BIG BROTHER SHOULD BE 'MR NICE GUY'

The process of Australian development might be likened to the downstream
passage of a volume of water. A multitude of streams of various sizes, intricacies
and overriding characters, represents its simple beginnings. The water-borne
creatures might at first choose to dwell in and select specialised environments
according to fancy and need. But the pressing uncertainty of the future security
of their small streams encourages a persistent migration downstream. At first,
the contrasts are slight, and natural gravitational pulls make the downstream
course relatively easy.

Perhaps, as the process develops, they may begin to feel some degree of
apprehension about what may lie around the next bend or beyond the next fall.
Whether they realise it or not, the ability to retrace their steps becomes increasingly
difficult and eventually impossible – because by now, the volume of water is great,
with its own momentum, and the downstream gradient becomes steeper.

The only course possible with banks becoming precipitous, is to adjust to the
inevitable, swim with the current, never against it, and gather with all the others
in the largest of pools, at the downstream end. The only escape from this pool is
through the floodgates in times of desperate emergency.

309

Although the final destination is not without its benefits – some measure of comfort and security – the creatures all begin to grow alike. They look alike, do the same limited things and choose from the same very limited places within the great pool. The humble beginnings of a somewhat precarious existence, with all of its compensating colour and intrigue, become a forgotten thing of the past.

This fantasy will serve to make two points:

– Even extensive survey and sampling of the opinions and desires of the large pool's population will have a limited value because of the restrictive nature of its environment and history.

– Changing the quality or character of the environment will be far beyond the capabilities of individuals or small activist groups.

The only way to promote change and improvement within existing and future built environments is by real action from centrally organised planning bodies. Unfortunately, anything 'centrally organised' in the planning of people's environments, in our democratic society, conjures the repugnant image of 'Big Brother'. Anything less, in my mind, is unrealistic, inadequate and quite undemocratic. People should be helped to understand the significance and inescapable reality of broad-scale comprehensive planning.

In turn, the planning bodies must adopt development policies and processes which are in scale with the magnitude of the task. A vital part of its task in these circumstances is to gain the total support of the population. Substantial energy has to be injected into this particular role and even then, success won't be achieved unless the common good is being served and the rationale is effectively communicated.

Serving the common good is the key to the whole question of our future environment and in its neglect, the possible indictment of the past. Herein lies, for the planners, tremendous demands upon their expert energies and moral responsibilities including that which embodies genuine humility. Bureaucrats earn disfavour in various ways. Most prominent is the too-typical serving of sectional power-interests, or even that of simply oiling the hinges of the squeakiest gates.

At the other end of the scale is the superconservative gentleness which denies its own convictions and sets out merely to preserve the status quo of present and past well-documented failures. No amount of public relations work will earn respect for such a system.

'Planning' I take to cover the activities of a host of disciplines and institutions which, in different ways, are instrumental in shaping our environment, destructively or otherwise. Of greatest importance, is not the certificated man at the drawing board measuring house-lots or vehicle movements, but the policy maker, the leader of political power – Prime Minister, Premier of the State, Departmental Head, Mayor of the Municipality, Dean of the Faculty or Chairman of Directors. Strong directives from these sources can set all of the cogs of the system into urgent motion forwards or backwards. Lack of inspiration at the top ensures a constant ticking to and fro leaving the smaller moving parts with one alternative – maintenance of current processes, the self-perpetuating status quo.

Any further comment directed towards a more enlightened management of our environmental house is pointless, unless the basic motivating forces are re-ordered intelligently and humanely. The conscientious professional or concerned

310

layman can continue to hit his head against the brick wall forever, unprofitably, without the vital support from the top. Presumably there is a wealth of talent and imagination bottled-up in frustration and resignation. Some others instead, have thick heads and continue to try to soften the brickwork or else they are helplessly addicted to optimism.

LIFE STYLES AND LANDSCAPE PERCEPTION
AND EVALUATION ARE INSEPARABLE

Having set out to produce yet another doctrine for future action, I appear to have effectively blocked my gambit. It would be reasonable too, to expect that I should engage in matters related directly to landscape qualities in the typical sense. However, landscape in all its forms and people in all of theirs, are inseparable. Their life styles, opportunities and their institutions shape the environment of landscape and determine its values.

Broadscale environmental issues are debated in a context that would suggest that the last Australian child had been born; that the current population would never become 26 million and beyond; as though our responsibilities to the people of the nation terminate in ten years time; that the acknowledged minority in the community, keenly interested in such things could not become a substantial majority in future periods. The simple observation that natural environments of grandeur may be either preserved or destroyed forever by our actions seems to be of little significance. The short-term gain of a destructive interest is measured against an imagined short-term community loss – as if our inconsequential present numbers are the beginning and end of all communities. Short-term interests include not only the obvious extractive industries but also the super-highways and their redundant motor cars, the parochial ambitions of local real estate investors and the apparently important expansion of rates revenues.

National parks and broad-scale natural environments of quality are made more valuable by *frequency* and their proximity to the populations. A diversity of preserved environment and a consequent multiplicity of destinations, enhances the desire to visit and increases the motivation to organise the effort. A distinction must be made here between those who can jet-set their escape to anywhere and the majority whose means are far more humble.

Pursuing the theme at a lesser scale, it is interesting to note the growth and popularity of lion parks, animal worlds, reconstituted 'historic' villages and the like. The demand for escape destinations is obvious. But it is often sad to experience the degraded nature of these environments, sought after by people desperate for a change.

Private enterprise is our system and as such it should be reasonably free to exploit its opportunities. But these opportunities should occur in balance with the community's own appropriately exploited recreational development, not in a barren environmental void where anything goes. Diversity and ease of access are vital components of a community's recreational needs, and must not be left to chance.

From the scale of National Parks through to that of the local open space within walking distance, every advantage should be taken by planners to retain and exploit potential resources. As stated earlier, the random and readily available diversity of places, inherent in a partly occupied built-environment, no longer occurs – unless planned for.

311

Landscape planning, including analytic inventories of environmental qualities, must be a prerequisite to the decision-making process. All facets of proposed development must be justly represented when sharing the landscape cake. In this scale of priorities the people's freely available spaces are diverted from left-overs to the choicest cuts.

Closer to the literal home lies a major problem that can continue to blight the community environments of the future – suburbia. We are born in it, we grow up in it and inevitably aspire to it. The planner (remember he is a multi-faceted institution) recognises this, and builds more of it – lots more, and quicker than ever before. He can justify his position by doing it more nicely than before, secure in the knowledge that it is what the people want. Concessions to nagging doubts about its implications, are made in terms of small indulgences in other methods of providing accommodation at increased densities.

The smallness of such innovative projects assures them a place of oddity and an inability to achieve any sort of real impact as an alternative. Their poorest traits are emphasised and the hoped-for potentials never realised. As examples, they continue to promote the compulsive need for the traditional house lot. And the traditional house lot, with its low density consumption of land, is the greatest inhibitor of open space reservations and maintenance demands – because so much precious land is already gobbled up in impotent backyards – and so much of the community's revenue is expended in supporting the far-flung web of its inadequate services. I am not advocating a ban of traditional quarter-acre house lots – just desperate to see logic applied, and confident that people can break from habitual patterns, given the chance of real and attractive alternatives. The quarter-acre house lot should be only a part of the choice.

In Sydney, it is pertinent to note the new vitality of older inner-city living areas, gained in the last ten years. Their growing popularity is reflected in their soaring commercial values.

A variety of housing types may enhance environmental quality in many ways. Apart from a choice of life-styles amongst different people, there are also the choices that people can make throughout a lifetime, as their needs and attitudes vary. The building structures create a diversity of visual characters and the spaces between differ accordingly. People's lives are affected and their responses stimulated by the variety of patterns.

In the central business district of the city there are defects similar to those of suburbia in that distinct boundaries and alienation of space from neighbours is also typical of central urban areas; such a waste it represents. Without any real cost to the individual development, co-operative amalgamation of pedestrian spaces and pathways could create marvellous adventure mazes. The city block could be a delight – a small world in itself instead of a complex of rigid entities all competing at the expense of the pedestrian. The pedestrian bustle, stripped of its dignity, crams into the narrow corridor between the competitors and the traffic torrent on either side.

Permeating all scenes of the total landlocked environment, but progressively more destructive as the vital cores of civilisation are approached, is traffic. No small or large part of the areas discussed is unaffected by the visual invasiveness, the time-wasting inefficiency, and the nerve-racking distress of traffic. The costs of the built-in redundancy of cars and road systems is commonly understood and further comment is not warranted.

I do not want to ban motor cars – they can be a joy – they can provide access to places otherwise beyond reach and they can be comfortable and convenient. But I want a choice. The community desperately needs it. As with suburbia, future built-environments are largely predetermined, to their far-reaching detriment, by the need to design around motor cars and their gluttonous road systems.

The immediate solution of efficient public transport systems is too well acknowledged to need any description. Instead of progressing along logical paths, our existing public transport system, already in decline for some years, appears set upon a certain path of self-destruction. Increased fares, reduced services and barely tolerable accommodation are its means of certain extinction. Apparently it has to balance its books before it can be a respectable member of our society. Surely such matters, in the comprehensive scale of community requirements, can be if necessary, an unprofitable component of its essentially efficient nervous system. Similarly, profitability can't be measured simply within the parameters of its own limited function. Every facet of the community's establishment and operation is affected visually, physically and economically.

The planner's dilemma lies between two extremes – authoritarian imposition of subjective judgments as to how his design elements, people, should live and behave – and denial of authoritative responsibility, allowing everything to tumble along its own established way. The planner's role, I believe should be to combine the forces of each extreme. In effect, it means the application of design skills, inventiveness and experiment born out of past experience and future predictions. The important result for people is a choice amongst many rational and cohesive alternatives influencing the way they live, work and play.

David Yencken* and Graeme Gunn†

Perception, expectation
and experience

There have been some fascinating speculations about the manner in which landscape architecture reflects the prevailing attitude of a society towards its natural surroundings. The formal Renaissance garden, it has been said, was the expression of a philosophy in which man is dominant, establishing his order over nature; and the Chinese garden, the expression of a Buddhist and Taoist oneness with the cycle of life. Is there a discernible if changing philosophic thread which runs through the history of landscape architecture in Australia?

In Victoria, the first great landscape tradition was established by Governor La Trobe; by Arthur and Dallachy, the first and second directors of the Royal Botanic Gardens in Melbourne; by Von Mueller the third, and above all by Guilfoyle the fourth and greatest.[1] Under their hands, the inner Melbourne parks, the river bank and the Botanic Gardens took their present shape. Guilfoyle brought this remarkable early interest and activity in botany and landscape to its great climax. The Botanic Gardens, and his other public and private gardens in Victoria, such as Dalvui; Colac Botanic Gardens which were never finished; Coombe Cottage Estate at Coldstream designed for Nellie Melba; Mwallok near Beaufort in the Western District, to mention a few of his gardens, are in the great tradition of English landscape design, and Guilfoyle is the equal of its best practitioners (Figures 105, 106, 107, 108).

Guilfoyle died in 1912 and the tradition seems to have died with him. There remained only a little fuse spluttering in that unpleasant Melbourne climate – a climate which Ian Burnley has now confirmed for us statistically – flaring up a little with Burley Griffin; a flame kept burning by Edna Walling[2] through the thirties and eventually handed down through Edna Walling to Ellis Stones.[3] Ellis Stones is still actively designing.* His practising life has seen some very important changes, both in his and Edna Walling's approach to landscaping and in the community's response to it.

In what way is Ellis Stones different from William Robert Guilfoyle? Before describing the major differences in approach between the landscaping of Ellis Stones and that of Guilfoyle it is worth considering some of the similarities in their work. Both obviously enjoyed designing landscapes which were broad, encompassing, and total. Their landscapes are generally bold compositions which control and manipulate external space in which other man-made elements such as buildings are not granted pre-eminence, although they are used as focusing and identifying devices. *Their gardens reflect the prime function of landscape architecture,*

---

* David Yencken is Joint Managing Director of Merchant Builders Pty/Ltd.
He was a member of the Committee of Inquiry into the National Estate during 1973-74 and is now Chairman of the Interim Committee on the National Estate.
†Graeme Gunn, Head of the School of Architecture and Building at RMIT, is also in private practice in Melbourne.

* Editor's note: Ellis Stones died on 4 April 1975.

314

*to harmonise the interaction of man and nature in the treatment of outdoor space for
human use.* Both understood, grasped, and sensitively employed the elements of
design in their landscapes. Composition, scale, form, control of space, exploitation
of light and shade, sympathetic relationships of materials, are all clearly shown in
their work (Figure 109).

With all these similarities, what major areas of difference could remain? The
differences do exist and are clearly reflected in the gardens they have produced.
Essentially, the differences are of time and consciousness. Guilfoyle operated at a
time when the early settlers alienated themselves from the natural Australian landscape. In order to reproduce traditional European experiences, Guilfoyle's designs
incorporated exotic plants and delicate, high maintenance lawns, as this description
of *Ercildoun* in 1885 illustrates:

> The last of three gates gave onto high trimmed hedges of evergreen, catching a
> sight at intervals of a sheet of water over-hung with weeping willows, a moment
> more and we were at the door of what might have been an ancient Scotch Manor
> House, solidly built of rough hewn granite, the walls overrun with ivy, climbing
> roses and other multitudinous creepers, which formed a border to the diamond
> paned, old fashioned windows. On the north side was a clean mowed and carefully
> watered lawn, with a tennis ground and cricket ground, flower beds, bright with
> geraniums, heliotropes, verbenas, fuchsia – we had arrived in fact at an English
> Aristocrat's country house reproduced in another hemisphere and under another
> constellation.[4]

.This description typifies gardens in this period. Although the character of all
Guilfoyle's gardens is predominantly exotic, Guilfoyle was not unaware of native
plants and even produced a book called *Australian Plants Suitable for the Garden.*[5]
Like Ellis Stones, he was also strongly influenced by his earlier contacts with the
Australian countryside. In Guilfoyle's case it was by the semi-tropical and tropical
plants he discovered during the five years he spent on the Tweed River in northern
New South Wales. Unlike Ellis Stones, however, he used these plants as individual
specimens. They are, as it were, indigenous exotica in his gardens.

Why do Ellis Stones or Bruce Mackenzie or other of the handful of talented
landscapers we have, use native plant material? There are immediate and obvious
answers. Native plants are well adapted to our soils and climate, will survive
better, need less maintenance.[6] Landscape design often takes place on sites which
either have an existing native character or which adjoin other sites which still
retain their native vegetation. The marriage of the new and designed, with the
existing and natural, takes place most comfortably and satisfactorily with similar
plant materials. Native plants have great beauty. There are many other similar
arguments.

The arguments to us are now redundant and self-evident, but they were not so
in the thirties and indeed, much later than that.

Ellis Stones has talked to us about growing up in Melbourne at the beginning
of the century. He has spoken about the then current preoccupation with individual
plants, the cult of camellias and rhododendrons, the serpentine path to the door
of the house flanked with standard roses, his father's passion for gardening, his
own hatred of it, the punishment of Sundays working in the garden. He has talked
about the influences, the prevailing artistic ethos 'never copy nature' and the slow
change. The main change did not take place until ten years after the Second

315

Figure 105. Royal Botanic Gardens Melbourne

Figure 106. Royal Botanic Gardens Melbourne

Figure 107. Royal Botanic Gardens Melbourne

Figure 108. Royal Botanic Gardens Melbourne

Figure 109. Royal Botanic Gardens Melbourne—outdoor space for human use

World War, influenced by growing self-confidence about Australian traditions; by the evident destruction of the natural landscape; in Melbourne, by the Eltham school; and by new concepts of the relationship of house and garden expressed in the house designs of architects such as Robin Boyd[7]; by seasonal wild-flower festivals in places like the Grampians in western Victoria; in fact by a whole complex range of forces.

Ellis Stones' vision was forward looking. He searched for a way in which to integrate this emerging Australian consciousness through landscape, and he found it first by recognising and then by using natural components in the design and execution of his landscapes. His use of native plants, rock forms and water emulate and extend that landscape which is peculiar to Australia.

If today the best landscapers reach naturally for native plants, what about their clients? There seems to be much evidence that public response has moved with the landscape designer, not perhaps as far or as well, not consistently, into the suburban garden still dominated by Robin Boyd's 'featurism', but often spontaneously into the suburban garden. Two examples illustrate the point. During a study of the satellite town of Elizabeth, just north of Adelaide, a part of the survey included such evidence as there was of the residents' response to the physical features of the town. The tree planting – mostly native – seemed to draw nearly universal praise and satisfaction. This was particularly interesting because the residents of Elizabeth were predominantly migrants who had only recently come to Australia.[8]

The second example concerns a development carried out by Merchant Builders in Melbourne. Here, houses designed by a number of architects like Graeme Gunn were placed in a landscape setting designed by Ellis Stones; we called it *Elliston* in recognition of his work (Figure 110). The houses were very different from the surrounding neighbourhood. The gardens were very different too. A survey carried out by a group of sociologists found that, predictably, the owners liked what they had. They had, after all, chosen it. The survey also found that the owners in the neighbouring areas thought the landscaping excellent but disliked the buildings intensely.

Elliston was one of those rare opportunities in which a group was encouraged toward, and to a marked degree achieved, a co-ordinated and sympathetic approach to a development problem. A landscaper and four architects restrained their individuality in an attempt to produce a simple, coherent and liveable environment which offered variety and identity for each of the prospective home owners. The difficulties inherent in a group of this type coming together were obvious, but even so, the result was effective and commendable. However, of all the design elements used in the *Elliston* development, houses, carports, fences, and landscaping, it was the landscaping which proved to be the most effective, not only in establishing *Elliston* as a place, but in providing a unifying theme in which the various and different houses managed to retain their identity.

Elliston is a special case of a form of landscape with which we are all familiar. It is an introduced landscape imposed on a previously undistinguished suburban environment (in landscaping terms). But what of those vast areas of Australian landscape that have not, so far, or too greatly, been affected by the onslaught of urbanisation? What of the forests, the coastlines, the foreshores, the lava flows, the treeless plains, the rock formations and those Mallee areas which have proved too uneconomic to stock and cultivate, and which for centuries have supported an

Figure 110. *Elliston*—ride between houses running into parkland, Rosanna, Victoria

Figure 111. Arid landscape, Australian interior

indigenous culture? Have we really perceived those flat endless monochomatic plains, that continuous horizon, that stratification of water, land and sky? Are they landscapes to which we can respond with any degree of consciousness?

Ellis Stones discovered and perceived those landscapes, not only for himself – through translation and conviction he introduced them to others. He helped people become aware of the conceptual and visual forms inherent in those landscapes and pointed out that men need not be humiliated by being in such an environment. He taught us of the transcendent quality of Australian landscape which sometimes defies cultivation and is not always able to suffer human intrusion without disastrous results.

For too long we have believed that the only landscapes that matter are treed landscapes with open spaces contained and controlled to limit the horizon and in doing so create a physical container of appropriate scale. Spaces to which man related. Spaces in which he perceived himself as the Corbusian unit of measure.

Some Australians have discovered and appreciated the arid treeless plain and the monochromatic grasslands, uninterrupted except by undulations or the pale mauve silhouette of a mountain range on the horizon (Figure 111). There are few people, however, who possess the industry, skill and sensitivity to position elements within this form of landscape in a complementary manner.

Sea Ranch,[9] a resort development north of San Francisco on the coast of California, to which Philip Cox has already referred, is one example of this art. Barragan's[10] work in Mexico is another. The interaction of man and his physical environment in Mexico is dynamic, vivid and sometimes startling. Even so, there remains a strong conscious effort to integrate the essence of the natural with the man-made and to give to open space a value equal to that of structure. Barragan's landscapes portray a subtlety of relationships which is not dependent upon the creation of a contrasting oasis of exotica. His landscapes demonstrate that by restricting the number of elements, more subtle yet positive landscape can be achieved, capable of stimulating new perceptions (Figure 112). Barragan's integration of buildings with landscapes is without par in the Western world. He has been an intermediary capable of extending and relating the natural and the built environments.

We have mentioned the reaction of neighbouring householders in the *Elliston* study. What the reaction showed was first that there was a very consistent and positive response to imaginative landscaping using native plants, from people of widely different backgrounds. It also showed how very different is the response to new building designs and how strongly influenced we are by the preconceptions we bring to buildings.

There are, however, some very interesting analogies between attitudes to landscape and attitudes to structure. The strongest emotional reaction seems to be to materials – the plant materials in landscaping and the building materials in architecture – not to layout and design. The reaction to materials could be primarily a reaction to the unfamiliar. The long exposure which Australians have had to their country seems to have at length conditioned them to accept native plants from their designers. No such exposure has conditioned them to accept concrete and plastics, especially in their houses. The reaction is not only to new materials, it is also to a different use of old materials, to changes in surface, texture, pattern, and colour.

Figure 112. A lava rock landscape designed by Barragan

Figure 113. The *Black Dolphin Motel* at Merimbula, N.S.W., by Robin Boyd

The reaction can be very real and very fierce. Robin Boyd designed the *Black Dolphin Motel* for us, on a site in Merimbula on the south coast of New South Wales (Figure 113). When it was first built, attitudes were quite savage. In the local area it was voted the ugliest building put up for decades. Then the *Black Dolphin* won an award, and the architect and owner composed a notice to go on the back of the doors in all the rooms. The effect on the guests was magical. The few who had approved before became convinced, the many who were doubtful became approving, the most who actively and positively disliked became at least a little uncertain.

Ten years later, a somewhat similar building, a house designed by Graeme Gunn, was built in the district. The Baronda house uses the same local brick and the same timbers and timber stains which blend most easily with the bush. The building is, furthermore, very much more extravagant in its shapes and projects (Figure 114). Yet local reaction was quite different. Many people from the district went out of their way to say that they found the house very exciting. There was no evidence of a reaction which in a way mirrored the reaction to the *Black Dolphin*. It is difficult to find a conclusion other than that the extra years of exposure, and perhaps some growing reputation for Robin Boyd's building, had brought about a major change of attitude.

Both the *Black Dolphin Motel* and the Baronda house were designed in response to local materials and to their natural surroundings. In both instances the client was the same. The motel also had a user client, called the public. The user requirements for the two buildings were therefore noticeably different. The motel called for separate and identifiable apartments with private usable external space. The

324

house on the other hand, being for one family, could tolerate integrated spaces with minimum separation.

In plan the *Black Dolphin* is a series of blocks linked by colonnades which provide shelter and which help to define and control the external spaces. Each of the apartments opens on to and enjoys the spaces so defined. The low profile building-form relates to the ground except where the public areas are elevated in response to their function, views, and rising ground. The natural poles which support the roofs, colonnades and upper floors appear at regular intervals, punctuating the spaces in a similar fashion to that of the trees of a forest.

By contrast, the Baronda house is a concentrated form, elevated to make the best of the marvellous views and to obtain relief from the dreaded sand fly. Its planning arrangement is reflected in a series of interlocking platforms, each stepped 1370 mm above the other and achieving the modicum of privacy through the vertical separation provided. It is a tree house which offers views of the inlet and the coastline and which suggests a relationship with the tree tops.

As in the *Black Dolphin*, natural poles are used as structure, although in this case they are used vertically and horizontally, i.e. in a grid form. The grid defines the internal space and as required the horizontal poles are cantilevered to support overhanging rooms and decks. The house is somewhat fractured in form and because of its elevation and exposed belly it induces upward glances. Both buildings use a limited range of materials in a simple and straightforward, nearly crude, manner. Both would produce an appropriate result in terms of the natural surroundings.

Figure 114. House at Baronda, N.S.W. by Graeme Gunn

At one time, of course, restraint in the selection and use of materials was not required. There weren't any options. The natural, simple, local, and common materials were the only ones to be had, with the result that natural, simple, and beautifully common buildings were often produced. Nowadays the proliferation of materials has removed the natural constraint, and simple buildings will only be produced if clients and architect perceive them that way, and in so doing provide their own constraints in the selection and use of materials.

The concept for the Baronda house seemed to have great appeal to the adjudicating authorities of the day! One had this to say of the proposed building:

Bega District News – 24 October 1972

An unusual building that would initially have no windows or doors was not approved by Mumbulla Shire Council on Friday. The application was submitted for approval by Mr David Yencken as a dwelling at Nelson Inlet, near Tathra.

The following information about the building was submitted to the meeting by Mr Brasington.

1. It has posts in the ground nine feet apart (treated by Penders).
2. No bearers or floor joists. The floor consists of planks of 10' x 2" hardwood.
3. Ant capping will not be possible.
4. There are no partition walls.
5. No windows, or glass at all, just canvas blinds.
6. No doors except to bathroom.
7. No studs as we know them.
8. No painting.

Mr Brasington recalled that the architect who designed the building had stated the reason for having no doors or windows was mainly because of fear of vandalism at a place that would for the present be empty for long periods. 'The architect thought that the windows and doors would come later,' Mr Brasington said.

The house was built to conform with regulations, including doors and windows, and has since been broken into seven times.

Nothing illustrates the complexity of perceptions better than housing. As we all know, the house in our society is no longer a mere matter of shelter. It is a cluster of values and preconceptions. It is the householder's view about his current place in society and a sign of his aspirations. It is an object by which he will be judged by his peers. It is the individual's prime source of capital raising. It is only then a place to live in.

It is quite extraordinarily difficult to make the house buyer concentrate on those aspects of his house and its surroundings which will most affect the way he lives and the satisfaction he may or may not enjoy. We at Merchant Builders have some evidence from the little research we have done that some of the things we have tried to introduce into the design of the house (Figure 115): good orientation for view and sun; relationship of living area to the garden; the greatest opportunities for the greatest number of different family activities to be carried out easily at the same time without destroying the spaces, and many other such considerations; that all these things are indeed the things which do matter in the end. These are not, however, the features which sell. What sells the house is the emotion it generates. Perhaps the issues are sufficiently marginal and man is so adaptable that most people can accept minor inconveniences in their houses without any consciousness of deprivation – provided that they have made the choice

Figure 115. Cluster development at *Winter Park*, Doncaster, Victoria, by Merchant Builders Pty Ltd

themselves. It is an important point. But it does seem that, to some people, poor solutions to these problems are more than minor inconveniences.

In group developments where we have experimented with shared facilities and communal open space, initial reactions have been highly responsive to the environmental gain, and highly suspicious of the communal use of the shared facilities and open space. But initial perceptions and actual experience seem widely at variance. Most observers assume as a matter of course that the provision of the shared open space implies a dramatic change in life styles. The implicit question always is, 'Would I like to make that total change?' The results of surveys suggest that the real situation is rather different. Most owners eye each other for a little while and then settle into a perfectly normal life within their private holdings. Some do go a lot further. There are also widely different reactions within the family itself. However, the real significance of the community facility – the extension of freedom to choose a wider range of interactions – is very rarely perceived by casual observers. They are far too occupied with their immediate emotional reactions.

How can initial perceptions be brought closer to the likely experience? There seem to be two possible answers. The first is more exposure to a much greater variety of residential opportunities. The second is a serious attempt to educate the potential customer before he buys. The problem is not simply one of producing check lists for buyers. It is much more that of dramatising the issues so that they assume an emotional significance equal to the other powerful emotional appeals which the private builder is carefully massing against his customers: the tumbled bricks, the coach lamps, the panelled front door, the plush carpets, the wallpapers, the furnishings, the armorial decorations on the wall. What a challenge to housing departments to find techniques to compete with these emotional lures. How good for them to learn to deal with people's feelings instead of just bricks and mortar and concrete panels. How good for architects, too.

We have been talking about environments which depend upon and only exist because of the interaction of man and his natural surroundings. A similar inter-action is essential to the realisation of built environment. In this case, however, more emphasis is placed on the interaction of man and man and his surroundings. Or, more realistically, the client, the architect designer and his surroundings.

It has been stated that architects and designers create for self-gratification at the expense of their clients' interests, as if there was a search for identity in the design process. Often the architect is identifying himself so closely with the design problem that it seems that he is primarily developing his own perceptiveness and extending his own experience, an experience which might, of course, be of some value to the next client, but is of little value to the current one.

There are some architects and designers however who have sufficient assurance and understanding of their role that they are both able to relate to the perceptions of the client and work objectively on the problem. This process is totally dependent upon input and interaction with the client. It would seem, however, that many architects and many clients are not prepared to be involved in this interaction, as if they were both afraid to expose their perceptions to one another. How much better it would be if both groups were more honest with each other. How much better it would be if in the early stages of the relationship, clients clearly stated their perceptions and admitted their limitations. How much better would it be if architects also defined what they really are – human resources, resources with problem solving abilities and a perceptiveness which should be in a continuing state of development. That architects and designers should operate as objectively as possible in solving problems does not mean that they are outside the problem. On the contrary, they are part of the problem.

Both architect and client need to grasp the fact that the effective environment for the perceiver is the environment he perceives. Prior, present, and even expected experiences define the meaning of conceptual input.

The phases of perception which exist in a client architect relationship could be categorised as follows:

First, the conscious or unconscious perception developed in a client in relation to a proposed problem or requirement. Secondly, the introduction of an architect into the client's area of perception, and the emerging interaction of the client and architect. Thirdly, the architect extending his perceptiveness and the transmission of that perceptiveness to the client. In this final phase, the architect acts as a pacer in psychological terms; that is, his developed perception moves ahead of the client but never to the extent that the client cannot readily or sympathetically understand.

These issues bear upon wider interests in the experiments of the environmental psychologists. There seems a growing hope that these experiments will provide a solid base for effective design and planning. It is indeed fascinating to learn that random relationships will be more easily established across the corner of a table than face to face across the table or side by side along the table; to read of the spatial relationships and relative dominance of patients in psychiatric wards; to consider the relationship of privacy and the bathroom. However, it is not very easy for the planner or decision maker who is dealing with a wide range of potential users to find a useful application for these intriguing studies, except perhaps to lock himself in the bathroom when inspiration fails.

Environmental psychology does however have a significant message. The message concerns the extraordinary diversity of human response, the complexity of cultural conditioning, the importance to the individual or the opportunity to choose and to adapt his envionment.

Environmental psychology also tells us that we are remarkably unaccomplished in our capacities to predict human reactions. Robert Gutman in an article called 'Site planning and human behaviour', says, 'Most efforts by social scientists to forecast behaviour patterns given a knowledge of site plan characteristics have not been successful'. To the planner it doesn't sound very promising. There is, nonetheless, a very important lesson. What our society should be attempting to provide for all its members, not just for a privileged few, is the greatest freedom of opportunity to choose environments and the greatest range of environments from which to make that choice. This has great implications for the way society provides housing for the poor. But that is another story.

Talented designers play a very important part in providing alternative environments. During the course of this paper we have suggested many examples of the influences which they exert. We have suggested that exposure to new and unfamiliar deas does demand reassessment and readjustment. We have described and illustrated typical Australian landscapes and talked about forms and structures and architectural spaces which would be responsive to the grandeur and size of those landscapes. We have discussed the confused and widely different views which exist about man-made environments appropriate to these landscapes. We have discussed the significance of new materials and reactions to those materials. The talented designer reaches instinctively for any material which is available to him. In doing so he teaches us to change our perceptions about materials. We have also tried to demonstrate how emotionally charged are reactions to new materials, both plant materials and building materials. (It might be questioned whether native plants could be described as new materials, but in an important sense they once were.)

Of course, the talented designer is doing much more. He is not only showing us new forms and spaces and opening our eyes to new perceptual possibilities. He is also making us re-order the attitudes we bring to function, and helping us to appreciate that there are alternatives to the ways we live and work and relax.

In confronting us with these new visions, the designers enrich our experience. In offering us new alternatives they widen our opportunity to choose. There are of course many, many processes and systems which need to be shaken up, broken down, reorganised, and redistributed before we will give the whole community the opportunity to share these benefits. We would like also to see the whole community sharing in the design exercise.

It can be done, and has been, in a number of projects in which very poor communities in New York took part in exercises in urban design. The community selected the projects, worked on the general ideas and took part in the execution, regardless of expertise or formal training. Some of the results were extraordinary.

There is a very real professional skill required from the co-ordinators of such projects, but it is a rather different skill from that which has been described by most of the architects and planners contributing to this Symposium.

Notes and references

1. See PESCOTT, R. T. M. *W. R. Guilfoyle, 1840–1912: the master of landscaping.* Melbourne, Oxford University Press, 1974.
2. WALLING, E. *Gardens in Australia: their design and care.* Melbourne, Oxford University Press, 1943.
3. STONES, E. *Australian garden design.* South Melbourne, Macmillan, 1971.
4. FROUDE, J. A. *Oceana, or England and her colonies.* London, Longmans, 1886.
5. GUILFOYLE, W. R. *Australian plants suitable for gardens, parks, timber reserves, etc.* Melbourne, Whitcombe and Tombs, 1911.
6. Or so it is said, although there is an element of nationalistic self-deception in this claim. In a disturbed environment – and all gardens are that by definition – introduced plants often fare better than native ones, although much turns on just which native ones.
7. BOYD, R. *The new architecture.* Melbourne, Longmans, 1965.
8. Elizabeth: an unpublished study by David Yencken.
9. See Ecological architecture: planning the organic environment. *Progressive Architecture.* 47:120–137, 1966.
10. Luis Barragan, Mexican architect, born Guadalajara, now living in Mexico City. Influenced and taught by Le Corbusier and landscape architect, Ferdinand Bac. He transformed the barren stony area near Mexico City known as the Pedregal by integrating houses and gardens with the volcanic rock, lava, cacti and indigenous vegetation of the area. See Smith, Clive Bamford. *Builders in the sun: five Mexican architects.* New York, Architectural Book Publishing, 1967, pp. 51–92.

*R. B. Lansdown**

Changing values towards the environment as exemplified in Canberra

INTRODUCTION

> Purely untutored humanity interferes comparatively little with the arrangements of
> Nature; the destructive agency of man becomes more and more energetic as he
> advances in civilisation.[1]

The force of this statement is now clearly apparent. By Marsh's standards, man is
now wonderfully civilised; energetically interfering with and manipulating nature's
arrangements in a highly advanced and technical fashion. From our early ancestors,
who used only enough of nature's resources to meet their immediate needs, to the
present generation, with its massive demands for raw materials, the effect of
civilisation has been to free us from the in-built controls of nature. The present
generation has seemingly escaped the natural laws which govern the evolutionary
process.

Evolution has been described by Julian Huxley as a tripartite process. The first
part is inorganic – the nuclear and molecular processes of matter. The second is
biological – the evolution of plants and animals. The third is psychological, and is
concerned with the development of human culture. It is the interaction between the
second and third parts of the evolutionary process with which this Unesco
Symposium is concerned.

Man has had a profound impact on the habitat in which he lives. In many
parts of Britain, for example, it is true to say that the process of change is so well
advanced that the landscapes, both rural and urban are largely man-made. In
Australia, similar changes can be seen to be occurring. The wide open plains have
been invaded by sheep and cattle, the forests have been felled to provide timber,
paper and agricultural and grazing land, and the coastal fringe has been the site
of intensive and little-controlled urban development. The pristine state which is
regarded by so many as the essence of nature has been sacrificed in the process
of cultural evolution.

The landscape is not a static background inhabited by man; rather it is the
dynamic interaction of a society and the habitat in which it lives. If either man or
the habitat changes then so inevitably must the landscape. Landscape can be
regarded as the natural environment changed by a creature who is himself constantly changing. It is the result of an equation:

Landscape = Habitat + Man

The equation can never be stable, and if on occasions it may seem so, it is
because the pace of landscape change has been slow compared with our brief
human generations. The potential for human beings to alter their habitat has been
greatly increased by technological advances. The advent of heavy earth-moving

---

* R.B. Lansdown was the administrative head of the Department of Urban and Regional
Development in Canberra. He was previously an Associate Commissioner with the National
Capital Development Commission.

331

machinery and new construction technology has greatly facilitated the speed and scale of changes to our habitat. Today's changes occur within a fraction of one man's lifetime and new habitats are created seemingly overnight.

Landscapes can be considered to have two sets of qualities; first, those which are intrinsic and act as determinants of a landscape's potential for use in a particular way; and secondly, those which are extrinsic and are the result of human interpretation and appreciation. Many of our environmental problems have arisen because of failure to understand the intrinsic merits of particular landscapes, the ecological processes which have operated, and continue to operate, throughout their slow evolution. They have also arisen because of the narrow perspective of western society, a culturally derived trait that places man above nature rather than in nature.

Nowhere in Australia have these changes and problems been more clearly illustrated than in Canberra. In the short space of 154 years since Joseph Wild[2] and a constable named Vaughan first camped near Duntroon, the open grasslands of the Canberra plain have been transformed into a thriving community of some 180 000 people.

THE EARLY CANBERRA LANDSCAPE

Dr Throsby's account of a trip to the Murrumbidgee appeared in the *Australian Magazine* for June 1821, and he describes the country as: 'perfectly sound, well watered, with extensive meadows of rich land on either side of the rivers; contains very fine limestone, in quantities perfectly inexhaustible, slate sandstone and granite fit for building with sufficient timber for every useful purpose; and, from the appearance of the country, an unbounded extent to the westward'.[3] This is the first recorded statement of a European explorer, but it should be remembered that he was not the first human being to set foot in this area. Tindale records that three Aboriginal tribes – the Ngunawal, the Walgalu and the Ngarigo – occupied the area at the time of European settlement.[4]

The role of Aboriginal man in the development of the landscape is not well known. The Aborigines were essentially hunters and gatherers and their role in that regard in the Canberra area is attested to by two small cave painting sites at Gudgenby.[5] The paintings are mostly red or white figures of animals and hunters. There can be little doubt that the use of fire by the Aborigines has also contributed to changes in the landscape, a reduction in the area of forests and an increase in the area of open grassland. The surveyor T.S. Townsend for example, denounced the Aborigines of the southern tablelands as incendiaries, and blamed them for the burnt scrub through which he passed and the clouds of smoke which obscured his sighting points. Whatever the contribution of the Aborigine, the landscape first seen by those early explorers in the 1820s already bore their mark.

It was not long after the Molonglo River had been discovered that the first permanent settlers arrived. Toward the end of 1823, stockmen squatted with their animals in the valley between Black Mountain and Mount Ainslie, the future site for the Civic district of Canberra. They built their first huts and yards where the Canberra Community Hospital now stands.[6] By the early 1930s, all the good land between Ginninderra in the north and the Murrumbidgee in the south had been settled, and visitors to the area were already seeing it as the site of a future provincial town.

Changing values towards
the environment
exemplified in Canberra

These early settlers grazed their flocks and herds with shepherds, making use
of natural grasslands and water courses. Crops of wheat were planted in a few places
but generally their acreage remained small. Toward the end of the 19th century
the form of settlement began to change in response to changes in agricultural and
grazing techniques. Hand tools were replaced by primitive machinery and paddocks
were fenced; greater specialisation occurred with agriculture being concentrated
on the more fertile flat land adjoining the rivers and grazing in the more marginal
hilly areas. The demand for timber for homes, fences, firewood and the other needs
of an expanding settlement, the need for more grazing land, and the need for
timber-free arable land – all resulted in the clearing of the hills and the fringes
of the plains.

These early settlers saw in the landscape the opportunity to create a habitat
which would provide for their material and social needs. There was little thought
given to the future consequences of their actions. The natural environment was
regarded not as something to be husbanded and conserved but as something to be
used and controlled – a place in which each settler could leave his mark. As a
consequence many have left their marks. It is possible to find areas where the hills
are actively eroding because trees were cleared where trees should have been left,
and because the pressure of grazing has been too great for too long. Grass species
which were once prevalent such as *Themeda australis* have been replaced by short
grasses and the grasslands have been invaded by exotic species. These were changes
about which the early settlers were unconcerned. This pattern of settlement and
landscape development continued until the end of the 19th century.

A NEW LANDSCAPE

In 1901 the six sovereign States of Australia agreed to form a Federal government and a condition of their federation was that the new government would have
its seat in a territory, not less than 100 square miles in area, situated within the
State of New South Wales not less than 100 miles from Sydney. After exhaustive
investigations, and several years of political wrangling, the Seat of Government Act
designating the Yass-Canberra district as the chosen territory, was passed in 1909.
In the same year the surveyor C.R. Scrivner[7] was directed to locate the site of
the future city.

The instructions he received gave the first indication that a change in attitude
toward the Canberra landscape was about to take place. In relation to the site
of the future city they said:

> the surveyor will bear in mind that the federal capital should be a beautiful city,
> occupying a commanding position with extensive views, and embracing distinctive
> features, which will lend themselves to the evolution of a design worthy of the
> object, not only for the present, but for all time; consequently the potentialities
> of the site will demand most careful consideration from an hygiene standpoint,
> with a view to securing picturesqueness, and also with the object of beautification
> and expansion.[8]

In February 1909, Scrivner reported that Canberra was the best city site available
in the area.

Scrivner's survey was followed in 1911 by an international competition for a
design for the capital. The competition was won by Walter Burley Griffin[9] with

a plan which has been described by the National Capital Development Commission as being, 'in essence, a piece of landscape design at a major scale'.[10] In designing the future city, Griffin emphasised the grand formal landscapes using avenues, water features, and the hills and mountains; he took advantage of all the natural features of the site.[11]

Griffin used the topography as the dominant element in his design; the ranges formed the background to the city as a whole, while the major hills on the Canberra plain formed the foci for vistas or the site of important public buildings. Griffin's plan was an attempt to compromise between the formality, dignity and scale befitting a national capital and the intrinsic qualities of the landscape in which it was to be sited.

While Griffin had envisaged a new landscape for Canberra, it was to be some years before it began to take shape. His plan was first criticised as extravagant and then 'cannibalised' by a Department Board appointed by the then Minister for Home Affairs, King O'Malley. Toward the end of 1913, Griffin was appointed Federal Director of Design and Construction, and he continued in that office until 1920. During this period, Griffin ensured as far as possible that the frame-work of his plan was firmly established on the ground, so that it would be difficult to depart from it in the future.

In 1921, the Federal Capital Advisory Committee was established to advise the Government on the implementation of the initial development of Canberra. The establishment of this Committee ushered in a new attitude to the Canberra landscape. While the Committee was not empowered to make major changes (in fact, when they recommended a return to the plan produced by the Departmental Board the government refused) they did recommend in their 'First General Report' that: 'utilitarian development and economy should be the aim in the first stage, leaving to future decades – perhaps generations – the evolution of the national city on lines that are architecturally monumental'. The Federal Capital Advisory Committee was succeeded in 1925 by the Federal Capital Commission which assumed responsibility for the planning, construction and administration of the newly developing city.

The Federal Capital Commission pursued the policy of utilitarianism that had been espoused by the Federal Capital Advisory Committee in their 'First General Report'. During the period 1925-1957, with an interlude during the 1930s and World War II, the Commission organised the construction of the public buildings and accommodations which were required for the efficient functioning of Parliament and government. The buildings that were constructed can in no way be described as architecturally outstanding. The 1954 Senate Select Committee on the Development of Canberra[12] reported that there were buildings: 'so unsuited to grace a national capital that those responsible for them plead as a mitigation of their offensiveness that they will be screened from the public gaze by trees, as though the function of trees were to hide ugliness, not to enhance and create beauty'.

While the Federal Capital Commission may have been criticised for its efforts regarding public buildings, its achievements in the field of landscape development remain today as some of the more important landscape components. The appointment by the Commission in 1926 of G.J. Rodger as Chief Forester resulted in the

Changing values towards
the environment
exemplified in Canberra

formulation and implementation of a forestry program. This program has given us the conifer forests which form a backdrop to many parts of Canberra in 1974. The Commission was also responsible for the establishment of a number of parks such as Haig Park and Telopea Park, and for the planting of hedges in lieu of fences, and of large numbers of street trees. There can be no doubt that the activities of the Commission in this regard have left the Canberra landscape considerably enriched.

The 1954 Senate Select Committee believed however that the policies of utilitarianism and 'living from hand to mouth' that had 'characterised all governments and departments since 1929' had to be changed and accordingly they recommended the establishment of a commission with responsibility to 'plan and develop Canberra and be guaranteed sufficient finance to permit it to carry out a long-term balanced program'. For the second time since 1900, the evolving attitude to the Canberra landscape was again at a threshold.

The Federal Government established the National Capital Development Commission and its associated National Capital Planning Committee in 1957 and at the same time invited Lord Holford (then Sir William), to examine and report on the problems of Canberra's future development. From this point onward a positive determination to complete the National Capital can be discerned, and with this determination a desire to blend the natural and man-made elements of the landscape in a unified whole.

A COMPREHENSIVE APPROACH

Lord Holford reported that if a unified whole was to be created, then there would need to be an acceleration of a building program on a scale that would catch the imagination of people, and in order to carry this out there would be a need for 'immense effort and considerable administrative courage'.[13]

The Commission began in a bold fashion by beginning the design and construction of the long delayed lake and Commonwealth and Kings Avenue bridges. Griffin's plan for the National Capital placed great emphasis on the lake and these two links between north and south Canberra. The lake, the bridges and the major avenues were planned to focus attention on the Parliamentary Triangle and its associated national buildings. Accordingly the Commission designed the lake and bridges as a unified scheme and programmed its development so that the emergence of the new landscape component would be co-ordinated. The foreshores of the lake were planted with native and exotic trees which would provide shade and shelter and a pleasant outlook soon after the lake filled and was available for use; although it would be a decade or more before this newly created landscape would take on a mature appearance. Likewise the bridges represented a new and holistic approach in which the product was not only one which was of engineering excellence but was also an integral and unobtrusive part of the landscape.

The Commission also responded to the immediate needs of the expanding community by providing office accommodation and pleasant residential environments.

The landscape envisaged by Griffin in 1911 had at long last begun to emerge. The community was generally pleased with the new environment which was being created around it. While some people were concerned at the disappearance of old familiar landmarks and favourite sites, the majority were happy with the new and increased opportunities which would be provided by the newly created landscape. It should however be explained that the majority represented people transferred from other cities who were unfamiliar with the past and quite probably found the new environment more pleasant than their previous one.

By 1965 the Commission recognised that the immediate needs of the community had been met and that the time was now right to look at longer range problems. Since the early 1960s the Commission had been investigating the long-term needs of the city and in 1965 published *The Future Canberra* as a statement of the long-term plan for the development of the National Capital.[14] The same landscape components which inspired Griffin's original plan can be identified in the Commission's choice of future development strategies.

The 1965 outline plan reaffirmed the landscape envisaged by Griffin and in order to cope with an expanding population chose to develop new districts in adjoining valleys. The hill tops and intervening ridges would be retained in their natural state in order that the future residents might continue to have a view of tree-clad hills as a backdrop to their daily routine. The plan also contained a new concept of 'special areas' which included the important national areas, the hill tops and ridges, the approach routes to the city and the system of parklands.

The period 1965-1968 saw the continued planning and development of the new districts of Belconnen and Woden. Planning and development was based on the identification of the important structural elements in the landscape and their incorporation in development plans. Landscape development was assisted by advance plantings of trees and shrubs. Throughout the Commission's reports for this period there was a strong emphasis on the need to create a pleasant environment in which to live. The emphasis was on the creative aspects and the obvious recognition that the landscape in each area had certain intrinsic qualities which needed to be retained. This can be seen in the arrangements of the major structural elements in the plans for each area; the use that has been made of the natural landscape in the siting of major buildings and access routes and the combination of topography and natural water courses which were incorporated in the plan for Lake Ginninderra in the Belconnen district. At the neighbourhood level considerable attention was given to the natural landscape in planning the arrangement of streets, parks and amenity areas, and the suburb of Aranda in the Belconnen district is a good example.

By 1970 the planning and development of Woden and Belconnen were well advanced and consideration was being given to the planning of the new district of Tuggeranong in an entirely new area, some ten miles to the south-east on the Murrumbidgee River. Planning began with a few firm ideas about what the future town should look like. The Commission had begun to respond to the emerging concept of ecologically based planning – planning based on the intrinsic merits of the landscape. In July 1970 it commissioned a report on the ecological considerations which might be involved in land use decisions in the A.C.T., and an ecological and physiographic report on the Tuggeranong district. The Commission also involved the community and groups of experts in the formulation of possible policies for the development of the district.[15]

The planning of Tuggeranong was the first evidence that a more sympathetic attitude to the natural landscape was emerging. The attitude was one which not

Changing values towards
the environment
exemplified in Canberra

only reflected the extrinsic merits of the landscape and its potential for certain uses but also reflected the intrinsic values attached to it by the community. A further refinement of these processes can be seen in the studies and seminars which were conducted during the formulation of the structure plan for the district of Gungahlin.

In the Gungahlin district, detailed studies were made of the extrinsic merits of the landscape and the potential of specific areas for particular uses was evaluated on the basis of these studies. Public participation was achieved through a week-long seminar and workshop involving young people aged 16-25. The detailed studies showed that there were areas in which the natural landscape placed constraints on future development. The seminar and workshop indicated that the people who were potential occupants of this future district were concerned that the total design, including the landscape, should provide for greater community interaction and should provide for new life styles associated with a leisure oriented society.[16] During this same period when the attitudes and techniques of the planners were changing, so were those of the community.

COMMUNITY VALUES

The early 1970s saw the development of a number of community groups concerned with the impact of technology and development on society. The Canberra College of Advanced Education began its life with new courses and new ideas, and a general shift in emphasis occurred in a number of the activities of the Australian National University as a result of a world wide recognition that more concern for our habitat was necessary if the human race was to survive beyond the 21st century.

In March 1970, the Society for Social Responsibility in Science was established to provide a forum and action group concerned with the impact of advancing science and technology on society. This organisation was largely responsible, through its INSPECT program and its use of the local press, for raising the level of public awareness about environmental issues.

The end of 1971 saw the beginning of a long and often bitter battle over the decision to construct a communications tower on the top of Black Mountain. The public feeling which was generated by this decision is an illustration of the attitude of people to a significant part of the Canberra landscape. To many Canberra residents, Black Mountain became a symbol of all that was good and beautiful in the landscape. They placed such a high value on its protection that a public appeal was launched to support an approach to the A.C.T. Supreme Court. In October 1973, the Hon. Mr Justice Smithers found in favour of the plaintiffs (14 Canberra citizens); not on environmental or landscape grounds, but on points of law relating to the activities and responsibilities of the Postmaster-General and the National Capital Development Commission. These points of law are now the subject of an appeal and cross appeal to the High Court of Australia, which has not at the time of writing handed down a decision, although it has heard the evidence.

Similarly, 1973 saw the announcement by the National Capital Development Commission that it proposed to construct the Molonglo Parkway along the base of Black Mountain and across Sullivan's Creek linking up with Parkes Way. Not

337

altogether surprisingly, there was public opposition to the proposal because of
the possible destruction of some of the landscape surrounding the man-made
lake. This case, more than any other, illustrates the change in attitude of the public
towards the landscape. Here was a landscape which had been artificially created,
and yet in the short space of ten years, it had become highly valued in the minds
of people.

These examples are used to illustrate the change in attitudes that have occurred
over the past few years. Other examples such as the development of cluster housing
projects might also be cited as examples. There remains however a double standard
on the part of the public. While they are vociferous in their protests regarding
the possible destruction of important parts of the landscape through planning and
development of the total urban environment, they are content to allow its destruction by increasing recreation pressures, motorists who drive cars into fragile areas,
and by people who leave their litter.

THE FUTURE

This paper has attempted to show that over the period of 150 years since
Europeans first settled in the Canberra district there have been a number of
changes in people's attitudes both to the natural landscape, and to the artificially
planned, man-made landscape. These changes have been mirrored in changing
patterns of land use, changes in planning techniques and changes in public attitudes
to planning decisions.

The future physical form of our landscapes will be a response to a particular
mix of human desires and attitudes, economic pressures at a national and local
level and the potentiality of particular habitats. In short they will be the result
of the equation outlined in the introduction.

Landscape = Habitat + Man

The landscape will continue to evolve as man's culture continues to evolve.
If one were to make any particular predictions about the future, they would focus
on the changes which are occurring in family life, the changes in educational practice
and standards, changes in transportation, and changes in the amount of leisure.
These changes will bring about a demand for more open space close to residential
areas, a greater diversity of landscapes where human potentialities can be developed
to their fullest extent, and more comprehensive planning which has regard for the
intrinsic merits of the landscape.

These changes will create challenges for the planners. Greater attention will
have to be paid to the blending of future settlements and industrial development
with the natural landscape. Greater attention will have to be paid to the assessment
of public attitudes and values and the involvement of the public in the making
of planning decisions.

These will be the challenges for the future.

Changing values towards
the environment
exemplified in Canberra

Notes and references

1. MARSH, G. P., 1864. in LOWENTHAL, D. (ed.). *Man and nature: or physical geography as modified by human action.* Cambridge, Mass., Harvard University Press, 1965.
2. Joseph Wild (1759–1847) was the convict overseer of Dr Charles Throsby, a former naval surgeon who turned pastoralist and explorer. During expeditions in search of the Murrumbidgee River, Throsby, Wild and Vaughan are thought to have reached a point near Hall cn the north western boundary of the A.C.T. In the early part of 1820 while again looking for the Murrumbidgee River, Wild, Vaughan and Throsby's nephew, discovered the Molonglo River and climbed Black Mountain.
3. FITZHARDINGE, L. F. 'Old Canberra and district 1820–1910', in WHITE, H. L., (ed.). *Canberra: a nation's capital.* Sydney, ANZAAS, 1954, p. 15.
4. TINDALE, N. H. 'Distribution of Australian Aboriginal tribes: a field survey', *Transactions of Royal Society of South Australia.* 64(1), 1940.
5. McCARTHY, F. D. 'Aboriginal antiquities in New South Wales', in McCARTHY, F. D. (ed.). *Aboriginal antiquities in Australia: their nature and preservation.* Canberra, Australian Institute of Aboriginal Studies, 1970.
6. *op. cit.* FITZHARDINGE, 1954, p. 16.
7. Charles Robert Scrivner, Surveyor, New South Wales Lands Department, and later Federal Director-General of Lands and Surveys.
8. FITZHARDINGE, L. F. 'In search of a capital city', in WHITE, H. L. (ed.) *Canberra: a nation's capital.* Sydney, ANZAAS, 1954.
9. Walter Burley Griffin was invited to Australia to develop the plan. He became Federal Capital Director of Design and Construction in 1913, and was associated with the plan until the end of 1920.
10. National Capital Development Commission. *Tomorrow's Canberra: planning for growth and change.* Canberra, ANU Press, 1970, p. 8.
11. HARRISON, P. '. . . Aft Agley: the development of Canberra', *Journal of Town Planning Institute.* Canberra, Sept.–Oct. 1953.
12. Senate Select Committee Appointed to Inquire into and Report on the Development of Canberra. Canberra, 1955.
13. *op. cit.* National Capital Development Commission, 1970, p.17.
14. National Capital Development Commission. *The future Canberra.* Sydney, Angus and Robertson, 1965.
15. National Capital Development Commission. *Sixteenth Annual Report 1972–73.* Canberra, AGPS, 1973.
16. National Capital Development Commission. 'How to build a Utopia: or not to bomb out by much!' A report of a seminar held at Guthega, 21–25 May 1973. Canberra, 1973.

*Sir Paul Strasser**

The developer

When considering the role of land and urban developers, it is important to understand who the developers are. Contrary to the belief of their critics, developers are
not a race apart. They are part of the race of man. Their actions reflect the values
of the community in which they live and work. Their achievements are praised
by this community and their potential mistakes curbed by its responsible legislation.
As with all vocational groups, they include skilled concerned practitioners and,
inevitably, a small number of spoilers – whom the industry could well do without.
I stress that these are a small number, and their actions should not be allowed to
mar the contributions of the rest.

A quick glance into history reflects the way in which the developer, or his
counterpart, reflected prevailing attitudes. The developer's counterpart in Roman
times obviously did a commendable job in terms of planning for a clean environment. His actions reflected community concern.. In the 18th century, however, his
counterpart reflected the attitude of the gentry, who desired water closets in their
houses but who cared little for the destination of their contents.

If the developer is a man of his time, what are the current attitudes to these
problems? Today there is an upsurge of concern for the environment. But although
voices are raised, their cries are often contradictory. Conservationists protest
vehemently against the flooding of a lake, the mining of a resource, the developing
of an area of bushland which is claimed to be unique. Governments and business
'experts' on the other hand attack these claims and accuse the protesters of
ignorance and self-interest. Academics can be found on both sides of the fence.

In the absence of comprehensive planning and accurate forecasting, the
developer then moves ahead as he sees fit, guided by legislation which many would
regard as outmoded. In an age of dissent he may be considered by his critics to
reflect this confusion.

Obviously this situation leaves much to be desired. It we are to have enlightened
developers embarking on projects which will blend in with and enhance the environment, our planners and legislators must work harder and faster on the guidelines
on which the developers will base their work. It would seem that concerned
members of Government have their sights fixed on this direction but the problems
are many and the implementation of their ideas is unfortunately a long way off.

Some people generally regard developers as money-hungry businessmen, with
no concern for proper planning and the environment. We are usually made the
scape-goats for all urban problems, particularly the high cost of land and accommodation, and for haphazard planning. Few people realise the positive things that
developers do and have done for the community. Over the last twenty years it has
been the developer who has taken the risk and the initiative. Developers have
assisted in providing this country with one of the highest home ownership rates in

---

* Sir Paul Strasser is Joint Managing Director of Parkes Developments Pty Ltd.

340

the world – just over 70%. We have provided more dwellings for the communtiy than any Housing Trust or Commission. We have produced the goods, we have arranged the finance, we have satisfied the consumer to the best of our ability at a time when environmental considerations were unknown. Unlike developers, however, planners, sociologists and environmentalists do not have to worry about the economics of providing a product which is within the economic reach of the consumer.

Of course, it would have been better if master plans had existed which allowed for environmental considerations – but they did not. In few other places in the world has it been possible for young couples to choose and purchase land or a home of their choice, on a minimal deposit, as it has been in Australia.

Gone are the days when the developer could operate without any interference, or concern for resident action groups or the environment. Citizen participation, whether in the form of resident action groups, union pressure groups or even the more zealous representatives of the media amounts to a powerful force in the community. The existence and influence of such groups has been attributed to the shortcomings of our democratic system, which although generally is felt to be a good political system, is not and never will be a perfect one.

However, while I express sympathy for these action groups, there are some worrying aspects about their role in society and the power they can wield, which must be faced. Although a socio-political vacuum – which may be an inevitable by-product of our type of democracy – can be seen as largely responsible for the frustration of these people, the dangerous philosophy of 'ends justifying the means' too often holds sway in such situations. This philosophy of expedience, coupled with the doubtful validity of representation by a vocal minority must give concern.

While I question the mandate and methods of such people, I acknowledge that they may well have very real grievances which our present system is inadequate to handle with sufficient machinery, knowledge or speed. Hence the developers' dilemma. One may well ask what meaningful role he can possibly have in this pluralistic society. Those developers who heed only legal restraints are fast discovering that there are some other restraints in the community today. They soon discover that an unyielding stance will scarcely result in a satisfactory solution. Citizen groups are an unmistakable reality and they demand to be treated seriously.

The developer also has a clear social responsibility. Despite the extra time and expenditure involved, he should hear the opinions of all interests involved. Only when this is done can an unemotional assessment of present and future needs be made. Such opinion sampling would wisely avoid the easily manipulated atmosphere of a public meeting.

Government recognition of the need for the development of a new democratic planning process in our society to deal with this developmental and environmental problem is vital. The costs involved through delays in development caused by such consensus-seeking programs, should be easily outweighed by the savings made as a result of avoiding strikes, bans and delays. The benefits of such community co-operation cannot be calculated in terms of dollars and cents, although we will never get 100% agreement on any environmental issue.

Over the next thirty years in Australia, we will probably be living in a mixed economy where part of our activities will be directed by the Government and the balance will be left in the hands of private enterprise. I believe that the production,

manufacturing and retail function is best performed by private enterprise. In our
economic system, absolute government control over the development function
would be disastrous, but in matters like environmental protection and the protection
of the National Estate then Government control and regulation is essential.

Control over historic buildings is often non-existent. In some States there is no
control over demolishers. The National Trust has been restricted in taking public
stands on preservation issues. The State Governments have been lax in taking the
initiative on these issues, while private contractors have often taken the brunt of
confrontation. The Government should require demolishers to be registered, and
demolition applications should include a Declaration of Environmental Factors
which takes into account historical, environmental, social and economic effects.

The ownership and preservation of buildings or sites of national or historic
importance should be placed under the control of an Historic Properties Commission and the cost of preserving such properties should be borne by the community at large and not by individual developers. Consideration must be given to
incentives to retain and restore historical buildings by way of: rate concessions,
development rights, land tax reductions, compensation and covenanting. Government must offer incentives to the public, including developers, for the great majority
of historic buildings are not owned by developers. It should initiate such controls
and regulations and it must do so urgently.

The standard of the built environment is closely connected to its price. Many of
the critics of developers on environmental issues also criticise them in relation to
the price of land and houses. One of the most important aspects which tends to
be overlooked by these critics is that subdivisional and developmental standards
are constantly rising, and now we have environmental standards. For example,
in 1958 when we first entered the development field, the subdivisional standards
were very much inferior to those which apply today. We were able to sell land at
Blacktown for approximately $800 and our gross profit was around 30%. We
were not required to provide kerb and guttering, there were minimum drainage
requirements, the water service was temporary and the carriageway was only
6 metres wide, tar sealed with earth shoulders.

Today the same block would sell for around $12 000 and our gross profit
(and risk) would be reduced to 10-15 per cent. Water and sewerage, underground
wires, higher road standards, kerb and guttering, public reserve contributions and
now environmental considerations, all add to the cost to the consumer; in my
opinion all necessary items, but very costly. These higher costs, labour and materials
are all being passed on to the buyer. If the developer has to make Environmental
Impact Studies, if he has to wait the approval and if he has to go to an Appeals
Tribunal to have the study finally approved then the delay and expense will be
passed on to the consumer. Such items although necessary and desirable should not
add to the cost.

Local Government must properly play its role in the planning and decision
making process. Continuous and frustrating time-consuming delays to Appeals
Tribunals must be avoided. Whenever we engage expensive experts the product
becomes more expensive. We should never forget that the people who are crying
about environmental protection are also crying about the high cost of land.
Whatever the private developer has to spend on the product he has to add to the

cost. You have to get out of the product what you put into its production – a simple economic rule.

At Mindarie, 30 kilometres north of Perth, one of my Companies is planning an environmental city of 3000 hectares. Our planners and consultants first defined the intrinsic stability of the land for human use by combining a study of the major features of the land and the factors that would affect its development. A system was evolved which took account of the existing environmental conditions, and the suitability of the land for urbanisation or recreational use.

The roads were designed to conform to sound environmental principles. Every effort is being made to preserve the extensive ocean frontage and sandy beaches. Care has been taken to ensure that the overall development is related to the natural environment in an harmonious manner, so that open space and natural bush will be integrated with residential development wherever practicable. In all our developments we preserve as many trees as possible. We now employ landscape architects and planners. In the bad old days we just bulldozed out the trees; but now we go around them. Of course, the cost is much greater, but most genuine developers today are trying to preserve as much of the environment as possible.

I am very much in favour of Radburn-type planning, where living is not dominated by the motor car, and the network of footpaths is independent of the road system. Much of our 300 hectares in Menai, just south of Sydney, is being planned on this basis.

The Green Ban issue has occurred because of the concern of certain sections of the community for planning, environmental and social matters. The result has been that Federal, State and local authorities, as well as all those involved, have had to re-examine their philosophies and to effect the improvements necessary.

It is important to see Green Bans in their real context. They are a tactic to achieve an end – effective participation, social and physical planning. Green Bans have been used to halt developments on which there has been no opportunity for citizen participation. The Urban Development Institute of Australia, N.S.W. Division, has had discussions with various union groups who acknowledge that Green Bans are not an end in themselves.

The Institute has recommended to developers that until such time as the desirable legislative changes can be made, residents who are affected by their proposals should be involved in meaningful discussion before the development application is lodged, and before major commitment of finance is made. Where a Green Ban exists it should be open to any party, be it local residents, the union, the developer, or Resident Action Groups to seek a meeting of the primary parties.

Developers do not believe that environmental, conservation and preservation matters can be considered separately from overall planning. The N.S.W. Government's decision to establish a Department of Planning and Environment, for example, is timely and progressive. Where such bodies are not already operative I believe that planning and development, and its effect on the environment, would be improved by the following recommendations which the U.D.I.A. made recently to the Inquiry on the National Estate:

1. Establish a position of Co-ordinator General who would be directly responsible to the Minister.
2. Establish Regional Planning Authorities, similar to Western Port and Geelong

Regional Planning Authorities, which would be responsible for the planning of their region within the framework of the planning policies established by the Ministry of Planning and the Environment and adopted as policy.

Ideally such Authorities should have powers similar to the Auckland Regional Planning Authority with responsibility also for services and transport and hence prevent the ridiculous situation now occurring in N.S.W. where service authorities are not programming in cohesion with the State Planning Authority.

These Authorities should be comprised of representatives of local councils, supply authorities, the planning and environment authority, and also representatives of the professions, industry and citizen and/or union groups. These Regional Planning Authorities could be for the same areas as the various decentralisation and development regions adopted by Government.

3.   Give citizens far more participation in the planning and decision making process, e.g. as along the lines of the Skeffington Committee Report,[1] the basis of the United Kingdom's Planning Act 1968-69, and also to consider schemes proposed by such organisations as Intermet,[2] and the Regional Plan Association of New York, with such participation to be in the early stages of the formulation of the structure plans.

Such plants must have flexibility and reflect the needs of the total community, and, with proper participation, should nullify or reduce a considerable degree of the opposition to planning schemes.

Citizens' rights of appeal should exist to a proper tribunal or court at this stage.

4.   Establish far better communications between the Ministry of Planning and Environment and the new Regional Planning Authorities and the public, but, at the same time, naturally recognising the need for secrecy in respect of some matters. As planning policy would be established and adopted by State Governments (in co-operation with the Australian Government), local government would then have the principal responsibility for the preparation and implementation of the flexible development plans within the framework of overall planning policies.

Such a course would ensure that the new Planning and Environment Department would be a policy-determining body rather than being weighed down with the detail now being carried out by the State Planning Authority, for example. Government and private enterprise must support wider programs of social and environmental research.

It is very difficult to find out what people want. There is always the danger that vested interests are involved. There is a difference between asking: 'Do you want a properly planned environmental development?', and asking the same question with the alternative that it will cost $1000 more. Those who have their own homes no doubt will give a different answer to the question 'Do you think medium density would be desirable for the area?', to those who live in rented accommodation for whom anything would be better than where they are.

It will be necessary in the future for much more effective continuous liaison and dialogue with developers and Resident Action Groups, Unions, Federal and State Government, the Australian Finance Conference and other kindred institutes to the U.D.I.A. The establishment of links between the U.D.I.A. and the International Association of Metropolitan Research and Development, which is a world-wide network of study groups investigating urban problems, is surely a further important step towards an enlightened industry.

We must realise that the big cities are here to stay and as they continue to grow, must be made more efficient and better places to live. Decentralisation will take a long time to work. It took 60 years to get Canberra really started, and to develop other cities will take a minimum of twenty to thirty years or more. The Government has to give generous incentives to industry, otherwise the people will not easily move. The new cities must be planned now.

More work must be done by government and industry on inner urban low-income accommodation and consideration should be given to density bonuses, specific tax concessions. There is today no such thing as low-cost housing, only low-income. If the lower income groups are to be catered for, it can only be through direct government subsidy, whether to bodies such as the Housing Commission or to private enterprise.

It is no longer possible for members of the industry to masquerade as dis-interested, objective professionals, applying our techniques with equal ease to those clients we agree with as well as to those we disagree with. We are the client for all our developments, for it is our own society we are affecting through our actions.

I hope that we will reach a time when all members of the community can freely contribute and share in creating and developing an environment which meets the needs of today and satisfies the aspirations of the future.

References

1. Great Britain. Committee on Public Participation in Planning. *People and planning: report*. London, HMSO, 1969. Chairman: A. M. Skeffington.
2. International Association for Metropolitan Research and Development.

*Jack Mundey**

The common man

I believe that the role of unions in modern society means that unions must engage
in new areas of activity. As long as unions exist, of course, a primary obligation
is for that union to defend the often hard-won living standards of the workers
they represent and to try to improve them. Yet in a society in which life is becoming
more complicated with the passage of each year, unions must also consider quality
of life issues. I'm not using 'quality of life' as the cliché which it sometimes is,
but to refer to how we spend leisure, the nature of spiritual and cultural pursuits,
the implications of going beyond the thirty-five hour week – because even if we are
successful in winning a thirty hour week, we still have to live the whole 168 hours.
And what is the good of winning higher wages and shorter hours if we are living
in cities that are polluted; if we are living in cities without parks and bare of trees;
if we live in a city without a soul.

Would anybody disagree with me when I claim that despite some improvement
in the materialistic standards of the people as a whole – and that is allowing for
the poverty that does exist in our very affluent society – life in Melbourne and
Sydney ten years ago was better than it is now?

Ninety per cent of Australians live in ten cities; if you take Melbourne-Geelong
and Sydney-Wollongong-Newcastle, you have almost half the population of the
whole country, a highly urbanised and yet sparsely populated country. The
problems of those cities are immense.

I think it is noteworthy that in 1972, in addition to the inertia of the then
Liberal Government, there had been almost a quarter of a century of mis-rule.
When you consider where Labor won the 1972 election, it turns out that it was
won in the city of Melbourne. It is my opinion that the oft repeated promises of
Gough Whitlam and Tom Uren that 'We are going to tackle the crises in our
cities', played a significant part in the swing to the Labor Party.

To date, even if we allow for the many problems of the new national Government, the deeds of Uren and Whitlam in tackling the crises in our cities certainly
haven't matched their words. Maybe it is premature to say that, but it would appear
that at this stage, they haven't made much progress. We have witnessed the
preposterous decision to have a place like Geelong as a growth centre. Already
Geelong is filling out, and Melbourne is spilling over into Geelong. Life in the
western suburbs of Melbourne and Sydney – probably better described as a valium
belt – remains at an all-time low.

I am not talking about an ecological crisis that is coming up next century –
we are in an ecological crisis now, and yet our existing societies, all of them,
whether they be capitalist or whether they be socialist, still worship the holy cow
of gross national product – it is still a question of growth, often for growth's sake,
without any real concern for the quality, or style, or direction of that growth.

* Jack Mundey was national president of the Communist Party of Australia and secretary of the
N.S.W. Builders Labourers' Federation.

346

As a socialist, of course, I believe that capitalism, by its very nature, is predatory and rapacious, but the so-called socialist countries, with their stunted democracy and the lack of adequate rights, especially the right of dissidence, are also, in the environmental sense, making just as tragic errors as the capitalists. The Soviet Union in 1969 showed me with pride how, by 1975, two factories would be producing over a million cars, at a time when young people question that it is a liberator of man; when cars choke the main arteries of the major cities of the world and bring about unprecedented pollution. The socialist countries have also managed to cause pollution in their rivers and lakes with an efficiency equal to that of the U.S.A.

We used to hear about 'the miracle of Japan', the 15-25 per cent growth rate experienced there for a number of years. I saw in one of the heaviest industrialised areas of Tokyo, workers, not only putting on their overalls, but also their gas masks. They told me that during the worst period of the year, the children in this area also had to wear gas masks for some hours a day at the local schools. Is this progress? Is this a raising of living standards? I think that is all upside down – I believe that if mankind is going to have a future, then a new ethic has to be worked out, and very quickly indeed.

There are two fundamental problems. The first is over-population, especially in the under-developed world; population will reach a minimum of 15 500 000 000 (fifteen thousand, five hundred million) by twenty years into the next century. The second is consumerism in the so-called advanced world, destroying our natural resources in the most wanton way. I am one of those who question very much whether mankind can withstand these pressures and maintain a reasonable hope of going very far into the next century unless there is a dramatic change.

Let me now come back to the question of unions and to the role of resident action groups. If the ecological crisis is so serious, then unions have to be more concerned about the result of their labouring. No longer is it good enough for workers to say: 'Right, I demand full employment'. That surely is a demand, but increasingly, I believe workers, whether by hand or brain, have to question the end of their labour; whether the labour is socially beneficial to the community at large, or whether it leads to the further destruction of our environment.

We now have over five hundred resident action groups throughout Australia, precisely because of the breakdown in government, particularly at State and municipal and shire levels. Incredible though it may seem, there are over nine hundred and fifty shire and municipal governments throughout Australia, and the degree to which real-estate and developer interests influence these councils cannot be underestimated. Isn't the civic consciousness of real estate agents at local government level remarkable? They don't show the same sort of interest at other levels – other living levels – or in other organisations of people. When you consider the booming periods of the sixties, one council in Sydney was sacked three times for proven collusion between some of the councillors, developers and property developers and real estate interests. Another council, twice, and six other councils in New South Wales, once. In Randwick, a 'better-deal' team of candidates got in after continual allegations of corruption, and promptly rezoned whole areas of Coogee and Randwick for high rise development.

This can be repeated many times over. I believe that future governments, surely, should see a two-tiered system, with one national government – despite

the ideas of Lionel Murphy, I think we could do without the Senate, which isn't
a house of review – and another tier of government below. I believe that this
should be a system of regional governments, with twenty or thirty regions – State
governments have outlived their usefulness. Such a system might work, provided
that regional government had more powers; provided that the community interests
within the regional governments had a right to recall the people that they elect,
and could participate in the planning and life of the council, which should not
be run by people who are elected and who then answer only to bureaucrats. Is
this possible? I think it is. I think that the resident action groups have played a
very important role in breaking down apathy in Australia. Whether the battles
be against freeways in Darwin or in the major cities, whether it is to save the
Palace Hotel in Perth or to save Fremantle or to save Battery Point, we find people
right throughout this country, ordinary people, not allowing councils and governments to have all the say, starting to assert themselves, and to me this is very
positive and most desirable.

I would like to give a few examples of the crisis that have lead to the coalition
of the resident action groups and the Builders Labourers and other unions in
combined action. I put it to you that I think it has been a very positive development.

In Sydney now there are over three thousand million dollars worth of so-called
development or proposed freeways or destruction of homes held up – three thousand
million. This had its origin, not in the forward thinking of Mundey or any of the
builders labourers, but in the women from a middle-class or upper-class suburb
in Sydney – Hunters Hill – where we haven't got too many builders labourers,
believe me. A.V. Jennings Industries Ltd., a well known Melbourne building firm,
came up to Hunters Hill and brought a choice piece of land called Kelly's Bush,
the last remaining bushland on the Parramatta River, for the construction of
luxury homes. After going through all the normal procedures of petitioning the
local council, calling in to the local council, and petitioning the local member of
parliament, after they had tried all these methods, the women felt helpless – but
they did not give up. As a last resort, the women came to us and said: 'It will be
too late when the bushland has been destroyed – can the union do anything?'
They had heard my statements about unions having to broaden their vision, and
be concerned about the environment, and they put it to us that we had now a
chance to show it in action. We in turn said that provided there was a real
expression from the people of Hunters Hill, we would be prepared to put a ban on
construction. (In those days we were old-fashioned, and had so far called them
black bans.) So we put a ban on it, to allow negotiations to continue between the
community that wanted Kelly's Bush retained, and the councils and the government who voted for its destruction. Over six hundred people came along to a public
meeting and we acceded to their request. So the Green Bans were born. I might
say that 'Green Ban' was deliberately chosen, because 'Black Bans' had the
connotation of workers using their industrial muscle to improve their wages and
conditions, whereas 'Green Ban' showed that the workers were socially aware,
and were prepared to take action in the interests of the environment.

Jennings announced that the company wasn't going to be concerned with the
ban, that they would use piece-work labour, even non-union labour if need be.

The line in the *Sydney Morning Herald*, which used to average about two editorials a week at that time against us, was that Mundey and a few leaders were duping the members of the Builders Labourers. We called a meeting on Jennings' biggest job in Sydney, a half-completed seventeen-storey building in North Sydney. The workers decided unanimously that if one tree or one blade of grass was touched in Kelly's Bush, that half-completed building would stand as a monument to Kelly's Bush for ever.

Now, this was illegal. We soon saw the politicians and other people in the establishment throwing their hands up in horror and saying: 'This is union power gone mad – people taking direct action, workers taking direct action with residents'. 'It is rather ironic', they said, 'that these women should go to the builders labourers, with whom they have nothing in common'. But we had one thing in common; despite the economic and social difference, we at least were all concerned with the rape of our city, and were prepared to take action.

After that action, I might say that Kelly's Bush still remains natural bushland, and community values have changed. I don't think there will be any council or any government that would suggest that it now be destroyed.

But to show you the frustration of people, and how helpless they felt; within the course of months there were over forty bans all urgently needed, in Sydney and other parts of New South Wales, and this doesn't mean that we willy-nilly imposed every ban that residents asked for. For example, there was a request from a handful of people at Vaucluse – again, we don't have too many members in Vaucluse, which is one of the exclusive suburbs, meaning that it excludes working men – to oppose a town house development. We consulted Milo Dunphy and a number of other conservationists and architects who are not concerned with vested interests (as too many architects are) and we decided against imposing that particular ban.

I want you to have a look at some of the bans that were imposed, looking back in retrospect. Whether or not they were all later proved justified, they were certainly urgent at the time: it is not much good holding a court of inquiry when more than half the building is gone. I remember when the Bank of New South Wales, on the corner of George and King Streets in Sydney was being demolished, a number of progressive architects approached us and said – 'Now look, it is a lovely building, Parisian, the last of its kind in Sydney, and it's going – it concerns us, and we want to do something'. We said: 'All right, when the next building considered worthy of preservation by the National Trust comes under threat of demolition, we will impose a ban on it'. The next ban was thus imposed on the Congregational Church in Sydney. The Minister, the Rev. Bryant, immediately wrote to Bob Hawke, (I believe Bob Hawke's a marvellous Congregational minister) and he wrote to the Premier and everybody else: 'The terrible Builders Labourers are at it again, and they are led by an atheist who is going to end up saving the church!' I did say to Rev. Bryant in an interview one time: 'Well, it is rather odd. Whilst I may be an atheist, at least I am showing a bit of concern for our heritage, while you want to build a twenty-storey building and knock down this building that is a hundred and forty years old; it appears to me that you are far more materialistic than spiritualistic'. He didn't particularly like that!

Anyway, the Congregational Church still stands, and around Australia there are over a hundred buildings in our capital cities and major provincial cities that otherwise would have been razed to the ground. Neither the States nor the Federal Government have yet introduced legislation adequate to protect our historical buildings. If you let the big developers and the like loose in Rome they'd knock down the Coliseum and St Peters and everything else and put up nice, shiny, new office blocks – such is their understanding of the needs of our cities.

Perhaps our action will bring about a situation where governments are willing to enact suitable legislation. We have not confined ourselves to bushland and buildings – Sydney is ill-provided with open parkland. Certain people had the crazy hope in 1972 that they might get the Olympic Games in 1988 to celebrate 200 years of white Australian rule, and for this they were prepared to destroy Centennial Park one of the loveliest parks in Sydney – one of the loveliest parks of all – to build a giant sports stadium, with swimming pools, gymnasia, and, of course, as always, plenty of space for the car. They were prepared to destroy Centennial Park for that.

People rose up in anger – staunch communists and Builders Labourers, like Cardinal Gilroy, Professor Runcie, Patrick White, Kylie Tennant the novelist, Vincent Serventy the naturalist, and for good measure, Jack Mundey. A ban was imposed on building in Centennial Park. The uproar was so great against the proposal to destroy the park that the Government quickly changed its mind and made another recommendation.

The Royal Botanic Gardens in Sydney were another battleground. We are very proud of our Opera House; even though it is not much good for opera, it is a lovely house! I want to make it quite clear that we are prepared to build opera houses and cultural centres and some of those architecturally odd buildings that we have been building in Sydney and other cities. But two successive Governments, spending a hundred million dollars, clean forgot the place of the car. We had visions of Bob Askin having to walk from Parliament House to open it. Right at the last moment, they were going to knock down part of the Botanic Gardens, destroy three Moreton Bay figs, more than a century old, spoil the contours of that part of the gardens, and also deface the cliff-face on the east side of Macquarie Street. A ban was imposed, the Botanic Gardens remained, the Opera House was opened, and functions without a car park. There won't be any car park built at the Opera House while the present leadership of the Builders Labourers' Federation remains.

We might now turn from individual buildings and parks to historic precincts, whole areas of interest. Look at The Rocks, or Woolloomooloo. There are millions of square metres of office-space in all the major cities now, yet materials and labour and financial resources continue to be ploughed into superfluous office buildings, and away from housing, unit flats, creches, kindergartens, universities, cultural centres. At the same time the establishment has plans to destroy The Rocks, the oldest urban survival in Australia. I think The Rocks belongs to the people of Melbourne as much as it belongs to the people of Sydney. In The Rocks, which is an area of only 20 hectares – that particular part of The Rocks – they were going to spend five hundred million dollars, mainly on high-rise, and another four hundred million dollars on a little base in Woolloomooloo. Well, that's what they were hatching, until we stepped in with Green Bans.

Let me repeat that I see Green Bans not as an end in themselves – I see Green Bans as a tactic to bring about people's participation and not just allow the engineers, architects, town planners, developers and their friends in high places in government to determine how the community should develop. When I speak of Centennial Park and Kelly's Bush and that type of Green Ban, I believe that changing values will ensure that they last forever. But when it comes to The Rocks, Woolloomooloo and other areas where the residents have taken action and proposed bans, I see that ban as a holding operation, to allow more time for discussion between the people who live in the area, and the Government bodies that make the decision.

We are now told that we are to have a completely new look for Sydney, under the auspices of George Clarke and some of the people who wanted to destroy Centennial Park. The proposal was announced two weeks before the election, I might add, but with a great fanfare. We are now going to lower the skyline to have greater interest, greater public participation and the tag that is written up on the Town Hall is 'Planning with People'. Anyone who knows the Sydney scene would question very much whether 'planning with people' would be taken seriously if it hadn't been for the Green Bans. They really had an impact.

So I think that in this sense, Green Bans have been positive. A combination of resident action groups and unions has done nothing but good. For those concerned souls who feel that unions might go too far and that power drunk union leaders will go around all day putting on Green Bans, let me point out that there are a couple of things that stand in the way. Not every builders labourer is a galloping conservationist. Some of them are more interested in the next race at Randwick or Flemington and the poker machines, and the rank-and-file members will always be a constraint. Nevertheless, the conscious element of the union was prepared to display a social consciousness and link up with people so that action could be taken.

To those who claim that we were usurping the role of government, I can only say that this was the failure of government to assert itself, to listen to people, and to plan with people, that drove the resident action group to become more militant, that led to the unity of residents and unions. In many of the bans we imposed, residents and unions were poles apart in political and theological thinking. I remember going to a meeting on Eastern Hill, Manly, only a stone's throw from Bob Askin's place. The protest was against a proposal to build a high-rise building. A barrister, one of the few Labor people there, said: 'Sitting out on that hill this morning, there are four or five hundred people; ninety per cent of those people would never vote Labor in their lives'. When the motion before the meeting was that it press the Builders Labourers to impose a Green Ban so that further negotiations could take place with the State Planning Authority and the Manly Council, one fellow strode to the microphone, introduced himself and said: 'I want to warn you all here this morning that it is easy to invite the Builders Labourers in, so long as you know how you are going to get them out again'. That was his thinking – we are like white ants. I suggested to him that his speech might have passed muster back in 1953, but that it was out of date in 1973, when Macarthyism hadn't got quite as much power.

I think the same humorous story can be told about out first sitting with the

National Trust. When we imposed the ban on the demolition of historical buildings, behind the scenes, the National Trust was delighted. Then came the first protest meeting at The Rocks, in support of The Rocks resident group, who wanted to draw up a plan using their own planners and architects. Tom Uren, then in opposition, was at the meeting, full of ideas and enthusiasm. The local Catholic priest was there, different business groups from the area, and a very wide range of people on the platform. I rang the bloke from the National Trust: 'Why don't you come along and make it clear that legislation should be enacted so that it won't be necessary for unions to impose bans – at least do that'. He said: 'Oh, I couldn't be in that'. 'Well', I said, 'can I come down and see you'. 'No, no, don't do that'. I said: 'Well, you come down to the Trades Hall'. 'That's even worse.' So he suggested that what we might do was meet in *The Royal George* saloon bar at 12 o'clock on Monday. 'I will be wearing a check sports coat and I've got a closely cropped red beard' he said. So I arrived on time, to find one person in the bar with a check coat and a red beard; so I said, 'Well, really, what is your hang up? You've got a wide range of people coming to this protest meeting; why don't you identify yourself with it and the need to keep those buildings on The Rocks?'. He said, 'Look it is wonderful what you are doing, it's great – but if I went along to the meeting those big shots on Bellevue Hill would never understand'. That was his thinking – the big shots of Bellevue Hill, which as you know is one of the most fashionable parts of Sydney, would never understand his rubbing shoulders with the Builders Labourers' Union, even though they are thankful enough to the Builders Labourers' Union for saving their historical buildings.

Things have changed since then. There is more ready acceptance, and I think that one of the things that the resident action groups have done, is to break down a lot of social class barriers. Of course, self interest is at work. But not only self interest. The king of writing, Patrick White, who is more or less a recluse, is concerned not only about Centennial Park, which he lives near (and he has enough money to live elsewhere if he wanted to). He tramped the streets of Redfern and Malabar assisting Aboriginal and other causes. Community action, even though it can be in the interest of your particular house, your particular community, can, in fact, lead to a wider social understanding.

So when people argue that the workers are going too far, I would remind them, first, that not all workers are so environmentally concerned as the Builders Labourers, and second, that the members of that union, which has imposed so many bans, have never rejected or seriously challenged the direction their leadership has taken. As for usurping the role of government, I would say that no progressive legislation was ever introduced anywhere in the world that didn't begin outside Parliament and our formal institutions, whether it be protest by way of petitioning, or action by the workers, or agitation for the forty-hour week, back to the Tolpuddle martyrs and everything they did. I believe that action by people – extra-parliamentary action – has a vital role to play in bringing greater degrees of democracy into being. Democracy, like everything else, is relative, and I believe that it is the extra-parliamentary activity that persuades our legislators to bring laws up to date.

I believe in every-day democracy. Surely democracy doesn't mean going to a ballot box once every three years and casting a ballot paper. To me, democracy is acting on one's conscience every day and facing up to responsibilities.

Workers have a responsibility to examine the results of their labour. Very soon I shall have finished my years as secretary in the union, and will voluntarily stand down – a practice I think which should go on in more unions and other organisations so that we don't get a perpetuation of the entrenched bureaucracies. When I look back would it be good enough to say: 'Well, I picked up the wages and conditions of the Builders Labourers; we lifted up their second-class status; we won a degree of permanency, or some degree of permanency; we've won accident pay'. Could we then honestly blame the development companies for destroying Sydney, the Sydney where in some streets built on bullock tracks you now never see the sun? The building workers are also to blame, because we built those bad buildings and I think that we've got a responsibility for what we do with our labour. We can't just say, 'Thank you boss, I've got a job, I will do anything, anywhere, at any time'. To me, that's out. Think now of the motor vehicle industry, for example. I think we should start to think about the iron monster now crippling our cities, and divert workers from making cars we would be better off without, retraining them, and putting them into building public transport, which has just about collapsed in every major city, because of the oil companies and the vested interests and the tie up between the motor vehicle and multi-national companies. We should divert those workers so that they're building trains and trolley-buses and trams that are less polluting. We should use and upgrade the badly run down public transport service. In the building industry we should divert workers away from ugly, high-rise, surplus building into areas that are socially beneficial.

I think these are the things that workers have got to think about as we go into the last part of the twentieth century – not just be tied down as unions have been for far too long to purely economic issues. I think ordinary people and the resident action groups and unionists with a conscience have a very vital role to play if our environment is going to be habitable at all by the end of this century.

Conclusion

*David Lowenthal**

Perceiving the Australian environment: a summary and commentary

A camel is a creature created by a committee; a discussion in book form might be considered a kangaroo. Much about this symposium was indigenous – the topic, the participants, the locale – but a good deal was not, including the Unesco sponsorship, the comparative focus and the assignment of this summary to a foreigner who had never been in Australia before. Or maybe this last is a truly Australian initiation, in which a neophyte is asked to bring order out of chaos.

Confusion is an inevitable and perhaps desirable concomitant of such occasions. Forty folk from twenty different professions, preparing papers in isolation and with little time for afterthought, are unlikely to reach cogent joint conclusions. Nor were they asked to do so. The purpose of the exercise – and of this book – was not to contrive a consensus, but to explore manifold insights. Multifarious and often conflicting ideas about Australian landscapes and attitudes emerged, insights drawn from history and geography, science and behaviour, and the special perspectives of architects and developers, governmental agencies and labour unions, poets and painters.

An Australian conversant in all these approaches would find an equitable summary no small task; for a stranger to the country and to most of the realms of expertise, it is manifestly impossible. I shall instead tease out a few common – and some uncommon – themes, whose concordances and contradictions surfaced in so many contributions. And I shall review them as an American resident in Britain concerned with similar themes in both lands.

UNITY IN DIVERSITY

That an Australian environment and viewpoint existed, few participants questioned. None needed Moorhouse's reminder of the power of local particularism, or Bolton's of how few Australians moved between States, even between cities. But most seemed to concur with a recent conclusion that regional differences tend to be 'strangled at birth' by centralist forces and that Australian culture displayed 'almost incredible uniformity'.[1] As a nation with a continent to itself, Australia's internal diversity is often minimised. Seddon's opening assertion that 'there is no such thing as an Australian environment', but rather 'a great variety of different places', elicited no response. But the biotic diversity Frankel characterised indeed bore out that 'Balmain is not much like Eucla'. The range of milieus is so great that only the eucalyptus serves as a symbol of continental continuity. And the gum tree's casual, informal, opportunistic growth form commended it as an apt metaphor for the Australian social environment too.

But the eucalyptus fails as a national emblem on at least two counts. Australians still regard it, like the kangaroo, less with devotion than with rueful amusement: as Elliott noted, it is jokey or banal. And the eucalyptus does not reflect the built environment at all. In fact, no man-made feature yet acceptably symbolises what Australia looks and feels like.

* David Lowenthal is Professor of Geography at University College, London.

357

A unified Australian perspective, though one that changed through time, thus seemed to be taken for granted. Most participants touched lightly on the diversity of environments, the absence of consensual attitudes. But as Australian diversity is not yet encompassed, true unity has yet to be forged.

MAN AGAINST NATURE

Three particular polarities stood out as persistent themes in Australian environmental life: the opposition of man and nature, the dichotomy of city and country, and the conflict between utility and amenity. Though these realms of discourse substantially overlap, the distinctive quality of each calls for separate treatment.

Modern man at odds with nature is by no means an exclusively Australian notion; thanks to traditional distinctions that set mankind apart and to modern concern with environmental mismanagement, the subject suffuses contemporary Western thought. (Its origins are explored in detail in John Passmore's *Man's responsibility for nature*,[2] and need no recapitulation here.) The man-nature opposition in Australia, however, struck many symposium participants as peculiarly strong, sweeping and strident; 'the people are at war with the land', in A.J. Rose's words.[3] Nowhere else, it was implied, had technological man lately occupied so fragile an ecosystem; nowhere else had settlers so utterly failed to identify with their new landscapes; nowhere else was man's environmental impact so patently reprehensible. Yet an outsider is soon aware how closely Australian attitudes and impacts resemble those of newcomers to New World shores. If colonial Australians hated trees, as Bolton noted, American colonists chopped them down with a vengeance. Like early Australians, pioneer Americans viewed the wilderness mainly as a hostile encumbrance.

More striking was the concurrence that nature in Australia was right and good, man wrong and heedless or evil. Perceptions ought to be 'more finely attuned to the needs of the land that is now home', Seddon felt, 'more sensitive to the special needs of their unique landscapes'. Australians remained hostile to their physical milieus because, Wright argued, they tried to manipulate them for their own needs, instead of adapting themselves to the landscape. The undisturbed environment embodied virtue to conservationists in Canberra; Lansdown reported that Black Mountain, menaced by a rotating restaurant atop a communications tower, had become 'a symbol of all that is good and beautiful in the landscape'.

Those who find such virtue in nature may overlook environmental facts, however. Urbanites and suburbanites who may never have seen the bush substitute a romantic image for the reality. Much of Australia 'is really pretty scruffy, straggly bush', Robin Boyd has observed. 'Yet in the Australian dream all the land is evenly beautiful, and beautifully even.'[4] Similarly, they sometimes mistake artificial landscapes that they like, for natural ones, as Lansdown noted in public responses to plans for development around Canberra's man-made lake.

The belief in nature's virtue and man's vice underlies the general neglect of the Australian social environment – a neglect deeply rooted in Australian history, as Kramer recalled from Darwin's account of human degradation amid natural beauty. Environmental reformers 'tend to restrict their concern with humanity to the things it makes', Horne charged. 'The reactions of so many Australian intellectuals

358

have tended to be as alien to the Australian social landscape' as early explorers were to the physical environment. Their attachment to the wilderness excludes concern for inhabited areas – an imbalance mirrored in America. The overdesign of Australian urban buildings, Murray thought, reflected an exaggerated compensation for this neglect. And the back-to-nature movement – the trendy abandonment of laundromat for bush that Moorhouse eloquently limned – was again analogous to, and partly derived from, the ecofreak, mother-earth, commune syndrome of the United States.

Yet the character of the social environment matters more than the physical in everyday Australian life, as Buchanan's survey showed. And Australians are bound to destroy the wilderness, Horne pointed out, whether they intend it or not. Ever more numerous and more mobile, they are now entering and inevitably altering environments heretofore accessible to only a few. But until Australians cease to polarise man and nature, attributing evil to one and good to the other, the Australian landscape cannot become a general medium for exploring personal and social identity, such as Kramer noted for Patrick White's *Voss*. The man-nature connection is crucial, but the relationship is not yet one of loving or even of accepting.

CITY AGAINST COUNTRY

Confrontation between city and country, like that between man and nature, is a common Western experience writ large in Australia. There the two polarities tend to converge because the countryside is so unpeopled and so many Australians live in cities and suburbs, but the distinction remains. The Australian city is a more satisfying target of attack than Australian man, perhaps because it seems more corrigible. And 'countryside' is a more attractive ideal than 'nature'.

The symposium order reflected the urban-rural polarity. The first group of papers focused almost exclusively on the rural landscape. Later presentations redressed the balance, giving exaggerated attention to urban and suburban scenes. Few tried to bridge these two apparently incompatible types of milieus.

The gulf became poignantly clear in Smith's account of Sali Herman, whose Kings Cross picture was almost rejected for the Wynn Art Prize in the 1940s on the ground that it was not a landscape. But the urban-rural dichotomy goes far back in Australia, Horne makes clear, and was especially prominent among city reformers of the late nineteenth century.

Country and city values are as explicitly moralised as those of nature and man. Such characterisations were Moorhouse's express theme: 'The country has symbolised innocence and purity, the city artificiality, decadence, and pestilence'. Crusaders have at various times fostered urban resettlement in the countryside, abetted by artists and writers. Most persuasive novelists, in Kramer's view, have hated cities, while painters seek refuge in their art, as some folk do in wild nature, from the urban jungle. 'Even the most sophisticated minds seem to go bush for their images of innocence', Horne notes elsewhere: 'to some poets and painters the desert seems to be the Australian symbol of hope'.[5] The behaviour of urban populations reflects such views. The typical Australian, in Horne's phrase, thinks of the countryside as one big nature strip and worships it as divine (though worship does not prevent desecration). Grass-roots conservationists oppose urban development, Lansdown notes, but seldom voice objections to the recreational

development of natural landscapes. Urban sprawl is viewed askance, rural preservation, for whatever use, is applauded. Anti-urban feeling is more exclusive and
intense in Australia even than in America, with its decaying city centres and
traditional urban links with vice and corruption. And the Australian back-to-earth
movement Moorhouse describes is more hapless, ecologically and economically,
than parallel movements in the United States, where subsistence farmers can at
least find fertile and well-watered land.

Yet Australian urban hatred and rural devotion could easily be exaggerated.
As Smith pointed out, the whole environmental history of most Australians is
profoundly urban and suburban. While the countryside induced fear, the city made
one a man, as a Christina Stead figure puts it; Kramer notes that this admission
is atypical, but it is nonetheless true to life. Melbourne residents queried by Buchanan
professed themselves happy enough, however aware of pollution and other urban
ills. Suburban 'prisons' reappear even in remote weekend hideaways, Moorhouse
comments, conceived not as jails but as shelters against the implacable hostility
of open space.

Australian cities and suburbs, unlike the countryside, are said to contain little
that is uniquely Australian, instead replicating unprepossessing forms of urban
Europe and North America. But the visitor finds too many unique perspectives and
pleasures to accept so negative an appraisal. The low density sprawl of city and
suburb do, however, impede many Australians from experiencing anything else,
even as uncontrolled development rapidly diminishes the choicest sea shores and
mountain playgrounds. A viable urban-rural synthesis requires the residential
common-land innovations of designers like Yencken and the 'natural' urban
parks of planners like Mackenzie. Only an urban and suburban Australia that
embraces rather than rejects the countryside will enable Australians to enjoy an
amalgam, however modified, of their own unique and characteristic environments.

ENVIRONMENT AS HERITAGE

A positive sense of the past was an essential but heretofore neglected aspect of
environmental appreciation in Australia, many participants agreed. Until recently
most Australians preferred to forget history than to celebrate it, because nothing
in Australia seemed old, interesting or virtuous enough to be historic.[6] The lack
of a rich indigenous tradition explained the paucity of tangible historical remains.
But without such a landscape, there was little consciousness of continuity, little
sense of local heritage. Lacking a tangible past, Australians could not truly appreciate their present human environments or plan constructively and compassionately
for the future.

The past decade, however, had brought a heightened awareness of the Australian
past, a new acceptance of that past in its entirety, and a concern for preserving
typical along with outstanding artifacts of occupance. Historical appreciation at
both national and neighbourhood levels, Smith noted, was no longer the sole care
of the cognoscenti; Australians of all kinds now took Sunday outings to folk
museums and pioneer gold mining towns. 'History and nostalgia have become the
perfect idea for filling motel beds.'[7]

Historical like environmental awareness is a pan-Western trend. But the new
Australian nationalism has revalued both environmental and human history.
Moreover, both the advent of various State and city centennials, noted by Heath-

cote, and the arrival of large numbers of European immigrants, documented by Burnley, have served as occasions for stocktaking and reminiscence. Both similarly animated the American preservation movement a century ago; the first centenary celebration stimulated Americans to review their past, and large-scale European immigration moved older Americans to cherish their native origins and to exalt them to newcomers.

The quality as well as the quantity of Australian historical traces perturbed several participants – the eclectic architecture, the nostalgia Spooner found for relics of bush life, the huge market for Ned Kelly mementos. Why did Australia so venerate its villains, Bolton wondered, when other countries had heroic exemplars? But America similarly immortalises the exploits of Jesse James and other frontier bandits. Admiration of the outlaw is typical of recently settled lands with mobile, egalitarian peoples. 'Americans and Australians were pleased to think they resembled their respective frontiersmen', Russel Ward has suggested, 'because he was more American or Australian than anybody else'.[8]

Historical perversion, some felt, threatened the survival of a true Australian heritage. The demand for scenes and objects from the past had outstripped the supply of actual sites and relics, encouraging the fabrication of substitutes. But the pressure of public demand and the necessary protection of popular historic sites likewise make substitution inevitable in the Australian historical environment.

The segregation of historical scenery from the modern world, a tendency deplored by Clarke,* is similarly unavoidable. Just as 'beauty spots in Australia run the risk of becoming professional beauties, ...tiresome and objectionable... exotics',[9] so do historic sites. Visitor pressure is bound to segregate and separate the past and thus to make it unreal. Yet only a sophisticated program of education can enable Australia both to cherish and to display artifacts that vividly convey the meaning of the country's history. Both British and American experience have much to offer by way of example here.

The urgent need for preservation and public education programs was underscored by Green, who warned that large-scale, durable engineering works today required greater awareness of the pace of environmental change. And as technology and scale expand man's impact on the Australian environment, so, Frankel noted, should his concern extend further into the future. Australians should be aware of both their immediate and remote environmental impact. The rediscovery of the past thus presages a lengthening but increasingly unpredictable future.

UTILITY AGAINST AMENITY

The neglect of amenity for economic planning is another characteristic of recently settled nations that is shared by Australia. Participants remarked on the almost unrelieved use of landscape for production, the often deliberate dismissal of aesthetic considerations. Canberra's Federal Capital Development Committee, Lansdown noted, early gave priority to utility and economy, leaving 'architectural monument' and similar considerations to later generations. As a consequence,

* Editor's note: George Clarke's symposium paper, titled 'Planning theory in the twentieth century: a story of successive imports since 1945', was not submitted for publication. Fred Ledgar's paper, covering much of the same ground, was solicited to fill the gap. George Clarke is director of Clarke Gazzard and Associates and related planning companies.

361

Australian urban and rural landscapes alike attest more to hard work than to affection.

This bias stemmed, participants judged, from a persisting view of the Australian landscape as not only strange but hostile. The scene settlers commonly confronted, Wright noted, was one they could neither understand nor enjoy. Because they found the Australian landscape 'not as a rule immediately hospitable to human needs', in Seddon's phrase, newcomers sharply segregated utility and beauty. Their practical response to the new landscapes was quick, their poetic response slow. 'You mightn't love a gum tree, but you could cut it down and make a durable home', as Elliott put it. 'But it was hard to live with emblematically, because it wasn't an oak.'

Exceptions to utilitarian behaviour were rare, trivial, or jesting. Spooner observed that pioneer women habitually sought to humanise their lonely homes with flowers. Picturesque canons borrowed from Britain dominated the domestic landscapes of the well-to-do and, Kramer commented, their poetry and painting. To be sure, Adelaide evinced early large-scale amenity planning, influencing the layout of many South Australian towns; but the impulse soon perished for want of local interest. Few current examples of amenity planning won the notice of participants.

The Australian conditions described and deplored closely resemble those in the United States, where use and beauty have been similarly polarised. But quite different explanations in each country account for practical emphasis and aesthetic neglect. Americans were too busy making a living in a new land and too close to the hard facts of life to devote time or effort to beauty; the plough left no place for the picturesque. Notwithstanding Australia's roughly similar pioneer conditions, only Kramer advanced a parallel explanation. Instead, participants emphasised estrangement from familiar English scenes as the cause of settler bias against Australia. Newcomers were unable to appreciate the unfamiliar landscape or to imagine that beauty could be created in it. Whereas Americans postponed amenity considerations, Australians abjured them altogether or limited themselves to transplanting replicas of European environments.

EGALITARIAN CONSENSUS

Participants emphasised that environmental evaluations should be made not by authoritarian fiat but by the great Australian majority. The people themselves should determine what kind of environment they wanted and were willing to work for. This was Mundey's central message, an object lesson in the effectiveness of public participation. Environmental custodians should cease to treat public landscapes as their private property; Moorhouse likened the proprietary manner of some national park rangers to librarians defending books from potential readers. Environmental management, in Clarke's view, required that planners function not simply as landscape experts but also as conflict managers. Lansdown reiterated the need for public participation, and several speakers recognised that citizen action groups are already a powerful force.

The attitude these views reflect is, again, more than Australian; all over the world, but especially in America, the public is demanding to be consulted on environmental decisions. Former citadels of expertise, schools of architecture are becoming centres of advocacy planning. Egalitarian waves now roil the waters of environmental design even in Great Britain. In Australia, planners at all levels of environmental management are relinquishing unilateral action in favour of public consultation. The man in the street, not the 'objective' expert, Clarke noted, validated environmental decisions.

No one gainsaid the propriety of democratic landscape management. Indeed, without it Australians could never bridge the gulf between ideals and realities, and environmental reform stood no chance. Yet the enthusiastic reception of popular control did arouse some misgivings. The proliferation of a showy but shoddy vernacular seemed one likely outcome of an enlarged public voice. If Horne could trace Australian interior decor through the genteelisms of Edna Everage and her forebears, most Australian exteriors were no more distinguished. Public preference as much as architectural ambition, both Cox and Clarke reminded us, accounted for the featurism that Robin Boyd has so memorably associated with the Australian built environment.[10] New South Wales poker machine palaces, Horne implied, were only the latest manifestation of an authentic vernacular style. An affluent and vigorous public confronted perhaps too vast an array of possibilities to make any coherent choice, Cox thought; no consensually satisfying pattern could emerge from such superabundant alternatives.

Ecological fears were also voiced. Participatory deliberations might prove too slow and cumbersome to cope with pressing problems. It was one thing to offer bounties for tree preservation and planting; it was quite another, Davidson pointed out, to persuade people to take essential action. The environmental impact of, say, mining operations might be irreversible by the time public awareness could lead to effective control. Perhaps Big Brother – government and industry alike – would be needed after all, Mackenzie suggested, to stimulate public participation in environmental matters.

No less alarming were the ecological pressures diffused by public interest – pressures that endangered just those environmental qualities the public was learning to value. Perhaps Australian man, McAuley suggested, was a natural litterer like the gum tree. At all events, increasing use of beaches, national parks, and the bush beyond the suburbs was taking a heavy toll of fauna, flora and landscapes. What was open to some ought ideally to be accessible to all, but the practice of this democratic principle posed grave threats to Australian ecosystems from desert to Barrier Reef.

Majority rule posed analogous problems for the built environment. The prevalence of newcomers, the propensity to pull up stakes and move on, stripped Australian communities of continuity, stability, and recollection, the meaningful accretions of generations. Thus Canberra's transformations, Lansdown pointed out, suited the many who lacked attachment to Canberra's past landscapes, but deprived both the rooted minority and future heirs of a time-honoured, durable milieu. Australian environmental decisions ought to involve not only present-day preferences but ancestral values and artifacts and the landscapes of potential inheritors.

SOME CONCLUDING CAVEATS

To stress these common themes, however disparate participants' views about them, would give a false general impression of the symposium. Heterogeneity not homogeneity, catholicity not unity, variety rather than uniformity featured both presentation and discussion, tone and content. Everyone seemed at pains to recognise the multiplicity of perceptual worlds and, still more, to accept the potential validity of them all. Attitudes ranged from admiration for the works of Australian man to horror at their blight to eye or to biosphere, from nostalgic fondness for introduced plants to nationalist acclaim for native flora, from sympathy with early settlers' fears about Australian landscapes to fervent pleas for conserving fragile ecologies and preserving historical artifacts. The subject matter was no less multifarious: trees and houses, agricultural processes and mineral extraction, tract development and tourism, and all the sciences and arts of depicting environmental activities and contemplations.

As each participant naturally stressed his specialty, we learned little about how he viewed his everyday Australian environment, and still less – except from Buchanan – about what other, mainly non-reflective, Australians made of their environmental experience. (Indeed, ignorance of public perceptions precludes valid generalisations about man-environment relations in Australia as elsewhere.) Moreover, participants striving for lofty – notwithstanding often impassioned – overviews of their areas of expertise screened out conflicts common to all environmental actors. We heard advocates of preservation and of development, of elite and of popular visions, but each of us is at various times a resident and a traveller, a conserver and a polluter, a mystic, a seer, a poet and a painter, now environmentally aware, now oblivious. It is the combination of all these amateur and professional roles that may one day yield an Australian environmental consensus.

Participants were particularly alerted to the interaction of local and imported environmental ideas. But Australians vary enormously, Heathcote and Seddon made clear, in how far they have grown up in transplanted or indigenous landscapes. Just as environments vary in their nativism, so do folk differ in their awareness of what is or is not native. At first the contrast is continually underscored; one is torn between alarm and fascination with the new land and nostalgia for one's homeland. Australia's radical dissimilarities made British settlers hold it at arm's length, in the words of Elliott, Kramer and Frankel, as a formidable adversary. With the transition to a settled society and an increased proportion of born Australians, the sense of disparity (though not the distaste for what was local) began to diminish; one was surrounded by landscapes familiar from childhood, whose imported or local provenience was learned rather than directly experienced. A combination of indigenous and imported now becomes natural, normal, expectable, although 'we are still learning to see our own land', Seddon has written elsewhere, 'and to forgive it for not being England'.[11] A compensatory nationalism may deliberately favour the indigenous.

At length a mature people, while knowing its historical antecedents and the difference between imported and indigenous forms, will feel enough at home to make the distinction purely academic, remote from everyday life and landscape. Perception will so fit experience that whatever the proportion of foreign and local in the landscape, Australians will consider it essentially their own. Environmental attitudes and behaviour will accord both with ecological constraints and with social well-being. That Australia has not arrived at this stage is clear from every essay in this book, but the extent of perceptual synthesis reached differs with each author's perspective.

What common perspective then have these essays? It is a matter of mood: a sense of being on the road to a mutual destiny and of being able, far more than the Old World or North America, to influence that destiny. Whether or not adumbrating solutions to particular problems, participants seemed to assume that things were malleable, alterable, accessible to reason. This was the more noteworthy in view of the recognised constraints – the fragility of ecosystems and the necessity of large-scale government planning. Most participants viewed themselves not as individuals planting solitary gardens in a wilderness but as partners in a greater and more orderly enterprise.

This co-operative spirit was partly responsible for the respectful attention paid to every contribution. Strong disagreements emerged when issues were joined. But highly diverse viewpoints were expected throughout the dialogue. Australia's environmental amenity problems seemed so complex that one welcomed potential insights from every quarter. No considered view of the matter was dismissed as wholly mistaken or valueless.

Yet if no perspective was rejected, none presented has the cogency of a widely acceptable solution. And in the absence of any predominant hypothesis, the diversity sometimes seemed diffuse, eclectic, or superficial. A grand structure is needed to contain all these varied standpoints and to specify directions where future analysts may find coherent views about this manifold set of problems.

The word problem is intentional. If any notion dominated the symposium, it was that man-environment relations in Australia embodied problems that urgently required resolution. Neither the built nor the natural landscape are adequately appreciated, and the pace of change threatens serious deterioration. Every developed country and many others today exhibit profound malaise about environmental impacts and relationships, ranging from risks to life to questions about its quality. But in Australia – both a developed and a developing country – the cutting edge of the debate is now as sharp as anywhere in the world.

Notes and references

1. ROSE, A. J. 'Australia as a cultural landscape', in RAPOPORT, AMOS (ed.) *Australia as human setting: approaches to the designed environment*. Sydney, Angus and Robertson, 1972, pp. 58–74.
2. PASSMORE, JOHN. *Man's responsibility for nature*. London, Duckworth, 1974.
3. ROSE, *op. cit.* 1972, p. 73.
4. BOYD, ROBIN. *The great great Australian dream*. Sydney, Pergamon Press, 1972, p. 115.
5. HORNE, DONALD. *The lucky country*. Harmondsworth, Penguin, 1964, p. 80.
6. SAUNDERS, DAVID. 'Man and the past', in RAPOPORT, 1972, *op. cit.*, pp. 124–136.
7. DUNSTAN, KEITH. 'There's no time like our past'. *Sun*, 25 May 1974, p. 27.
8. WARD, RUSSEL. 'The social fabric', in McLEOD, A. L. *The pattern of Australian culture*. Ithaca, N.Y., Cornell University Press, 1963, pp. 12–41.
9. WOOD, THOMAS. *Cobbers*. 3rd edn., London, Oxford University Press, 1953, p. 130.
10. BOYD, ROBIN. *The Australian ugliness*. Harmondsworth, Penguin, 1963, espec. pp. 23–26.
11. SEDDON, GEORGE. *Swan River landscapes*. Nedlands, University of W.A. Press, 1970, p. 3.

Index

Format: International B5

Typeface: Monotype Times Roman Series 327, 10 on 12 point

Text paper: New Spectrum Matt Art 103 gsm.

Cover: Shoalhaven Satin Finish Ivory Board, 235 gsm.

R77/101 Cat. No. 77 29846